I0880135

'Wonderful and Confessedly Strange':

Australian Essays in Anglican Ecclesiology

Editor
Bruce Kaye

Associate Editors
Sarah Macneil and Heather Thomson

ATF Press
Adelaide

‘Wonderful and Confessedly Strange’:

Australian Essays in Anglican Ecclesiology

Editor
Bruce Kaye

Associate Editors
Sarah Macneil and Heather Thomson

ATF Press
Adelaide

Text copyright © 2006 remains with the authors for all papers in this volume and with ATF Press for the collection and introduction.

All rights reserved. Except for any fair dealing permitted under the Copyright Act, no part of this book may be reproduced by any means without prior permission. Inquiries should be made to the publisher.

First published 2006

This publication was made possible by a grant from the Australian Theological Research Foundation.

National Library of Australia
Cataloguing-in-Publication data

'Wonderful and confessedly strange': Australian essays in Anglican ecclesiology.

Includes index.
ISBN 1 920691 67 7.

1. Anglican Church in Australia. 2. Church. 3. Church and education–Australia. 4. Australia–Church history.
1. Kaye, Bruce Norman, 1939– . 11. Macneil, Sarah, 1955– . 111. Thomson, Heather, 1954–.

283.94

ISBN: 978-1-925612-29-5 soft
978-1-925612-30-1 hard
978-1-925612-31-8 epub
978-1-925612-32-5 pdf

ATF Press
An imprint of the Australasian Theological Forum Ltd
P O Box 504
Hindmarsh
SA 5007
ABN 90 116 359 963
www.atfpress.com

Brilliant Printers Pvt. Ltd., Bangalore - 94

Contents

Part Three: Bridging

Part Four: Context

Preface

This book has had a long gestation which began in 1996 when the first of the National Anglican Theology Seminars was held in Perth on Australian Anglican Identity. Subsequent seminars have been held on:

- A Theology of the Laity: Australian Anglican Perspectives (1997)
- Reconciliation in Church and Society: Perspectives from Australian Anglicans (1998)
- Spirituality and Society: Tasks and Challenges for Australian Anglicans (1999)
- A Question of Authority: Anglican Responses to the ARCIC Report, 'Gift of Authority' (2000)
- Australian Responses to 'Radical Orthodoxy' (1999) by John Milbank and others (2001)
- Violence and Theology: A Study of the Work of Rene Girard and Phyllis Trible (2002)
- Towards an Australian Anglican Ecclesiology (2002).

This book stands in the tradition of these annual seminars and follows on directly from the 2002 seminar. The authors have in the main been drawn from the members of these seminars. The book, like the seminars, is aimed at encouraging the development of a theological contribution to the life of the Anglican Church in Australia. The book, like the seminars, could not prosper without the voluntary support of all those concerned.

This book in particular could not have happened without the unstinting work of the two Associate Editors Sarah Macneil and Heather Thomson. They have carried a large burden on editorial and detailed work. We salute the authors who have turned their minds to this important topic. We acknowledge the financial support of the Australian Research Theological Foundation for a grant to support the preparation and publication of the book and have been grateful for institutional support from St Paul's College in the University of Sydney and St Mark's National Theological Centre in Canberra. The ATF Press, particularly in the person of the indefatigable Hilary Regan, has been encouraging and supporting.

Bruce Kaye

Part One: Setting The Scene

Part One: Setting The Scene

Introduction

Introduction

This book attempts to do something which is at once controversial and daring. It is controversial because it attempts to deal with some of the 'undiscussable' issues of ecclesiology in Australian Anglicanism. Such is the nature of the diversity, to use a generously euphemistic term, in Australian Anglicanism, that the underlying issues of ecclesiology are often kept in the background of the political arguments that are the bread and butter of ecclesiastical life. We seek here to bring some of those ecclesiological issues into the foreground. The project is daring in that it has brought together people who write out of very different contexts within the Anglican Church of Australia, and who are naturally influenced by those contexts. Having done that, it has sought to encourage a conversation on vital issues to do with ecclesiology for Australian Anglicans.

The project is also daring in the sense that it seeks to engage with the divine origins of the Christian community. In an age when the political dynamics and public disputes within the church appear to many to be little different from the power politics of government or of business corporations, it is reasonably daring to suggest that this community has something to do with a God of Grace, with a suffering and serving Christ. Yet that is the claim of the essays in this book. The Christian church has long been described as a pilgrim community made up of people whose citizenship is in heaven; a community of resident aliens. It is not surprising that this vocation appeared to the ancient writer Diognetus to be 'wonderful and confessedly strange'. We have taken this phrase for our title in order to draw attention to the divine character of the vocation of the church.

The difference between this project and those of the General Synod Doctrine Commissions in recent years has been that this project has not been set within the politics of a Commission and it has encompassed general issues of ecclesiology, rather than specific matters which were the subject of intense political debate in the church. The project involved several meetings of the authors and continuing contact between them, though mostly through the editors. The diversity in attitude and style is very marked and this in itself reflects something of the character of Australian Anglicanism. It points to the significant challenge of listening to others, especially as they seek to pursue their Christian vocation within a context of significant diversity. It also points to the peculiar and pressing difficulty of understanding and engagement with difference that Australian Anglican theologians have to struggle with. This book thus does not present a coherent unified ecclesiology. Rather it points to the mixture, one might even say the fruit cake, that is the result of two centuries of cooking; not to strain too many images!

These kinds of considerations have influenced the shape of the book. It begins with a 'Setting of the Scene', which seeks to introduce issues of methodology in ecclesiology conducted in this Australian context and also the historical context in which the Anglican tradition has existed. The subsequent sections reflect different ways into the subject. Part II looks at aspects of the inheritance with which the present generation must work. Part III looks at aspects of the life of the church which cross boundaries of time or framework. Part IV looks at various contexts within which ecclesiology is shaped and created.

This book is an 'essay', what German theologians might call an *Untersuchung*, an attempt. The chapters are also essays in this sense. They are attempts, trials, testings of where the church is, that is to say, where God is bringing into existence and life a people who will be witnesses to Christ the crucified king.

1

Foundations And Methods In Ecclesiology

Bruce Kaye

From the very earliest times Christians believed that Jesus of Nazareth was also and at the same time the Son of God incarnate. Their belonging to this Jesus Christ committed them to live according to a heavenly vocation in the earthly circumstances in which they believed God had placed them. The early Christians' struggle to understand how Jesus was both human and divine was also at the same time a struggle reflected in their own lives as a group of people. Paul encouraged the Philippians, who lived in a Roman garrison town, to think of their circumstances in terms of a heavenly citizenship. Jesus told his disciples that they were to set their hearts on a treasure in heaven.

The point is well made in the second century letter of Diognetus. He was concerned to show that the Christian faith appealed to all throughout the known world and therefore it underlined a continuity across cultural and social differences. The continuity was provided between believers through a common heavenly citizenship:

> For the distinction between Christians and other men is neither in country nor language nor customs. For they do not dwell in cities in some place of their own, nor do they use any strange variety of dialect, nor practice an extraordinary kind of life . . . while living in Greek and barbarian cities, according as each obtained his lot, and following local customs, both in clothing and food and in the rest of life, they show

> forth the wonderful and confessedly strange character of the constitution of their own citizenship. (V,1)[1]

This shared vocation constitutes them as Christians and together with the character of their lives marks out the heavenly kingdom to which they belong.

Just as Christians have sought to understand the nature of their faith so also that search has been a quest to understand the nature of the group or community which together they are becoming. As a consequence ecclesiology has been an implicit part of the Christian conversation from the beginning. This has been so especially at times of significant social and cultural change and at times when Christians have found themselves in contact with each other across different cultural divides.

Not surprisingly the engagement of the early church writers in the key theological questions of Christology and the doctrine of the Trinity was accompanied by attempts to make sense of the nature and foundations of the community which increasingly came to be called church. Institutional arrangements developed such as a canon of scripture, sacraments, an ordered ministry, and also patterns of authority and power began to be visible amongst the Christians. Groups such as Gnostics and Montanists emerged and sharpened the perceptions of other Christians on issues of authority, scripture and community order. This early period in Christianity also highlighted the question of how a Christian conversation on these issues might properly be conducted: according to what criteria and in the light of what authority? How could it be a conversation which encountered the changing social circumstances of Christians and at the same time was faithful to the word of God in Jesus Christ and the reality of the Holy Spirit in the Christian gospel?[2]

These questions did not go away with Constantine's deal with the bishops and the recognition of Christianity as the official religion of the Roman Empire, indeed they only multiplied and became more intense and more difficult. Undoubtedly Constantine's was a political act born of a recognition that the widely spread and astonishingly

---

1. K Lake, editor, *The Apostolic Fathers*, with an English translation by Kirsopp Lake (Cambridge: Harvard University Press, 1965).
2. See B Kaye, *Web of Meaning: The Role of Origins in Christian Faith* (Sydney: Aquila Press, 2000), 132.

numerous Christians offered the best hope of providing the unity which his empire required and that the bishops appeared to be the significant leaders in this religion.[3] Nonetheless his decision introduced into the life of the Christian community new and alien versions of authority, power and institutionality which sharply challenged the heavenly vision of the Christians' vocation.

These changes have echoed down through the history of the Christian church. The revolutionary creation of Christian Europe in the time of Gregory the Great and its division and dispersion in the seventh century were moments of similar magnitude.[4] The shattering of the world of Gregory the Great by the reforms of Gregory VII, which created a separate and overarching identity for a clerical vision of the church, laid the groundwork for the political divisions in Western Europe which in turn formed the social and political shape of the sixteenth century Reformation.[5] All of this meant that Western Christianity was driven into a different image of its coherence than had prevailed under the Constantinian model or the later Carolingian version of a universal Christian Empire.

The early modern emergence of nation states and the attempt by Christians to live out their heavenly vocation in such differentiated social and political contexts meant again the Christians had to adjust their image of how they were as a group to testify to their true identity as people of God. The pluralism of the modern period in Western Christianity has provided the base challenge for Christians. The ecumenical movement and the consolidation of the centralised concept of the Roman papacy are but two of the more prominent responses to

---

3. See HA Drake, *Constantine and the Bishops: The Politics of Intolerance* (Baltimore, MD: Johns Hopkins University Press, 2000) and also R Stark, *The Rise of Christianity* (San Francisco: HarperSanFrancisco, 1996).
4. RA Markus, *The End of Ancient Christianity* (Cambridge: Cambridge University Press, 1990) and RI Moore, *The First European Revolution: C 970–1215* (Oxford: Blackwells, 2000).
5. See B Kaye, *Reinventing Anglicanism: A Vision of Confidence, Community and Engagement in Anglican Christianity* (Adelaide: Openbook, 2004).

this challenge.[6] The Anglican form of this story has had some characteristic markers of its own; an early experience of nationalism and encounters with domestic and exported imperialisms. The current crisis in worldwide Anglicanism is but the consequence of the desiderata of this story and its exportation as part of the colonial phase of the English and American imperial experiences. All these moments have to do with Christians in their interrelations dealing with complexity and coherence, change and faithfulness.

But this story only raises more questions. The history of Christianity has clearly shown that this particular form of faith with its heavenly dimension and earthly engagement has produced a number of clear discrete traditions of faith. These traditions are exemplified in groupings or communities of Christians who align themselves with the tradition which provides the overarching framework for their practice of the faith. Not only so, it is also clear that these traditions change over time in terms of their precise form and structure. Each encompasses the challenges of continuity and change which can be seen on the broader canvas in Christianity generally. Some change more obviously than others. Some have change more prominent in their self-understanding; others give prominence to continuity. Thus Lutherans speak of the church as always reforming while being constant and Roman Catholics use the rhetoric of consistency while changing. Discrete traditions and change inevitably raise both the coherent vision of the heavenly character of the Christian vocation and also of the contingency of the life of the Christian and the pilgrimage of the Christian groups. That in turn draws attention to the contingent character not just of the Christian life but of the institutional arrangements by which the different traditions sustain their life of faith and witness to their vocation.[7]

It is in this context that we should understand the preoccupation of writings on ecclesiology with both the empirical reality of the church

6. See the interesting references to Mott in the US context in IT Douglas, *Fling out the Banner: The National Church Ideal and the Foreign Mission of the Episcopal Church* (New York: Church Hymnal Corporation, 1996) and also Kaye, *Web of Meaning*.

7. See E Cameron, *Interpreting Christian History: The Challenge of the Churches' Past* (Oxford: Blackwells, 2005) and also R Williams, *Why Study the Past? The Quest for the Historical Church* (Grand Rapids: Eerdmans, 2005).

and the so-called theological ideal of the church. Michael Ramsey's influential Anglican treatment of this subject illustrates the interdependence of the empirical and the ideational. 'Michael Ramsey wished to recall both Evangelicals dismissive of church order, and legalistic Catholics to a truly catholic awareness of the continuity and interdependence of the Gospel and church order'.[8] Ramsey sought to sustain an argument that catholic order, by which he meant episcopacy in an apostolic succession, arose from the character of the gospel which he found to be focussed in the death and resurrection of Christ. This is a different argument from that of Charles Gore who wished to argue that the same catholic order was a consequence of the institution by Jesus of an organic community, the church, and this particular order. Despite the confidence of Gore, Ramsey's argument is less vulnerable to the criticisms of historical investigation about such an institution and the emergence of this order of ministry and at the same time is a more substantial theological account of the issue. The Gore position relies for its force on a notion of legitimacy that arises from institutional pedigree.[9] In nineteenth century England the rhetorical power deriving from the status of the position of the bishop in the social structure of the day gave weight to Gore's point of view. No doubt there is some sense in such an argument, but it carries significantly less cultural valency now than it did in Gore's time. Where Anglicanism was located in a different cultural context the dynamics of this argument changed. Gore's position has also been seen to be quite fatally open to historical investigation. Ramsey makes a more substantial argument precisely because he addresses the question in terms of the nature of the gospel.

There is a significant issue here about the nature of theology which can be illustrated by a comparison of the way in which Schleiermacher in the nineteenth century and Barth in the twentieth century dealt with the relation between the church and the task of theology. Schleiermacher opened his account of *The Christian Faith* by declaring that since 'dogmatics is a theological discipline, and thus pertains solely to the Christian Church, we can only explain what it is when we have

8. Geoffrey Rowell, 'Introduction', in M Ramsey, *The Gospel and the Catholic Church* (London: SPCK, 1936, Second edition 1990), iii.
9. See S Sykes, 'The Basis of Anglican Fellowship: Some Challenges for Today', *Journal of Anglican Studies*, 1/2 (2003): 10–23.

become clear as to the conception of the Christian Church'.[10] He then goes on to a discussion of the general nature of church as a communion of people constituted by certain qualities, principal amongst which is piety. In the Christian church this piety is the feeling of absolute dependence. Religious self consciousness on his analysis leads inevitably to communion and thus to the formation of a church marked out by the Christian monotheistic beliefs. As the argument unfolds it is clear that Schleiermacher understands the church as the present community of people who share this piety and whose theology arises out an understanding of the self consciousness which goes with that piety. It is in this sense that he thinks that theology grows out of church. This Christian theology is the theology of this Christian church.

Barth, in the twentieth century, also thought that theology and church were intimately connected. He opened *Church Dogmatics* (1.1) with startling words for a Reformed theologian: 'as a theological discipline dogmatics is the scientific self-examination of the Christian Church with respect to the content of its distinctive talk about God'.[11] At first blush this might look like the point Schleiermacher was making in the previous century. And it is true that in a certain sense they are making the same point, a point that is relevant to our concerns here, namely that the actual experience of church is intimately connected with the kind of theology we espouse.

However for Schleiermacher this is because theology is the adumbration of the nature of this pre-existent community which he calls church. This could hardly be more different from the point of view Barth takes up. For him church is the consequence of an ongoing creative work of God. When therefore he says that dogmatics is the scientific self-examination of the church with respect to its talk about God, he means that this is an examination of an event which is brought into existence by the gracious act of God. There is no sense in which that theology is born out of that pre-existent community. Theology is about the creative grace of God in the witness of the church, and that witness is faithful when it testifies to this grace.

10. F Schleiermacher, *The Christian Faith* (Edinburgh: T&T Clark, ET of second German edition, 1928), 3.

11. K Barth, *Church Dogmatics*, volume 1, The Doctrine of the Word of God, Part 1 (Edinburgh: T&T Clark, 1975), 3.

Barth comes to the empirical life of the church when he argues that just as Jesus was for the world so the church must be for the world. It lives out the mission character of the grace of God and in doing so it is an empirical phenomenon. Barth's insistence on the church as a community for the world brings him to the very point with which Ramsey struggled, though from a significantly different point of reference. How are we to make sense of the empirical reality which is the Christian church in the light of the Christian gospel? Ramsey honed an argument which led through the sacraments to a specific conception of ministerial order which he regarded as normative. Barth developed an argument which caught up the significance of the sacraments but which did not envisage any kind of continuing ministerial order and underlined the occasional character of a church which was, in its particular instances, a creation by God.

The general project of Christian theology, the systematic attempt to understand and imagine the meaning of Christian faith in the circumstances in which we find ourselves, is a part of and thus shapes and is shaped by the Christian community. This has significant implications for any endeavour in ecclesiology and especially so in one which is appropriate to a particular tradition of faith. That issue is magnified when we are concerned with an ecclesiology, for example, of such a tradition considered in a specific cultural, social context such as Australia. No particular circumstance or tradition can, nor should it want to, avoid the wider generality of the Christian faith and the wider Christian community in its endeavour to live out the gospel faithfully. In that sense an attempt at an ecclesiology for Australian Anglicanism for the present time cannot be conducted in isolation. Generality and particularity must be held together in such an enterprise. These polarities provide a context for the key issues in ecclesiology, namely an understanding and imagination of the character of the Christian gospel and some account of the empirical realities of the Christian church. Clearly different authors and different traditions represent different emphases in their consideration of these two issues, but these are the keys.

The empirical realities of the Christian group often come to bear in the unconscious assumptions of the theologian. Someone in a Roman Catholic, Eastern Orthodox or Anglican tradition would find it hard to avoid a consideration of ministerial order if for no other reason than the power of the practices of these traditions. Many theologians consciously address this element, as did Michael Ramsey. In recent Australian writing Kevin Giles addresses it under the general heading of 'denomination'[12] and it is quite determinative in some recent essays by Peter Carnley.[13] The role of social and political assumptions in shaping the practical understanding of the church is evident in every chapter of church history: the political structure of the Roman administration in the church in late antiquity, the communal legal traditions in conciliarism and nation state assumptions in the sixteenth century Reformation. Notions of empire in the nineteenth century shaped some English conceptions of church and practices of episcopacy. Different conceptions of nation and empire played a role in the formation of a national church ideal in the Episcopal Church of the USA in the nineteenth and twentieth centuries.[14] The formation of synods in Australia in the nineteenth century reveals democratic political assumptions, even perhaps Chartist notions of social structure and power. The dynamic is at work in other authors and in the actions of individuals and groups within the church. This aspect of the shaping of ecclesiology is not so often remarked upon in theological literature on ecclesiology, but it is nonetheless an important and significant issue for any serious ecclesiological analysis.[15]

There is a good deal more in the standard ecclesiology literature on the nature of the Christian gospel, and the place of the church in the kingdom of God. However, the way in which that vision of the Kingdom of God is approached is very varied indeed in ecclesiology generally, and even within the smaller body of Australian Anglican writing.

Appeal to the notes of the church as drawn from the third clause of the creed features in many if not most discussions of the church. It is a

---

12. K Giles, *What on Earth Is the Church? A Biblical and Theological Enquiry* (Melbourne: HarperCollins Dove, 1995).
13. PF Carnley, *Reflections in Glass: Trends and Tensions in the Contemporary Anglican Church* (Pymble, NSW: HarperCollins, 2004).
14. See Douglas, *Fling out the Banner*.
15. See the important point made by Paul Marshall in relation to the contribution of the North American tradition of Anglicanism to modern Anglicanism in relation to such things as what he calls spiritual episcopacy, synodical government and the sending of missionary bishops in PV Marshall, 'A Note on the Role of North America in the Evolution of Anglicanism', *Anglican Theological Review*, 87/4 (2006): 549–57.

touchstone issue in Hans Küng for whom the political issues are very clear.[16] Schillebeeckx uses the notes of the church while trying to underline the human aspect of the question.[17] It plays a confirmatory and interpretative role in Karl Barth's *Church Dogmatics*. As we have already seen, Michael Ramsey takes what he regards as the core of the gospel, namely faith in the death and resurrection of Christ, as the key point of entry and also the principal interpretative issue for ecclesiology. Though that core is differently construed, that is essentially the way in which Barth comes to this question also. In *Church Dogmatics* it is the creative act of God to form the church and it is done by the preaching of the word of God. Similar attempts to give priority to the action of God are to be found in Leonardo Boff[18] and Edward Farley.[19]

In the 1960s a very notable attempt to draw together the empirical, entered through an historical investigation of the early history of Christianity and the essential marks of the Christian church, was given by Emil Brunner. He argued that the *ekklesia* as gathering or group emerged into institutional patterns. This 'church' he proposed should be thought of as the instrument and shell of the *ekklesia*.[20] A strictly biblical linguistic approach to the issue has marked a tradition on ecclesiology amongst some Anglicans in Australia. That approach was given early expression in an influential small booklet by Donald

---

16. H Küng, *Structures of the Church* (New York: Thomas Nelson & Sons, 1964); H Küng, *The Church* (Tunbridge Wells: Burns and Oates, 1968); and most clearly in the personal reminiscences in H Küng, *My Struggle for Freedom: Memoirs* (London: Continuum, 2003).
17. E Schillebeeckx, *The Church with a Human Face* (London: SCM, 1985).
18. L Boff, *Church, Charism and Power: Liberation Theology and the Institutional Church* (London: SCM, 1985); L Boff, *Ecclesiogenesis: The Base Communities Reinvent the Church* (New York: Orbis Books, 1992).
19. E Farley, *Ecclesial Man: A Social Phenomenology of Faith and Reality* (Philadelphia: Fortress Press, 1975).
20. E Brunner, 'The Christian Doctrine of the Church, Faith and the Consummation', in *Dogmatics*, volume 1, ii (London: Lutterworth, 1962).

Robinson entitled *The Church of God: Its Form and Unity.*[21] The booklet was written in the context of disputes amongst Australian Anglicans about the World Council of Churches and the Delhi Assembly of the WCC. However the general approach of the booklet has been of more enduring significance in the Sydney context, even though Robinson may have moved in his views somewhat. The material provided by Robinson was taken up by Broughton Knox to develop an ecclesiology and has been taken by a number of commentators as the 'Knox–Robinson' view of the church.[22] Whether there is such a thing as the 'Knox–Robinson' view is open to doubt in any strict sense that Knox and Robinson put together a view. It does appear to be the case though that Knox took up some of the points made by Robinson in his strictly biblical approach to the issue and used them to develop his own views on ecclesiology, views which have been much debated and proved to be very influential in the local scene.

Robinson uses the New Testament to argue that *ekklesia* is best understood as the gathering of Christians. It is a meeting and thus is intermittent and occasional. It is not the continuing group and it is certainly not the institutional structure that has developed in relation to the *ekkelsia*. Church, seen as *ekklesia*, is a meeting of Christians under the headship of Christ.[23] The book is notable for its determination to stay with what the bible says about church. Throughout the appeal which finishes the argument is that the New Testament, or the Bible, say such and such, even if it means disagreeing with a quotation from the Anglican bidding prayer about the church as the whole people of God scattered throughout the world. It is in this respect an extraordinary piece of theological method. There is no attempt at a

---

21. D Robinson, *The Church of God: Its Form and Unity* (Sydney: Jordan Books, 1965).
22. See for example, Giles, *What on Earth Is the Church?*. Peter Carnley also refers to what he calls a 'Sydney position' even though it is hard to see how a city could have an opinion or a diocese as large as that in Sydney could be held to have a common opinion.
23. This view is not unprecedented in theological debate, nor unrepresented in New Testament Studies. On the linguistic aspects of the question see JY Campbell, *Three New Testament Studies* (Leiden: EJ Brill, 1965). On the more general theological side the Congregational debates of the sixteenth and seventeenth centuries in England cover this material. See for example, G Lawson and C Condren, *Politica Sacra Et Civilis* (Cambridge: Cambridge University Press, 1992).

theological explanation of the empirical reality of the Christian groups while at times there are social assumptions hidden in the text which are quite unexamined. Yet in a curious way the broad outlines of what he says has a number of important points of contact with the introductory section of Karl Barth's *Church Dogmatics*, not least of course in the emphasis on the preached word of God, though the semantic fields of that phrase are not quite the same for the two authors.

A primarily biblical approach is taken in Australia by Kevin Giles in a number of publications. However, he is clearly not content with the local meeting conclusions and seeks to develop an interpretation of the institutionality of Christianity and also seeks to show a more nuanced approach to the New Testament texts and a different conclusion, namely that church in the New Testament means the community of Christian people.

A quite different approach can be found in Scott Cowdell's book *God's Next Big Thing*.[24] Cowdell begins with an analysis of the current cultural condition in which the nature of the church is being sought. He looks at what he calls the 'signs of the times' and the challenges that the present form of the church faces. He contrasts what he sees as the old church with the new church which is emerging. He considers, and puts aside, deductive (fundamentalist withdrawal) and reductive (secularising adaptation of the gospel) options as dead end desperate measures. We need, he says, to go beyond these and confront the theological and institutional failure of the present church. There is a new church emerging, he claims, and it will be mature, mystical and militant. With this in mind he outlines the way forward in terms of liturgy, laity and a better character of organised religion.[25]

At first blush this looks like an attempt to give theological legitimacy to a sociological analysis. But it is clear from the beginning that the analysis is theologically shaped and motivated. Throughout it is clear that he has in mind some idea of what the church might look like in general terms. At the conclusion this underlying theologically informed framework is manifest.

24. S Cowdell, *God's Next Big Thing: Discovering the Future Church* (Mulgrave: John Garratt, 2004).
25. These target groups for Cowdell are similar to those Michael Ramsey had in mind, though the proposals are very different.

The emerging church will be One, Holy, Catholic and Apostolic, as ever. It will be a Church of prophets and apostles, saints and martyrs, as ever. It will be a Church of Eucharistic celebration, of changed lives, of public witness and of world-transforming holiness. It will be a Church where much from the past will be lost. And it will be a joyful Church. Where Jesus is present, how can we tolerate it being otherwise? The question is simple. Will we put our money on the emerging church or not?[26]

This book represents a very particular approach to the question of ecclesiology. It highlights the issues of the relation between the empirical reality of the church and the theological 'ideal', though the ideal is cast in terms of fairly traditional markers. In this respect he has similar ambitions to Michael Ramsey. He casts the matter in such a way that it is difficult not to see the two aspects of the question as necessarily held together. In this respect the impulses of his earlier book, *A God for this World*,[27] seem to me to be apparent. There is not the same distance between nature and grace as in some other authors, but there is still a sense of the determining criteria of grace, of the gospel, in shaping what a church might more appropriately look like.

Behind this method however lurks a further question, namely how has the theology which has informed these shaping considerations been developed, and how has it been developed in relation to the actual experience of ecclesial reality to which the conclusions point? That that question is there yet again illustrates how far ecclesiology is at the heart of any question of theological method and the shape and character of any theological endeavour. A great virtue of Cowdell's book is that it displays this fundamental question with the utmost clarity.

In recent ecumenical writings it has become common to approach ecclesiology through a variety of theological motifs. The church as communion, or *koinonia*, became an important theme in Vatican II and has come to have a central role in the ARCIC documents.[28] The Inter

26. Cowdell, *God's Next Big Thing*, 230.
27. S Cowdell, *A God for This World* (London: Mowbray, 2000).
28. See for example J Tillard, 'The Church of God Is a Communion: The Ecclesiological Perspective of Vatican II', *One in Christ*, 27 (1981): 117–31; J Zizioulas, *Being as Communion* (Crestwood: St Vkadimir's Seminary Press, 1985). See also other essays in *One in Christ*, 28 (1992).

Anglican Theological and Doctrinal Commission used the kingdom of God and the people of God as the entry point in an early report,[29] though the 1998 Virginia Report turned to *koinonia* for its key.[30] The doctrine of the Trinity has become widely used and used to justify a variety of different models of church and even of hierarchy.[31]

It is apparent from even these most sketchy remarks that ecclesiology has been a current topic of considerable interest in the last century and especially in the last fifty years, no doubt encouraged by the documents of Vatican II. Within Australian Anglicanism there has been some limited discussion of ecclesiology. It was an underlying issue in debates on the national constitution for the church,[32] and, in particular areas of ministry and power, it was an issue in the debates over the ordination of women. In general theological debate, much has centred on ecumenical issues or the local conceptions referred to above.

An ecclesiology for Australian Anglicanism is simply an example of the general ecclesiological project set with a particular context. The elements in that context are the Anglican tradition of Christianity, insofar as that is consciously available to Australian Anglican writers, and the Australian tradition of rationality and life. The last twenty years has seen a remarkable renaissance of Anglican history and this

---

29. Anglican Consultative Council and Inter-Anglican Theological and Doctrinal Commission, *For the Sake of the Kingdom: God's Church and the New Creation* (London: Published for the Anglican Consultative Council by Church House, 1986).
30. The Virginia Report can be found in *Being Anglican in the Third Millennium*: The Official Report of the 10th Meeting of the Anglican Consultative Council: Panama, 1996 (Harrisburg: Morehouse Publications, 1997). See also B Kaye, 'Unity in the Anglican Communion: A Critique of the "Virginia Report" ', *St Mark's Review*, 184 (2001): 24–31.
31. On the general question see M Volf, *After Our Likeness: The Church as the Image of the Trinity* (Grand Rapids: Eerdmans, 1998).
32. See for example RA Giles, *The Constitutional History of the Australian Church* (London: Skeffington, 1929); J Davis, *Australian Anglicans and Their Constitution* (Canberra: Acorn Press, 1993); B Kaye, *A Church without Walls: Being Anglican in Australia* (Melbourne: Dove, 1995) and B Kaye, editor, *Anglicanism in Australia: A History* (Melbourne: Melbourne University Press, 2002).

has placed at the disposal of theologians a wealth of information and analysis not previously available.[33]

This particular project on ecclesiology is thus addressed to and speaks out of the present circumstances in which Australian Anglicans are called to be disciples of Christ. These elements are not solipsistically unique. Australian Anglicans share a faith tradition and story with Anglicans elsewhere, just as they share a social and cultural history with their fellow Australians. The demand on the theologian in the particular is to be faithful to apostolic Christianity in the light of the tradition to which they belong in the particular contexts in which

33. See for example S Judd and K Cable, *Sydney Anglicans* (Sydney: AIO, 1987); D Hilliard, *Godliness and Good Order: A History of the Anglican Church in South Australia* (Sydney: Wakefield Press, 1986); D Hilliard, 'Anglicanism', in *Australian Cultural History*, edited by S Goldberg and F Smith (Melbourne: Cambridge University Press, 1988); D Hilliard, 'The Ties That Used to Bind: A Fresh Look at the History of Australian Anglicanism', *Pacifica*, 11 (1998): 272–3; JA Moses and KJ Cable, *From Oxford to the Bush : Catholic Anglicanism in Australia. The Centenary Essays from the Church Chronicle 1932–1933* (Adelaide: Broughton Press & SPCK/Australia, 1997); B Porter, editor, *Colonial Tractarians* (Melbourne: JCBE, 1989); B Porter, editor, *Melbourne Anglicans* (Melbourne: Mitre Books, 1997); B Kaye, editor, *Anglicanism in Australia: A History* (Melbourne: Melbourne University Press, 2002); B Kaye, 'The Baggage of William Grant Broughton: The First Bishop of Australia as Hanoverian High Churchman', *Pacifica*, 8 (1995): 291–314; B Kaye, *The 1850 Bishops' Conference and the Strange Birth of Australian Synods* (Melbourne: Trinity College, 2000); T Frame, *A Church for a Nation: A History of the Anglican Diocese of Canberra and Goulburn* (Sydney: Hale and Iremonger, 2000); C Holden, *From Tories at Prayer to Socialists at Mass: St Peter's Eastern Hill, Melbourne 1846–1990* (Melbourne: Melbourne University Press, 1996); C Holden, *Ritualist on a Tricycle: Frederick Goldsmith* (Perth: University of Western Australia Press, 1997); B Dickey, *Giving a Hand: A History of Anglicare SA Since 1860* (Adelaide: Anglicare SA, 2003); RM Frappell, 'The Anglican Ministry to the Unsettled Rural Districts of Australia, 1890 to 1940', PhD thesis, University of Sydney, 1991; RM Frappell, *Anglicans in the Antipodes: An Indexed Calendar of the Papers and Correspondence of the Archbishops of Canterbury, 1788–1961, Relating to Australia, New Zealand, and the Pacific* (Westport: Greenwood Press, 1999).

they are called to fulfil their vocation as theologians. That is what this project is about. It is part of a long conversation amongst Anglicans and in the present it involves a number of connecting and competing elements. It is for these reasons that this work of ecclesiology contains chapters which deal with all aspects of the life of the church community, including such things as education and welfare. These are activities of the church and they properly come within the compass of any work on ecclesiology.

From time to time voices can be heard amongst Australian Anglicans which suggest that a theological opinion or formulation can be simply read off some aspect of the tradition, the canon of scripture, the constitution, the current practice of ministerial order, a view about the practice of the sacraments or what is going on the wider society, to name but a few of the leading examples. The fundamental work of theology cannot be so selective of the tradition and the experience of faith both in the church community and in the wider Australian society. In ecclesiological matters the nature/grace, human/divine dimensions, so clearly at the forefront in Christology, are crucial to the way we approach the question of ecclesiology and how we formulate any proposals for an ecclesiology for Australian Anglicanism.

There are some serious inherited difficulties facing the theologian in this task. Australian Anglicanism has historically been divided on ecclesiastical and theological dispositional grounds in ways which create very serious obstacles for fundamental theological endeavour. Other national entities of Anglicans have the same kinds of dispositional differences, but in Australia these differences have been embedded in the institutional structures of the dioceses in a way which is very distinctive if not unique in world wide Anglicanism. For the theologian the most serious problem this creates is the failure of a habit to listen to those who differ. There is no real necessity in the organisational arrangements for theologians to listen to those who hold significantly different views. Moreover the nature of church life means that theology is colonised into inter-diocesan politics and real differences amongst theologians are overlaid with institutional political considerations and feelings, which inevitably diminish the possibility of genuine theological encounter and thus creativity.

In principle this is a common problem in every national expression of Anglicanism. The difference in Australia is the institutional level at which the diversity and commonality is set. In Australia it is set predominantly at the diocesan level. The challenge in each case for the theologian is similar. Furthermore, because power, and its first cousin property, are held at the diocesan level, the diocese can easily tend in the Australian environment to become a self referencing totality and thus to constitute an empirical reality which is often overwhelming and seriously corrosive of open conversation both within its own arena and in relation to the wider church. How to engage with this empirical reality of ecclesial and social life and how to listen to other theologians in the common task of attending to the God and Father of our Lord Jesus Christ thus becomes one of the most pressing issues for Australian Anglican theologians.

Given this kind of framework in which Australian theologians work, theological method, especially in regard to ecclesiology, assumes a significance and priority which is quite distinctive. The conversation is often so difficult, and often so overlaid with the noise of solemn assemblies, that the necessity to return to basic issues of methodology is a recurring one. Even in this collection of essays, the preparation of which involved significant meetings and encounters, that challenge to engage at the level of assumptions and method is quite manifest. That it is so manifest shows that any movement towards an Anglican theological endeavour which is truly Australian is still in the early stages of what is increasingly a difficult and challenging journey. However, more optimistically, the project shows that the journey is at least being enterprised.

2

Historical And Global Contexts

Keith Rayner

The emergence of the Anglican Communion was not driven by a predetermined ecclesiology. It paralleled, and was intimately associated with, the evolution of the nation state of England into the British Empire and Commonwealth; and as often happens, theological reflection followed, rather than determined, changes that occurred. The articulation of an ecclesiology for the Anglican Communion is in fact a work in progress. Behind it lies the conviction that the emergence of the Anglican Communion of autonomous churches represents not merely an accident of history but the providential unfolding of something of theological significance for the church universal.

The word Anglican has a long history: the English church was known as *Ecclesia Anglicana* for centuries before the Reformation. But the word Anglicanism to describe a particular theological tradition is found only from the 1830s;[1] and the term Anglican Communion was first used in public discourse in the middle of the nineteenth century.[2] Initially Anglican simply meant English, so it was not considered an appropriate appellation for churches in Scotland or the newly independent United States, which both chose the term Episcopal. In Ireland, too, the English connotations of Anglican led the Bishop of Meath in 1878 to plead for a more appropriate term than one which for many Irishmen was linked with 'the church of the Anglo-Saxon

1. B Nockles, *The Oxford Movement in Context: Anglican High Churchmanship 1760–1857* (Cambridge: Cambridge University Press, 1994), 40. Initially the term denoted a High Church or even Puseyite understanding of the church.
2. AMG Stephenson, *The First Lambeth Conference: 1867* (London: SPCK, 1967), 55.

invaders'.[3] The fact that Anglican has survived as the name of this communion of churches, despite similar understandable sensitivities in newly decolonised countries, indicates that it has come to signify much more than English.

Robert Bosher has argued, with some justification, that the formal organisation of the Protestant Episcopal Church in the United States in 1789 really marked the birth of the Anglican Communion, though of course this was not recognised at the time.[4] The American church continued to be recognisably Anglican in doctrine and liturgy, but unlike the Church of England it had no relationship with the English Crown. It was therefore seen in England as 'a dubious offspring' (to use Bosher's words); and because it was not legally possible for the Archbishop of Canterbury to consecrate the first American bishop, Samuel Seabury obtained consecration instead at the hands of the Scottish bishops. It also explains why clergy ordained by American bishops were not permitted to exercise their office in British territories. In fact for some decades there was virtually no contact between the American and English churches.

At the time of his consecration, Seabury made a concordat with the Scottish bishops listing seven points of agreement, one of which was independence of the lay power of the state.[5] Herein lay the essential difference in polity from the mother church, for the principle of royal supremacy over the church, promulgated by Henry VIII in 1534, was integral to the self-understanding of the Church of England.[6]

In the English Reformation there had been no sense of a new church being founded: it was still the *Ecclesia Anglicana*, the church of the English nation. Papal jurisdiction was rejected and the authority of the Bible was affirmed; but this was seen as restoring a purer

---

3. AMG Stephenson, *Anglicanism and the Lambeth Conferences* (London: SPCK, 1978), 7.
4. Robert Bosher, 'The American Church and the Formation of the Anglican Communion 1823–1853' (The M Dwight Johnson Memorial Lecture in Church History, 1962), 4. The Scottish Episcopal Church could well claim, however, that it was the earliest example of an Anglican Church distinct from the Church of England.
5. The seven points are listed in full in PHE Thomas, 'Unity and Concord: An Early Anglican Communion', *Journal of Anglican Studies*, 2/1 (2004): 13–16.
6. For the terms of the Supremacy Act 1534 see GR Evans and J Robert Wright, editors, *The Anglican Tradition* (London: SPCK, 1991), 136–7.

catholicity, expressed in formularies which maintained the creeds, ministry and sacraments of the catholic church. The Elizabethan Settlement succeeded because these formularies allowed a diversity of interpretation—catholic and protestant—but within the limits of the common liturgy prescribed by successive Acts of Uniformity. The concept of a church of the nation accorded with the spirit of the age in which the nation state was coming into its own; and freedom from the centralised control of the papacy gave the church liberty to express itself in the culture and ethos of the English nation. Church and nation were bound together in a symbiotic union signified by the joint supremacy of the Crown.

The royal supremacy was a key element in these arrangements. Later theologians were to see the significance of this as a restoration of the authority of the laity in the life of the church. This was hardly uppermost in the mind of Henry VIII: his emphasis was on the authority of the king, not of the layman; yet latent within it was the possibility of restoring to the laity a real place in the governance of the church.

Richard Hooker in particular developed this theme. He argued, and this was one of his strongest objections to papalism, that authority resided in the whole church and not the bishops and clergy alone. Taking the royal supremacy out of the context of Tudor despotism he interpreted it to mean that no ecclesiastical law should be made without the consent of the laity (in Parliament) and the clergy (in Convocation), though always with the consent of the monarch.[7] With the development of the power of Parliament and the emergence of constitutional monarchy during the seventeenth century, Hooker's ideal seemed possible of realisation. But it was not to be. The English Convocations virtually fell into desuetude from 1717 to the middle of the nineteenth century; while the opening of Parliament to non-Anglicans following the reform legislation of the 1820s made it

7. Richard Hooker, *Of the Laws of Ecclesiastical Polity*, 8.6.1 and 8.6.2. See R Hooker, *The Works of That Learned and Judicious Divine Mr Richard Hooker*, arranged by John Keble, seventh edition, revised by RW Church and F Paget (Oxford: Clarendon Press, 1870). See also John Gascoigne, 'Church and State Unified: Hooker's Rationale for the English Post-Reformation Order', *Journal of Religious History*, 20/1 (February 1997): 23–34.

progressively less representative of the laity of the Church of England. So even in England by the middle of the nineteenth century the royal supremacy, while providing a pragmatic basis for the exercise of ecclesiastical authority through Parliament and the courts, was problematic as a basis for a satisfactory ecclesiology.

The situation in Australia by this time was even more problematic. The church in Australia had begun its life simply as an extension of the established Church of England. The earliest clergy were chaplains in the penal settlement and were part of the military and administrative structure of the colony, subject to the governor. Even when New South Wales became part of the new diocese of Calcutta in 1814 distance prevented the bishop from exercising any effective control. When it became an archdeaconry of Calcutta in 1824, the archdeacon was ranked next to the governor, thus recognising the church's official status. This was underlined by the proposal to set aside one seventh of the land in the colony for the endowment of the church and its schools. The fact that the proposal was never carried into effect indicated that by the early 1830s the principle of an Anglican establishment was already coming into question.

In 1836 the diocese of Australia was created, with William Grant Broughton as bishop. Broughton was a high churchman for whom the Church of England represented and upheld the spiritual side of the English nation. He was a man of determination who saw it as his responsibility to maintain the privileges and responsibilities of the established church in the colony. For him the royal supremacy placed upon the Crown the responsibility of ensuring that the church had the authority and the means to fulfil its spiritual role.

Another event of 1836, however, implicitly called into question Broughton's understanding of the place of the Church of England in the colony. Governor Sir Richard Bourke's Church Act provided financial assistance from colonial funds not only to the Church of England, but also to the Roman Catholic and Presbyterian Churches (and subsequently to others too). For the first time other denominations were placed on an equal footing with the Church of England.

Bishop Broughton reluctantly acquiesced in the Act (which in any case improved the financial position of his church), but he worried about its long term implications. Those implications became even clearer for Broughton in 1842 when, for the first time in the British Empire, a Roman Catholic hierarchy was formally inaugurated in Australia without protest from the representatives of the Crown. The governors and the Colonial Office were in fact more realistic than the bishop in recognising the realities of the situation. New South Wales was not simply English in ethnic composition. The Irish and Scots were well represented in the population, and it was their predominant churches that were recognised in the Church Act. Besides, the position was changing in England itself, where the repeal of the Test and Corporation Acts and Catholic Emancipation had in effect recognised the plurality of English religious life. In the colony the anachronism of the Church of England being understood as the spiritual side of the state under the common authority of the Crown was now exposed more sharply than in the mother country.

As New South Wales, and in due course the other Australian colonies, were granted an increasing measure of responsible self-government, the relationship of the Crown with the church became more complex. The authority of the Crown was now exercised partly through the Colonial Office and partly through the colonial legislature. Even though that legislature was largely Anglican in membership, it was unwilling to act in such a way as to imply a privileged status to the Church of England. In effect the Anglican Church became one voluntary religious body among others in the colony. The fact of ethnic and religious plurality, the influence of liberalism and the inapplicability in many respects of English ecclesiastical law in the life of the colony combined to create dysfunction between the legal status of the church in Australia and its real situation.

For Bishop Broughton this was a cause of real tension. As a conservative high churchman he respected the royal supremacy; yet in the colony the Crown was unable to protect the church and provide an authority structure to enable it to fulfil its proper ministry. Indeed, the opposite was true. The church was tied to a legal system which was not working but from which it could not escape. As a bishop he was particularly faced with difficulties of clergy discipline. In England bishops operated within an enforceable framework of law, but that framework was not operative in the colony. If he tried to act on the basis of authority inherent in the office of bishop, the law was unlikely to back him up; and the local legislature was unwilling to empower what they regarded as a voluntary body with legal sanctions.

The creation of a diocesan structure in New South Wales was paralleled in other British colonies around the world. By 1841 the Church of England had ten overseas dioceses. The establishment of the

Colonial Bishoprics Fund in that year—an underrated event in the history of the Anglican Communion—gave great stimulus to that development. 'We must plant the Church . . . in all its integrity', declared CJ Blomfield, bishop of London and chief architect of the fund; and he added that the church must 'proceed on her own principle of Apostolical order and discipline'.[8] The language is significant. Blomfield was no Tractarian, yet his words reflected Tractarian principles of the church's divinely given authority independent of the state. This added a further dimension to disquiet about the royal supremacy as the fount of church governance.

This diocesan expansion was reflected in the creation of the dioceses of New Zealand in 1841 and Tasmania in 1842 and in the subdivision of the diocese of Australia to form the dioceses of Sydney, Melbourne, Adelaide and Newcastle in 1847. By letters patent Bishop Broughton was appointed metropolitan of Australasia, with the other five bishops as his suffragans. The new structure was not however termed a province in the letters patent, and though the suffragan bishops were required to take the oath of canonical obedience to the bishop of Sydney, the metropolitan himself was to be subject 'to the general superintendence and revision of the Archbishop of Canterbury for the time being, and subordinate to the archiepiscopal see of the province of Canterbury'.[9]

By the time the new dioceses and the quasi-provincial structure were in place, the cracks in the system of governance for the colonial church were apparent, so Broughton summoned his suffragans to meet in conference in Sydney in 1850. But they had a problem: were they inhibited by Henry VIII's legislation from assembling as a formal body empowered to make decisions about the life of the church? The minutes reflected their uncertainty:

---

8. WL Sachs, The *Transformation of Anglicanism* (Cambridge: Cambridge University Press, 1993), 114–5.
9. The letters patent constituting Broughton as Metropolitan of Australasia are reproduced in full in RA Giles, *The Constitutional History of the Australian Church* (London: Skeffington & Son, 1929), 231–7. For the letters patent constituting Charles Perry as Bishop of Melbourne, see A de Q Robin, *Charles Perry: Bishop of Melbourne* (Nedlands: University of Western Australia Press, 1967), 205–12.

> We, the undersigned Metropolitan and Bishops of the Province of Australasia, in consequence of doubts existing how far we are inhibited by the Queen's Supremacy from exercising the powers of an Ecclesiastical Synod, resolve not to exercise such powers on the present occasion.[10]

While ensuring that they kept within the bounds of the law, the bishops' statement nevertheless presaged change. That they were meeting at all was significant, for it was the first time that colonial bishops had met in this way. They spoke of being a province, thus implicitly paralleling the church in Australasia with the English provinces of Canterbury and York. They also pointedly declined the powers of a synod on this occasion. First among the objects of the conference was:

> to consult together upon the various difficulties in which we are at present placed by the doubtful application to the Church in this Province of the Ecclesiastical Laws, which are now in force in England; and to suggest such measures as may seem to be most suitable for removing our present embarrassments.[11]

The chief measure which the bishops proposed was the formation of synods composed of the bishops and representative clergy which would determine 'Rules of Practice and Ecclesiastical Order'. Alongside the synods would be conventions of representative laity who, together with the clergy, would decide upon 'all questions affecting the temporalities of the Church'.[12] It was made clear, however, that the synods should have no power to alter the Thirty-Nine Articles, the Book of Common Prayer, or the Authorised Version of the Bible.[13] In this way the identity of the Church of England would be maintained in matters of doctrine and liturgy while there would be

---

10. Giles, *The Constitutional History of the Australian Church*, 237. The full minutes of the conference are printed on 237–47.
11. Giles, *The Constitutional History of the Australian Church*, 237.
12. Giles, *The Constitutional History of the Australian Church*, 239.
13. Giles, *The Constitutional History of the Australian Church*, 238.

freedom locally to decide on issues of discipline and practical administration.

This was a turning point for the colonial church. The vexed issue of the royal supremacy was tackled, not by denying it (for it still existed legally and there was sentimental attachment to it) but by tacitly recognising that it could no longer be fully operative in the conditions of a distant colony moving to self-government. The hiatus left by the breakdown of the royal supremacy would be met by constituting synods empowered to exercise authority formerly residing in the Crown and the English ecclesiastical law. The place of the laity in church government was restored, albeit in a limited fashion.

The role to be accorded to the laity was a vexed issue. Broughton believed strongly in the place of the laity in the church. Following Hooker, he held the view that the essential principle of the royal supremacy was that the monarch was invested with 'this supreme authority on behalf of the laity of the Church and as its representative'.[14] The Crown was no longer able to exercise this role in the colony, so some other form of lay representation must be devised. Broughton's problem was that in the rudimentary circumstances of early colonial life the laity were not sufficiently educated in church affairs to fit them for decision-making in spiritual matters though they had a proper role of restraint on the clergy. Charles Perry, the evangelical bishop of Melbourne, was less pessimistic. He wanted a full role for the laity, with clergy and laity meeting in one body,[15] and when synods were established in Australia it was this view that prevailed.

This conference marked a turning point for the Anglican Church. Though the break with the royal supremacy and the introduction of synodical government had been accomplished in a more thoroughgoing way in the American Episcopal Church—a precedent of which the Australasian bishops were well aware—that church was no longer part of the Church of England after the Revolution. The changes proposed by the Australasian bishops were to be effected within the Church of England, of which the colonial churches were still part.

Already at the 1850 conference there were theological differences among the bishops, which were to be magnified in subsequent years.

---

14. BN Kaye, 'The Laity in Church Governance According to Bishop Broughton', *Journal of Religious History*, 20/1 (1996): 86.
15. Robin, *Charles Perry*, 70.

Evangelicals like Charles Perry in Melbourne (1847–76) and Broughton's successor Frederic Barker in Sydney (1854–82) wanted to maintain the royal supremacy as far as was practicable and in particular wanted the protection of the English courts and ecclesiastical law against what they perceived to be the doctrinal and ritual threat associated with the growing Tractarian movement. This sense of dependence on the state inclined them to the view that new constitutional arrangements embodying synods should be instituted by parliamentary enactment. If Westminster was unwilling to act, then enabling legislation must be obtained from the colonial legislatures. The evangelicals were also wary about any proposals for provincial synods (or a General Synod) to which diocesan synods would be subordinate. From the early years regionalism was a characteristic of Australian Anglicanism, and as churchmanship differences tended to harden along diocesan boundaries, evangelical dioceses were concerned to maintain their independence against potential high church or anglo-catholic majorities in a superior synod.

High churchmen, increasingly influenced by the principles of the Oxford Movement, had a different stance. For them the church was a divine society in which bishops in apostolic succession had the responsibility to teach and guard the faith. They were happy to approve the involvement of the laity in church governance, but only in temporal matters. They strongly opposed erastian attitudes which regarded the church as subservient to the authority of the state, so they tended to be lukewarm about the royal supremacy and decidedly cool about the authority of the Judicial Committee of the Privy Council to determine matters of law involving doctrinal issues. As the church should possess spiritual authority within itself, dioceses should accept constitutions and establish synods not by permission of the legislature but by voluntary agreement of members of the church in what was known as consensual compact. They also favoured a graduated system of synods in which diocesan synods would be subordinate to those above them.[16]

---

16. This principle was endorsed by the 1867 Lambeth Conference, Resolution 4. See Roger Coleman, editor, *Resolutions of the Twelve Lambeth Conferences 1867–1988* (Toronto: Anglican Book Centre, 1992), 1.

As diocesan synods were established in Australia, beginning with Adelaide in 1855, they tied themselves firmly to the Church of England so far as faith, order and worship were concerned. In making no provision for any alteration of the basic formularies of the Church of England, however, they sowed the seeds of future problems. An unalterable Declaration in the Constitution of the Diocese of Adelaide was typical:

> The Diocese of Adelaide in South Australia is part of the United Church of England and Ireland, and doth maintain the Doctrine and Sacraments of Christ, as the Lord hath commanded, and as the said United Church of England and Ireland doth receive the same; together with the Book of Common Prayer, and of ordering of Bishops, Priests and Deacons.[17]

By this kind of constitutional provision each of the Australian dioceses remained attached to the Church of England. In fact, constitutionally, their ties were to the mother church rather than to each other. Clearly the mechanism was effective because, half a century later in 1911, eminent English and Australian counsel gave their considered opinion that 'the Anglican Churches in Australia and Tasmania are all organised upon the basis that they are not merely Churches "in communion with" or "in connection with" the Church of England, but are actual parts of that church'.[18] It was only in 1962 that this legal nexus was broken.

By the middle of the nineteenth century there were signs of the emerging awareness of an Anglican Communion and of the need for consultation on matters of common concern. A significant factor was improved communication, particularly with the advent of the steamship. Bishops and others from the American and colonial churches were visiting England more frequently and formerly abstract issues

17. Giles, *The Constitutional History of the Australian Church*, 255. A superficial reading of John Davis, *Australian Anglicans and their Constitution* (Canberra: Acorn Press, 1993), 35, might suggest that this Declaration was alterable; but the provision for alteration applied only to the 'Fundamental Provisions'.
18. Giles, *The Constitutional History of the Australian Church*, 166.

became more personal.[19] Meanwhile in the American church there was a sense of spiritual isolation stemming from the absence of visible bonds of communion with other Anglicans with whom they shared a common history, faith and order. In 1851 John H Hopkins, bishop of Vermont, took up a phrase in a letter from JB Sumner, Archbishop of Canterbury, about the 'close communion' binding the two churches. Hopkins looked to the time 'when we shall prove the reality of that communion in the primitive style by meeting in the good old fashion of Synodical action', and he hoped for 'a Council of all the Bishops in Communion with your Grace'. It was significant that Hopkins assumed that being in communion with the Archbishop of Canterbury would be the test for participation in this common action. This would be a natural assumption for the colonial churches which looked to Canterbury's metropolitical status; coming from the bishop of an autonomous church it was an important pointer to the pivotal role of the see of Canterbury in the Anglican Communion.[20]

By the 1860s the constitutional difficulties of the colonial churches became increasingly pressing. Up to this time colonial dioceses had been created, bishops appointed, and the powers to be exercised by them specified in letters patent of the Crown. In points of detail these were sometimes deficient;[21] but the difficulties were even more deep-rooted. In the judgment of the New South Wales Supreme Court in the

---

19. In 1853, for example, when Bishops Broughton of Sydney and Mountain of Quebec visited England to press for action to meet the constitutional problems of their respective churches, they were able to meet with the bishops of Newfoundland, Nova Scotia, Cape Town and Antigua, who were there at the same time.
20. Hopkins to Sumner, 15 May 1851, quoted in Stephenson, *The First Lambeth Conference: 1867*, 43.
21. For example, when a dispute occurred in 1864 in the diocese of Brisbane as to whether the bishop or the congregation had the right to appoint an incumbent to the parish of Ipswich, the advice of the Queensland Attorney General was that the letters patent conferred this power neither on the bishop nor the congregation. 'If such a legal power exists anywhere', the Attorney General advised, 'it is to be found in the Governor, acting provisionally on behalf of the Crown'. This was an intolerable situation in a self-governing colony where there was no established church. Quoted in Governor Sir George Bowen to Secretary of State for the Colonies, Despatch number 6, 1865.

case of Long v the bishop of Sydney, in 1861, the Chief Justice opined that 'the King's Ecclesiastical Law of England has no applicability to the circumstances of this colony' and that the letters patent on which the bishop relied purported to convey more powers than they legally could.[22] Then judgments of the Judicial Committee of the Privy Council in the case of Long v the bishop of Cape Town, in 1863, and the Colenso case, in 1865 and 1866, made it clear that in colonies with an independent legislature letters patent of the Crown could have no legal effect or operation.

The disarray in which this left the colonial churches was a major reason for the calling of the first Lambeth Conference by the archbishop of Canterbury, Charles Longley, in 1867. But there were other considerations too: doctrinal concerns, particularly associated with the publication of *Essays and Reviews* in 1860; a fear that the revival of the English convocations might lead to the promulgation of new canons for the Church of England which would put it out of kilter with other Anglican churches; and a desire to counterbalance the influence of the Roman Catholic Church, particularly following the promulgation of the dogma of the Immaculate Conception of the Blessed Virgin Mary in 1854. More positively there was the sense that the family relationship among Anglicans resulting from their common origin and common faith, which was both catholic and reformed, should find tangible expression in mutual consultation to maintain and enhance the communion between them.

It was not immediately obvious what should be the nature and authority of such a meeting and who should be invited to it. The first formal request came in 1865 from the Canadian provincial synod which proposed 'a National Synod of the Bishops of the Anglican Church at home and abroad'.[23] The term 'National Synod' reflected the continuing understanding that the colonial dioceses were part of the one Church of England; it also implied an assembly with power to make and carry out decisions. This would have excluded the American and Scottish Episcopal Churches. In the end those churches were included but not, as someone had suggested, the Presbyterian Church of Scotland (being established under the Crown) nor the Church of

22. R Border, *Church and State in Australia 1788–1872* (London: SPCK, 1962), 259–66.

23. Quoted in Stephenson, *The First Lambeth Conference: 1867*, 151.

Sweden.[24] The term 'synod' was controversial because it implied decision-making powers which could not accord with the royal supremacy and was anathema to English broad churchmen and evangelicals. Archbishop Longley recognised this and insisted that it would be a conference, not a synod, with a consultative, not juridical, character. So from the start, a pattern was set not only for the composition and authority of the Lambeth Conference but for the Anglican Communion itself.

Only one of the eight Australian bishops, Mathew Hale of Perth, attended the first Lambeth Conference. The absence of the others did not signify either apathy or hostility. Distance from England was great, notice of the conference was short, and pressing commitments could not readily be shelved.[25] A good picture of the outlook in the Australian dioceses is given, however, in their responses to a pre-conference questionnaire circulated by AC Tait, bishop of London, in 1866. They revealed a wide diversity of opinion. From the evangelical bishops and their dioceses, notably Sydney, Melbourne and Goulburn, there was a high degree of consensus. It was summed up by Dean W M Cowper of Sydney: the bonds needed to maintain Anglican unity were 'the Royal Supremacy, the relation we hold to the See of Canterbury, and the right of appeal in all causes of grave moment to Her Majesty in Council'.[26] Bishop Perry of Melbourne only differed in arguing that bishops should take their oath of obedience to their own metropolitan, not to the archbishop of Canterbury.[27] Nevertheless he was clear that colonial church independence would be dangerous: it would promote sacerdotalism and alienate the laity.[28]

At the other end of the scale the high churchman, William Tyrrell, bishop of Newcastle, argued for the independence of the colonial

---

24. Stephenson, *The First Lambeth Conference*: *1867*, 163.
25. Longley Correspondence, Lambeth Palace Library, volume 6, 1867, admirably summarised in R Frappell, R Withycombe *et al*, editors, *Anglicans in the Antipodes* (Westport, CT: Greenwood Press, 1999), 16–17.
26. WM Cowper to AC Tait, 23 January 1867, Tait Correspondence, Lambeth Palace Library, volume 160, 24–7.
27. C Perry to AC Tait, 26 December 1866, summarised in *Anglicans in the Antipodes*, 33.
28. C Perry to AC Tait, 13 November 1866, *Anglicans in the Antipodes*, 33.

church, with its bishops receiving their mission not from Canterbury but from the local provincial synod which should also be the final court of appeal. The royal supremacy was now inoperative, and rightly so. The unity of the Anglican Communion would be preserved by the voluntary adoption by the daughter churches of the classical formularies of the Church of England, namely the Book of Common Prayer, the Articles and the Ordinal.[29] Adelaide agreed about the formularies but revealed mixed views on the value of personal allegiance to the archbishop of Canterbury. Its synod even implied that Archbishop Longley had dangerously sanctioned the Colenso schism in South Africa.[30]

These varied responses already foreshadowed what would be continuing differences among the Australian dioceses as to the nature of the bonds that should hold the Anglican Communion together. No one questioned that unity of doctrine and liturgy was necessary, and no one wanted to diminish the reality of communion. But those who feared high church innovations put their reliance on remaining an integral part of the Church of England under such degree of royal supremacy as was still possible. High churchmen were more inclined towards autonomy of government within the doctrinal and liturgical limits required by the classical formularies and with the breadth of interpretation which they permitted.

Constitutional anomalies and differences of opinion about them made little impact on ordinary Australian Anglicans. Most of them were British by birth or descent, and imperial sentiment was strong at least until the second World War. In the parishes the same varieties in the expression of faith and worship developed as in the home church. While little concerned about royal supremacy as a theory, Australian Anglicans were proud to belong to the church of the monarch, for whom there was affection and loyalty. It was still the Church of England, and if not 'established' in any legal sense, it was both the largest denomination and the one generally called upon to provide the spiritual input into national and civic occasions.

This was one reason the church in Australia was slower than in other self-governing dominions to break the legal nexus with the

29. W Tyrrell to AC Tait, 22 March 1867, *Anglicans in the Antipodes*, 32 (wrongly dated there as 22 January).
30. AR Russell to AC Tait, 25 February 1867, *Anglicans in the Antipodes*, 35.

mother church. The other major factor was the regionalism which was strongly entrenched in its history. In part this reflected the size of the nation-continent and the separate history of its six colonies before Federation in 1901; but also the way in which differing ecclesiastical traditions had developed along diocesan lines.

Even when a General Synod was inaugurated in 1872 (significantly almost thirty years before the colonies federated) its unifying effect was minimal. Its constitution provided that its Determinations would only become operative in a diocese when that diocese accepted them. Real power remained with the dioceses, for which the General Synod provided a loose federal structure. The primate was simply the first among equals without jurisdiction over the other bishops. Until 1900 the mother diocese of Sydney was the fixed primatial see, but the unwillingness of that diocese to give any say in the appointment of its bishop to the rest of the Australian church caused it to lose that status. As internal provinces were formed, roughly coinciding with state boundaries, it was only the province of Queensland, with its fairly uniform anglo-catholic tradition, which followed the principle proposed by the 1867 Lambeth Conference that synods should be subordinate to the higher authority of a synod above them.[31] In consequence, the Australian church continued to be essentially a diocesan, rather than a national, church.

In the latter part of the nineteenth century, and increasingly in the twentieth, the traditional formularies of the Church of England came under pressure. The Bible was being subject to a variety of interpretations; doctrinal and ritual controversy accompanied the growing influence of the catholic movement; and changes in society meant that liturgical rigidity and seventeenth century language were inadequate to meet all the needs of worshippers.[32] This last was particularly true in Australia, where conditions were so different from England. One outcome of these pressures was the movement for revision of the

31. K Rayner, 'The History of the Church of England in Queensland' (University of Queensland, unpublished PhD Thesis, 1962), 276–7.
32. In England the Royal Commission on Ecclesiastical Discipline concluded in 1906 that 'the law of public worship in the Church of England is too narrow for the religious life of the present generation'. Quoted in GKA Bell, *Randall Davidson* (London: Oxford University Press, 1935), 471.

Prayer Book. In Australia, particularly among anglo-catholics, there was restiveness at the legal inability of the Australian church to modify the existing formularies and at its bondage to the judgments of English courts. Yet imperial sentiment was still strong, and for those who feared anglo-catholic encroachment, the ties with the Reformation formularies and the English legal system were seen to be more necessary than ever.

It was in this climate of divided opinion that the long struggle for the constitutional autonomy of the Australian church took place in the decades after the first World War. The laity more than the clergy were influenced by the pro-Empire argument against 'cutting the painter'.[33] Though the need for autonomy was increasingly obvious, evangelicals (particularly in Sydney) argued for caution lest Reformation principles be lost. They initially insisted on the rigid, unalterable entrenchment of the classical formularies in any constitution and on an appellate tribunal which would have a majority of lay rather than episcopal members.

From the end of the nineteenth century Australian Anglicans played a significant part in the wave of missionary enterprise which led to the spread of Anglicanism around the world. As early as 1825 the Reverend Samuel Marsden had formed a New South Wales Auxiliary of the Church Missionary Society and he personally engaged in the evangelisation of Maoris in New Zealand. The church's missionary responsibilities were officially recognised by the bishops at their 1850 conference when they established an Australasian Board of Missions. But it was the beginning of the New Guinea mission in 1891 and the formation of Church Missionary Associations in New South Wales and Victoria in 1892 (which became branches of CMS Australia in 1916) that gave impetus to the Anglican overseas missionary enterprise. While ABM concentrated on the southern and western Pacific (particularly New Guinea), CMS majored on East Africa (particularly Tanganyika) and parts of Asia. The numbers who served as missionaries were considerable, reaching their peak in the years after the second World War.[34] It meant that Australian Anglicans

---

33. RSM Withycombe, 'Imperial Nexus and National Anglican Identity: The Australian 1911–12 Legal Nexus Opinions Revisited', *Journal of Anglican Studies*, 2/1 (2004).
34. Stuart Piggin, 'Australian Anglicanism in a World-wide Context', in B Kaye, editor, *Anglicanism in Australia* (Melbourne: Melbourne

played a critical role in the development of what would become autonomous churches in the Anglican Communion, notably Papua New Guinea and Tanzania, and others to a lesser degree.[35] It was part of the process of decentralisation by which the once dominant role of the Church of England in the Anglican Communion was diminishing.[36]

Meanwhile the struggle to achieve an Australian church constitution, which had begun in the 1920s, was still unresolved by 1950. The heart of opposition lay in the predominantly evangelical diocese of Sydney, which feared that autonomy would permit anglo-catholic encroachment by permitting alteration of the seventeenth century formularies and removing the protective jurisdiction of the English courts. One factor which led to the reconsideration of Sydney's opposition was the outcome of the 'Red Book' case. Leading Sydney churchmen supported a court case against Arnold Wylde, bishop of Bathurst, for authorising rites which were not provided in the Book of Common Prayer. Although Wylde lost his case both in the lower court and on appeal to the High Court of Australia in 1948 (in a 2-2 judgment), the nature of the judgment made it clear that evangelicals could not in future rely on the civil courts for protection.[37] The other factor was the work being done in England on a proposed new code of canon law which, among other things, would legalise eucharistic vestments. These were in widespread use both in England and Australia; but for Sydney evangelicals they symbolised anglo-catholic

---

University Press, 2002), 208, reports that in the mid 1960s CMS supported 265 missionaries and ABM 213.

35. For the work of ABM in Papua New Guinea see David Wetherell, *Reluctant Mission: The Anglican Church in Papua New Guinea* (St Lucia: University of Queensland Press, 1977). For the role of CMS Australia see Keith Cole, *A History of the Church Missionary Society of Australia* (Melbourne: CMS Publications, 1971).

36. There was some initial reluctance in England to accept Australian recommendations as to the appointment of Australians as bishops of Central Tanganyika. See Davidson and Fisher Correspondence, Lambeth Palace Library, summarised in *Anglicans in the Antipodes*, 225–7 and 292–4.

37. John Davis, *Australian Anglicans and their Constitution*, 111–30. See also Ruth Teale, 'The "Red Book" Case', *Journal of Religious History*, 12/1 (1982): 74–89. Also F de Witt Batty to GF Fisher, 4 April 1949, summarised in *Anglicans in the Antipodes*, 286.

doctrine and practice, and their use was banned by the Sydney synod. So the legal nexus with the Church of England became a potential threat rather than a protection.[38]

The intervention of Geoffrey Fisher, Archbishop of Canterbury, facilitated a breakthrough. Fisher was the major architect of the decolonisation of Anglican churches around the world in response to the political decolonisation which occurred after the second World War. His vision of pan-Anglicanism led to a great increase in the number of autonomous provinces and shaped the modern Anglican Communion. The achievement of a constitution for the Australian church was an important part of his vision.[39] After a complicated legal process involving both federal and state parliaments the constitution came into effect in 1962 and the Church of England in Australia (as it was still called until it became the Anglican Church of Australia in 1981) became an autonomous church in the Anglican Communion.

The constitution makes clear that the Anglican Church of Australia understands itself to be 'a part of the One Holy Catholic and Apostolic Church of Christ'. It binds itself to the faith as set forth in the creeds, the canonical scriptures as 'the ultimate rule and standard of faith', the gospel sacraments and the ministry of bishops, priests and deacons. Its ruling principles—now alterable, but only within strict limits—tie it firmly to its Anglican heritage in the principles of doctrine and worship in the Book of Common Prayer, the Thirty-Nine Articles and the Ordinal. It remains in communion with the Church of England and with churches in communion therewith. The diocese is specified as the basic unit of organisation, and on major matters of order and good government canons of General Synod only have effect in a diocese when accepted by the diocesan synod. In contrast to most churches of the Anglican Communion this gives the Australian church a federal and diocesan character. The General Synod consists of the houses of bishops, clergy and laity, who meet together in one assembly; but the opportunity to vote by orders gives each house the possibility of veto on significant matters. Though the bishops meet informally in annual conference, the house of bishops does not (except in one or two minor areas) fulfil constitutional functions apart from the whole synod. This potentially increases the lay influence in church governance, as does

38. HWK Mowll to DWB Robinson, 12 August 1955, quoted in Davis, *Australian Anglicans and their Constitution*, 150.
39. See Stuart Piggin in Kaye, editor, *Anglicanism in Australia*, 210–14.

the composition of the appellate tribunal which consists of four lay lawyers and only three bishops.

In the constitution the catholicity of the church, derived through the mother Church of England from the Church Universal, is foundational. So is its reformed, scriptural character. At the same time it is an Australian church, autonomous and able to be inculturated in Australian life. This national character assumed greater importance in the latter part of the twentieth century as Australia diverged further from its English roots. Yet membership of the Anglican Communion is seen to be important. It gives expression to the sense of 'family' which, if less obvious than in the days of Empire, is still real;[40] it enables participation in global mission in an increasingly globalised world; it helps guard against narrow bondage to local culture; it allows for the possibility of outside fraternal critique if deviant doctrinal trends should emerge; and it expresses the gospel imperative for Christian unity, initially with fellow Anglicans, and through that global fellowship with other world communions.

In the last quarter of the twentieth century the ready availability of rapid travel and the revolution in electronic communications enhanced the visibility of communion among Anglican churches worldwide. Anglicans at every level from primates to ordinary worshippers travelled to one anothers' churches. Every Archbishop of Canterbury after Geoffrey Fisher visited Australia, and Australian church leaders were playing significant roles in inter-Anglican activities. The Lambeth Conference of bishops continued to meet every ten years. From 1971 the Anglican Consultative Council met at three yearly intervals, bringing together representative clergy and laity as well as bishops. After 1978 there were regular meetings of primates, initially biennially but by the late 90s annually. There was now talk of four 'instruments of unity' binding the Anglican Communion together—the Archbishop of Canterbury, the Lambeth Conference, the Anglican Consultative Council and the Primates' Meeting.[41]

---

40. David Hilliard, 'The Ties that used to Bind: A Fresh Look at the History of Australian Anglicanism', *Pacifica*, 11 (October 1998): 265–80, makes interesting observations about the diverse ties binding Anglicanism.

41. See 'The Virginia Report', M Dyer *et al*, editors, *The Official Report of the Lambeth Conference 1998* (Harrisburg: Morehouse Publishing, 1999), 56–63.

In one sense the emphasis on these 'instruments of unity' was a response to perceived threats to the unity of the Communion. In the western world increasing secularisation was diminishing the church's influence and confidence. Changing gender relationships and sexual mores in society raised questions for the church about its traditional understanding of an all-male priesthood and sexual morality. At the same time the growth in numbers and confidence of the church in the 'two-thirds world' was changing the balance of power in worldwide Anglicanism. Controversies over the ordination of women, homosexuality and biblical interpretation were often exacerbated by cultural differences; and reactions in some parts of the world to the sole superpower status and encroaching culture of the United States contributed to a sense of unease at innovations in the American church. Also, instant communication across the world which enhanced the possibilities of communion at the same time magnified the possibilities of disunity by immediately transferring local controversy to the global stage.

In this environment adherence to the classical formularies, which had been seen as a safeguard of unity among Anglican churches, was no longer adequate for that purpose. These were subject to diverse interpretations. The Bible itself was being read differently; the Book of Common Prayer was falling out of use, even though the new liturgies owed much to it; the Articles did not satisfactorily address many of the theological questions of the twenty-first century; and there were strong differences on matters like the ordination of women and sexual morality. Even the bonds of a common English heritage were losing their force as the numerical weight of the Communion moved.

In Australia the tensions resulting from these new circumstances took a distinctive form. The federal character of the church meant that differences were catered for by dioceses adopting different policies. There had in fact been a long tradition of diocesan diversity, for example in biblical interpretation, in permitted variations in worship, and in provision for remarriage after divorce. When new issues arose—notably, the ordination of women, homosexuality and proposals in Sydney for lay presidency at the Eucharist—they posed real threats to unity, but they tended to be contained within the Australian tradition of diocesan diversity. Most dioceses, for example, opted to endorse the General Synod's approval of the ordination of women but some did not.

Underlying other differences lay the emergence of a distinctive ecclesiology associated with Sydney's Moore College, which interpreted 'church' to mean only the local congregation or else the assembly of the saints in heaven.[42] On this view it was a misnomer to apply 'church' to a national church or a diocese. This built upon earlier evangelical emphasis on the church as the invisible body of true believers known only to God rather than on the structured visible church. Previously this tendency had been tempered for Anglican evangelicals by their commitment to Anglican order and liturgy. For the new breed of radical evangelicals this was less important. For them pan-evangelicalism took priority over pan-Anglicanism, and organised ecumenism (to which Anglicanism had traditionally been a significant contributor) was given short shrift.[43] They saw 'biblical orthodoxy' as the only basis for christian fellowship. The problem is that many fellow Anglicans who stand firm to biblical faith see this 'orthodoxy' as partial and sectarian in character, representing an ecclesiology that fails to do justice to the Anglican tradition and to the founding fathers of the Australian church constitution.

In the face of significant diversity in belief and practice the question of the nature and exercise of authority has become critical in Anglican ecclesiology. It is not that diversity is evil in itself: it is evident in the New Testament and throughout church history. Anglicans are suspicious of over-centralisation and the desire for rigid uniformity which often accompanies it, and the principle of subsidiarity has received recent emphasis.[44] But what if particular differences are seen by some members of the church to be so fundamental as to breach communion? Who is to adjudicate, and how ?

The Tudor royal supremacy had been one answer. It depended however on an understanding of church and nation as twin sides of one entity of which the sovereign was the head; and it allowed, at least in theory, for the exercise of authority by the whole church—clergy

---

42. Bill Lawton, 'Australian Anglican Theology', in Kaye, editor, *Anglicanism in Australia*, 188–90.
43. This lay behind the decision of the diocese of Sydney in 1992 and subsequent years to withhold that part of its contribution to the general synod budget which supported the work of the Anglican Communion and the Australian (later National) Council of Churches.
44. 'The Virginia Report', 44–7, 53–4.

and laity together under the headship of the Crown. That principle could no longer exist in post-Revolution America, where the relationship of clergy and laity had to be rethought. Less dramatically, it gradually ceased to exist in workable form in the colonial dioceses of the Church of England in the nineteenth and twentieth centuries as the colonies achieved self-government and the jurisdiction of the Crown and English law diminished. In Australia, for example, a system of synodical government was developed involving bishops, other clergy and laity, with internal disciplinary tribunals and an appellate tribunal empowered to interpret church law. There is still recourse to the civil courts in matters such as breach of trust, but it is apparent that those courts have become increasingly unwilling to adjudicate on matters of doctrine. Even in England, though the trappings of royal supremacy and establishment have continued into the twenty-first century, the trend is inexorably in the direction already taken elsewhere in the Communion.

Each church of the Communion now has its own juridical structure. But what if one church disagrees with others on potentially communion-breaking issues? This has become a reality, most recently with the consecration of an actively gay bishop of New Hampshire and with formal approval in New Westminster of the blessing of same-sex unions. From the first Lambeth Conference, inter-Anglican entities have consistently disclaimed juridical authority over member churches of the Communion. Each church is autonomous. The archbishop of Canterbury is a focus of unity who 'gathers' but does not rule the churches. The other 'instruments of unity' are consultative, and their authority is one of 'moral suasion', not compulsion. For a church which eschewed papal centralisation and uniformity at the Reformation these are important principles. But are they sufficient to maintain communion ?

Two opposite responses have been proposed. One tends towards some kind of authoritative central authority for the Communion. The Lambeth Conference in 1998, for example, asked the Primates' Meeting, under the presidency of the archbishop of Canterbury, to be prepared to intervene 'in cases of exceptional emergency' and to give guidelines 'on the limits of our Anglican diversity in submission to the sovereign authority of Holy Scripture and in loyalty to our Anglican tradition and formularies'.[45] Subsequently the primates of the West Indies and the Southern Cone of South America built upon this resolution by proposing procedures through the Primates' Meeting for the possible suspension of communion with an intransigent church.[46]

The alternative view emphasises the constitutional independence of member churches, arguing for tolerance and cross-cultural understanding. Prophetic initiatives have often failed to win widespread assent initially, and premature authoritative judgments can inhibit new understandings of the truth. A period of 'reception' is needed in which the Holy Spirit can guide the whole church into fuller understanding of God's will.[47] In the end each church must be free to act according to its own convictions, even if this means a rupture of communion with others.

Against the background of the crisis in inter-Anglican relationships provoked by the New Hampshire and New Westminster actions, the archbishop of Canterbury in consultation with the primates set up a commission on Communion which produced *The Windsor Report*. This report was a creative attempt to apply the principles of consultation and moral suasion, which had characterised inter-Anglican relationships since the first Lambeth Conference, to the polarised situation within the Communion. Taking seriously the authority of scripture, the report pointed out that the phrase 'the authority of scripture' is really shorthand for 'the authority of the triune God, exercised through scripture'.[48] The autonomy of the churches of the Communion does not imply isolated individualism: 'The key idea is autonomy-in-communion, that is, freedom held within interdependence'.[49] This places upon each church the responsibility of bringing potentially contentious initiatives to the rest of the Communion for consultation and agreement before they are implemented. It proposes

---

45. Dyer *et al*, editors, *The Official Report of the Lambeth Conference 1998*, 396, Resolution III, 6.
46. Drexel Gomez and Maurice Sinclair, editors, *To Mend the Net* (Carrollton: The Ecclesia Society, 2001), 13–14.
47. Stephen Pickard, 'Innovation and Undecidability: Some Implications for the Koinonia of the Anglican Church', *Journal of Anglican Studies*, 2/2 (2004): 87–105, gives an interesting perspective on the undecidability of some critical issues.
48. *The Windsor Report* (London: Anglican Communion Office, 2004), 39.
49. *The Windsor Report*, 48.

that this should be voluntarily agreed in the form of a Covenant to be formally adopted by each church.

This proposal is strangely consonant with the experience of Australian Anglicanism. In a sense the Anglican Church of Australia, with the limited power and resources of its central organs of governance, is a microcosm of the Anglican Communion as a whole. It holds together in tension dioceses which embrace a wide diversity of biblical interpretation, doctrinal emphases and liturgical practice. The leadership of its primate does not depend on formal jurisdiction over dioceses other than his own. The framework provided by its constitution requires a high degree of voluntary acceptance by the dioceses of a common pattern, which is based more on 'moral suasion' than on formal juridical authority. Agreement has to be worked at; and in controversial issues that is not easy and takes time. It displays that degree of apparent weakness which is evident in any polity where authority is not imposed by organs of governance from above. Yet despite predictions from time to time of impending disintegration, the common life of the Australian church continues, albeit with an element of impaired communion which establishes a constant imperative to continue working at differences.

The parallels between the mutual relationships of dioceses within the Australian church and those of member churches within the world-wide Anglican Communion are not of course precise. Obviously the racial and cultural differences are greater on the international scene; also the Australian church is governed by a constitution, which is lacking in the Communion as a whole. The proposal in the Windsor Report for a common Anglican Covenant would however provide a framework for the Communion not dissimilar to that given to the Australian church by its constitution.[50] In the end, both require a high degree of voluntary compliance. It is a framework which displeases the tightly ordered legal mindset; but perhaps it sits well with the freedom inherent in the christian gospel.

It is too early to assess the response to *The Windsor Report*. The danger is that it could inhibit genuinely prophetic action and impose a stagnant conformity. Its virtue is that it could foster an ecclesiology enabling worldwide communion across boundaries of nationalism, culture and sectarian narrowness but without the deadening hand of centralised enforced authority. If that should be achieved, it would be a major contribution of Anglicanism to the ecclesiology of the church universal.

---

50. *The Windsor Report*, 62.

Part Two: Inheritance

Introduction

The essays in this section deal particularly with the Anglican inheritance. The first three essays look at the biblical and theological underpinnings of an Anglican approach: the place of the Scriptures in the life of the church and what it means to be an incarnational church. The second three essays consider particular aspects of Anglican ecclesiology through contemporary lenses: episcopacy, worship and spiritual gifts.

Richard Treloar argues that deep within the Anglican tradition is the notion of the church as a hermeneutical community. Openness, mutual listening and conversation are the key ingredients of an Anglican approach to hermeneutics.

Peter Adam passionately defends the local congregation as the place in which theology should happen. Biblically grounded, intellectually rigorous theology is the heartbeat of the life of the church and should be encouraged among the people of God meeting at parish level.

Heather Thomson reconsiders the implications of the Anglican understanding of the church as incarnational. She links this with JB Metz's idea of Jesus' life and teaching as offering a 'dangerous' memory to the church, encouraging it to be true to its prophetic calling.

Through his analysis of current models of church leadership, Stephen Pickard critiques a managerialist approach to episcopacy. He calls the church back to a vision of episcopacy linked more closely with the historic focus on oversight and pastoral care of eucharistic communities.

Jane Foulcher takes the reader through a rich exploration of worship both as expressing and forming belief and as providing a place of connecting everyday lives with the Christian tradition. She encourages Anglicans to be confident and to reclaim the breadth of the tradition as we construct common worship in the future.

In a postmodern environment of individualism Scott Cowdell asks us to rethink the communal dimension of giftedness. He sees the Anglican tradition as offering a propitious environment for the discernment and nurture of the gifts of its members for the well-being of the whole.

These chapters show the richness of the tradition within which the church of today stands, the importance of holding to the strengths of that tradition and its potential to speak of authentic discipleship to the present generation.

3
'How Do You Read?': The Anglican Church of Australia As A Hermeneutical Community

Richard Treloar

> There is no intellectual, cultural, political, or religious tradition of interpretation that does not ultimately live by the quality of its conversation; there is also no tradition that does not eventually have to acknowledge its own plurality and ambiguity.[1]

> Love your ties to their last splendour, and you will be free.[2]

Introduction

As an intellectual, cultural, political, and religious tradition of interpretation, Australian Anglicanism has long since learned to acknowledge its own plurality. Bringing that plurality and its attendant ambiguity to bear constructively upon its hermeneutical tasks—reading and applying Scripture; reading and reappropriating its own ecclesial heritage; reading and interpreting itself to the context in which it is set, and that context to itself—is a much greater challenge.[3]

1. David Tracy, *Plurality and Ambiguity: Hermeneutics, Religion, Hope* (San Francisco: Harper & Row, 1987), ix.
2. Reb Elat, as cited by Terry A Veling, *Living in the Margins: Intentional Communities and the Art of Interpretation* (New York: Crossroad, 1996), 25.
3. Bruce Kaye offers a neat definition of the hermeneutical task facing Australian Anglicans: to 'make sense of their inheritance in this particular social and political context', *A Church Without Walls: Being Anglican in Australia* (Melbourne: HarperCollins/Dove, 1995), 4.

This chapter asks of Australian Anglicans Jesus' question to the lawyer in Luke 10:26 (NRSV): 'What is written in the law? What [as in 'how', or 'in what manner'] do you read [as in 'know', 'own', or 'recognise it', 'deduce or persuade from it'] there?'[4] It does so mindful that, in Luke's gospel, this question prompts the telling of the parable of the good Samaritan—modelling a sort of hermeneutical circle in the interplay between interpretation and praxis. In short, how do Australian Anglicans read and interpret Scripture? What is the influence of their Anglicanism and of the particular social and cultural forces of their context upon this hermeneutical enterprise? And how might the Anglican Church of Australia ensure that the quality of its conversation around these issues is ultimately something it and others can live by?

What follows falls into three unequal parts. First, and unavoidably briefly, we consider some aspects of Australian society that seem relevant to these questions. Second, an Anglican doctrine of Scripture is adumbrated, with particular attention given to those theological instincts and methodological presuppositions which have characterised Anglican approaches to the reading of Scripture. Last, a short case study on the homosexuality debate in the Anglican Communion illustrates how a current hermeneutical problem is being addressed.

Some relevant aspects of the Australian context

In the state of Victoria, at least, an act of weekly 'religious' observance is watching Friday Night Football (of the Australian Football League, or 'AFL', variety) on television. In one such game of 'Aussie Rules' between Adelaide and Collingwood during the 2004 AFL season, commentator and former footballer, Dermott Brereton, revealed of a Collingwood player: 'His team mates call him "the Bible"—they reckon they can't read him!' This light-hearted, but no doubt factual, remark says much about the challenges of the context in which Australian Anglicans seek to read and interpret Scripture.

The rituals and spiritual traditions of Aboriginal and Torres Strait Islander people—the first inhabitants of Australia—are among the oldest in the world, stretching back tens of thousands of years.

Although Christianity has been the dominant religion since European settlement in the late eighteenth century, Australia is a

4. See Henry G Liddell and Robert Scott, *An Intermediate Greek–English Lexicon* (7th edition) (Oxford: Clarendon, 1952), 53, 714.

'secular' state in the technical sense that none of its public institutions are ecclesiastically controlled, nor are any of its churches established by law, such as many of its first white occupants would once have known the Church of England to be.

That is not to say that Australians are irreligious, but that religious activity in Australia is widely regarded as belonging to the private sphere.[5] In the 1996 census, only sixteen and a half per cent of people identified themselves as 'non-religious' or 'agnostic'. Whilst seventy per cent declared themselves Christian, as in other developed Western democracies, the second half of the twentieth century has seen something of a marginalisation of the influence of the churches on popular culture in Australia.[6] Alongside this, the presence of other major world religions is growing, and, according to one commentator, 'Spirituality is making a comeback'.[7]

Substantial post-World War II immigration has helped Australia grow from its Anglocentric colonial origins into a pluralist and multicultural society. Religious pluriformity, however, has been provided for by the state since at least 1836, when what became commonly known as the 'Church Act', sponsored by the eighth governor of the colony of New South Wales Richard Bourke, was passed. This Act provided state aid to churches of *any* denomination—not just the Church of England—and is thus described by Naomi Turner as a liberalising piece of legislation:

> It stood for tolerance of another man's views, for justice towards all, for equality of persons no matter . . . their origin or their religious denomination, and so for a Utopian future where all . . . would live harmoniously as one race.[8]

---

5. Kaye, *A Church Without Walls*, 34.
6. These figures are provided by the Federal Parliament of Australia, Research Note 27, 1997–98, Census 96: Religion. Cited 3 May 2004. Online: http://www.aph.gov.au/library/pubs/rn/1997–98/98rn27.htm.
7. David J Tacey, *ReEnchantment: The New Australian Spirituality* (Sydney: HarperCollins/Dove, 2000), 2, see also 3.
8. Naomi Turner, *Sinews of Sectarian Warfare? State Aid in New South Wales 1836–1862* (Canberra: Australian National University Press, 1972), 4; see also 2–3, 10, 12.

The egalitarianism of the 1836 Church Act is consistent with a self-understanding widespread among Australians, as belonging to a fairly flat social structure in which authority is dispersed and is accountable to the electorate, the media, and—most importantly—the satirists. This is partly attributable to the circumstances of colonisation, including Australia's convict origins and federated political structure,[9] but is also a function of the vast but lightly populated physical landscape and the 'tyranny of distance'[10]—both internally and externally—which Australians experience. In reality, a significant degree of socio-economic stratification has always existed, and has—if anything—increased in recent years.

Anglican views of Scripture[11]

A 'high' doctrine of the inspiration of holy Scripture, and of holy Church

Writing on the subject of inspiration in that celebrated collection of late-nineteenth-century Anglican essays, *Lux Mundi*, which he himself edited, Bishop Charles Gore makes a bold claim: 'The Church has in Scripture the highest expression of the mind of Christ.'[12] At the same time as acknowledging an intrinsic or derived authority,[13] Gore

---

9. William J Lawton, in *The Better Times to Be: Utopian Attitudes to Society Among Sydney Anglicans 1885–1914* (Kensington: University of New South Wales Press, 1990), 8–9, 55–6, depicts the first chaplains' brief as a moralising or civilising force in the new colony as being self-defining with respect to Anglican origins in Australia. The colony's emerging political model also found an echo in Australian Anglicanism's 'excessive diocesanism'. See John Davis, *Australian Anglicans and Their Constitution* (Canberra: Acorn Press, 1993), 15; see also 24.
10. See Veronica Brady, 'Called by the Land to Enter the Land', in *Creation Spirituality and the Dreamtime*, edited by C Hammond (Sydney: Millennium/E J Dwyer, 1991), 35–49, and especially 46; see also Davis, *Australian Anglicans*, 18.
11. We are reminded by Stephen Sykes in *The Integrity of Anglicanism* (London: Mowbrays, 1978), 67, that what is *distinctively* Anglican is not necessarily *uniquely* Anglican.
12. 'The Holy Spirit and Inspiration', in *Lux Mundi: A Series of Studies in the Religion of the Incarnation*, edited by C Gore (8th edition) (London: John Murray, 1890), 326.
13. Evan L Burge has argued that the premise underlying Anglicanism's high doctrine of Scripture is implicit in the second of Article of Religion.

cautions that the biblical texts need the Church no less if their revelatory genius is to shine, and that the Scriptures have 'suffered greatly from being isolated' as a source of authority for belief.[14]

Because of an understanding of the nature of revelation that is both historically grounded in paradigmatic events and continuously recapitulated in the present experience of the community of faith,[15] 'belief in the Holy Scriptures as inspired requires . . . belief in the general action of the Holy Spirit upon the Christian society and the individual soul'.[16] Anglicanism then, in Gore's view, preserves the dialectical model of the early Church whereby Scripture, 'as the highest utterance of the Spirit, the unique and constant test of the church's life and teaching', is itself interpreted by that same Spirit at work in the Church.[17]

Centuries earlier, with respect to the Anabaptist view of Scripture as all- and self-sufficient, Richard Hooker countered, 'for mine own part, I dare not so lightly esteem of the Church'. The Church, constantly tested by Scripture, remains faithful to the authority of that instrument by its 'constant wrestling with the problems involved in discovering the force and relevance of the biblical story to the circumstances of Christian living today'.[18]

'The Authority of Scripture—An Anglican Perspective' (paper presented to a meeting of the Australian Church Union, Melbourne, 17 November 2001), 3.

14. Gore, 'The Holy Spirit and Inspiration', 337.
15. *Ibid*, 338. The Church's life in every age, Gore reflects, 'reproduces the original "witness" . . . and brings down remote and alien incidents into close and intelligible familiarity', *ibid*.
16. *Ibid*.
17. *Ibid*. More recently, Gerard Loughlin has made a similar case: 'The Scripture makes the Church and the Church makes the Scripture; they are mutually constitutive', in *Telling God's Story: Bible, Church and Narrative Theology* (Cambridge: Cambridge University Press, 1996), 36. 'The location of biblical inspiration', he adds, drawing on the work of John Henry Newman, 'is not the text itself, but the life of the community in which the text is read and celebrated', 114.
18. Anthony Harvey, 'Attending to Scripture', in The Doctrine Commission of the Church of England, *Believing in the Church: The Corporate Nature of Faith* (London: SPCK, 1988), 25–44, and here at 30.

A 'relative' view of the authority of Scripture

This inescapable relationship between Scripture and Church is reflected in the Thirty-Nine Articles, the Lambeth resolutions of 1958, and in the formularies of the Anglican Church of Australia. Articles of Religion 6 and 7, in setting out the 'sufficiency' or 'adequacy' of Scripture, implicitly acknowledge the Church's hermeneutical task.[19] Echoing the language of Article 20, Resolution 3 from the 1958 Lambeth Conference describes the Church as 'guardian and interpreter' of holy Scripture. The Committee Report from this conference insists that neither Bible nor Church can be understood independently of the other, reminding Anglicans, with particular reference to the New Testament, that:

> the Church preceded it in time, and it was within the Church, with its Sacraments, Creeds, and Apostolic Ministry, that [it] was canonized. The Church is the witness and keeper of Holy Writ, charged to interpret and expound it by the aid of the Spirit of truth which is in the Church.[20]

In short, Scripture is authoritative because the Church accepts it and privileges it as such.[21] When the Church speaks of the Bible as 'word of God' it speaks sacramentally no less than it does when speaking of bread and wine as the 'body and blood of Christ'. So

---

19. The conviction that Scripture contains 'all things necessary to salvation' does not reflect a reductionist tendency in Anglican theology. Hooker, for example, understood Scripture as presupposing the wisdom of art, philosophy, and science, and cautioned that 'the benefit of nature's light be not excluded as unnecessary'. *Of the Laws of Ecclesiastical Polity*, I.xiv.4, see also I.xiv.i, II.v.2, in Volume 1 of Isaac Walton, *The Works of that Learned and Judicious Divine, Mr. Richard Hooker: With an Account of His Life and Death*; edited by John Keble (Oxford: The University Press, 1841), 1:271; see also 1:267–8, 1:300.
20. 'The Holy Bible: Its Authority and Message', in *The Lambeth Conference 1958: The Encyclical Letter from the Bishops Together with the Resolutions and Reports* (London: SPCK and Seabury, 1958), 2.4–5.
21. See Harvey, 'Attending to Scripture', 42–4. Of course, the extrinsic authority conferred on biblical literature is not independent of its intrinsic authority or the experienced reliability of those writings. See *Ibid*, 40–1.

privileged in the life of the believing community, Scripture functions something like currency: conveying what it signifies (in this case, the word of God) and becoming what it conveys.[22]

That an understanding of biblical authority as being, at least in part, extrinsic or conferred, need not necessarily lead to a purely instrumental view of Scripture is evident in the Fundamental Declarations of the constitution of the Anglican Communion in Australia (1962), which nominate the Bible as 'the ultimate rule and standard of faith' (I.2). We note with interest, however, that the declarations on either side (I.1 and I.3) refer to the one holy catholic and apostolic Church of Christ, its creeds, sacraments, and structures of ministry. As the *ultimate* source of authority for belief, then, Scripture is never the *only* reliable authority for Anglicans—including Australian Anglicans, whose constitution's Ruling Principles (II.4–6) indicate that the doctrines and principles of the Church of England, which it retains and approves, are to be found in the Book of Common Prayer (1662), the ordinal, and the Thirty-Nine Articles.[23]

This same instructive tension is also at the heart of Hooker's classic triangulation of Scripture, reason, and tradition as sources to be appealed to in concert,[24] and of the Chicago-Lambeth Quadrilateral (1886/1888) which pegged out the Scriptures, creeds, sacraments, and the historic episcopate as the framework over which the 'sacred deposit' of Christian faith can be stretched.[25] In both of these foundational Anglican schemas, Scripture's authority is relative rather than absolute. As Hooker warns, 'we must . . . take great heed, lest in attributing unto Scripture more than it can have, the incredibility of that do cause even those things which indeed it hath most abundantly to be less reverently esteemed'.[26]

---

22. Reginald H Fuller, 'Scripture', in *The Study of Anglicanism*, edited by Stephen Sykes and John Booty (London: SPCK, 1988), 80.
23. Kaye, *A Church Without Walls*, 59; see also 55.
24. With reference to the Reformation catch-cry *sola scriptura*, Hooker argues that the Scriptures do not so much direct all courses of action as shape in the Church a Scripture-informed reason. *Laws* II.i.2–3, see also II.v.1, II.viii, 5, in Keble, *Works*, 1:287–9, 1:299, 1:333.
25. See *Quadrilateral at One Hundred: Essays on the Centenary of the Chicago-Lambeth Quadrilateral 1886/88–1986/88*, edited by J Robert Wright (Cincinnati: Forward Movement Publications, 1988), vii–ix.
26. *Laws* II.viii.7, in Keble, *Works*, 1:336.

Receiving the authority of Scripture in relative rather than in absolute terms is entirely in keeping with an Anglican (and Australian) polity of dispersed authority more generally—in fact the two are inherently connected, as Stephen Sykes observes:

> it is of the essence of the Anglican view of authority that . . . the means of judging matters concerning the faith are in the hands of the whole people of God by reason of their access to the Scriptures; and further . . . it is distinctively Anglican that this means is given to them in the liturgy of the church, backed by canon law.[27]

An 'incarnational' view of revelation and Scripture

The reference in Article 6 to what may be proved from Scripture assumes 'the possibility of development or application of more general principles to changed circumstances'.[28] Those changed circumstances must include major shifts in human self-understanding through the social sciences.[29] Moreover, what may be proved from Scripture will, to some degree, be influenced by changes in the field of biblical studies, including what the very nature of biblical literature is thought to be by the community that receives it as Scripture. With the rise of the historical-critical method in view, Gore acknowledged, 'We are being asked to make considerable changes in our literary conception of the Scriptures, but not greater changes than were involved in the acceptance of heliocentric astronomy'.[30]

Likewise, in distinguishing between non-binding 'civic' and 'ritual' aspects of the Mosaic law and the binding 'moral' force of the Ten Commandments, Article 7 implies that what constitutes a faithful reception of Scripture for Anglicans is not fixed by original or

---

27. Sykes, *Integrity*, 93; see also 90, 91, 99. Burge ('Authority', 1) notes that the 'ordered, comprehensive, intelligible reading of both Old and New Testaments . . . is a fundamental principle of Anglican worship'.
28. Kaye, *A Church Without Walls*, 70.
29. Sykes, *Integrity*, 92, cites the 1928 revisions to the Book of Common Prayer wedding service as an example of this process involving the use of Scripture, 'including the scriptural grounds for allowing Christian doctrine to be responsive to changes in human self-understanding'.
30. Gore, 'The Holy Spirit', 356; see also 361. This openness to advances in biblical criticism was anticipated in an earlier volume, *Essays and Reviews*, edited by Henry Bristow Wilson (London: Longmans, 1860).

originating reading contexts.[31] Rather, as Hooker insists, careful attention to aspects of the provenance of biblical texts is part and parcel of their interpretation:

> The several books of Scripture having had each some several occasion and particular purpose which caused them to be written, the contents thereof are according the exigence of that special end whereunto they are intended.[32]

Thus he sees a danger in generalising from biblical prohibitions, and in the use of so-called 'proof texts'.[33] Anthony Harvey, writing for the Church of England's Doctrine Commission, makes a similar point on the basis of Scripture's literary form, which 'is not such that we can easily deduce from it general statements of what it is that we believe'.[34] Such a view does not compromise the high doctrine of Scripture with which we began; rather, it casts an understanding of Scripture's 'perfection' in terms of its aptness to particular ends. Adopting a high view of Scripture's inherent particularity also squares well with Anglicanism's distinctively incarnational spirituality,[35] as Harvey explains:

> If Scripture is 'inspired', it is inspired by the same God who accepted the constraints of the incarnation. It is not invested with an other-worldly, totally self-authenticating power; as with the incarnation itself, its uniqueness and authority can be glimpsed only through the limitations imposed upon it, as upon any other book, by the circumstances of composition, editing, copying and circulation.[36]

---

31. See Kaye, *A Church Without Walls*, 71.
32. *Laws* I.xiv.3, see also II.viii.5, in Keble, *Works*, 1:269–70, 1:333–4.
33. *Laws* II.vi.4, II.vii.6, 9 in Keble, *Works*, 1:317, 1:325–6, 1:328–9.
34. Harvey, 'Attending to Scripture', 30.
35. See, for example, John E Skinner, 'An Incarnational Spirituality', in *Anglican Spirituality*, edited by William J Wolf (Wilton, Conn: Morehouse–Barlow, 1982), 135–61.
36. Harvey, 'Attending to Scripture', 30. See also Fuller, 'Scripture', 80.

A 'canonical' approach to the reading of Scripture

Article 20 urges Anglicans to apply a canonical approach to the reading of Scripture; that is, one in which its various parts are understood in light of a sense of the whole. To adopt such a reading strategy does not imply that the various voices within Scripture must be syncretised, or their differences repressed under the influence of some unifying and supposedly pervasive biblical motif (such as 'covenant', or 'redemption', or 'salvation history'), nor that any notion of Scripture as a site of contest for theological or ideological meaning need be lost.[37] It does, however, demand that Scripture be read coherently, and that particular texts not be read in isolation from their context. In so far as any canonical hermeneutic is concerned with Scripture's interactive and mutually formative relationship with believing communities,[38] there can be said to be at least three aspects to such an approach, all of which will be in view in the example considered later in this chapter.

The first and most obvious has already been alluded to in the previous section, namely the interpretive significance of a given text's full *literary* context. This extends beyond the scope of any one individual biblical 'work' or 'author'.[39] It includes all of the reading-and-still-writing (or at least *re*-writing) believing communities responsible for generating the asynchronous textual dialogue which the canon of Scripture represents by virtue of its sheer 'binding' artefactual existence as a single literary volume—'the Bible'.[40] Scripture, in its final and canonical form, itself bears witness to this interactive and mutually formative relationship between texts and communities, preserving a plurality of disparate and sometimes

---

37. For an exposition and analysis of this set of approaches, see Mary C Callaway, 'Canonical Criticism', in *To Each Its Own Meaning: An Introduction to Biblical Criticisms and Their Application*, edited by Steven L McKenzie and Stephen R Haynes (revised edition; Louisville, Ky: Westminster John Knox, 1999), 142–55.
38. See Callaway, 'Canonical Criticism', 142.
39. The use of quotation marks here indicates that biblical texts and authors are not regarded as artistic objects and subjects in the same way as their modern counterparts.
40. Veling, in *Living in the Margins*, 17, uses 'conversation' as a metaphor for Christian tradition—conversation that generates writing, including and extending (although never simply as appendices) the pages of Scripture.

dissonant voices, allowing none absolute hegemony, and offering later readers a long-exposure view of the literary traces of their interplay.[41]

The second aspect of a canonical approach as one which both imposes and enables coherence has also been referred to earlier: the interpretive significance—or what Hans-Georg Gadamer has called the 'effective-historical consciousness'[42]—of tradition. *The* Tradition,[43] experienced always and only ever via one or more *traditions*, has been described as 'the stream in which we live and move'—mostly unconsciously, so encompassing, so close is its influence on us.[44]

Tradition, Walter Wink avers, 'furnishes us with our conceptions, it hides itself in our language, it provides the "available believable"; which sets the parameters of belief, and it provides an orientation for the process of reasoning'.[45] Scripture, as such, therefore, 'has no unmediated presence in the community, precisely because it is a "holy book", whose primary use is in worship'.[46] Our reading of Scripture

---

41. See Callaway, 'Canonical Criticism', 153 and 147.
42. *Truth and Method* (translated by DE Linge: Berkeley: University of California Press, 1976), 300–7. This phrase could also be translated from the German 'historically-effected consciousness'.
43. Tradition with a capital 'T' is used here in the same sense as in *A Treasure in Earthen Vessels: an Instrument for an Ecumenical Reflection on Hermeneutics* (Faith and Order Paper 182; WCC: Geneva, 1998), §15, following the 'Montreal Report'. It connotes the Gospel—'the self-givenness of God in the self-giving of Jesus Christ'—as transmitted from generation to generation in and by the Church, in various forms and expressions, or 'traditions'. See Faith and Order Paper 40, 'The Report of the Theological Commission on Tradition and Traditions', II.39, in *Faith and Order Findings: The Final Report of the Theological Commissions to the Fourth World Conference on Faith and Order, Montreal 1963*, edited by Paul S Minear (London: SCM, 1963), 1–63, and especially 18 (note that the page numbering in this volume starts over with each new report).
44. Walter Wink, *The Bible in Human Transformation: Toward a New Paradigm for Biblical Study* (Philadelphia: Fortress, 1973), 20.
45. *Ibid*, 21.
46. Sykes, *Integrity*, 107–8.

within the canonical context established by tradition(s) is thus always a 'ruled reading', determined in part by the rule of faith.[47]

That the Church's proclamation of Scripture takes place principally in this setting presents no conceptual difficulties for a communion which lives by the adage *lex orandi, lex credendi*. The corporate and fideistic nature of this hermeneutical context[48]—and more especially its impact on the imperative for coherence between readings of Scripture and other aspects of the Church's common life and worship[49]—is significant for our current purposes. The Church's identity as an interpretive community is first and foremost a function of its nature as a believing community: one that is constantly 'living into' its own collective experience and memory, a process evident within Scripture itself.[50] A good example is George Lindbeck's plea that the cross 'is not to be viewed as a figurative representation of suffering nor the messianic kingdom as a symbol for hope in the future; rather, suffering should be cruciform, and hopes for the future messianic'.[51]

Collective experience and memory, as a canonical force,[52] is at once catholic and contextual, universal and particular. In its discussion of this dialectic, the Faith and Order Commission of the World Council of Churches identifies the continual exchange between catholicity and

---

47. See James G Dunn, 'What Makes a Good Exposition?', *ExpTim* 114.5 (2003): 147–57, and especially 150; see also Loughlin, *Telling God's Story*, 50–1. Both Dunn and Loughlin make the point that the ruled reading of Scripture is an ancient practice in the Church, identifiable in the reading strategies of patristic theologians (Loughlin) and again during the Reformation (Dunn).
48. See Harvey, 'Attending to Scripture', 44.
49. Lambeth Conference 1958, 'The Holy Bible', 2.13–18.
50. See Anthony Thiselton, 'Knowledge, Myth, and Corporate Memory', in The Doctrine Commission of the Church of England, *Believing in the Church: The Corporate Nature of Faith* (London: SPCK, 1981), 45–78, and here at 73, following CH Dodd.
51. GA Lindbeck, *The Nature of Doctrine: Religion and Theology in a Postliberal Age* (London: SPCK, 1984), 118.
52. Wink's image of tradition as a stream is helpful when thinking of the force it exerts as a canon. Similarly, Delwin Brown thinks of canons as galaxies: given realities with their own gravitational pull. See *Boundaries of Our Habitations: Tradition and Theological Construction* (Albany, NY: State University of New York Press, 1994), 76–7.

contextuality as precisely that which characterises the Church as a hermeneutical community:

> The Church, whether embodied in a local congregation, episcopal diocese, or a Christian World Communion, is called to interpret texts, symbols and practices so as to discern the Word of God as a word of life amid ever-changing times and places. This hermeneutical task undertaken by the Church, with the guidance of the Holy Spirit, is a condition for apostolic mission in and for the world. To speak of the Church as a hermeneutical community is also to say that this community is a proper locus for the interpretation and the proclamation of the Gospel.[53]

There is an inevitable circularity to this interactive and mutually formative relationship between Scripture and tradition—between texts and believing communities—which is neither to be despised nor overlooked.[54]

The third aspect of a canonical approach is, in some ways, the hardest to appeal to from *within* the circle just sketched, although still very much concerned with the relationship between texts and communities: specifically that imputed by the believing community between Scripture and the wider world, by virtue of the Spirit's activity with respect to both.

Hooker's 'Scripture-informed reason' (see note 24, above) is in no way anti-scientific. It simply recognises that 'reasoning is always embedded in an inherited tradition, and tradition always extends itself through reason'.[55] Rehearsing the classic typology of God as author of both the 'book of nature' and the 'book of Scripture',[56] Hooker pleads

---

53. *A Treasure in Earthen Vessels*, §49.
54. Faith and Order Paper 40 discusses precisely this issue from an ecumenical perspective. See Minear, *Faith and Order Findings*, 36–41, and 50–3.
55. Brown, *Boundaries of our Habitations*, 35.
56. The concept of two organically related revelations in Scripture and creation can be traced back to Origen, and was developed by Hugh and Richard of Saint Victor, among other medieval scholars. See Henri de Lubac, *Medieval Exegesis: The Four Senses of Scripture*

that each of these texts be read in such a way that their respective world-views are seen as mutually illuminating, and never incompatible, for 'both jointly and not severally either of them be so complete'.[57]

Much later, the 'Noetics'—a group of influential nineteenth-century Anglican clergy based around Oriel College, Oxford, and Trinity College, Cambridge—advocated an understanding of the revelatory quality of biblical texts in which the historicity of the human condition, and their historically- and culturally-conditioned account of the same, is assumed. Scripture, accordingly, is to be studied with a spirit of openness to ongoing revelation comparable to that which might be expected to accompany the investigation of nature, or of anthropology.[58]

At the turn of that same century, Bishop Brooke Foss Westcott also argued strongly for a progressive view of revelation encountered in the Bible, which is to be 'read in the light of our own time, by the help of that same Spirit through which it was written'—asserting that 'the Church welcomes the experience of the past not as exhaustive or finally authoritative, but as educative'.[59] More recently, Delwin Brown has made a similar claim, describing the past as 'not a building but a wave, with direction and potential . . . impacting upon the present in a different form to what it was at the source of origin'.[60]

Attentiveness to this dimension of the reading context prevents the 'canon' of the Church's life and worship from becoming a *closed* hermeneutical system or circle in its relationship with Scripture. Rather, when our reception of this form of canon and our present circumstances—when catholicity and contextuality—are allowed to exist as 'mutually critical correlations', then tradition can provide both

---

(Ressourcement; translated by Mark Sebanc; 2 volumes; Grand Rapids: Eerdmans, 1998), 78.

57. *Laws* I.xiv.5, see also II.iv.5–7, in Keble, *Works*, 1:271, 1:297–9.

58. See William L Sachs, *The Transformation of Anglicanism: From State Church to Global Communion* (Cambridge: Cambridge University Press, 1993), 43.

59. As cited by Sachs, *Transformation*, 150, and 152. Fuller, in 'Scripture', 84, likewise, describes Scripture's 'normativity' for Anglicans as illustrative rather than prescriptive. So too Oliver O'Donovan speaks of Articles 6–8 as pertaining to the realm of theological 'epistemology' (see Kaye, *A Church Without Walls*, 71).

60. Brown, *Boundaries of Our Habitations*, 36.

'effective hold' and 'productive possibility',[61] *both* of which are vital to the identity and mission of the believing community. This is especially important for Anglicanism as 'essentially a "church in society" tradition',[62] because, like it or not, 'the adequacy of the identities a canon creates and sustains is tested in the unprotected space of contemporary public discourse',[63] the searching light of our own time.

In Australia, this 'ecclesial expression of the Anglican emphasis on the presence of God in the world and in human society'[64] means taking fully seriously—even 'canonically'—our pluralist, secular, postmodern context, and contributing to the formation of identity and self-understanding within it.[65] In fact without this broader canonical structure, the opportunity and 'freedom to reconstruct [an] identity which is responsive to new and changing circumstances'—what Terry Veling regards as a key hermeneutical task[66]—may be denied, the energising and identity-maintaining exchange between catholicity and contextuality defused, and the Anglican principle of liberty (see below) lost.

To summarise, then, Anglicans could be expected to be accountable for their reading of particular biblical texts (a) to the whole of biblical literature, (b) to other readers of biblical literature within the Church,[67] and (c) to texts from the 'book of nature' as appropriated and interpreted by the wider culture in which the Church is set and sent.

A 'libertarian' view of the reading of Scripture

Notwithstanding these canonical structures of accountability, the final feature of an Anglican view of Scripture to be considered here is one that many Anglicans—and Australian Anglicans, particularly—may identify with most readily and surrender least willingly. Gore's sense

61. These are David Tracy's terms, as used by Veling, *Living in the Margins*, 56.
62. Kaye, *A Church Without Walls*, 7.
63. Brown, *Boundaries of Our Habitations*, 90.
64. Kaye, *A Church Without Walls*, 7.
65. *Ibid*, 198–9.
66. Veling, *Living in the Margins*, 28.
67. There is an important ecumenical dimension to this line of accountability, see Faith and Order, *A Treasure in Earthen Vessels*, §59.

of an Anglican idea of authority which 'leaves much for the individual to do' applies no less to the interpretive authority of tradition.[68]

The essential point of Article 6 in this regard is what it negates. Sykes puts it neatly: 'It is not saying that everything which can be read in scripture ought to be believed; but rather that what a plain reader cannot himself find in the text can in no sense be required . . . as an article of belief.'[69]

The Anglican principle of liberty resonates with that of dispersed authority—including its dispersal between, and relativity with respect to, Scripture and tradition—as it does, in Australia, with a spirituality that is 'radically and significantly private'.[70] Indeed, in Gore's opinion, individual illumination serves as 'a purifying force upon the common mind of the Christian society'.[71] That said, liberty remains in the service of the catholicity of the Church, as AEJ Rawlinson, amongst the next generation of Anglicans in Gore's tradition, insisted:

> Belief in the principle of liberty does not mean simply belief in the liberty of those with whom one happens to be in personal agreement. It means the refusal to have the church turned into a sect . . . Any and every particular manifestation or expression of the Church . . . —for example the Church of England—ought . . . to aim at being catholic, in the sense of being comprehensive of all that is Christian . . . It ought to exclude none whom our Lord Jesus Christ would not exclude. It ought to rule out in principle no type of thought or of temperament, and no forms of devotion, which are in any sense genuinely and defensively Christian.[72]

Rawlinson's plea for a shared identity predicated on establishing (even by pushing back) those limitations or boundaries which circumscribe a 'field of play'—however expansive—rather than on a more categorical unity, is echoed by Brown,[73] and is, arguably, a

68. Gore, 'The Holy Spirit and Inspiration', 326.
69. Sykes, *Integrity*, 90.
70. Kaye, *A Church Without Walls*, 34.
71. Gore, 'The Holy Spirit and Inspiration', 326.
72. From a sermon preached in 1925, as cited by Sykes, *Integrity*, 23–4.
73. See Brown, *Boundaries of Our Habitations*, 77.

distinctively Anglican way of finding the freedom which comes from loving one's ties to their last splendour.

Living by the quality of our conversation: A short case study on hermeneutics and homosexuality

Rawlinson's remarks on liberty bring us back to Tracy's opening challenge: that any tradition of interpretation must ultimately live—survive its inescapable plurality and ambiguity—by the quality of its conversation. In the light of what has been argued to this point, we can think of that conversation as taking place on several levels: within Scripture, within the Church's living Tradition (including the Anglican tradition), and between traditions and their wider cultural contexts. All three are in view in the case study that follows, but the latter two will receive greater attention.

If Veling is correct in claiming that 'every true and responsible conversation puts all its participants at risk',[74] then perhaps the quality of the Anglican Communion's conversation on the issue of homosexuality—both nationally and internationally—is better than might first appear. Continuing to develop the metaphors of 'stream' and 'galaxy' (see note 52, above) for tradition—forceful spaces 'in whose pluriform swirls we are placed'[75]—responsible and honest risk occurs when:

> inhabitants of a tradition enter its stories, enact its rituals, play its roles, explore its visions, try its arguments, feel its sensibilities . . . negotiating the identity of this space in relation to themselves, and themselves in relation to the space.[76]

At the same time, Anglicans the world over in these early years of the twenty-first century will feel the sobering force of Veling's parallel observation, that 'to engage a tradition is to engage its darkness as well as its light . . . to engage it as something we are responsible for'.[77]

---

74. Veling, *Living in the Margins*, 61.
75. Brown, *Boundaries of Our Habitations*, 86.
76. *Ibid.*
77. Veling, *Living in the Margins*, 61.

At the heart—and heartache—of this particular question, with which Anglicans are currently engaging their tradition, lies an issue that is fundamental to the outcome of this and any interpretive task: whether the governing hermeneutical goal is 'productive' (in terms of new insight) or 'reproductive' (in terms of original meaning or 'intent').[78]

A reproductive hermeneutic clearly has its place in better appreciating and understanding Scripture's perfection in terms of its aptness to particular ends, but that very same principle must issue in the conviction that the hermeneutical task does not end with establishing 'original meaning' or reconstructing an 'originating context'. Veling describes the refusal to be constrained by their history of production as 'the gift of classic texts—their meaning, their reference, their subject matter, can continuously stand out in front of the text (not behind it) to awaken interpretive possibilities'.[79] On the basis of the Anglican views of Scripture presented hitherto, one can assume that Anglicans would want to include biblical texts in this company, and, with Brown, to regard the experience they connect us with in terms of 'wave' rather than 'building', impacting upon the present in a different form to what it was at the source of origin.

Leviticus 18:22 and 20:13

With these considerations in mind, let us review three recent Anglican treatments—one from England and two from Australia—of a pair of biblical texts frequently introduced into the homosexuality debate.[80]

a) Ian Duffield[81]

Ian Duffield (from the Urban Theology Unit, Sheffield) takes issue with the oft-rehearsed claim of those who opposed the appointment of Canon Jeffrey John as Bishop of Reading that homosexuality is against

78. *Ibid*, 67.

79. *Ibid*, 62.

80. *To Set Our Hope on Christ: A Response to the Invitation of 'Windsor Report' ¶135* (New York: The Office of Communication, the Episcopal Church Centre, 2005), published after the drafting of this chapter, contains another specifically Anglican reception of these texts (see §2.21a).

81. I Duffield, 'The Clear Teaching of the Bible? A Contribution to the Debate about Homosexuality and the Church of England', *ExpTim* 115.4 (2004): 109–15.

the clear teaching of the Bible, examining a number of Old and New Testament texts, including Leviticus 18:22 and 20:13. In the process, Duffield illustrates several aspects of a canonical approach to the reading of Scripture.

Although his exegetical conclusions are not uncontested,[82] these interpretive strategies include appealing to the 'inclusive trajectory' of Scripture,[83] arguing that the 'purity laws of the Old Testament (which appear to outlaw male homosexual expression but not lesbian activity) are clearly set aside in the New Testament',[84] and critiquing the lack of coherence with which those who would see here clear biblical teaching against homosexuality read these twin texts. For example, on the basis that 'the specific concern of these verses appears to be about . . . avoiding the shame associated with *confusing* social roles in the community',[85] Duffield contends that, in so far as this concern assumes a hierarchical differentiation in the social order between men and women, the prohibition of sexual practices which blur that (flawed) distinction must cease to apply when viewed in light of broader canonical (that is, theological and moral) considerations.[86] Significantly, in terms of pursuing 'productive' or 'reproductive' hermeneutical goals, Duffield has no difficulty in concluding that it is entirely appropriate to make decisions on non- or meta-biblical grounds about what biblical teaching is applicable and what is not.[87]

My own reading of these texts leads me at once to agree and to disagree with Duffield in relation to his central point that these verses are chiefly concerned with the consequences of confusing social roles in the community. There seems to be little support for readings which

---

82. See Ron Cassidy, 'The Clear Teaching of The Bible on Homosexual Practice: A Response to Ian K Duffield (*Expository Times*, January 2004, 109–15)', *ExpTim* 115.9 (2004), 298–301.
83. Duffield, 'Clear Teaching?', 110; see also 112.
84. *Ibid*, 110.
85. *Ibid*, 111, original emphasis.
86. Duffield, 'Clear Teaching?', 112. Other charges of incoherence relate primarily to the practice of an arbitrary—or, rather, theologically biased—selectivity with respect to the authority of various prohibitions in the Holiness Code, and the application of their associated penalties. *Ibid*. See also Charles Cosgrove, *Appealing to Scripture in Moral Debate: Five Hermeneutical Rules* (Grand Rapids: Eerdmans, 2002), 50.
87. Duffield, 'Clear Teaching?', 112.

cast these texts as anything other than prohibitive with respect to male homosexual acts. That is to say, their 'plain sense', linguistically and syntactically, is clear enough, and not much is gained, for example, by the suggestion that מִשְׁכְּבֵי אִשָּׁה (*mishkh'vey 'ishah*), literally 'the lyings [down] of a woman' or 'as one lies with a woman', indicates the sort of non-reciprocal or 'pederastic' relationship that Paul is reacting to in 1 Corinthians 6:9–11.[88]

However, the literary and, inasmuch as we can reconstruct or posit it, the socio-political and religious context of these texts is essential to their meaning. They must be read as part of the 'Holiness Code' (Leviticus 17–27), wherein the imperative for ritual purity sees the domain of the sacred expanded, 'embracing the entire land, not just the sanctuary, and all of Israel, not just the priesthood'.[89] As Jewish commentator Jacob Milgrom explains:

> Israel's separation from the nations is the continuation (and climax) of the cosmic creation process. Just as YHWH has separated the mineral, vegetable, and animal species to create order in the *natural* world, Israel must separate from the nations to create order in the *human* world . . . [So much so] it is possible H [the postulated 'holiness' source or 'author'] carries the belief that the very order of the natural world rests on Israel's ability to maintain its sanctity by separating itself from the nations that surround it.[90]

Given that its borders were surrounded by more populous and powerful nations, and contained numerous groupings of Canaanite peoples, it is 'understandable that Israel was obsessed with increasing its birth-rate without endangering harmonious relationships within the

88. Duffield, *Ibid*, 111, 113–14, implies this. See also Robin Scroggs, *The New Testament and Homosexuality: Contextual Background for Contemporary Debate* (Philadelphia: Fortress, 1983), 62, 101, 113, and Robert A Gagnon, *The Bible and Homosexual Practice: Texts and Hermeneutics* (Nashville: Abingdon, 2001), 111 note 177, 116.
89. Jacob Milgrom, *Leviticus: A Book of Ritual and Ethics* (Continental Commentary series; Minneapolis: Fortress, 2004), 175.
90. *Ibid*, 179, original emphases; see also 258, and Jacob Milgrom, *Leviticus 17–22: A New Translation with Introduction and Commentary* (AB3A; New York: Doubleday, 2000), 1764.

extended family'.[91] As such, the Holiness Code is concerned principally—although not solely—with questions of discrete identity and ordered procreation, which helps to explain the otherwise puzzling omission of any reference to female homosexual acts (in which no semen is 'lost' and hence no life symbolically lost) here or anywhere else in Scripture, even though the practice is unlikely to have been unknown.[92]

Robert Gagnon has demonstrated that male homosexual acts are clearly attested in other ancient Near Eastern sources.[93] Differentiation—בדל (*bdl*), 'to separate' (Leviticus 20:24; see also 18:3, 24, 26, 30; 20:23)—from the practices of neighbouring peoples is therefore an index or expression of Israel's holiness understood in these terms (Leviticus 19:1; 20:7–8, 26). One form this takes is the proscription for Israel against male-male anal intercourse that, with its uniform attendant punishment for both parties (Leviticus 20:13) and the lack of exceptions to the interdiction in respect of the scope of its address (namely the *paterfamilias* and other male extended family members),[94] is unique amongst the texts of the entire ancient Near Eastern and classical world.[95]

Thus, in answer to his own question, 'Does the Bible prohibit homosexuality?', Milgrom responds, 'Of course it does (18:22; 20:13), *but the prohibition is severely limited*.'[96] It is not, as Gagnon would attest,

---

91. Milgrom, *Leviticus: Ritual and Ethics*, 256.
92. See Milgrom, *Leviticus 17–22*, 1787, and Gagnon, *The Bible and Homosexual Practice*, 133.
93. Gagnon, *The Bible and Homosexual Practice*, 44–56.
94. Although he does not appeal to it, the fact that 18:7, 14 refer to exposing the nakedness of one's father and uncle, respectively, strengthens Milgrom's somewhat tentative argument that the prohibitions of 18:22 and 20:13 are directed towards the same set of prohibited heterosexual relationships, that is, those within the extended family group (see *Leviticus 17–22*, 1569).
95. See *Ibid*, 1412 and 1565–6; compare Gagnon, *The Bible and Homosexual Practice*, 115.
96. Milgrom, *Leviticus: Ritual and Ethics*, 196, emphasis added.

an unqualified pair of prohibitions,[97] but is qualified precisely by its inclusion in the Holiness Code with all its parameters: literary, theological, sociological, and historical. Specifically, Milgrom insists, it is limited to Israel (and resident aliens) as distinct from the nations, and, further, to those Israelites who would reside in the land (Leviticus 18:24–30), and, further still, to Israelite men in that category.[98]

The Hebrew repeatedly bears out these considerations of the specificity—with respect both to theological vision and to applicability—that is assumed in the wider passages in which these texts appear. The word translated in NRSV as 'statutes' (Leviticus 18:4, 26; 20:8, 22, 23), חֹק (*khoq*), suggests 'limit' or 'boundary', echoing both the language of creation/procreation (Jeremiah 5:22; Psalm 148:6; Job 28:26) and of separation or distinction. Conversely, illicit sexual unions are described as a 'confusion' or 'mixing'—תֶּבֶל (*tevel*)—of such boundaries (Leviticus 20:12; 18:23). This is rendered in the NRSV (unhelpfully or imprecisely, perhaps, in view of Milgrom's comments above and the word's modern associations) as 'perversion'. The same 'mixing' takes place in the 'anti-creation' story of the Tower of Babel (Genesis 11:7, 9).[99] So too, with תּוֹעֵבָה (*to'evah*), 'an abomination' (Leviticus 18:22; 20:13), the sense is primarily cultic, and only secondarily—as a consequence of that sacral disruption—moral.[100]

In essence, then, we would read with Milgrom and others: the prohibition in these parallel texts is obvious; its universal application, however, is far less obvious. One might disagree with Duffield, therefore, on the question of what constitutes 'clear biblical teaching' in this instance, whilst supporting his 'hermeneutic of resistance' in respect of that teaching. If space allowed, this hermeneutic could be

97. Gagnon, *The Bible and Homosexual Practice*, 142.

98. See Milgrom, *Leviticus: Ritual and Ethics*, 196–7, 256.

99. See Stephen K Sherwood, *Leviticus, Numbers, Deuteronomy* (Berit Olam: Studies in Hebrew Narrative and Poetry; Collegeville: The Liturgical Press, 2002), 74.

100. See William L Holladay, *A Concise Hebrew and Aramaic Lexicon of the Old Testament* (Grand Rapids: Eerdmans, 1988), 388. טמא (*tm'*), 'to become unclean' (Leviticus 18:20), has the same cultic or ceremonial connotation. See *Lexicon in Veteris Testamenti Libros*, edited by Ludwig Koehler and Walter Baumgartner (Leiden: EJ Brill, 1958), 353. For a contrary view see Gagnon, *The Bible and Homosexual Practice*, 113.

strengthened by appealing to the second and third senses of canon outlined above. Other Hebrew Bible texts, such as Ruth, and a number of texts in the New Testament (Mark 3:31–5 and parallels, for example), implicitly or explicitly challenge an understanding of the *paterfamilias* ('extended family') that is constituted biologically or ethnically as being determinative of identity for the faith community—be it 'Israel' or 'Church'. The sacrament of baptism functions similarly within the Church's tradition. Once the centrality of this socio-economic unit is deconstructed for the community of faith, interdictions that pertain to its surviving and thriving *as such* cannot be simply or neatly transposed into new polities.

More broadly still, the injunction to be fruitful and multiply (which clearly functions as a point of reference or orientation for the Holiness Code in some foundational manner) has had to be reinterpreted and qualified by the prior demand of ecological stewardship in an age in which creation can no more bear the consequences of an anthropocentric hermeneutic than can our current geo-political environment bear an ethno- or religio-centric one.[101]

In the Australian context, these texts are further problematised by the way the relationship between the land and its indigenous inhabitants is presented. In Leviticus 18:26, 'native'—אֶזְרָח (*'ez'rah*)—denotes the Israelite settler, as 'citizen', possessing full civic rights.[102] Non-Israelite sojourners are denominated as 'resident aliens'—גֵּר (*ger*)—with restricted civil rights.[103] The indigenous 'people of the land'—אַנְשֵׁי־הָאָרֶץ (*an'shey ha'arets*), 'those living in it' יֹשְׁבֶיהָ (*yosh'veyah*)—are described as the cause of the land's pollution or defilement, and as being 'vomited out' by it (18:25; see also 18:27–8; 20:22–3; Numbers 33:50–6; Genesis 3:17, 23).

---

101. For a more detailed discussion of this issue see Norman Habel, 'Geophany: The Earth Story in Genesis 1', in *The Earth Story in Genesis*, edited by Norman C Habel and Shirley Wurst (The Earth Bible, 2; Sheffield: Sheffield Academic Press, 2000), 34–48, and especially 45–7.

102. See Koehler and Baumgartner, *Lexicon*, 26, a category which, interestingly, would include the refugee or asylum seeker: one who 'on account of war, troubles, famine . . . or other misfortune has been constrained to leave his original place or tribe'. See also Milgrom, *Leviticus 17–22*, 1705–6.

103. Koehler and Baumgartner, *Lexicon*, 192.

Such an outworking of H's doctrine of differentiation—regardless of its contingency upon prior understandings of God's action in creation—is surely intolerable in view of the treatment that both the Indigenous and, more recently, the would-be citizen/sojourner have received in *this* land, and must cast the applicability—even in part—of any code derived from this doctrine further into doubt in the present time and place. Indeed to suggest anywhere on the globe today, as Milgrom claims Leviticus 18:24–30 does for its first audience, 'that exile is the automatic, built-in punishment for land pollution'[104] (in the sense of 'defilement') is as theologically untenable as positing HIV/AIDS as some sort of divine (or quasi 'natural') judgment on homosexuals.[105]

b) John Dunnill[106]

Like Duffield, John Dunnill (Director of Biblical and Theological Studies at the Anglican Institute of Theology and Religious Education in Perth and Lecturer in New Testament at Murdoch University) demonstrates a canonical approach to the biblical witness to human sexuality, seeking at the outset 'to place that issue in the widest context' by looking at 'the Bible's understanding as a whole', and acknowledging that, in its full canonical scope, this view is 'richer and more complex than is sometimes supposed'.[107]

Dunnill is concerned to establish the particular ends which biblical texts are apt to meet, listing the Leviticus texts that prohibit intercourse between males as among a series of texts that render non-procreative

---

104. Milgrom, *Leviticus: Ritual and Ethics*, 208.

105. See, for example, the Episcopal Church's Resolution on Violence Against Homosexuals (1988), in *The Churches Speak on Homosexuality: Official Statements from Religious Bodies and Ecumenical Organisations*, edited by J Gordon Melton (Detroit: Gale Research, 1991), 104, and the comments of Pat Buchanan and John Stott as reported by Michael Doe, *Seeking the Truth in Love: The Church and Homosexuality* (London: Darton Longman and Todd, 2000), 79.

106. Dunnill, 'Human Sexuality and its Purpose from a Biblical and Theological Perspective', in Doctrine Panel of the Anglican Church of Australia, *Faithfulness in Fellowship: Reflections on Homosexuality and the Church* (Melbourne: John Garratt, 2001), 27–46, and 'Homosexuality in the Old Testament', in Doctrine Panel, *Faithfulness in Fellowship*, 47–61.

107. Dunnill, 'Human Sexuality', 27.

sexual activity as shameful. This, in turn, must be understood against the background of the honour which attaches to the continuance of the name of a patriarchal clan through the multiplication of progeny.[108] Dunnill also sees some New Testament themes as qualifying or transcending concerns with the social order addressed in the Hebrew Scriptures.[109] At the same time he acknowledges the limitations or 'ambivalence' of Scripture—both Old and New Testaments—with respect to meeting the needs of a society whose questions regarding sexuality are of an entirely different order.[110]

This last difficulty applies *a fortiori* to homosexuality and the Hebrew Bible, although—again—what material there is must be viewed in its full literary context, including attention to questions of literary form.[111] With respect to the two texts in question, Dunnill observes that they form part of the Holiness Code, 'a section of the Priestly document that prescribes the conditions of purity needed for the worship of Yahweh',[112] noting further that amongst a list of offences that constitute ritual defilement, homosexual acts alone are connected with abomination-as-idolatry, תּוֹעֵבָה (*to'evah*).[113]

Dunnill suggests a number of ways in which the rationale for this particular Leviticusitical regulation might be understood, leaning towards a semiotic analysis which adopts the body (and what is in contact with it) as a metaphor for the identity and holiness of Israel. In recognising the provisional nature of any meaning so construed, Dunnill offers an excellent illustration of a characteristically Anglican canonical hermeneutic at work, which bears quoting in full:

> Such reflections are . . . part of the ongoing work of interpretation. But the task is not optional, for the meaning of the parts depends on the meaning of the whole context in which they are placed. Although the terms of these two verses are clear, prohibiting sexual intercourse between males, the effect of their placement

108. *Ibid*, 27–8.
109. *Ibid*, 39, 42.
110. *Ibid*, 40–1, thereby not 'attributing unto Scripture more than it can have' (see page 55, above).
111. *Ibid*, 47.
112. *Ibid*, 57.
113. *Ibid*, 58.

> within a system of ritual holiness . . . raises questions about how they are to be applied. Do they only apply in cultic contexts? Or only when signifying idolatry? And why does the ban specify intercourse only between males? Since the text, notoriously, offers no clear answer to such questions, the verses cannot simply be plucked out of their context and enforced as laws. It is necessary to seek to understand the meaning of the whole legal and symbolic system, before evaluating the ethical status of any individual rule . . . [whose] authority must be assessed and not assumed.[114]

c) Scott Cowdell and Peter Jensen[115]

Scott Cowdell (Rector of St Paul's, Manuka, Editor of *St Mark's Review*, and faculty member of St Mark's National Theology Centre in the School of Theology, Charles Sturt University) and Peter Jensen (current Archbishop of Sydney and former Principal of Moore Theological College) model a type of dialogue over this issue in the pages of a recent edited volume which gathers perspectives of members of the Doctrine Commission of the Anglican Church of Australia on the use of Scripture.

Cowdell, like Duffield, challenges 'the alleged incompatibility of gay and lesbian lifestyles with the plain teaching of Scripture'.[116] Again, a highly contextual, canonical approach to relevant texts is evident in the arguments adduced by Cowdell to counter this claim, including biblical 'silence' with respect to a range of homosexual practices.[117]

Helpfully, for our purposes, this author also attends directly to the quality of conversation currently taking place amongst Anglicans in relation to homosexuality and the Bible, as does his interlocutor

114. *Ibid*, 58–9.

115. Scott Cowdell, 'Homosexuality and the Clarity of Scripture: Reflecting with Peter Jensen', in *Lost in Translation?: Anglicans, Controversy and the Bible*, edited by Scott Cowdell and Muriel Porter (Melbourne: Desbooks, 2004), 114–30; Peter F Jensen, 'A Response to Scott Cowdell', in Cowdell and Porter, *Lost in Translation?*, 131–8.

116. Cowdell, 'Homosexuality and the Clarity of Scripture', 114.

117. *Ibid*, 114, 126–9.

correspondingly.[118] Cowdell's careful elucidation of Jensen's position with respect to the clarity of Scripture makes a valuable contribution in itself to ensuring that the quality of this conversation is, in fact, something we might live by, although neither Cowdell's nor Jensen's own discourse is always measured,[119] and Jensen challenges Cowdell's reading of his own work on several points.[120]

The central issue Cowdell takes up is Jensen's understanding that biblical clarity is 'located in the text itself, not in the inspired reading of it'.[121] This would appear to be a narrow view of the canonical imperative discussed earlier, and an 'absolute' rather than a 'relative' doctrine of the authority of Scripture. Cowdell offers a similar critique when he suggests that it is 'Dr Jensen's intent to replace the authority of Church tradition and modern culture . . . with the Bible's own authority', adding that such a move is unsustainable given Jensen's implicit appeal to both ecclesial tradition and the categories of modernity elsewhere.[122] In place of this, Cowdell advocates a more recognisably Anglican 'biblical approach, seeking the mind of God in a conversation with Scripture where Church tradition and the modern world are our partners'.[123]

For his own part, Jensen points to the ecumenical and historical consensus 'that Scripture clearly forbids homosexual practice'.[124] Diarmaid MacCulloch, enlisted by Jensen in support of this position, sets out in rather stark terms the decision effectively taken by anyone who, while participating in this consensus, would not regard the prohibition as binding:

> it is difficult to see the Bible as expressing anything else but disapproval of homosexual activity, *let alone having*

---

118. *Ibid*, 115; see also Jensen, 'A Response', 138.
119. See, for example, Cowdell, 'Homosexuality and the Clarity of Scripture', 115, 125; compare Jensen, 'A Response', 135–7.
120. Jensen, 'A Response', 132–3.
121. This is Cowdell's paraphrasing of Jensen in 'Homosexuality and the Clarity of Scripture', 118.
122. *Ibid*, 120; see also 121–5. Jensen rejects this view, 'A Response', 134–5.
123. Cowdell, 'Homosexuality and the Clarity of Scripture', 130.
124. Jensen, 'A Response', 131.

> *any conception of homosexual identity*. The only alternatives are to try to cleave to patterns of life and assumptions set out in the Bible, or to say that in this, as in much else, the Bible is simply wrong.[125]

Given what *is* known about homosexual identity today, the latter seems entirely unremarkable, provided that one's notion of biblical authority will cope with such a suggestion. If the features explored above give an accurate picture of an Anglican view of biblical authority, then Anglicans certainly *can* resist the Bible's 'plain teaching' in this matter, as they patently already do with regard to much else.

Jensen strongly endorses Gagnon's biblical work on the subject,[126] and yet Gagnon is inconsistent on this very question of reading 'canonically' in the widest sense. On the one hand he wants to appeal to continuing taboos in contemporary culture as a means of comparing the seriousness of homosexuality as a violation of the commandments with such practices as child sacrifice, adultery, some forms of incest, and bestiality—all of which share the same penalty in Leviticus 20.[127] Because these remain abhorrent to us, Gagnon would argue, so should homosexuality. But the hermeneutical authority he gives to culture with one hand, he takes away with the other, minimising the fact that homosexuality is *not* abhorrent to large sections of contemporary Western society—the reading context of most *Australian* Anglicans, at least—and then explicitly rejecting the legitimacy of any 'effective historical consciousness' exercised by culture:

> Contrary to the contemporary trend of Jewish and Christian communities to accommodate to the prevailing cultural approbation of homosexuality, the entire context of the Holiness Code stresses the distinctive holiness of the people of God.[128]

Gagnon's observation that there is a disjunction between the world-view of the Holiness Code and some expressions of contemporary

---

125. Diarmaid MacCulloch, as cited by Jensen in *Ibid*, 132, emphasis added.

126. Jensen describes *The Bible and Homosexual Practice* as 'magisterial', 'A Response', 134.

127. Gagnon, *The Bible and Homosexual Practice*, 114 note 182.

128. *Ibid*, 116.

Judaism and Christianity is self-evident. The question for Australian Anglicans, however, reading from our eddy in the 'Church in society' stream, is whether we can live with that sort of binary opposition between 'the unique authority of Scripture'[129] and the (presumably no less unique) authority of culture—an opposition which sets one over against the other hierarchically—or whether we need to discover a way of enabling a less hegemonic conversation between these two important sources of theology.

Furthermore, Jensen's reluctance to impute motive as part of the interpretive task[130] would seem to deny the validity of any attempt at the ideological criticism of Scripture (such as feminist and socio-economic reading strategies) as well as the more widely accepted historical-critical methodologies which endeavour to reconstruct authorial intent and *Sitz im Leben* ('setting in life', or 'life situation')—including attendant motivational forces and ideological concerns—as data available to the wider hermeneutical process.[131] Such a diminishing of the contextual impulse, which drives the canonical approach variously illustrated by Duffield, Dunnill, and Cowdell, strikes this reader as uncharacteristic of the Anglican Church as a community of inquiry, at least as represented here. It also fails Mary Callaway's test for reading incarnationally: 'Any move away from understanding the biblical writings in their historical context, at any stage in their development, opens the risk of absolutizing the words, at the expense of the Word.'[132] Anglicanism, generally, has done well to avoid this theological reductionism, not least in terms of its pastoral implications.

---

129. Jensen, 'A Response', 134.

130. *Ibid*, 137.

131. Gagnon does precisely this in relation to Leviticus 18:22 and 20:13 in *The Bible and Homosexual Practice*, 128–42, citing connection with idolatry, the impossibility of procreation, the mixing of defiling substances, and violation of the created order (such as by gender dis-complementarity) as possible motive clauses, each of which may be argued as being no longer operative in our reading context.

132. Callaway, 'Canonical Criticism,' 153. A text's 'development' is understood here to include its history of reception.

Conclusion

As these examples show, we can never possess absolute certainty with respect to the hermeneutical task. Yet, as Tracy notes, we can achieve 'good' and 'adequate' interpretations that are appropriate to the Church's identity as a hermeneutical community—one which must reason discursively, inquire corporately, converse and argue within itself, and whose knowledge is always embodied, collective, finite, and partial.[133] Good and adequate interpretations under such conditions are:

> relative to the power of disclosure and concealment of the text, relative to the skills and attentiveness of the interpreter, relative to the kind of conversation possible for the interpreter in a particular culture at a particular time. Somehow conversation and relatively adequate interpretations suffice.[134]

This describes, to some extent, the experience of Australian Anglicans. Given our history of 'excessive diocesanism' and current tensions in the national Church—not least over the use and interpretation of Scripture—which echo, without exactly replicating, those in the worldwide Anglican Communion, creativity has always been demanded in the way Australian Anglicans form community, including hermeneutical community. In Brown's estimation, this experience positions us well as a tradition to wrestle with the problems involved in discovering the force and relevance of the biblical story to the circumstances of Christian living today:

> The creativity of a tradition is the tensive character of the life lived within, and sometimes against, its boundaries. The viability of a tradition is the vastness of its collected resources, unified enough to sustain needed continuity and diverse enough to create something new for new times. The power of a tradition is the worth of its space, the productivity of its complementary and competing voices, as it progresses through the novelties of history

133. Tracy, *Plurality and Ambiguity*, 27.
134. *Ibid*, 22–3.

> . . . Tradition is lived canon—the negotiation of personal and corporate identities with/in canonical space.[135]

But whether we live or die as a discrete hermeneutical community—the importance of which, or otherwise, being its own topic for discussion—will, as Tracy foreshadows, depend on the quality of our conversation. Anglican divine, Jeremy Taylor, regarded as the 'Chrysostom' or 'golden-mouth' of England, recognised this a long time ago. His seventeenth-century counsel may help us, at least, to love our ties to their last splendour:

> Let all errors be as much and as zealously suppressed as may be . . . but let it be done by such means as are proper instruments of their suppression, by preaching and disputation . . . by charity and sweetness, by holiness of life, assiduity of exhortation, by the Word of God and prayer . . . Only let not men be hasty in calling every disliked opinion by the name of heresy; and when they have resolved that they will call it so, let them use the erring person like a brother, not beat him like a dog, or convince him with a gibbet, or vex him out of his understanding and persuasions. But all of us [are] to be united in that common term, which as it does constitute the Church in its being such, so it is the medium of the Communion of Saints; and that is the Creed of the Apostles; and in all other things an honest endeavour to find out the truths we can, and a charitable and mutual permission to others to disagree from us and our opinions.[136]

---

135. Brown, *Boundaries of Our Habitations*, 89.

136. J Taylor, *The Liberty of Prophesying* (first published in 1647), as cited by Burge, 'Authority', 4 note 22.

4
The Scriptures Are God's Voice: The Church Is His Echo

Peter Adam

Introduction

In this chapter we consider the local church as the place where theological education happens. Before the creation of universities or colleges, all theology was local church theology; the task of theological education was the task of educating and training lay people in theology; and theologians were not a special breed, but the clergy and lay people of the early church. We see in the *Didache*, and in the ministry of St Augustine of Hippo, a high level of theological training in the local church, not least by means of daily sermons designed to edify the faithful and to educate enquirers. This same commitment is seen in the churches of the Reformation. This theology will be responsive to the Scriptures, focussed on the Gospel, firmly founded in the practice of the local church, contextual and missional, educated and informed, and reflected both in liturgy and in life.

A responsive theology

At its heart, Christian theology is responsive theology, responsive to God's revelation, responsive to God's self-revelation, responsive to Jesus Christ and the Spirit, responsive to God's grace, responsive to God's saving works, and responsive to God's words.

We should not hold the view that words are merely human attempts to describe or express what is by nature wordless. We need not have a negative view of the use of words about God. For example, does speaking of God always imply an attempt 'to encapsulate him and have him on our terms'?[1] Peter Carnley approved Rowan Williams' warning that those who engage in building theological

1. Peter Carnley, *Reflections in Glass* (Sydney: HarperCollins, 2004), 29.

systems may use their body of clear and distinct truth as a weapon of power to browbeat and bludgeon others.[2] No doubt this has happened many times in the history of the church. However the misuse of something is not an argument against its usefulness or validity, and it is just as easy for those who assert the incomprehensibility of God to use this assertion as a weapon of power to browbeat and bludgeon others. We must defend the value and integrity of theological discourse.

God is so great and so transcendent that he is able to use human language, able to communicate effectively and truly by human discourse. Remarkably, Christianity holds that God has given this verbal revelation, and that this revelation is so powerful that it can work even in translation (unlike the Holy Books of Judaism and Islam). This verbal revelation is reflected in Jesus' description of his own revelation of himself and of the Father to his disciples: 'The words you gave to me I have given to them, and they have received them, and . . . believe that you sent me'.[3]

Words of revelation are God's promises, teaching, encouragements, warnings, and information, his personal communication to us. God's revelatory words in Scripture are powerful and personal, creative and effective. 'But this is the one to whom I will look, to the humble and contrite in spirit, who trembles at my word.'[4] Or, in the words of Jesus, 'My mother and my brothers are those who hear the word of God and do it'.[5] Sandra Schneiders remarks:

> In fact, experiencing the text as text is as integral to the work of biblical interpretation as hearing a Mozart symphony played in concert is integral to the work of the music critic or as seeing Hamlet in the theater is to the work of the literary scholar.[6]

2. Carnley, *Reflections in Glass*, 47.
3. John 17:5.
4. Isaiah 66:2.
5. Luke 8:21.
6. Sandra Schneiders, *The Revelatory Text: Interpreting the New Testament as Sacred Scripture* (Collegeville: The Liturgical Press, 1999), 173.

Paul taught that the Spirit of God's three-fold ministry was to search the depths of God, to reveal to the apostles, and to teach the apostles the words so that they may speak of what God has revealed.[7] So we are a listening church. In the words of Jeremiah Burroughs, a seventeenth century London preacher, when you sit to hear and read the Bible, 'you come to tender up your homage to God, to sit at God's feet and there to profess your submission to Him'.[8]

Modern Anglican theology seems reluctant to believe that words can effectively mediate God's self-revelation. This perhaps reflects an Enlightenment distrust of language, a neo-Platonic view of spirituality, and a Romantic commitment to wordless experience.

The traditional view of God's self-revelation was that God's revelation occurred through words and deeds, through the speech of God and the acts of God. For some curious reason, Christian theology in the twentieth century has found it necessary to assert either that God reveals through deeds and not words, or words and not deeds. Anglican theology has favoured the notion that God is present to act, but not to speak, while Bultmann and Marxsen have asserted that God is present to speak, but not to act.[9]

However, the cause is not lost. It is possible to retain the notion of the God who speaks. John Webster has shown that the expression 'Holy Scripture' contains a clue about the divine use of the common human words of Scripture.[10] For describing something as 'holy' in the Bible means that something of common use is set aside and used by God. This is a sacramental transformation of the 'common' to become 'holy', the mundane to be taken up and used by God. So the words of the Bible are 'holy words,' that is, they are set apart by God for his saving purpose, and mediate his grace.[11] In Austin Farrer's words:

---

7. 1 Corinthians 2: 9–13.
8. Jeremiah Burroughs, *Gospel Worship* (Ligonier: Soli Deo Gloria, 1990), 197.
9. Of course some more courageous theologians may claim that God neither acts nor speaks. See Nicholas Wolterstorff, *Divine Discourse: Philosophical Reflections on the Claim that God Speaks* (Cambridge: Cambridge University Press, 1995), 123–9.
10. See John Webster, *Holy Scripture: a Dogmatic Sketch* (Cambridge: Cambridge University Press, 2004).
11. John Dunnill, 'Theological interpretation', in Scott Cowdell and Muriel Porter, *Lost in Translation: Anglicans, Controversy and the Bible* (Thornbury: Desbooks, 2004), 73, 74, likened scripture to an icon.

> We must attend to the homely phrases, the soaring poetry, the figures of speech, and the changes of mood; for these are the alphabet of the divine utterance.[12]

So as we do theology, we are able to think God's thoughts after him, in response to the will of God, the saving will of God in Christ Jesus, and the articulated will of God in the Scriptures. The Ruling Principles of the Anglican Church of Australia state that: 'This Church receives all the canonical Scriptures of the Old and New Testament as being the ultimate rule and standard of faith given by inspiration of God and containing all things necessary for salvation'.[13] The basic material of theology is the verbal revelation of God in scripture: for this includes the stories of our salvation, our sacred history, the warnings of the prophets, the varied gifts of God's wisdom, the teaching of the Lord Jesus, and the writings of the New Testament apostles and prophets, the words and works of God. It is as we receive these words in a continual *lectio divina* that we are formed by God's words, and increasingly resonate to God's character and will, becoming the people we were created to become, and adorning the teaching of God our Saviour.[14]

Reason and experience are not pure sources of theology but the contexts in which we respond, and tools to help us understand it. Tradition at best is the attempt of the church of the past to understand and obey the Scriptures. We need the Tradition of the church because we realise that the people of God in every age have worked hard to understand and live the Scriptures. We need to learn from them.

Our theology is formed from many sources. We are undoubtedly shaped by our Christian provenance, by our social context, our character, all our human experiences, our experiences of God, and by the wisdom and blindness of our age. We may view this as an entirely negative reality; it still remains a reality. Peter Jensen's ideal of the

---

Schneiders, *The Revelatory Text,* wrote of scripture as sacrament, 40–3, and see Webster, *Holy Scripture,* 'God speaks in a veiled form, "sacramentally" ', 73.

12. Austin Farrer, *Interpretation and Belief* (London: SPCK, 1976), 12.
13. *The Constitution of the Anglican Church of Australia.* Available at http://www.anglican.org.au/index.cfm (accessed 23 March 2006).
14. Titus 2:10.

Bible as the sole source of theology is never realised.[15] Even if we interpret our varied sources of theology negatively, we must understand that it happens, for what is not acknowledged will influence us most powerfully. If acknowledged, then the ongoing process will be to assess every element by Scripture, and so attempt to bring every thought captive to the pure word of God.

So also it is true that 'the Gospel creates the church', not 'the church creates the Gospel'.[16] For faith comes by hearing, and hearing from the word of Christ. In the words of the *Didache*, 'Where the things of the Lord are spoken, there the Lord is present'.[17] As Old observed, 'Christ's presence in the worshipping congregation is understood to be by means of the teaching and preaching of the Word of God'.[18] In the time of the *Didache*, daily sermons were provided not only to edify the faithful, but also to educate enquirers about Christianity.

Some may appeal to words from John 16:13, 'When the Spirit of Truth comes, he will guide you into all the truth', as a general promise that the Spirit will gradually guide the church into the truth of God over the centuries. However the verse in context is addressed by Jesus to the disciples, and the context of John 14–17 makes it clear that these are specific instructions and promises to those disciples at that time. They were fulfilled in the preaching and teaching of those early apostles, teaching that resulted in the formation of the New Testament. Of course our reading and hearing of the Bible will be consciously in the context of the reading and hearing of the Bible in the whole of the one, holy, catholic, and apostolic church. We will also read the Bible in light of our own culture and society, and the issues and questions of

---

15. Peter Jensen, *The Revelation of God* (Leicester: Inter-Varsity Press, 2002).
16. John Webster, *Word and Church: Essays in Christian Dogmatics* (Edinburgh: T&T Clark, 2001): claims that Rowan Williams shows insufficient attention to the need for a theological statement of communicative presence of Christ and the activity of the Holy Spirit, 22, and that George Lindbeck's notion of 'mutually constitutive reciprocity' between church and word is also inadequate, 42. We need an understanding of both Bible and church that is theological and not just sociological.
17. *Didache* 4.1.
18. Hughes Oliphant Old, *Reading and Preaching The Scriptures: The Early Church*, volume 2 (Grand Rapids: Eerdmans, 1998), 265.

our age. But in the midst of this we will feel that the Bible reads us, as much as we read the Bible.

The barrier to a right response to the revelation of God is not our humanity, but our sin. It is our sin that keeps us from the right response of faith and obedience. We often hear the words from Isaiah, 'My thoughts are not your thoughts, neither are your ways my ways, says the Lord',[19] quoted in support of the idea that there is such a gulf between ourselves and God that we cannot understand him. But the immediate context is an appeal for the people of God to repent:

> Let the wicked forsake their way, and the unrighteous their thoughts; let them return to the Lord, that he may have mercy on them, and to our God, for he will abundantly pardon.[20]

The barrier is not the limitations of humanity but sin of God's people. If they repent and return to God, then they will follow God's thoughts and ways.

So we respond to the Scriptures, not because they merely provide a notable attempt of previous generations of believers to describe their experience of God, not because they are merely the formative stories of our particular community, but because we believe that God continues to address us through these ancient texts. Austin Farrer has written of 'the power of these texts to enliven the soul and to open the gates of heaven',[21] that is, to achieve God's revelatory purpose. Walter Hilton wrote that:

> (Jesus) comforts them with His words in Holy Scripture . . . He gives gladness and joy to all who truly believe His promises, and humbly abide the fulfilment of His will.[22]

John Goldingay quoted Fishbane's *The Garments of Truth*: 'One of the great contributions of Judaism to the history of religions is its

---

19. Isaiah 55: 8.
20. Isaiah 55: 7.
21. Austin Farrer, *The Glass of Vision* (Westminster: Dacre Press, 1948), 36.
22. Walter Hilton, *The Ladder of Perfection*, translated by Leo Shirley-Price (Harmondsworth: Penguin, 1957), 244.

assertion that the divine reality makes itself humanly comprehensible through the structures of language'. Goldingay then commented: 'it is through a written text . . . that God is known'.[23] No wonder Jesus quoted from Deuteronomy in these words: 'It is written, "One does not live by bread alone, but by every word that comes from the mouth of God".'[24]

A frequent claim is that the Bible is not the revelation of God, but the witness to that revelation. There are two versions of this claim.

One is that there were revelatory events of fundamental importance for the people of God in every age in the history of salvation recorded in the Bible. However though the events were revelation, their interpretation was not. In this case the writings of Scripture represent the attempts of the church at that time to make the best sense they could of the meaning of the revelatory events. So the Bible is the witness that these events happened, and the interpretation of those events by God's people.

The other, more extreme, version of this claim is that the events recorded in the Bible have no special revelatory significance for any other generation, and that God works equally in every age. Then the Bible becomes the attempt of earlier people of God to witness to what God was doing among them, as we must also attempt to identify and interpret God's saving works among us today.

Both versions of this claim have a fatal flaw: they restrict God's revelatory activity to events, not their interpretation. In both, revelation comprises God's works but not God's words. This arbitrary restriction is clearly expressed in the artificial dichotomy so unfortunately articulated by William Temple: 'What is offered to man's apprehension in any specific revelation is not truth concerning God, but the living God Himself'.[25] There need be no separation between God's words and God's works: both are deeds of God, and both reveal the character of God who is present in his words, and present in his works.

---

23. John Goldingay, *Models for Scripture* (Grand Rapids: Eerdmans, 1994), 4.
24. Matthew 4:4, quoting Deuteronomy 8:3.
25. William Temple, *Nature, Man and God* (London: Macmillan, 1934), 322.

A gospel theology

There are varied claims made about the identity and heart of Anglican theology. It is frequently claimed that the heart of Anglicanism is the doctrine of the incarnation, though this is more a tribute to the pervasive influence over the last 100 years of the authors of *Lux Mundi*, than a substantiated interpretation of nearly 1500 years of theology within and beyond *Ecclesia Anglicana*. The *Lux Mundi* school was criticised because, as AM Ramsey commented, 'in their intense concentration upon the incarnation as the key to the understanding of the world, these writers and their subsequent followers were minimizing the Cross, the divine judgement and the eschatological element in the Gospel'.[26]

Stephen Sykes expressed a clearer appreciation of the centre of Anglican faith when he wrote:

> The public commitment of the Anglican is to the full doctrine of the Holy Trinity, as Articles 1 to 5 of the Thirty-Nine Articles make plain . . . the incarnation and atonement are likewise taught within this trinitarian context. The centrality of the atoning work of Christ becomes evident in the BCP Order of Holy Communion. God is addressed as follows; '. . . who of thy tender mercy didst give thine only Son Jesus Christ to suffer death upon the cross for our redemption; who made there (by his one oblation of himself once offered) a full, perfect, and sufficient sacrifice, oblation, and satisfaction, for the sins of the whole world.'[27]

Or again, 'The heart of the matter may be spoken of as the paschal mystery ('Christ our Passover is sacrificed for us; therefore let us keep the feast').[28] Or again, 'What is it then that holds Anglicans together? First and primarily, we must focus on the gracious, reconciling and unifying act of God in Jesus Christ'.[29]

---

26. Arthur Michael Ramsey, *From Gore to Temple* (London: Longmans, 1960), 9.
27. SW Sykes, in *Celebrating the Anglican Way*, edited by Ian Bunting (London: Hodder and Stoughton, 1996), 28, 29.
28. Sykes in Bunting, *Celebrating the Anglican Way*, 23.
29. Sykes in Bunting, *Celebrating the Anglican Way*, 31.

As Sykes explained, the Book of Common Prayer, the Thirty-Nine Articles and the Ordering of Bishops, Priests and Deacons constitute 'the inheritance of faith' (Canon C 15) of the Church of England, and therefore define the nature of being in communion with Canterbury, and therefore the meaning of what it is to be Anglican.[30] Of course these documents are also definitive for Australian Anglicans, as our Ruling Principles make clear.

So Trinitarian faith lies at the heart of Anglicanism, and this Trinitarian faith protects the central doctrines of the incarnation of the Son of God, his atoning work on the cross, and his resurrection from among the dead.[31] This Gospel is at the heart of the message of the Scriptures, and is the meaning of the two Gospel sacraments, Baptism and the Lord's Supper. Anglican theology is Gospel theology.

An ecclesial theology

The Bible assumes that the people of God carry the responsibility to receive, hear, understand, and implement the Word of God.

One of the declared aims of the 1662 Book of Common Prayer is the 'edification' of the people. In the words of the preface 'Of Ceremonies', 'Christ's Gospel is not a Ceremonial Law . . . but a religion to serve God . . . to stir up the dull mind of man . . . whereby he may be edified'.

In the Old Testament, the people of God were addressed by the Word of God. On the plains of Moab, Moses addressed Israel, the people of God, with the words of God, and instructed them, 'You shall love the Lord your God with all your heart, and with all your soul, and with all your strength'.[32] He then explained how they were to love their God in the life of their community, 'Keep these words that I am commanding you today in your heart. Recite them to your children and talk about when you are at home and when you are away . . . '[33]

Paul expressed the same imperative for New Testament believers: 'Let the word of Christ dwell in you richly; teach and admonish one another in all wisdom, and with gratitude in your hearts sing psalms,

30. Sykes in Bunting, *Celebrating the Anglican Way*, 23.
31. Peter Adam, 'The Trinity and Human Community', in *Grace and Truth in the Secular Age*, edited by Timothy Bradshaw (Grand Rapids: Eerdmans, 1998), 52–65.
32. Deuteronomy 6:5.
33. Deuteronomy 6:6.

hymns, and spiritual songs to God'.[34] For the faith has been 'once for all entrusted to the saints.'[35] Within this general framework, church leaders have a particular responsibility to guard the Gospel, and help the church to be the pillar and bulwark of the truth.[36]

I regard the local church as the gathered church meeting on Sunday under the direction of the clergy appointed by the bishop. It seems to me to be unworkable to imagine that the local church is the Diocese, for if this is the case, then the local church never meets, as even in the annual Synod service, there are only representatives of parishes. Furthermore, though children are clearly members of the church, they may not be members of Synod. It is bizarre to assert a local church which never meets.

On the other hand, it is not inappropriate the use the word church by extension to describe a diocese or national church. This wider use of church is in Colossians 1:18, 24, and a theology of 'church' needs wider material than an exegesis of *ekklesia.*

Ironically enough, I believe that the liturgical practice of many Anglicans actually illustrates a weak view of the church as the people of God. Certainly in Sunday School and as a server I was trained to exhibit great respect for objects, but not for people! However it is the people of God who are the temple of the Holy Spirit, and not the building.

However it remains the duty of the people of God to reflect on Scripture, to understand its message, and to work out its meaning in their lives in the church and in the world. It is the *consensus fidelium,* the agreement of the faithful, which determines how God's grace will be lived and shared in the world. Each service should include a *lectio divina,* a corporate reflection on the Scriptures.

However the ideal is not always realised. Some of the pressures that restrict the practice of theology by the people of God can be briefly outlined:

- In churches where the preaching of the pure Word of God has been largely replaced by personal reflections, contemporary social comments without theological basis, or explanations of the latest liturgical innovation,

34. Colossians 3:16.
35. Jude 3.
36. 1 Timothy 3:15.

then we should not be surprised if the people of God are ill equipped to engage in any kind of theological reflection action.

- In churches where any disagreement with the leader is interpreted as rebellion and it is assumed that the preacher shares the infallibility of the Scriptures, then we should not be surprised if lay people engage in theological reflection as an underground activity.
- In churches where the preacher makes no attempt to enable lay ministry, or to educate or train the laity, they will be ill equipped to engage in theological reflection.
- Where the minister exhorts people to action, but makes no provision in the life of the Parish for practical lay training and empowering for ministry in the church or in the world, the laity will be hindered in their capacity for effective response.
- The traditions and structure of our liturgy make it a difficult context in which to engage in theological debate or discussion. It is therefore the case that where there are no other meetings of occasions for lay people to ask questions, debate and discuss, then the theological training of the lay people is unlikely to happen.
- Sometimes 'Theological Reflection' actually inhibits the practice of true theology, when it is merely sociological or psychological reflection. There is no serious theological reflection without interaction with the Bible and the theological traditions of the church.
- Lay training must include equipping for daily work in the world, for healthy participation in the local community, in Australian society, and as citizens of the world.
- A society which does not value ideas or principles will not provide a good context for the development of theological debate. We need to provide a counter-cultural alternative in a cynical and pragmatic world.

The health of churches is defined by the health of the whole community. Church communities are healthy when everyone is able to contribute to theological reflection, theological decisions, and theological actions.

Some ways in which we should see theological formation happening in the churches are:

- Parish discussion groups, Bible studies, or other adult Christian education activities, lay training schemes, where lay people are empowered to do theology.
- Lay people, theologically trained by the clergy, well equipped to use their theology in their ministries in the church and in the world, and also equipped to train others also.
- Theological formation happening in daily conversations, in personal reading and prayer, and in joint ministry (as people learn by example).
- Theological formation happening in structured courses. Some examples include evangelistic courses such as Alpha, Credo, or Christianity Explored. More intensive lay training programs have become common in churches, especially those that provide a context of internship, mentoring, ministry and reflection. There are also Discipleship Schools and Institutes of Spiritual Studies.[37]
- Good use of the resources of theological training and empowering of the laity provided by other church agencies, such as Theological Colleges or Institutions, or by Missionary Societies. Distance education has the possibility of extending these ministries.

A practical theology

It is worth reflecting on the fact that before the creation of universities or colleges, all theology was local church theology: the task of theological education was the task of educating and training lay people in theology, and theologians were not a special breed, but the clergy and lay people of the early church. We see in the life and ministry of St. Augustine of Hippo a high level of theological training

37. Peter Adam, 'Theological Education', in *Melbourne Anglicans*, edited by Brian Porter (Melbourne: Mitre Books, 1997), 173.

in the local church, not least by means of daily sermons designed to edify the faithful and to educate enquirers.

In *Reading and Preaching the Scriptures*,[38] Old points to the following features of Augustine's preaching:

- He was determined to let the people hear the eloquence of God in the words of Scripture, and not to fill their minds with his own eloquence (345).
- He practised expository preaching, that is preaching through books of the Bible in his daily or weekly sermons (346).
- His preaching reflected the big theological themes of the Bible, the big themes of human existence (362).
- He believed in the power and effective authority of the Bible, so his aim was to let the text speak (363).
- He interpreted Scripture by Scripture, so that his hearers built up a coherent theology of God and his grace in Christ (364).
- He used Biblical stories to illustrate Biblical teaching (364).
- He engaged in an effective dialogue in his sermons, addressing the pastoral issues of his congregation (365).
- He used simple speech so that everyone could understand his words (366).
- He used variety to help people to listen and to see the point of what he was saying (367).
- His preaching was marked by the vitality of his personal engagement with God, with the Bible, and with the congregation (368).
- His sermons were intended to convert people to Christ as well as to edify the congregation (382).

This practice of Augustine's ministry of the word resulted from a deep sense of the spirituality of the Word, and of the Word as the God-given nourishment of the congregation. For Augustine believed that

38. Page references to Old's *Reading and Preaching the Scriptures* follow each point in brackets.

God spoke through the reading and teaching of the Bible, as we find in references provided by Polman.[39]

- A fire blazes in God's Word. It is the fire of the Holy Ghost (127 = Sermo 22, 7).
- The Gospel is the mouth of Christ. He is in heaven, but never ceases speaking on earth. Let us not be deaf, for He calls. Let us not be dead, for he thunders (127 = Sermo 85, 1).
- His Word is read out to us, and He does not keep silent. His Word is preached, and inasmuch as the preacher speaks the truth, Christ speaks through him. He does not keep silent, and it is our duty to listen, but with the ears of our hearts (127 = Sermo 17, 1).
- If we preach Christ's Word, Christ himself feeds through us (133= Sermo 46, 2).
- The daily bread of the children is the Word of God, which is given them daily . . . Our daily food on this earth is the Word of God which is dispensed in the churches (174 = Sermo 56, 10).

So the Bible is not only the Word of God, but is also God's own speaking to us, God's familiar speech.[40] As both the Bible and the sermon are God's words to his people, they must be central to their spirituality and theological formation. The congregation must come ready to hear God, and to respond with trust and obedience.

This exercise in corporate theological formation was practised in the church at Hippo, and the same kind of model was found in later times, for example in the daily sermons of the Reformation era.[41]

A contextual and missional theology

The Catholic and Reformed identity of Anglicanism should lead to theology which is deeply contextual, reflecting God's universal grace, universal Saviour, and universal Gospel. Sadly, the reality often does

39. ADR Polman, *The Word of God according to St Augustine* (London: Hodder and Stoughton, 1961).
40. Polman, *The Word of God according to St Augustine*, 127.
41. Peter Adam, *The Church 'Halfly Reformed': The Puritan Dilemma* (London: St Antholin's Lectureship, 1998), 7–20.

not reflect the rhetoric, and Anglican churches often look like 'Little England'. Attempts to render Anglicanism genuinely Australian must grapple with the fact that the perceived Australian identity is often far from the reality. Our perceived identity is of outback life, whereas real Australian life is increasingly urban. Grappling with Australian identity is complex!

Perhaps the most serious issue is that of the membership of our churches. Certainly in the cities, the Anglo-Saxon identity of the church is a major barrier. A genuinely Australian church would have to be multi-ethnic and multicultural. This requires the desire and the practice of evangelising people of every ethnic group. And this will not happen unless we are willing to assert and defend the uniqueness of faith in Jesus Christ, and the universality of the Gospel. Here is a paradox! Anglicans who prefer to believe that all religions are the same, or that we should not expect people of other religions to become Christian, are most likely to continue Anglican churches which are white Anglo-Saxon ghettoes. Whereas Anglicans who want people of any religion or none to become Christians are more likely to produce churches which reflect the eschatological hope of 'a great multitude . . . from every nation, from all tribes and peoples and languages, standing before the throne and before the Lamb'.[42] It would be an irony for those who delight in the diversity of the worldwide Anglican Communion not to continue the energetic cross-cultural mission which produced it. The Anglican Church of Australia will be genuinely contextual when it reflects the eschatological vision of Revelation 7.

In our multi-cultural and rapidly changing society, any person in public ministry will need to learn cross-cultural ministry, and congregations will need to learn cross-cultural life as well as cross-cultural mission.[43]

---

42. Revelation 7:9.
43. Adam's culture rules: The better you function naturally in a culture without recognising it, the more difficult you will find it to work in any other culture, and the more likely you are to produce disciples who will have the same difficulty. The more unaware you are of your own culture, the more difficulty you will have working in any other culture. The more unaware you are of your own culture, the more you will force people from other cultures to change to adopt your culture.

An informed theology

The responsibility of the ordained ministry is to read and teach the Bible to the people of God, to enable the people of God to do their theological work, so that they can serve God in the church and in the world.

It is interesting to contrast the pre-Reformation ordination services with those of 1552 and 1662. In the earlier services the 'means of ministry' handed to the priest was the chalice and paten for use in Holy Communion. In the Reformation services the only 'means of ministry' handed to deacon, priest or bishop was the Bible. This reflected a focus on the priority of the task of education and edification in the ordained ministry. This in turn demanded clergy who were themselves well trained. The Renaissance and Reformation had profound effect on both the task of ordained ministry, and the preparation required for it. For example, in the Diocese of Worcester, the percentage of clergy who were university graduates increased from nineteen per cent in 1560, to eighty-four per cent in 1640.[44] At one stage, learned Anglican clergy were *stupor mundi*, the wonder of the world. If we are to have well trained lay people, we need well trained clergy. If the clergy do not bring deep resources of Bible, tradition, and contemporary missional perspectives, then the life of the church will be trivial in every respect. Without good theological education for the clergy, the life of the local church will be limited by a merely local and trivial perception of the meaning of Scripture, and Tradition will be no more than 'What the last Vicar did'!

Not only should lay Christians be educated and edified for their lives in the world and in the church, but also we need well trained lay people so that our bishops can assess who should be candidates for ordination. For the primary formation of ordination candidates is the formation they receive in their local church. Without good quality lay people, we will not be able to find good quality clergy for the future. Good theology in local churches depends on good theological education for the clergy. It is very difficult for a church to rise above the level of its clergy!

It is ordinary members of churches who are treated as theologically responsible in the New Testament. Romans, Ephesians, and Revelation are written for the members of local churches. It is ordinary believers who together are 'the church of the living God, the pillar and bulwark

44. Adam, *The Church 'Halfly Reformed'*, 12.

of the truth'.[45] It is members of churches who are instructed to 'build yourselves up in your most holy faith'.[46]

Anglicanism has often valued conformity. A pluralist society calls for a church which is able to be 'all things to all people in order to win some to Christ'. We are called to a pluriformity of integrity, in which essential values are expressed in a variety of ways, for the effective mission of the church to our society.

The task of the church as a theological community is not only for its own life by the truth of the Gospel, to 'adorn the doctrine', but also to engage in the theological task of presenting the Gospel to the world and of living for God and serving God in the world.

The church needs four effective instruments to develop as a theological community

1. Sermons

Development as a theological community depends on a solid diet of good Biblical, theological, pastoral, practical, creative, educative and empowering preaching of the word of God. For the sermon is the moment when the intersection between God's story and our story is articulated, through a thoughtful and relevant meditation and application of the text of the Holy Scriptures. In the words of Gabriel Hebert:

> Such preaching will be 'theological' in the true sense. It will deal with God, God's work of grace, and man's reconciliation with God . . . For every sermon that is a good sermon is, so to speak, dated and addressed.[47]

In our sermons we either train our people to read and interpret the Bible for themselves, or we leave them untrained and ill equipped for responsible Christian life and action. In our preaching we either model and teach sound theological exegesis, or we leave people to use the Bible badly or to ignore it. We either enable our churches to be effective and responsible hermeneutical communities, or we silence God, and infantilise God's people.

---

45. 1 Timothy 3:15.
46. Jude 20.
47. Gabriel Hebert, *Liturgy and Society: The Function of the Church in the Modern World* (London: Faber, 1961), 223.

2. Bishops

The bishop's throne is a place from which to teach. It follows in the tradition of the seat for the synagogue teacher (Luke 4:20–2, Matthew 23:2). It is meant to honour the teaching ministry of the bishop. If the bishop is not a teacher of God's word, then the diocese will lack theological direction. The bishop will not be a preacher of God's word, if that bishop does not have a firm foundation in biblical studies, and the ongoing practice of the study of God's word. Administrative stability or administrative inertia is a poor substitute for the people of God growing up into true godly stability: 'the unity of the faith and of the knowledge of the Son of God, to maturity, to the measure of the full stature of Christ' (Ephesians 4:13). Bishops must be accountable for the theology of their dioceses, that we might 'no longer be children, tossed to and fro and blown about by every wind of doctrine' (Ephesians 4:23).

3. Centres for academic research and training

Our theological colleges have a crucial role in setting a standard in biblical studies, church history, theology, ethics, liturgy, and training in theological reflection and in practical ministry. It is difficult for a church to rise above the level of its colleges. Colleges must be credibly Christian, intellectually rigorous, educationally effective, and well able to train students in the Bible, Christian thought, and the practice of ministry.

Colleges need the full support of the church in terms of qualified and expert faculty, excellent libraries, a plentiful supply of good quality students and candidates for ordination, bishops who will set and maintain high standards for ordination training, and the prayers and financial support of the people of God.

4. Engagement with the world

We should set ourselves the aim of planning to set the intellectual and visionary agenda for our society. This will not happen without a deep appreciation of the foundations of Christian faith, a rigorous and ongoing study of the Scriptures, and contact with our society at the deepest level, both in ideas and the reality of human lives. It will be expressed in a committed and long-term loving and listening dialogue with our society, in terms of the human, social, political, ethical and religious realities of our current world. We cannot avoid 'incarnation,' nor can we make it easy for ourselves by making it merely a superficial incarnation, or by denying or hiding our fundamental beliefs, world-views, and values. We rely on our bishops and the leaders of our churches to lead us in this engagement.

A liturgical theology

The context of the practice of theology in the life of the church is the liturgy or the meeting together of God's people, though as we have seen, it must also happen in discussion groups, Bible studies, training events, and general conversations. Anglican liturgy is based on the Bible in the following ways:

- The purpose of the lectionary is to ensure that both the Old and New Testaments are read in a systematic way, so that every part of Scripture is heard in the church.
- Every service includes the meditative use of the book of Psalms.
- The words of the liturgy reflect the language of the Bible.
- The shape of the liturgy reflects the Gospel of the Bible. For example, in Morning and Evening Prayer we are addressed by the Word of God, we confess our sins and are assured of forgiveness, we hear the Bible read, we respond with faith in the words of the Creed, and then we pray for the world and the church. This provides a permanent *lectio divina* for the people of God.
- Sermons are the corporate meditation on the Scriptures, and the application of those Scriptures to the life of the church and to the world around us.

In the words of Article XIX, 'The visible Church of Christ is a Congregation of faithful men, in the which the pure Word of God is preached, and the Sacraments duly ministered according to Christ's ordinance . . .'[48]

Because theological formation happens in the church, prayer and belief go together; *lex orandi* and *lex credendi* inform each other. As we engage in *lectio divina*, our minds and hearts are formed by the

---

48. See David Peterson, *Engaging with God: a Biblical Theology of Worship* (Leicester, 1992).

Scriptures. So both our prayers and our actions are attuned to God, and there should be no disparity or dissonance between our liturgy and our life.

A theology for the whole of life

The results of this theological exercise will be found in every aspect of the lives of the members of God's household. It will certainly be evident in the structures and relationships of the members of the church to each other, and in their joint activities in their meetings and life together. It will also be evident in the daily lives of the people of God, in their marriages and families, the paid and unpaid work they do in their local community, their political and social participation in their human communities, as members of the one holy catholic and apostolic church, as participants in the world mission of the gospel of Christ, as citizens of their nation, as inhabitants of the world, and as those who participate in God's great work of cosmic transformation, in fulfilling God's purposes for his creation.

This must profoundly influence the subjects and processes of the theological enterprise in the local church. The agenda for discussion and reflection will not only be set by the Bible and its message, but also by the issues and priorities of contemporary society, and the big issues of our daily world. It is in the integration of theology and life that true theological formation happens, as it is in the same integration that effective liturgy is formed.

The theological task must not be narrowly ecclesiastical, but must embrace and be lived out in the world loved by God, and being transformed by God.

Conclusion

Theology belongs in the life of the church: that is its God-given and normative place. In the language of *The Gift of Authority*, the church is 'a community which receives the canonical scriptures as the authentic Word of God'. As the church receives and re-receives the Word of God, it is saying its 'Amen' to that Word and Catholicity is 'The "Amen" of the Whole Church' to God's Word.[49] The practice of

---

49. Anglican–Roman Catholic International Commission 11 (ARCIC 11), *The Gift of Authority*, 21, 22 at www.ewtn.com/library/Theology/Arcicgf3.htm (accessed 17 May 2006).

theology in the local church is the process of receiving the Word of God, interpreting it, understanding it, reflecting on its significance, responding to it in meditation, prayer, and praise, and being formed by it so that we are transformed into increasing faith in, and obedience to, the Lord Jesus Christ.

Healthy Anglicanism is marked by obedience to Scripture, active and responsive theological reflection in churches, and lives transformed by the Spirit and obedient to Christ.

5

Dangerous Memory For An Incarnational Church

Heather Thomson

How are we to think, theologically, of the church in a particular context? To ask this question from a theological perspective is not to work from what *is* the case (sociological surveys) or what *has been* the case (history). Rather it is to work from what *might be* the case, from possibilities beyond the empirical world that call us forward and inform our choices and decisions and commitments in the here and now. In Christian theology, to be theologically driven is to seek the possibilities that God sets before us, as revealed in the scriptures and tradition, for being the people of God. We have then to think that through in our own context.

There are a number of associated terms that belong to the discussion of the church in context. I wish to explore these briefly and to explain why, in this chapter, 'incarnation' is the term chosen. First, the term 'context' itself. Developed in relation to biblical studies, context referred to the texts before and after the particular text being studied. To read a text in context means to read it in relation to the larger whole of which it is a part. It is to understand the place of a text in a larger situation, and the difference that makes to the meaning of the part and the whole when read in relation to each other. The term has been expanded in both biblical studies and theology to refer to the particular (text, church, mission program) within its larger context, read in relation to each other.[1]

Contextual theology is the self-conscious effort to do theology and to be the people of God in a particular time and place. More and more it is becoming the *responsible* way of doing theology, taking

1. S Bergmann, *God in Context: A Survey of Contextual Theologies* (Aldershot: Ashgate, 2003), 2.

responsibility for one's social location, and for the resultant social and political effects of one's work. Contextual theology involves reading around local efforts to the larger situation in which they are placed—their economic, social, historical, political, and geographical environments, to name a few.[2] Contextual theology is often driven by a desire for relevance and authenticity, so that the faith that is believed and lived in a particular place is not merely imported from elsewhere and imposed, but is lived and expressed according to the local culture and broader environment.

The desire for relevance and authentic expression is good and worthy, but there are two dangers when these are the prime motivators for contextual theology. First, in focussing on the local, the resultant theology and church life can become parochial, losing sight of and missing out on the richness of the larger Christian tradition across time and in other parts of the world. A parochial church has no message for others beyond its own small place, yet the Christian gospel has a proclamation that is universal.[3] Balance is needed between the local and the worldwide to avoid the problem of parochialism, or of reducing the gospel to a message and vision that is too small.

The second danger is that churches which seek to be relevant and authentic in their context sometimes end up merely assimilating into their culture in an uncritical process—Barth's criticism of liberal theology. The danger is that the source and the inspiration of the Christian church comes from the culture itself rather than anything beyond it that may stand as a critical vantage point from which to evaluate the church's life and mission. The church has played its part in sanctioning the status quo, and uncritically assuming that what privilege and power it does have, has been given it by God. Yet there

---

2. *Ibid.* For more on contextual theology see Stephen Bevans, *Models of Contextual Theology* (Revised and expanded edition, Maryknoll, NY: Orbis Books, 2002); Gideon Goosen, *Australian Theologies: Themes and Methodologies into the Third Millennium* (Strathfield: St Paul's, 2000).
3. This point is made by Joseph Galgalo in his unpublished lecture notes for 'Jesus Christ in the African context', taught at St Paul's Limuru, Kenya, 2004. Chris Mostert makes a similar point in his chapter, 'Is a Non-Contextual Theology Viable?' in *Mapping the Landscape: Festschrift in Honour of Professor Ian Breward*, edited by S Emilsen and WW Emilsen (New York: Peter Lang, 2000), 118–33.

have also always been traditions within the church that have questioned such assumptions, starting with the prophetic tradition in the Old Testament and the teachings and life of Jesus. As Daniel Migliore says, these prophetic traditions:

> knew very well the extent to which religion and its official custodians can stand in opposition to God's intentions for human life. Theology indeed becomes questionable when it ceases to ask itself what powers it is in fact serving and whose interests it may be promoting. It is clear that much of Christian theology has not yet learned to take these questions with the seriousness that they deserve.[4]

The church, as custodian of the Christian tradition, has a responsibility to hold and to pass on that which it has received. Yet what it has received is already a conversation and argument about what God is like and what God requires of us. In any context churches need to make choices as to which traditions they will side with, among all those they have inherited. The argument of this essay is that to think through the question of the church in context is to make conscious choices about what powers the church is serving and whose interests it is promoting. To do this is to stand firmly within the prophetic tradition, as Jesus himself chose.

There are various models of contextual theology, including the *translation model* (where culture is a vehicle for translating the unchangeable truth of the gospel), the *anthropological model* (where faith is communicated according to a particular group's symbolic worldview), the *praxis* or *liberation model* (where the point is not merely to understand a context but to change it to ameliorate suffering and oppression), the *correlation model* (that tries to balance the different demands of the other models between received faith and contemporary culture), and the *transcendental model* (from transcendental philosophy and its focus on the authentic, subjective experience).[5] I am

---

4. D Migliore, *Faith Seeking Understanding: An Introduction to Christian Theology* (Second Edition, Grand Rapids: Eerdmans, 2004), 9.
5. Bergmann, *God in Context*, 87–94. See also Goosen, *Australian Theologies*, 69–75. Both Bergmann and Goosen base their models on

working with the liberation or praxis model, because this is the model that overtly engages in the discussion about the powers and interests that are served and promoted by our theology and church life. Liberation theology seeks to recover the fullness of the meaning of salvation, and challenges the church to convey the 'good news' in their work and words within their contexts.

Discussions regarding church and context sometimes use other terms such as inculturation and enculturation to describe the process of a church finding its place in a new situation. The relation of faith to culture is not a simple question. As Katherine Tanner argues, faith is not abstract, but is already encultured. There is no expression of the Christian faith in thought and deed that is not already expressed in lives and communities, in languages and symbols of human cultures. It is not as though we can have an abstract 'faith' or 'church' and then work out what is its relation to culture. The 'Christ and culture', or 'Christ against culture' categories of Niebuhr are somewhat misleading in that way. The very exercise of theology is already a form of culture. What is needed is a critical engagement, a two-way conversation, between church and its surrounding context, such that each is open to the mutual critique and challenge of the other, as well as mutual efforts to make human life more humane.[6]

According to Rowan Williams, Michael Ramsey saw the task of theology in this way. Ramsey's concern was not the tension between religious belief and modern culture, or faith and society. Rather he was concerned to address the tension between the gospel vision of corporate human life (realised through Christ and the Spirit, epitomised in the eucharistic assembly), and all other forms of human corporate life. Sometimes this Christian vision of human community is most fully realised within church communities. Sometimes there are good, or better, examples of it outside the church. Thus the task is to address the tension through a mutual thinking by church and non-church, a reciprocal testing, which includes the church listening to

---

Bevan's, in his first edition, *Models of Contextual Theology* (New York: Orbis Books, 1992).

6. See Aylard Shorter, *Towards a Theology of Inculturation* (London: Chapman, 1988), 13, where he explores the terms inculturation, enculturation, acculturation, and interculturation as they relate to the work of the community of faith finding its expression in its surrounding culture. He advocates a two-way process between the culture of the church and that of its context, a 'bilingual' conversation.

voices of protest and anger, even against itself, and naming its own failures. In this way, in humility, it may return to its source.[7]

Rowan Williams comments that such a task is born from an incarnational theology that 'requires a fundamental commitment to that world as deserving of attention, as having depths worth sounding . . . '[8] Contextual theology, or the terms inculturation and enculturation, do not really convey the depth of commitment to the world as deserving of attention. Nor do they incorporate the reciprocal testing of both church and wider society with quite the same commitment. It is because I wish to tie a theology of the church closely to its *source* and to the *world* that I am opting for the term incarnational to describe the church in its context. To speak of an incarnational church holds even more dangers than the terms contextualisation, inculturation and enculturation. However, it also holds even more promise if it is linked with the prophetic tradition, and the notion of 'dangerous memory', which will be discussed more fully later.

The church as incarnational

Upholding an incarnational view of the church is a traditionally Anglican way of thinking about the church in the world. Thus to continue to employ the term is to participate in a longer conversation where it has been critically assessed. In reviewing this longer conversation, a number of positive implications can be discerned. For one, as mentioned above, incarnational theology takes the world seriously as God's own abode. Ecclesiology that derives from this does not seek to withdraw from the world but to engage with it, to work with God 'who so loved the world' (John 3:16). It gives the wider context some credit for having something to say back to the church, for having 'depths worth sounding'. Such an understanding of incarnational theology promotes openness and dialogue, humility rather than arrogance, and yet gives the church a warrant to stand firm and faithful to its gospel, as Jesus did in his context.

Another strength of incarnational theology applied to both Christ and the church is that the two are held together, allowing the church

7. Rowan Williams, *Anglican Identities* (London: Darton, Longman & Todd, 2004), 101–2.
8. Williams, *Anglican Identities*, 101.

no basis in self-justification. The church gains its existence and life, its mission and hope from Christ. As the body of Christ it receives its reason for being from the one whose body was given for us, who was the true icon of God to us, and whose gathered community remembers him and lives by his present life. Ecclesiology should not be separated from Christology, lest it loses sight of its foundation and source. As Bill Lawton argues, tying ecclesiology closely to Christology makes good theological sense.[9]

However, care needs to be taken that it is Christology that drives ecclesiology and not the other way around. This is a difficult point to discern at times, but there have been within the Anglican tradition assumptions made that the institutional Anglican Church (read back into the Christian tradition) has been derived directly from Christ and the apostles—a kind of extension of the incarnation. Such a view has also been roundly criticised within the tradition. Examples include Rowan Williams' critique of Ramsay who saw the institutional church as an 'epiphany' of God,[10] and Peter Hinchliff's critique of Walter Lock on 'The Church' from *Lux Mundi*.[11] In each case, what is criticised is that it is an incarnational view of the church that is used to argue for sanctioning the institutional Anglican Church in all its arrangements, orders and governance. Theology is reduced to an ideology, sanctioning the status quo, and upholding one form of church life over others. This is its great danger, and the reason that a critical appropriation is needed.

---

9. Bill Lawton argues that Christology and scripture are the rightful foundations for ecclesiology, rather than ecclesiology having its own starting point or justification. I agree with this, but wish to draw out the implications more so than he does. See Lawton's essay, 'Australian Anglican Theology', in *Anglicanism in Australia: A History*, edited by Bruce Kaye *et al* (Melbourne: *Melbourne University Press*, 2002), 178–9.
10. Rowan Williams, *Anglican Identities*, 91.
11. Walter Lock, 'The Church', in *Lux Mundi: A Series of Studies in the Religion of the Incarnation*, edited by Charles Gore (London: John Murray, 1902), 267–95. Peter Hinchliff's response is in his chapter, 'The Church', in *The Religion of the Incarnation: Anglican Essays in Commemoration of Lux Mundi*, edited by Robert Morgan (Bristol: Bristol Classical Press, 1989), 136–57. See: 'Lock's appeal is simply to the continuity of the church from the apostolic age to the Church of England of the late nineteenth century', 145.

Thinking of the church as incarnational has been a fruitful metaphor, and one that continues to be used by contemporary Anglican theologians.[12] However, the term continues to be used most often as a shorthand reference to tradition without being fleshed out, so to speak. We have only the bones of an idea, rather than a full-bodied theology. As Bruce Kaye notes after discussing Hooker's incarnational theology, Anglican theology needs a sense of the 'more fundamental importance of certain key theological themes, principal among which, in my judgment, is a better sense of the meaning of the incarnation and the relationship of God to his world'.[13]

To avoid the dangers of too close an association of the presence of God in the world with a particular church denomination (or a faction within it), a critical appropriation of the term 'incarnational church' is necessary. Fortunately, incarnational theology contains within it its own critical principles. From what we can know of the incarnation of God in Christ in the scriptures, the presence of God in human life was anything but a sanctioning of the status quo. Jesus was such a disturbing and powerful challenge to the prevailing culture, religion and political scene of his time that those in power conspired to kill him. He was a threat on many levels. Understanding this allows us to incorporate critical principles into our ecclesiology that are already within the doctrine of the incarnation itself. God did not just preside in a human body, nor merely dwell among us as another ordinary human being. Jesus of Nazareth did not merely adapt to his culture, so that his message may be more relevant to his hearers. Although this world became the domicile of God, it did not domesticate God, though it has tried and continues to do so.

Rather, God in Christ was a direct challenge to the powers of his world, and continues to confront us with the questions: what powers

---

12. See Rowan Williams, *Anglican Identities*, 33ff for an analysis of Hooker's 'governing narrative of incarnation'. For Australian writers see Bruce Kaye, *A Church Without Walls: Being Anglican in Australia* (North Blackburn: Dove, 1995), 104–5, 136ff. See also: Bruce Kaye's introductory chapter to this volume; Scott Cowdell, *God's Next Big Thing: Discovering the Future Church* (Mulgrave: John Garrett, 2004), 93, 96; Lawton, 'Australian Anglican Theology', 197.
13. Kaye, *A Church Without Walls*, 106.

are we serving and whose interests are we promoting? And what is the power of God in the world in which we are called to participate?

The notion of an incarnational church has to take up the challenge of these questions. Such a task is enabled by and modelled on the incarnation of God in Christ. Helpful in this task is the work of JB Metz in relation to the memory that lies at the foundation of the church, that of Jesus as the 'dangerous memory of freedom'.

Dangerous memory

Metz was concerned to develop a political theology, that is, one that was critically aware of its relation to social and political power structures in any given context. He argued that 'it is not possible, without self-deceit, to regard Christianity and theology as politically innocent and entirely without intention'.[14] In wanting to give an account of the hope that is in us (1 Peter 3:15) Metz related this hope to the actual historical and social contexts in which people live, rather than to some abstract realm, or to the pretence that the gospel does not concern such matters.[15]

Metz develops an understanding of the church as the bearer of a dangerous memory—that of Jesus' passion, death and resurrection.[16] As the community who keeps this memory alive, the church is founded on and justified by the memory of Jesus' suffering and liberation. Since Jesus' suffering and liberation was God's in human form, then the whole history of suffering is taken into this memory. Jesus' suffering was on behalf of others. Since Jesus revealed God's solidarity with the 'least of these' (Matthew 25), God's compassion and love reaches out to those who suffer, are neglected, scapegoated or oppressed by social, political and religious powers. Jesus engaged those same powers, and was crucified by them. Any community founded on this memory has to be concerned with the question of power and how it is exercised in human societies. That is why we need a political theology, one concerned with issues of power, when talking about the church in context.

---

14. JB Metz, *Faith in History and Society: Towards a Practical Fundamental Theology* (New York: Crossroads, 1980), ix.
15. Metz, *Faith in History and Society*, 3.
16. *Ibid*, Chapter 5: 'The dangerous memory of the freedom of Jesus Christ. The presence of the church in society'.

We learn more about God-like power from the resurrection. The power of God, that raised this crucified one from the dead, did not express itself as vengeance on those who had killed Jesus. What was vindicated in the resurrection was the power of love and compassion, a power that reached into the furthest realms of darkness. No other power, such as the power to dominate, control or kill, was expressed in the resurrection. Human oppressive, repressive, controlling power was transcended in the interests of peace, reconciliation and liberation. Metz's political theology enquires about this dangerous memory of freedom, freedom from human forms of power and control, and how that may manifest itself in contemporary ways to give a hopeful future to those who suffer.

For Metz, the dangerous memory of Jesus is not a mere remembering of past events, but the type of memory that makes demands on us now. It reveals new insights and challenges for the present as we contemplate and work towards the future.[17] It is subversive of the plausibility structures of our contemporary societies, and shocks us from ever being reconciled to the facts and trends of how things are. The church rather is called to live out of the possibility of how things could be, the possibility of the new creation in tension with and transforming the old.[18]

Metz's notion of dangerous memory has had, and continues to have, a significant influence in theology, liturgy and preaching. Liberation and feminist theologians use the term to keep alive the social and political dimensions of the gospel. These are often lost in theologies or Christian communities that have become too complacent, or who reduce the gospel to a matter of the individual before God. Elizabeth Schussler Fiorenza, for example, speaks of the democratic vision of a radical equality that characterised the church in the early Jesus movement. This understanding of church as a discipleship of equals is a dangerous memory for any church structure now that institutionalises inequality, such as those that do not ordain women. Further, the memory of those women and men throughout history who have been faithful agents of the vision of equality, against all that would marginalise, exclude and dehumanise them, is a dangerous memory for us. They inspire us to keep alive God's vision of human

17. Metz, *Faith in History and Society*, 109.
18. Metz, *Faith in History and Society*, 112–18.

community, of which the church is meant to be the sacrament. In this community all previous divisions between people in terms of status and privilege, no longer count. Our baptism into Christ overrides the earlier divisions. We die to our old selves and become a new people, recognising each other as equals.[19]

Metz's political theology has been brought into conversation with eucharistic practice in a book by Bruce Morrill, *Anamnesis as Dangerous Memory: Political and Liturgical Theology in Dialogue*.[20] Much liturgical theology does not think through the political implications of worship, and much political thought and activity does not include the liturgical practice that gives and sustains the vision for our action in the world. Putting the two in dialogue is a fruitful exercise.

Sharon Welsh is also a significant contributor to the notion of dangerous memory. She approaches the question through feminist theology and ethics, and is concerned to find a theology that will sustain the long-term effort towards social justice when it is all too easy for middle-class Christians to fall into despair or return to their comfortable lives and give up on the fray. Welsh contributes to a 'theology for the bearers of dangerous memory'.[21]

I will draw on this rich tradition of 'dangerous memory' as I try to flesh out what it might mean to be an incarnational church. Reflecting on Ramsey's contribution to incarnational theology, Rowan Williams wonders what an ecclesiology might look like if done by the victimised and excluded. Although Ramsey advocated continual reform of the church, and its need to acknowledge its failures, he nevertheless defended the hierarchy of the church as an 'epiphany' of God. Williams comments:

> If the theologies that emerge from the experience of the victimised and excluded, the theologies that deploy suspicion and ideological critique, are to be in any

---

19. See for example, ES Fiorenza, *Sharing Her Word: Feminist Biblical Interpretation in Context* (Edinburgh: T&T Clark, 1998), 49, 113ff.
20. BT Morrill, *Anamnesis as Dangerous Memory: Political and Liturgical Theology in Dialogue* (Collegeville: Liturgical Press, 2000).
21. SD Welsh, *A Feminist Ethic of Risk* (Minneapolis: Fortress Press, 1990). Part 3 of her book is called 'A Theology for the Bearers of Dangerous Memory', and consists of three chapters entitled 'The Ideology of Cultured Despair', 'An Ethic of Solidarity and Difference', and 'A Theology of Resistance and Hope'.

> sense *theology*, not just the expression of an assortment of resentments, they are bound to work with a governing critical model . . . a system of relations between persons established by the events of revelation—that is, by the history of Israel and Jesus.[22]

Through the idea of the church as the incarnation of dangerous memory, I hope to explore this further. What emerges is a particular system of relations between persons, established by the events of revelation, one that works from 'the least of these'. The church is the community founded on the memory of Jesus, the one who was excluded and crucified. But the stone that was rejected has become the cornerstone. The foundation of the church as the new creation lies with this rejected one.

In the following three sections I explore the implications of this understanding of the church. Each section has its own text around which the material is focussed. The first considers the stance of the present in relation to past traditions, with the text from Mark 2:27: 'The Sabbath was made for humanity, and not humanity for the Sabbath'. The second section reconsiders personal salvation, the healing and liberation that occurs within our selves and our relation with others as we take up the challenge of the dangerous memory of freedom in relation to Jesus. This section has as its focal point the story of the woman at the well. The third section explores the community of the church called into being in memory of Jesus, and in the power of his Spirit. The focus here is on community relations and how they are built up from the underside. Its text is from Mark 12:10, 'The stone that the builders rejected has become the cornerstone' (See: Acts 4:11; 1Peter 2:7; Psalms 118:22; Isaiah 28:16; Ephesians 2:19–22).

In each section I seek to understand what was dangerous about Jesus, dangerous enough that he was put to death. What power did he live by in his context and why was that such a threat? What may we learn from this as we situate ourselves in our own contexts, in relation to the past traditions of our church, our understandings of salvation, and to the community of the church built upon the dangerous memory of Jesus' freedom? I am searching for criteria by which the dialogue between church and non-church may fruitfully proceed, at least the

---

22. Williams, *Anglican Identities*, 99.

criteria which we in the church may wish to use in this dialogue, on how our lives together may become more human and humane. This is the challenge that Rowan Williams has given us—to seek a governing critical model for church, 'a system of relations between persons established by the events of revelation—that is, the history of Israel and Jesus'.

The sabbath was made for humanity, not humanity for the sabbath (Mark 2:27)

In this text, Jesus and his disciples had been seen eating the grains of wheat as they walked through a field and were accused of breaking the law, not for stealing, but for working on a sabbath.[23] In his defence, Jesus tells the story of David who entered the house of God and ate the bread of the Presence when he and his men were hungry and in need of food, even though this bread was reserved for the priests. By implication, Jesus and his disciples were hungry and in need of food as well. Jesus sums up by asserting that the sabbath was made for humanity, not humanity for the sabbath, adding that the Son of Humanity (wrongly translated 'Son of Man') is Lord even of the sabbath.

This was an unusual defence, since it did not really answer the accusation. There is no clear connection in the story told of David that indicated he was breaking a sabbath law. Rather, Jesus seems to turn the argument on the law and cult in general, with the sabbath being a test case. Should the law be upheld when it means people will go hungry? In Matthew's version of this incident, Jesus quotes Hosea in his defence, 'I desire mercy and not sacrifice'. Mercy is one of the clues to the interpretation of this text.

I am taking this story of the conflict over the sabbath to represent the conflicts Jesus was involved in regarding the law in general, and over cultic practices such as hand washing before meals. Jesus was not only challenged over his actions but at times deliberately provoked the conflict himself (Luke 11:37–53). Thorwald Lorenzen explains Jesus'

23. Ben Witherington III, *The Gospel of Mark: A Socio-Rhetorical Commentary* (Grand Rapids: Eerdmans, 2001), 128: 'The controversy is not over the disciples gleaning and eating a little grain, as that was allowed to the stranger or the poor by law (Deuteronomy 23:25). The issue in this text has to do with reaping, a form of work. This was an activity prohibited on the Sabbath at Exodus 34:21.'

actions as a passionate concern and struggle for the right understanding of God—a struggle to the death.[24] He says that we need to:

> appreciate the fact that Jesus' death was not an accident of history, that he did not die of old age, and that his execution was not the result of a judicial error . . . the opposition against him can be explained by the common struggle for the right understanding of God and its implications for the concrete shaping of human life . . . the question of God, who he is, how he relates to the world, and what he demands, cannot be eliminated if one wants to understand the opposition to Jesus.[25]

There are a couple of points I wish to draw from these stories of confrontation and conflict, to help us discern what powers Jesus was serving and what interests he was promoting. The first concerns our interpretation of Jesus' authority. By what authority did Jesus act, even against the traditions of his own religion? There is no doubt the gospel writers are making a point about the authority of Jesus in the claim that the Son of Humanity is Lord even of the sabbath. King David had broken the law when he ate of the bread of the Presence. In Jesus we have one greater than David—how much more, then, is he able to act with an authority greater than the law.[26]

But the next step in interpretation is crucial. Do we believe that Jesus was free to break the law because his status put him *above* the law? He is the Son of God, he can do what he likes? In our common language we use Jesus' name this way. If someone is strutting around in their own self-importance, acting as if they are above the law, we say, 'Who does he think he is—Jesus Christ?' If we assume it is Jesus'

---

24. Thorwald Lorenzen, *Resurrection and Discipleship: Interpretive Models, Biblical Reflections, Theological Consequences* (New York: Orbis Books, 1995), 249.
25. Lorenzen, *Resurrection and Discipleship*, 251.
26. Joel Marcus, *Mark 1–8* (Anchor Bible Commentary, New York: Doubleday, 1999), 245.

status as Son of God that puts him above the law we miss the point.[27] Further, we lock ourselves into thinking that if a person is important enough, he or she can do what they like.

There is another way of understanding Jesus' actions and the struggles he engaged in, that reveals something about God—the understanding of God that Jesus lived and died for. The authority and power by which he acted was in each case the practice of goodness and compassion. When Jesus encountered people in need, nothing had a greater claim on him than how goodness and care may be brought to bear on the situation—mercy, forgiveness, healing, alleviating burdens, reconciliation. It is not that Jesus was too important to be bound by the law, but that he wanted it to fulfil its purpose.[28] 'Is it lawful to do good or to do harm on the sabbath?' he asked. 'To save life or to kill?' (Mark 3:4). As recounted in John's gospel, when a group of accusers took up stones to kill him he responded, 'I have shown you many good works. For which of these good works are you going to stone me?' (John 10:31–2).

Jesus acted by the power of God's goodness, even when this clashed with some teachings and practices of his religion. This was the interest he served, and not a promotion of his own importance or status, though he could have pulled rank on anyone. But then he would have lost the argument about God that he was having—that God is good, God is merciful, God welcomes all to his table, God cares like a good shepherd, God's yoke is easy.

We sometimes miss how radical Jesus' actions were when he worked on the sabbath. Keeping the sabbath, with all that entailed, is so central to Jewish faith. It is not just a human tradition, but one understood to be given them by God. In terms of Christian theology it had the status of revelation, not something derived from natural theology. Yet not even that tradition was to be kept 'religiously' if by keeping it people suffered in some way.

---

27. Ched Myers, *Binding the Strong Man: A Political Reading of Mark's Story of Jesus* (New York: Orbis, 2000), 160. Myers refers to the term 'christological prerogative' used by most commentators to justify Jesus' actions in this story. For Myers this is missing the point. Jesus is leading his disciples into an act of civil disobedience against the Pharisaic codes on land and food, while himself choosing solidarity with the poor (*ibid*, 160–1).

28. Marcus, *Mark 1–8*, 245.

So my first point is that if we are to think of the church as incarnational, the authority by which we act in any particular context is through the exercise of goodness and compassion. In Anglican thinking about webs of authority, or dispersed authority, this practical criterion is sometimes lost.[29] Jesus' struggle for the right understanding of God contains a dangerous memory of freedom in relation to tradition, even those traditions held to be revealed by God. For us, our traditions have to be measured and reassessed according to different situations and contexts, and any possible harm they are causing.

There are three examples I have in mind that are pushing my agenda here. The first comes from the ordination of women debate that occurred in Australia from the 1970s and continues in some dioceses of the Anglican Church in Australia, though most have ordained women to the priesthood since 1992 or so. My point is about tradition. One of the arguments against the ordination of women early on was that it had not been done before, and that held the weight of providence, of God's will. Tradition, it was assumed, was guided by the Holy Spirit, so if women had not been ordained before, then God did not want them to be ordained. The weight of women's suffering under this tradition held no *theological* weight in this argument. The harm being done, robbing women's lives of their calling, and degrading women's natures as being not 'fit' for the office of priest, was seen as faithfulness to God's word and the tradition that came from it.

However, if we are to understand the saying of Jesus that 'the sabbath was made for humanity and not humanity for the sabbath', then arguments appealing to tradition can never hold out *theologically*

---

29. Alisdair MacIntyre in *Whose Justice, Which Rationality* (Notre Dame: University of Notre Dame Press, 1988) draws our attention throughout his book to 'practical rationality' as one form of knowing what a community believes—by the way they act. I am suggesting here certain practical criteria for knowing what 'authority' means, drawn from the life of Jesus as given in the gospels. Many Christian communities practise care and compassion to those within and outside the church, on the authority of Jesus' practice. However, I am interested in the authority by which Christians may criticise aspects of their own received tradition. This too is authorised in Jesus' practice, his 'practical rationality', given in the stories of him breaking the Sabbath rule.

over arguments that this tradition is causing hurt and harm and should be changed. The exercise of care and compassion is our primary authority, and if our tradition does not serve these interests and promote the power of this work, then where does its authority come from?

The second example comes from an encounter I had a few years ago with a young postgraduate student who was a Christian and was also gay. She had trouble finding a spiritual 'home'. Her friends in the homosexual community couldn't understand why she wanted to be involved in the church. 'Why don't you just leave?' they asked. Church members who knew her did not understand or did not like her association with the gay community. It seemed to compromise her faith and commitment. I thought she was being over-dramatic when she said that 'people are dying over this'. I asked her what she meant and she said that in the last year two of her friends had attempted suicide, one successfully, over being torn in two. Their very beings were unacceptable to church people, but they had faith and the love of God as any other Christian. I looked at her and she was shaking and holding back tears. It was then I realised that in the death and attempted suicide of her friends, and in her struggle for her own life, the church is culpable. Our traditions of seeing homosexuality as an 'abomination' and unacceptable to God, have played their part in the cultivation of hatred. These traditions have caused, and continue to cause, harm to individuals and to the whole church.

In Jesus' proclamation that the sabbath is made for humanity not humanity for the sabbath, and in his actions against the hurt and harm laid on people by tradition, we have a warrant to change our tradition on this matter. 'Is it lawful to do good or to do harm . . . to save life or to kill?' (Mark 3:4).

The third example concerns the alienation and foreignness of the Anglican tradition for some in the Australian context. Much has been done to address this, but it is still the case, for example, that Aboriginal people find the Anglican Prayer Book and Anglican styles of worship culturally foreign in a number of ways. Instead of enhancing worship, traditional Anglican forms, church buildings and music sometimes serve instead to stifle the authentic worship of Aboriginal people. This is not just a matter of different cultures, but is caught up in the history between Aboriginal people and white settlement where the so-called 'gospel' served colonialism and the imposition of Western culture. For healing and reconciliation to occur, new traditions need to be developed and allowed to flourish within the Anglican Church. What we need to guard is not the Anglican heritage but fresh forms of worship and the common life of local churches that are themselves forms of healing and reconciliation. We need to hold onto these so that the medium in which we gather and worship is also the message of good news.

My final point concerns the interpretation of Jesus' words and action in his conflicts over the sabbath. Sometimes Christians read these stories triumphally, that is, we read them as the ones who are the victors, the ones who now see clearly, who now have the fuller revelation of God in Jesus Christ. In this way we consider Jesus to be right to take the stance he did, and make the criticisms he did. However, we then read ourselves as having now received the right traditions which we then keep and guard 'religiously'.

To interpret the scriptures triumphally is also to miss the point. Jesus' criticisms against certain religious practices and beliefs of his day are founded on his understanding of what God is like and what God requires of us. These still stand whatever religion we are in. They are principles of living and acting, and if we Anglicans are to understand ourselves as an incarnational church, we will live and act them too, even if they take us into conflict with our own Christian and Anglican traditions. That is all part of the dangerous memory of freedom in relation to traditions—the freedom to change them in the interests of fostering goodness and care.

Within the Christian tradition and within Anglicanism there are many voices and different practices. This makes for a rich diversity but at times differences have divided us. It is a difficult thing to know when, for the sake of unity and harmony, to lay aside traditions that divide, and when to fight over one's understanding of God, as Jesus did. There are warrants for both, but my concern here is to get a better understanding of the *criteria* by which one decides. From what has been said in this section so far, the criteria come from practice as well as doctrine, from giving care and exercising mercy, offering forgiveness and cultivating life. These are the criteria by which our doctrines and traditions in general—in short, our religion—should be judged. Whether it is within the wider church or within Anglicanism, our lives of faith and our conflicts with each other should serve these interests and promote these powers.

'If you knew the gift of God . . .' (John 4:10)
The second section exploring the meaning of dangerous memory concerns the difference the gospel makes on a personal level. I am concerned that unless we know for ourselves the dangerous memory of freedom contained in the gift of God to us, we may not be free to serve the interests of goodness and compassion. Rather we would be acting out of our own needs and desires, from our own hurts and scars, guilt and fear. We need to know the gift of God—God's love and the cost of our salvation—but we need to know it more than in our heads. It takes a life-long journey to know this deeply, to be freed from our old selves as we become renewed in Christ. My interest in pursuing this theme is not to talk about personal fulfilment, but to think about the ways that church communities, theological schools and colleges and the practice of faith may enhance the process of personal healing, so that Christian people in their various contexts may more readily serve the interests of the gospel.

Those Christians whom I most admire as being quiet and wise souls have usually spent some time in counselling, spiritual direction, psychotherapy, meditation, tai chi, yoga or whatever it takes to bring healing from old wounds and an ability to move forward with much less baggage. I have heard psychotherapy described this way. It is as if you are travelling along the road of life, but are carrying much too much baggage with you. So you stop off by the side of the road with your therapist. Together you open up all the bags, sort through all the stuff you have in them, discard much of it, and repack the bags in a better way. Then you get back on the road travelling much lighter and with a sense of freedom.

Freedom is one of the gifts of God. We may find a measure of personal freedom directly from church life and liturgy, from reading the bible and praying, but we should not discount intentional work on ourselves, and certainly not discount it as a theology of works. Freedom is part of the interest we are called to serve and the powers we are meant to promote as people of the God of Jesus Christ. For the church, work is already being done to promote this in terms of Christian counselling and spiritual direction. Christian communities also play a part in healing, forgiveness and reconciliation. However, that is not always the case, and the message needs to be carefully contextualised.

Some churches have *such* a strong doctrine of sin that they have the effect of making people feel bad about themselves. I grew up in both

Baptist and Anglican Churches in Sydney having to live with the teaching that I belonged on death row. I know of kids who have asked their parents after church, 'Am I really that bad?' The secular newspapers have even commented on the church in this regard. I read in *The Australian* a few years back that the congregation at St Vincent's Catholic church in Redfern was complaining about the priest who had replaced Ted Kennedy there. The largely Aboriginal congregation said that he 'tells us we are sinners, corpses of sin'.[30]

It is bad enough calling anyone a 'corpse of sin'. It is even worse doing so in the Australian context when it is a white priest ministering to Aboriginal people. The examples I have given of churches too strong on sin have crossed denominations—Anglican, Baptist, Catholic—yet hold a certain theology in common, that of a low view of human nature that seems to require judgment of people rather than compassion and care.

My point is not to do away with judgment or the doctrine of sin. Rather it is to balance the message with the positive calling of faithfully imaging God in whose image and likeness we were created, and for which we were redeemed. This message requires an awareness of context. As in Mary's song, the work of God 'brings down the mighty from their thrones and lifts up those of low degree' (Luke 1:52). The message to people of low degree is not that they are corpses of sin, but that they are valued in the eyes of God, conferred with dignity and worth that nothing human can take away. If God so loves the world, in God's work of creation and of redemption, then no-body is a no-body. So if some people are rendered no-bodies in a particular society or historical time, we had better ask some questions as to why this is so, and who made them this way? What plausibility structures have put them there and kept them there, and what is the church doing about this?

I was privileged to attend a Jean Vanier seminar in Canberra 2004, where we explored the different perception of the gospel that comes from work with severely physically and mentally disabled people. Jean Vanier talked of his work and that of the *L'Arche* communities as 'liberating'. He explained it this way. Most people suffering disabilities have a low sense of self. Some can compare themselves with others and wonder why they have to live with disability when

30. *The Australian*, 22 September 2003, 6.

others don't. Some have been neglected and abused, vulnerable as they are, and have been on the receiving end of anger and frustration as well as having to live with these feelings within themselves daily. What has proved to be liberating, and it takes a lot of time and effort, is that *L'Arche* communities convey through touch and speech, music and daily care, the message that 'you are loved', 'you are beautiful', 'you are worthy of dignity and respect'. This is liberating, healing work. It frees these people from a false sense of self, and liberates the carers from the false assumption that human worth is founded on achievement or status, able-bodiment or good looks. There is no mention in these communities of 'corpses of sin'. Again, it is the exercise of goodness and compassion that makes the difference, and the testimony of the carers is that it transforms their lives as well. They see themselves and their society differently.

'If you only knew the gift of God' is taken from the story of the woman at the well in John 4. Though Jesus knew her, he did not judge her or call her a sinner. Rather he seemed to care for her and her restless life, what she was searching for. He was concerned that she was lost, not looking in the right place for the source of her being, the living water that he could give. Further, Jesus transcended the 'plausibility structures' of his society that made him more important as a Jewish man, than her a Samaritan woman. Such divisions go deep and are often unconscious. It takes some effort to be aware of the assumptions we carry about our relative importance in relation to others.

Therefore the message of an incarnational church is to offer people the gift of God, the living water, the love that is the source of their dignity and being beyond anything that society or history or biology may serve up. There is a tremendous freedom that comes from knowing the love of God at this personal level. Yet the message will not be known truly and deeply unless people are willing to work on themselves, to have all their baggage opened up and sorted and repacked. This is the life-long work of the Christian, and the church can play its part in giving people better scripts about themselves.[31]

31. I owe this idea to Bruce Stevens, Anglican priest and clinical psychologist, in an unpublished paper, 'What Ghosts do in the Parlour: Internalised Relationships and the Dynamics of Personality', Appendix on Spirituality, cited from a 24 June 2003 draft.

The dangerous memory of freedom is based on the work of God already completed and there for our taking. For the church to convey this message it needs to attend to context. For those who are the mighty on their thrones, they need to be given the message, 'you are *no more* important than anyone else on this earth'. For those of low degree, the message is rather, 'you are *as* important as anyone else on this earth'. The church is the bearer of this double message of judgment and care, of bringing down and of building up. This is the dangerous memory of freedom for individuals—that we are all equal in God's sight and all equally invited to drink of the living water. The social and political implications of this are radical, and it has a bearing on how the church lives its communal life. That brings us to the final section.

The stone that the builders rejected has become the cornerstone (Mark 12: 10)

This section considers the dangerous memory of a community built up from the cornerstone of this rejected one. It takes as its text Mark 12: 10, which comes at the end of the parable of the wicked tenants. The owner had sent his servants to receive the harvest, but the tenants beat one, wounded another and killed the third. Finally the owner sent his beloved son and heir. But they killed him and cast him out. The parable alludes to the tradition of the killing of the prophets and to Jesus' own death and casting out.[32] Jesus then sums up the parable with this quote from Psalm 118: 22–3, 'Have you not read this scripture: "The stone that the builders rejected has become the cornerstone . . . ?" ' Although most Rabbinic literature interprets David as the rejected one in Psalm 118, Mark and other New Testament writers use this text to refer to Jesus, from whom a new people will be built up, a people who will bear fruit.

Again there are dangers of interpreting this text triumphally—we in the Christian church are now the new people of God, founded on Christ, who bear the good fruit. But the parable's significance goes beyond the historical rejection and death of Jesus and the birth of the Christian church. It speaks of the reception of God's message in such a way that it bears fruit, and the cornerstone is significant as the foundation of such a community. In other New Testament texts, Psalms 118 is combined with Isaiah 28:16, which also speaks of a

32. Myers, *Binding the Strong Man*, 308.

cornerstone: 'Behold, I am laying in Zion a stone, a cornerstone chosen and precious, and he who believes in him will not be put to shame' (1 Peter 2:6). The Isaiah texts goes on to say that in this building God will make justice the line and righteousness the plummet (Isaiah 28:17). Paul in Ephesians speaks of the building up of the church is these terms:

> So then you are no longer strangers and sojourners, but you are fellow citizens with the saints and members of the household of God, built upon the foundation of the apostles and prophets, Christ Jesus himself being the cornerstone, in whom the whole structure is joined together and grows into a holy temple in the Lord; in whom you also are built into it for a dwelling place of God in the Spirit (Ephesians 2: 19–22).

Now there is a real mixing of metaphors here, but it is significant that the early church writers put the foundation stone, with its lines of justice and righteousness, alongside that of the stone that was rejected and became the cornerstone. In a social and political reading of these texts, Jesus, the rejected one, subverted the system from within. He challenged the plausibility structures of his religion and society, siding with those who suffered under them, and was violently rejected for it. He therefore revealed the violence at the heart of such a system.[33] If he, then, is our cornerstone, we too will side with those who suffer under the prevailing religious and social rules that cause some to be outcast and hated, while others are given importance on false grounds.

A church built on this foundation stone would have empathy for the victims of the abuse of power. If the only legitimate form of power we have is the exercise of goodness and compassion, then the church founded on the rejected one will seek out and side with the most

33. This reading comes from theological and biblical studies based on the work of Rene Girard. See for example, Robert Hamerton-Kelly, *Sacred Violence: Paul's Hermeneutic of the Cross* (Minneapolis: Fortress Press, 1992).

powerless, the victims and the rejected ones in its particular context.[34] That is our primary allegiance, not to any particular denomination or tradition. Yet at its best, a church tradition fosters the kind of community which can incarnate such a vision of the people of God, and bear its fruit.

Colin Smith, an Anglican priest I met in the slums of Nairobi, was initially sent to Kenya to do in-service training for Anglican clergy, and to serve the agenda of the Archbishop to give the clergy a better understanding of Anglicanism. However, over time, he felt that Anglicanism in that context was failing to engage with life in the slums, seeing its role as preserving the fixed deposit that was the Anglican tradition. He has renegotiated his role, and now works in the slums and teaches urban theology to theology students, still under the auspices of the Anglican Church.[35] He says:

> My sense of affinity lies more with people and churches committed to ministry in the slums than specifically with the Anglican Church. In some ways my agenda has moved from an initial question about the mission of the Anglican Church in the slums to think more generally about what it means to be the church and a sign of the Kingdom in this context, irrespective of denomination.[36]

Our primary allegiance is to the 'least of these' as Matthew 25 makes clear. Allegiance to a tradition is a good and legitimate enterprise in so far as it supports this aim. The Anglican Church, as an incarnational church, finds its place in its context as it eschews the kinds of power and interests that are self-protective and self-serving. Instead, it will build up its presence on the foundation of the cornerstone, Jesus Christ, the stone who was rejected.

---

34. Stephen Pattison attempts to spell this out for chaplaincy in mental health institutions, in *Pastoral Care and Liberation Theology* (Cambridge: Cambridge University Press, 1994): 221–39.
35. Colin Smith is attached to an Anglican church in Kibera, a large slum area in Nairobi, and is seconded by the Archbishop to Carlile College in Kibera to teach in the Centre for Urban Mission.
36. In an email to me, 28 April 2004.

6

The Travail Of The Episcopate: Management And the Diocese In An Age of Mission

Stephen Pickard

Introduction: the episcopal body

The nature and history of the Anglican episcopate in Australia has been well documented.[1] In many ways episcopacy operated as a 'pioneer ministry' in the developing Anglican Church on Australian soil. Australian bishops had both jurisdictional and pastoral oversight of large territories. The missionary nature of the episcopate was exemplified in the ministry of Bishop Tyrrell of Newcastle.[2] In other respects the Church of England in Australia proved quite innovatory in the development of modern synodical government with lay participation in the oversight and ordering of the church, through Bishop-in-Synod.[3] This embodiment of a personal, collegial and communal episcopate has a remarkably modern feel to it in the light of

1. See the extensive bibliography in *Episcopacy: Views from the Antipodes*, edited by Alan Cadwallader (Melbourne: ABCE, 1994).
2. For a recent assessment see Paul S Robertson, *Proclaiming Unsearchable Riches: Newcastle and the Minority Evangelical Anglicans 1788–1900* (Leominster: CSAC & Gracewing, 1996), chapters 4 and 5.
3. The 1850 conference in Sydney convened by Bishop Broughton marked the development of synodical forms of government outside America. See J Davis, *Australian Anglicans and their Constitution* (Canberra: Acorn Press, 1993) 13. For an important overview see KS Chittleborough, 'Towards a Theology and Practice of the Bishop-in-Synod', in *Authority in the Anglican Communion*, edited by SW Sykes (Toronto: Anglican Book Centre, Canada, 1987), 144–62.

the ecumenical reflections on ministry in *Baptism, Eucharist and Ministry*.[4]

Today the Anglican Church of Australia consists of five provinces and twenty-three dioceses covering over seven and a half million square kilometres of earth under the care of twenty-three diocesan bishops (including five Archbishops), eighteen regional bishops and four assistant bishops.[5] However, the geographical size of dioceses is uneven given the population distribution in a sparsely inhabited country with major urban concentrations. These preliminary remarks suggest a rather remarkable history in a relatively short period of time.[6] Are bishops in the Anglican Church of Australia very different now than when William Grant Broughton was consecrated as the first bishop in 1836? Certainly times have changed, the number of dioceses has multiplied, there are more priests and deacons; and there have been well over 200 bishops consecrated since Broughton. On the other hand the Anglican Ordinal specifies a range of responsibilities and raises expectations concerning a form of life that, on any account, points to some essential and enduring features of the episcopal brief.[7]

This chapter explores some of the ecclesiological issues relevant to a re-formed episcopate in contemporary Anglicanism. The notion of 're-form' is deliberate and points to a number of issues. First, even the briefest familiarity with the history of the episcopate in Australia would offer sufficient evidence that the episcopate has and continues to undergo constant re-forming.[8] As the environment in which

4. *Baptism, Eucharist and Ministry* (Geneva: WCC Publications, 1982), wherein these diverse and complementary forms of episcope are recognised.
5. See *The Australian Anglican Directory 2003* (Richmond: Angela Grutzner Publications, 2003).
6. On the other hand Australian Anglicans had to wait till 1962 before they had their own Constitution and a further twenty years before our church became officially 'The Anglican Church of Australia'.
7. See the 'Exhortation and Examination' (section 18) for the consecration of a bishop in *A Prayer Book for Australia* (Sydney: Broughton Books, 1995), wherein is set out the responsibilities and duties that belong to the episcopal office.
8. This begins with the episcopate of Broughton. For a helpful discussion see Bruce Kaye, 'Bishops and Social Leadership: What we might learn from the first and only Bishop of Australia', in *Episcopacy*, edited by Cadwallader, 91–108. Kaye examines the episcopate of Broughton, who

episcopacy has been practised changes over time so too this impacts in various subtle and not so subtle ways upon the form and function of the episcopate within church and society.[9]

There are two areas in which the re-forming of the episcopate, both in Australia and the wider communion, has been taking place, often with little critical reflection, but usually with significant anxiety. We might identify the two areas as the church in its *intensive* mode (its gathered life within the local ecclesia, the diocese) and its *extensive* mode (its life in relation to the wider *ecumenea*, in particular inter-church dialogues).[10] Space only permits this chapter to examine the first area relevant to reform of the contemporary episcopate, that is, the church in its intensive mode.

In the first area (intensive mode) the major influence upon the episcopate arises because the church, for better or worse, has been deeply influenced by prevailing management models of leadership associated with the emergence of the corporate life of modern Western institutions. In some respects this has been a question of survival and recovery of administrative efficiencies. Good management at least gives some possibility that bishops might be released to fulfil their

---

soon discovered that with the loss of his inherited framework of Royal Supremacy and church-state relationship he had to reappraise the kind of social leadership offered in Australian society.

9. For a general overview of the changing 'art' of episcopacy in Australia, see Alan Cadwallader's, chapter in *Episcopacy*, 1–21. The changing form and re-forming of episcopacy is an ambiguous occurrence for it is not necessarily evidence of the reformation dictum, *ecclesia semper reformanda*. When re-forming takes place in an uncritical manner, as it were by osmosis in response to changing environments and needs, or through canonical and legal apparatus of the church with minimal reference to deeper theological impulses then conditions arise in which re-forming might simply fail the test of *episcope semper reformanda*.

10. The terms 'intensive' and 'extensive' have been adapted from Daniel Hardy's notion of 'extensity' as the 'spread-out-ness' of the Christian faith *in situ* in the world and 'intensity' through the 'inner dynamic of the wisdom of God' which occurs particularly in worship and the living tradition of the church. This dynamic between intensity and extensity is fundamental to the formation of Christian life and service. See, Daniel Hardy, *Finding the Church: The Dynamic Truth of Anglicanism* (London: SCM, 2001), chapter 6, especially 109ff.

episcopal vows. Ruling and caring for the body is 'big business', made even more urgent with declining resources and increasing needs. The deployment of management technique is enmeshed within traditional hierarchical patterns of authority (tendencies to centric, 'top-down' decision making and communication) within a diocesan structure carrying heavy burdens for administrative and legal oversight. What has happened to the shape and form of the episcopate within this mix of contemporary management culture drawn from a secular corporate environment, and inherited patterns of authority and ecclesial structure? How might the re-forming that has occurred be critically assessed in the light of the gospel and mission of God's church? What would a theological assessment look like compared to an administrative stocktake of duties; or a management consultation designed to develop strategies for streamlining a diocese for mission? Or rather, how might the various approaches complement each other? And what inhibitors are operating at the systemic level; those unnoticed but powerful drivers of 'corporate life'? This discussion does not pretend to be able to offer a full answer to these questions but hopefully it can begin to prise open some of the issues. This ought to provide a clearer understanding of why a critical re-forming of episcopacy is so difficult and yet so necessary.

The following discussion comprises three parts. Part One briefly examines recent Australian reflection on episcopacy. Part Two examines the significance of management as a reforming instrument of the episcopate and in doing so identifies some systemic problems that thwart reform. Part Three briefly examines what a grounded and emergent episcopate might look like.

Part one: Antipodean episcopacy—a brief overview

The 1994 publication of a series of essays to mark the twenty-fifth anniversary of the consecration as bishop of the then Primate, Archbishop Keith Rayner, marked an important point in Australian theological reflection on the subject of episcopacy.[11] *Episcopacy: Views from the Antipodes*, contained twenty-four essays covering significant territory on the history, practice and theology of episcopacy and in doing so paid tribute to the fruits of reflection beyond these shores. What is interesting in terms of the present paper is the relative paucity

11. *Episcopacy*, edited by Cadwallader.

of discussion of the fundamental relation between episcopacy and ecclesiology. The ecumenical context for episcopacy appeared the most promising place for more developed ecclesial reflection on the subject.[12] Some brief reflections on the unity of the church were offered in relation to the 1990 Church of England report on *Episcopal Ministry*, wherein episcopal ministry was related to the doctrine of the Trinity.[13] James McPherson's chapter on the theory and practice of episcopacy in Australian Anglicanism critiqued the 'congregat-ionalism' implicit in the diocesanism 'dating back at least' from the 1872 Constitution whereby General Synod determinations were made 'subject to diocesan acceptance'.[14] McPherson proposed re-forming the episcopate along the lines of an episcopal college which would strengthen bonds between bishops and increase potential for prophetic engagement in the nation.[15] These recommendations arose out of a theology of episcopacy with minimal attention to matters ecclesiological. Generally the focus of the essays was historical and pastoral /theological but distinctly lacking in self-conscious engagement with ecclesiology as such. This makes practical solutions to problems of a structural nature appear piecemeal; larger systemic difficulties remain hidden and opportunities are lost for the development of new conceptual frames for the theology and practice of episcopacy.

In 1992 Allen Brent had developed a creative approach to episcopacy in the church, *Cultural Episcopacy and Ecumenism*.[16] Brent identified the enduring and debilitating impact of the development of a territorial/jurisdictional episcopacy and the eclipse of the earlier more organic Ignatian model. Originally bishops exercised *episcope* in respect to peoples and cultures rather than geographically defined areas. Brent's argument for a return to a 'cultural episcopacy' more in keeping with the Ignatian period was given added force through his deployment of Durkheim's categories of organic and mechanical

12. *Ibid*, 291–9.
13. *Ibid*, 36–8.
14. *Ibid*, 85f.
15. *Ibid*, 86.
16. Allen Brent, *Cultural Episcopacy and Ecumenism: Representative Ministry in Church History from the Age of Ignatius of Antioch to the Reformation with special reference to Contemporary Ecumenism* (Leiden: E.J Brill, 1992).

solidarity.[17] The latter form describes the functioning of societies in which social cohesion occurs through uniformities at all levels of society through law-like apparatus. It was a feature of the post Cyprianic jurisdictional episcopacy and eclipsed a more original organic episcopacy of Ignatius and Tertullian in which diversity and difference was given social cohesion through symbols such as a representative and sacral figure, for example a bishop. Brent's approach was fresh and showed the value of drawing upon the insights of other disciplines to gain a critical and constructive re-imagining of the practice of episcopacy. His approach is both historical/theological and sociological but does not develop in any depth a distinctly ecclesiological approach to the subject.

In Australia reflection on the nature of episcopacy has been driven by an emphasis on historical and biographical approaches[18]—after all we do have a responsibility to uncover and tell our story. And when it has been more self-consciously theological it has been done from a historical point of view—can there be any other![19] Certainly good ecclesiology ought not to be undertaken in a vacuum. What might a theological/ecclesial approach to episcopacy look like? A brief excursus in this area by Jeff Driver and myself in 1997 attempted to map out an approach to episcopacy within the framework of a Trinitarian ecclesiology.[20] The practical outcome of this argument was the proposal that the Anglican Church needed to embed the episcopate

---

17. *Ibid*, 185–95.
18. Cadwallader in *Episcopacy*, 4, notes that the major source of reflection on episcopacy in Australia is indirect through history and biography which in turn reflects a well established English model. He also notes the relative sparsity of *theological* reflection on episcopacy, not only in Australia but also more generally. Ecclesiological reflection is even more problematic as a mode of inquiry.
19. For an interesting example of the different modes through which theology can in fact be done see Stephen Sykes, 'Theology through History', in *The Modern Theologians*, edited by David Ford (Oxford: Blackwells, 1989), 229–51; and Daniel Hardy, 'Theology through Philosophy', in *The Modern Theologians*, 252–85. The Anglican tradition in recent centuries has been dominated by the former mode.
20. Jeff Driver and Stephen Pickard, 'Re-Placing Bishops: An Ecumenical and Trinitarian Approach to Episcopacy', *St Mark's Review*, Autumn (1997): 23–8.

closer to the 'ground' through diocesan downsizing.[21] In this way it would be possible to 're-place' bishops in the strict sense of the word, that is, put them back in their rightful place closer to the pastoral and eucharistic communities that had originally been the case. Of course such a move has significant implications across a range of areas and eventually leads to a reconfiguring of networks of authority and power in the church. The proposal has some resonances with Brent's recovery of the ancient Ignatian paradigm. Yet without a strong ecclesiological frame of reference discussion of episcopacy and proposals for change will inevitably reinvent a version of the jurisdictional/administrative model of episcopacy.[22]

If church and ministry are related reciprocally it should be important to explore this relation and its implications further for the practice of episcopacy. A strong theological foundation can give great confidence to engage in creative and faithful change in that most resistant area of structural reform. The following section explores the question of episcopal re-form from the perspective of the church's inner life and organisation: its intensive mode of being.

Part two: Episcopacy and managerial culture

Managing episcopal vows

In the 'Exhortation and Examination' for the consecration of bishops in *A Prayer Book for Australia* a bishop 'is called to maintain the church's witness . . . to protect the purity of the gospel . . . to proclaim Jesus Christ . . . guard its [Church's] faith, unity and discipline . . . promote mission . . . ensure God's word is faithfully proclaimed and sacraments administered . . . Church discipline applied justly, with mercy . . . to lead and guide priests and deacons . . . be faithful in

21. The suggestion was hardly novel though the theological underpinning and confidence this could give to the task was significant. The Anglican theologian David Ford made a similar proposal in a paper offered at the Anglican–Lutheran consultation on *episcope* in 1987. See Anglican–Lutheran Consultation, *Episcope in Relation to the Mission of the Church Today*, 1987 (Geneva: Anglican Consultative Council and The Lutheran World Federation, 1988), 151.
22. This is not totally without merit for it preserves the importance of a collegial episcopate and is a check on tendencies for isolation and loss of the interdependent nature of local churches.

choosing and ordaining of ministers . . . watch over, protect and serve the people of God . . . to teach and govern them and be hospitable . . . know and be known by them . . . and be a good example to all'. The exhortation ends: 'These are the duties of a bishop, and they are weighty. Are you willing to perform them?'[23]

Who can undertake such an Office in our present environment? Under what kinds of conditions is it possible for bishops to fulfil their promises at consecration? A bishop's daily, weekly, monthly and yearly diary tells the story of remarkable business, crowded days, few spare moments, rapid and constant travel between engagements, little space, time and peace for critical reflection (let alone writing), amidst immersion in a host of ecclesiastical and secular appointments. What is the relationship between the diary and the vow? That is the question that deserves examination. This is not only a practical issue of organising of time; it is also an issue of priorities and more particularly orientation of life. What does it mean any longer for a bishop to 'see over' the people of God? Is it possible? Do the consecration vows make any sense practically. Is it a hit and miss approach to 'solemn vows'? How do the vows made before God and the people inform the shape and dynamic of episcopal life?

Such issues are made even more urgent because the modern diocese is highly complex, requiring a high degree of management and financial care. A good case can be made that this has ever been so. Furthermore the medieval bishop had many affinities with a modern corporate CEO. Yet the highly competitive market economy of modernity, operating under assumptions of scarcity of resources and unlimited wants, is the new context in which the bishop has to exercise due care for the governance of the church. Within this environment there are significant pressures upon leaders, pressures generated from expectations in the church and wider public as well as those inner demands felt by individuals, particularly given the increasing scrutiny leaders are under in our society. Leadership is under suspicion in all quarters and this only increases the claim felt by those in authority to offer visionary leadership. This includes charisma and 'champions', for in uncertain times the charismatic leader is what is sought and expected. It also requires administrative savvy that makes for efficient and effective management of a diocese and its increasingly limited resources. Critical also is a pastoral genuineness—the common touch;

---

23. *A Prayer Book for Australia*, 802.

and quality teaching and preaching, that is, scholarly but well earthed. In many respects bishops are in no different position from a host of occupations these days that have a high public profile and concomitant accountability. A bishop:

> is at the beck and call of unreasonable expectations: constant availability and divine competence to solve all problems and right every ill of society. If he [sic] seeks to be an efficient manager, he is told that his is a 'spiritual' role; if the diocese lacks cohesion and direction he is to blame. He may well reflect that 'giving lead in the Church of England is like trying to take the cat for a walk'.[24]

Given these realities and the wider ecclesial and social context for episcopal ministry the vows made at consecration can look overwhelming. The most obvious strategy is to reinterpret the solemn promises in the direction of management: in the key areas of episcopal responsibility—teaching and defending the faith, pastoral oversight and personal holiness—the accent is on good and effective management.

Administration and management require significant time and energy and a focus on managerial theology is not to be despised.[25] Being efficient and effective in the business of the episcopate is critical *precisely* so that the ordination vows can be fulfilled with integrity, albeit never fully.[26] It is at this point that the need for good quality

---

24. Ian Cundy and Justin Welby, 'Taking the cat for a walk: Can a Bishop order a diocese?', in *Managing the Church: Order and Organization in a Secular Age*, edited by GR Evans and M Percy (Sheffield: Sheffield Academic Press, 2000), 26.
25. See the classic book on the subject, Peter F Rudge, *Ministry and Management* (London: Tavistock Publications, 1968).
26. It is a curious matter that the major review of the management of the Church of England, *Working as One Body: The Report of the Archbishop's Commission on the Organization of the Church of England*, Church House publishing, 1995, makes no causal link between the episcopal brief given at ordination through the vows and the overhaul of the church's management system. Whilst such a relation may have simply been assumed (for there was discussion of the episcopate)

management arises almost as a default move to streamline, repair, recover lost ground, and upgrade the system and structures of the local diocese and wider church. The influence of the management ethos upon church life has been immense. 'Ethos' is probably the right word for there is a world of difference between an ethos and the skilled application of quality management practices—so called best practice. The church for the most part has been enticed by the former but remains weak on the latter.

There may be nothing wrong with the incorporation of management models into the life of a busy diocese and world. The bishop as CEO of the diocese may be resisted in theory but inevitable in practice. Few would deny that in our present environment, where the church is big business[27] church leaders should avail themselves of the best management wisdom from the corporate sector. It is neither possible nor particularly Anglican to set one's face against the world. In any case the effort usually fails for church and culture are always in creative interaction, either consciously and intentionally or subliminally and without critical assessment of the process. Re-evaluation of structures, communication networks, development of strategic plans and mission statements, change management, use of management consultants—for the ostensible purpose of releasing the people of God for mission in the world—are all things to which bishops and their councils have become accustomed. Indeed, it would be irresponsible of the church and its bishops not to encourage the above; for how can the church be a generous giver of its life to the world for which Christ died, if it can't manage the resources (including its people!) of its household. The management paradigm is almost a given of our ecclesial world and bishops are the primary focus for authority and sanction of the forms of life and witness of the church. Drawing upon the best wisdom from management in the corporate sector and integrating it with the wisdom of the living tradition of the church may be precisely what Christians are called to do, both intentionally and with a focus on excellence. The Anglican theologian, David Ford, puts a most apposite question:

---

the fact that it was not expressly addressed is indicative of the orientation generated by an 'aims' and 'objectives' management culture approach.

27. See the provocative recent discussion from the United States context, M Budde and R Brimlow, *Christianity Incorporated: How Big Business is Buying the Church* (Grand Rapids, Michigan: Brazos Press, 2002).

> How can Anglicans . . . take account of the models and pressures of powerful modern forms of authority in corporate enterprises in such a way that *episkope* neither succumbs (as so often in the past and present) to patterns not adequately informed by the gospel, nor fails to learn from them where possible.[28]

Thus, one answer to the question of whether management is a good thing might be, 'yes', if it is undertaken wisely. For bishops the stakes are high, nothing less than the vows of their Office.[29]

Management as 'power of the keys'

However a danger arises when managerialism is incorporated in an uncritical way.[30] The matter is the subject of a sustained critique by a British theologian, Richard Roberts, who argues that 'the assimilation of managerialism into an organisation whose leaders have been—and remain—in a state of prolonged identity crisis endangers the "care of souls" '.[31] By reference to care of souls Roberts intends 'the fostering of that delicate ecology of spiritual opportunity that constitutes the fabric of real human community, *koinonia* itself'.[32] Roberts offers a

---

28. See *Anglican–Lutheran Consultation, 1987*, 148.
29. This underlies the statement in the report on Episcopal Ministry in the Church of England: 'The presenting practical problem in Episcopal Churches has come to be the manner in which a bishop today can, or should, hold his (sic) office in "totality". That is, as a personal, collegial and communal office, where it is clearly an impossibility for a single individual to carry out all the traditional and modern functions of a bishop.' See *Episcopal Ministry: The Report of the Archbishop's Group on the Episcopate* (London: Church House Publishing, 1990), paragraph 423.
30. This matter was the subject of a special edition of *Modern Theology*, 9/4, (1993): 'Ecclesiology and the Culture of Management'.
31. Richard Roberts, 'Ruling the Body: the care of souls in a managerial church', in *Religion, Theology and the Human Sciences* (Cambridge: Cambridge University Press, 2002), 164. A similar theme is developed by Roberts in a more recent contribution, 'Order and Organization: The Future of Institutional and Established Religion', in *Managing the Church*, edited by Evans and Percy, 78–96.
32. Roberts, 'Ruling the Body', 164.

powerful analysis of the state of English Anglicanism as he explores the dynamics and tensions between 'a long-standing crisis of identity and authority within English Anglicanism and the legitimation and actualisation of power provided by the prerogatives of managerialism and its employment as a means of ecclesial restoration'.[33] He analyses the restoration in two stages. First, the

> reinauguration of the ecclesial vision of the manager's 'right to manage' seen in the restructuring of an 'executive Church' . [Second], the introduction and implementation of the culture of performance and appraisal which may consolidate the oversight of episcope into an ecclesial Panopticon other than self-administered surveillance.[34]

Roberts argues that such managerialism amounts to a betrayal of the ecclesia and his focus is very clearly on the power elites of Anglican hierarchy, including of course its bishops. Much of the critique involves a deconstruction of two documents produced in the mid-1990s: *Working as One Body: The Report of the Archbishop's Commission on the Organization of the Church of England* and *Strategic Church Leadership*,[35] the latter co-authored by a former University Vice-Chancellor and the Anglican theologian and sociologist, Robin Gill. An important assessment of the tensions inherent in the 1990 report—between management, problems of governance and administration of the 'organisation' on the one hand, and on the other, the inherited traditions of order and 'ancient ecclesiological principles'—is contained in the book of essays *Managing the Church*,[36] an invaluable resource for Anglicans anywhere. It may be somewhat consoling for Australian Anglicans that Roberts' critique is directed to the English church though it is hard to resist the view that the dangers of the

---

33. *Ibid.*
34. *Ibid.*
35. See *Working as One Body: The Report of the Archbishop's Commission on the Organization of the Church of England*, Church House publishing, 1995; R Gill and D Burke, *Strategic Church Leadership* (London: SPCK, 1996).
36. Roberts, 'Order and Organization', in *Managing the Church*, edited by Evans and Percy.

rational management of the church have become part of the ecclesial culture of the West and highly relevant for our own life.

Roberts has drawn attention to the problem of episcopal leadership in the Anglican Church. On the one hand the exercise of episcopal ministry belongs to an ancient inherited 'right to rule' based on divine sanctions and historical consolidation enshrined, for example, in the Fundamental Declarations of the Anglican Church of Australia.[37] On the other hand there is a long running identity crisis for those in Holy Orders from which bishops cannot escape.[38] How then might the episcopate re-invent itself for a modern and post-modern world whilst holding firmly to ancient vows and responsibilities? The managerial option, which in effect transfers the 'right to rule' into the 'right to manage' is almost irresistible within the managerial culture of Western society. The danger in effectiveness and efficiency (and associated aims and objectives discourse)[39] is that it becomes another way in which real power is recovered for episcopal leadership. This is not to deny that power is irrelevant to the episcope of bishops.[40] But the danger is that it can easily occur at the expense of a more collaborative, negotiated and interdependent form of ecclesial life. This latter approach is made even more difficult for the narcissistic leader and those whose emotional intelligence for leadership is under-

---

37. *The Constitution of the Anglican Church of Australia*, chapter 1, 'Fundamental Declarations', paragraph 3: 'This Church will ever obey the commands of Christ . . . follow and uphold His discipline and preserve the three orders of bishops, priests and deacons in the sacred ministry'.
38. See my chapter, 'Orders of Praise: Ministry, Ordination and the *Missio Dei*', in *Prayer and Thanksgiving: Essays presented to the Rev'd Dr Graham Hughes on his sixty-fifth birthday*, edited by W Emilsen (Sydney: UTC Publications, 2003).
39. See Stephen Pattison, 'Some Objections to Aims and Objectives', in *Managing the Church*, edited by Evans and Percy, 128–52.
40. For a discussion see: *Bishops in Communion*, House of Bishops Occasional Paper, (London: Church House Publications, 2000), 33–7. 'The words and actions of bishops have the power to affect the lives of many people, especially devout church people, and are experienced as either affirming or undermining, building confidence or destroying it', 34.

developed.[41] Roberts notes that the 'right to manage' is related to the 'other'. The 'other' in such a framework is constituted as the 'trusting followership'.[42] Institutional and organisational efficiency becomes the overarching objective albeit for the sake of the mission of the church. What falls out of view is pursuit of 'active prophetic imagination' and 'effective pastoral care'. These latter two aims require a significant degree of 'professional autonomy' and the 'exercise of much discernment'.

The basic need to gain efficiency in organisational life may seem reasonable enough but there are systemic problems that skew the whole venture in the direction of an archaic power structure. Roberts brings to his support the historian Edward Norman who has noted that it has been a defining characteristic of the episcopal elite in the Church of England to 'absorb and transmit the dominant ideology of its peer group'.[43] This peer group is now constituted by senior executives and managers who are the leaders of the managerial revolution. Roberts' concern is that this revolution hands over 'imagination, thought, agency and control to management' in this case bishops and loss of 'spontaneity and creativity from below'.[44] In the new learning organisation simple command-obedience is inadequate; now it is more a matter of ownership of the new identity, generated from the top but in a manner (via management) that it is received and implemented from below. Management of the 'power of the keys' may singularly fail to facilitate the exercise of power among the baptised.[45] Motivation of the baptised within a post-modern environment might

41. See for example, Michael Maccoby, 'Narcissistic Leaders: The Incredible Pros, the Incredible Cons', *Harvard Business Review*, November–December (1998): 27–49, and Daniel Goleman, 'What Makes a Leader?', *Harvard Business Review*, November–December (1998): 1–25. Goleman addresses the relative paucity of studies on the affective dimensions of leadership. See his recent work, D Goleman, R Boyatzis and A Mckee, editors, *The New Leaders: Transforming the art of leadership into the science of results* (London: Little, Brown, 2002).
42. Roberts, *Religion, Theology and the Human Sciences*, 170.
43. *Ibid*, 172.
44. *Ibid*, 174ff.
45. The centrality of the problem of power in relation to the episcope and the ministry of the whole people of God has been recognised by Stephen Sykes. See 'Episcope and Power in the Church', in *Unashamed Anglicanism* (London: Darton, Longman and Todd, 1995), 178–98.

require patterns of relating quite inimical to the practices of management in a modernist framework.[46]

The travail of the episcopate: systemic distortions

A number of issues arise from the above discussion. First, it is hard not to feel sympathy for episcopal leadership in our difficult and insecure times. There have been and continue to be many areas of poor management and waste of resources. The crisis of leadership identity is profound and does impact upon those in Holy Orders. The episcopate is charged with the 'care of the churches' and oversight of the mission of the church. Proper accountability for those in leadership at all levels is needful and indeed urgent, especially in the light of such things as clergy abuse. Second, it is inevitable that the church will assimilate and imitate to some extent the managerial practices of the 'host' culture. This is not all loss yet a major concern is an uncritical appropriation of management programs, models and techniques. Problems in these areas surface in everyday activities such as intercession—a religious practice in which one's own powerlessness requires a certain habit and form of life very much at odds with the disciplines of management which are aimed at the efficient and accountable use of power.[47] Third, the discussion points to the need for ongoing education and vocational development for bishops. A central issue here would be a critical reflective approach to the practise of episcopal vows.

However, as suggested above, there are some enduring systemic issues that cannot be exorcised by reflection and careful weaving together of best management practice and gospel imperatives, though some degree of self-consciousness at this level is a minimum requirement for episcopal re-form. There are two issues of a systemic kind that have a profound impact upon the form and function of the church and its episcopate. Both issues are of an ecclesiological kind and press home to us the importance of the relation between ministry and ecclesiology in a discussion about management, leadership and the

---

46. See *Postmodernism and Organizations*, edited by J Hassard and M Parker (London: Sage, 1993), 96–9.
47. Michael Hanby, 'Interceding: Giving Grief to Management', in *The Blackwell Companion to Christian Ethics*, edited by S Hauerwas and S Wells (Malden MA: Blackwell, 2004), chapter 18 and especially 246.

episcopate. These issues concern the idea of the sacred and the ideology of the diocese.

Episcopacy and the migration of the sacred

The first concerns the purpose of the church in the context of modern /post-modern society. Contrary to many popular perceptions religion is not dead, nor in fact dying. As David Tacey has well documented, the search for 'primal spirituality' and the 'return of the religious' continues unabated.[48] It is the reason why, notes American theologian, Harvey Cox, Pentecostalism has exercised such a potent force throughout the world and, in its more domesticated forms, why the charismatic movement and its offshoots provided such an important impetus for renewal in the late twentieth century.[49] How well will mainline churches, like the Anglican Church, be able to connect people with the deep realities of human need expressed through such a 'primal spirituality'? It is a problem, for increasingly the traditional institutional embodiments for such religious searching are being jettisoned by the younger generations. Furthermore, as Philip Jenkins has recently convincingly argued, the Christianity of the twenty-first century will be significantly influenced by the religious and spiritual impulses from the southern globe.[50] Roberts contends that for the secular West the sacred has not been lost or abandoned so much as migrated.[51] In this context the church has to rediscover its significant resources as a 'form of life' through which it is possible to encounter a radical otherness beyond the 'sacralization of the self' and 'self-religion'.[52]

This discussion raises a fundamental question: management for what purpose? It can hardly do to speak glibly about the mission of God or the church or the service of love and care, without understanding the environment and the different cultures in which such a

---

48. David Tacey, *The Spirituality Revolution* (Melbourne: HarperCollins, 2003), especially chapter 8.
49. Harvey Cox, *Fire From Heaven* (London: Cassell, 1996).
50. Philip Jenkins, *The Next Christendom: The Coming of Global Christianity* (Oxford: Oxford University Press, 2002).
51. Roberts, *Religion, Theology and the Human Sciences*, 178f.
52. *Ibid*, 178.

mission occurs.[53] What do those who exercise episcope see on the horizon or in the depths? To what extent is the episcopal vision impaired by the demands of management and organisation? Management is only one instrument but in the absence of a robust and embodied theological vision for the church episcopal energy is easily diverted into strategic issues concerning managerial restructuring. So the first issue is a systemic problem: the force and inevitability of the management paradigm systematically distorts the vision. If the theological blur is overcome and the primacy of the recovery of the sacred is sensed, it can only be momentary before the organisational imperative re-asserts itself. What we end up with is an episcopal ministry which is constantly in danger of losing its prophetic edge and forgetting its fundamental brief to point to the holy in our midst.

Given the enduring search for 'primal spirituality', albeit in 'migrated' secular and quasi-religious forms, what is an appropriate 'form of life' for the episcopate to nurture through, teaching, preaching, pastoral care, and government? This requires an 'outside-in' approach to management in the church, allowing the presence of the 'other' on the outside to shape the management of the church. It is thus an ecclesiological and missiological matter: regard for the church in its extensive outward directed mode of life. To draw this to the attention of the ecclesia of God may be a prophetic episcopal responsibility.

Management and the diocese: reconsidering the relation

Related to the above issue is a second issue of a systemic kind. Here the question about the 'form of life' of the ecclesia becomes foreground. What is an appropriate form of ecclesial life that opens up and points toward the sacred and human longing? Actually it is not difficult to map out characteristics of a church given over to the nurturing of such needs in the world. One of the key words here is 'community'. The church is a *koinonia*—a communion of peoples joined in common life, worship and discipleship. Most mission statements of the church 'organisation' will embody this vision of

---

53. A criticism of the *Working for the Body* report is that it fails to give any attention to the nature of the 'mission field' (a very different thing from 'the mission of the church') and its significance for any restructured management of the church.

ecclesia somehow. We instinctively know what is required! We re-present a lost ideal and then struggle within our ecclesial structures to implement the plan.

Here we come face to face with the nature of the episcopal system as it is practised in Anglicanism. It is almost taken as read that the diocese has quasi-sacred status in the episcopal system. But in the history of Christianity the traditional diocesan structure came relatively late on the scene. The diocesan system owes its debt to Cyprian, Bishop of Carthage and became, in the course of the fourth century associated with a strong jurisdictional emphasis. In this episcope the bishop is an *alter Petrus* expressing the unity and communion of the church in space.[54] Such a bishop is a conciliar being connected to all other bishops. This offers the church a cogent symbol of the bond of unity between the local church and all other local churches. The Cyprianic office can easily become an 'external administrative office'. This jurisdictional model is particularly associated with Roman Catholicism but is also a feature of Anglicanism, the main difference being that in the latter conciliarity is not trumped by a jurisdictional primacy. In the Irenaean form of episcope the bishop is the authoritative teacher—the *alter apostolos* and as such serves as a living link with the apostles through a historical continuing in time. This is a continuity not merely of structure (Cyprianic) but apostolic faith. Anglicanism is indebted to both Irenaean and Cyprianic forms of episcope and in this way preserves both a synchronic (across territories) and diachronic (through time) unity in faith and life.[55] However, it is clear that in these forms of episcopal structuring the local church was the diocese. This was the logic of a theology of episcopacy focused on the unity of the ecclesia with its bishop.

Yet the price of this kind of episcopal unity has been high. The theory of the bishop in the local church has been maintained by redefining what 'local' means. The result is that the diocese becomes a complex network of 'local community' churches (parishes) organised on a territorial basis to secure 'coverage'. This does ensure at least two things: the bishop becomes an administrative figure who has jurisdictional as well as pastoral oversight of the whole; and the consequent loss of a sense of an embedded episcope at the micro level

54. Erikson, *Episkope and Episcopacy*, 82.

55. For a succinct and insightful discussion of the Cyprianic, Irenaean and Ignatian models of episcope see Erikson, *ibid*, 80–92.

of church life. The Anglican system deals with this through a theory of shared episcope, through delegation of a bishop's oversight responsibilities to priests who thus perform a representative role on behalf of the bishop. This conceals a systemic structural problem manifest in the management paradigm for episcopal ministry. In such a context any counteractive and critical movement to re-form episcopal management is undermined at the root by a systemic structural defect supported by a theory of delegation and representation which appears unassailable. An uncritical acceptance of a diocesan ecclesiology usurps the best theological intentions for re-forming the episcopate. *The diocesan system ensures the assimilation of the management revolution in the church.* Within this framework there are severely limited possibilities for an episcopate to model and exemplify that form of life appropriate for a community given over to the nurture of the sacred in the midst of the world. Of course 'others' (including the laity!) might be able to do this in a representative manner, in lieu of the bishop.[56] But what about the reform of the episcopate? The question is inescapable: is the episcopate trapped in a 'steel-hard casing' of an inflexible ecclesiology.[57]

The power of the prevailing Cyprianic ecclesiology in Anglicanism ought not to be underestimated. *The irony is that managerialism is a creative attempt to overcome the worst features of this ecclesial form*! But the problem is systemic and structural and therefore the jurisdictional/administrative model of episcopacy is transferred into the new managerialism. In this context the capacity of bishops to fulfil their episcopal vows is seriously weakened and/or compromised. We may be guilty of espousing a doctrine of the episcopate that does not and cannot exist. The reason being that such an episcopate belongs to a different church structure from the prevailing model.

---

56. Anglican polity contains a number of tensions including the issue of the relation between those in orders and the laity. The gifts and ministries of the latter do not simply devolve from the bishop nor do they erupt spontaneously from below but represent a dynamic ordering within the body of Christ with significant untapped potential. The unreconciled relation between orders and laity is manifest in a diocesan polity which is driven more by delegation than from emergent authorised ministries. Clearly this is an area that requires attention in Anglicanism.
57. Roberts, *Religion, Theology and the Human Sciences*, 179, quoting Max Weber.

What kind of ecclesiology could generate an episcopal office that made sense of the Anglican ordinal and vows? The Orthodox Church has long focussed on the Ignatian model of episcopacy. Here the bishop is the president of the local eucharistic assembly gathering the diverse gifts of the local community into a unity. Such a bishop is the *alter Christus*, a living icon who constitutes 'the focus and visible centre of unity within the local church'; who expresses 'the fullness, unity and multiplicity of the eschatological community in each place'.[58] This theology of the episcopate belongs to a eucharistic ecclesiology. Of course this episcopo-centrism can become an episcopo-monism. But it does put the bishop in the midst of the people. And this is appealing, though, as the Orthodox theologian and bishop, John Zizioulas has noted, the ancient Ignatian model has suffered the fate of diocesanisation. The bishop remained the bishop of the 'local' church (renamed diocese) but ceased to be the head of the eucharistic community. From Zizioulas' point of view, the diocesan system (as an aggregate of many local eucharistic communities) represents a corruption from an episcopal model developed in relation to a eucharistic ecclesiology centred around the bishop in the local church.[59] However, replicating the Ignatian structure in the context of a global village rather than the ancient *polis* may simply be a romantic ideal and only succeed in generating something very different from what Zizioulas has in mind.[60] Nonetheless, in terms of the present argument it may be important to explore how an Ignatian ecclesiology might be creatively deployed in the service of a modified diocesanism. Certainly the notion of re-placing bishops through diocesan downsizing has similarities and fundamental sympathies with the Orthodox approach and might say something to Anglicans about their long-standing affinities with Orthodoxy.

---

58. Erikson, *Episkope and Episcopacy*, 81.
59. For a discussion of Zizioulas' position see John Erickson, 'Episkope and Episcopacy: Orthodox Perspectives', in *Episkope and Episcopacy and the Quest for Visible Unity*, edited by P Bouteneff and A Falconer (Geneva: WCC Publications, 1999, Faith and Order paper number 183), 80-92.
60. *Ibid*, 85.

Part three: A 'grounded episcopate' for the 'emerging church'

From territoriality to places-in-relation

This chapter has argued that recovery and re-engagement with ecclesiology is critical for re-forming episcopacy in Anglicanism. The managerial paradigm pervades the practice of modern episcopacy. Its appeal is precisely as a foil to the loss of episcopal form and function in the contemporary church. Efforts to re-form through such a strategy necessarily fail due to an unexamined ecclesiology in which the modern Anglican bishop is systemically skewed towards an admin istrative/jurisdictional manager. A re-formed episcopate is correlative to a re-formed ecclesial structure. An important conclusion to this inquiry is that the integrity of the episcopal vows requires a differently structured church in which they may be fulfilled.

The proposal to reduce the size of dioceses is hardly new nor unproblematic, as the Church of England report, *Episcopal Ministry* made clear in 1990.[61] Though on that occasion it appeared as a practical measure to deal with the multiplication of suffragan bishops, a development at odds with the traditional theology of one bishop in one place.[62] Tensions *within* the theology of episcopacy—relationship between diocesan bishop and suffragan bishop—were only indirectly related to difficulties in the supporting ecclesiology.

Diocesan downsizing, which retained strong conciliar networks between dioceses, would represent a move towards a more grounded episcopate with affinities to the ancient Ignatian eucharistic ecclesiology whilst retaining the strengths of a wider episcopal collegiality. The result would be a modified territorial episcopacy in which the ideal of coverage of territory was more dynamically related to the

---

61. *Episcopal Ministry*, paragraphs 428–34. It noted that 'such a development would represent a return to what is judged to be the primitive model', yet the 'theological purity' would be purchased at the expense of a number of practical disadvantages: fear of greater administrative load, disjunction with prevailing economic and social orderings of society, impact on mission. These so-called disadvantages may not hold up to scrutiny. The Report appeared equivocal on the matter though it did finally state that 'our Group would like to see serious consideration of the possibility of reduction in size of some dioceses by the creation of more dioceses', paragraph 432.
62. *Ibid*, paragraphs 423–69.

kinds of groupings and cultures envisaged in, for example, Brent's 'cultural episcopacy'. The idea of a diocese would be formed in relation to an understanding of 'place' rather than the Western preoccupation with 'space' and its associated concerns with 'occupation' and 'territory'.[63] Does this mean the traditional notion of territoriality must disappear? Not exactly. Geography remains relevant, coverage remains critical. But how is it to be conceived? The 'normal system' is 'the bishop with restraint', that is, 'a territorial diocese ruled by a bishop, and divided into territorial parishes each in charge of an incumbent'.[64] The great advantage is coverage. But 'although the territorial principle is valuable, it is not part of the theological structure of the church *in the form we know it*' (my italics).[65] Whilst in theory each diocese constitutes a local church with its chief pastor, priest and teacher (the bishop) the tendency is to see the diocese as 'little more than a territorial subdivision of a larger unit'.

A different approach would first emphasise the universal church, 'the whole fellowship of which Christ is head and king, and in which he has set the apostolic ministry, and then to ask ourselves what a local church is and should be'.[66] This prompts questions about the 'desirable size of a particular church' and whether every 'true local church' should have a bishop. Considered from a theological point of view there may be a number of possible answers. Territoriality does not have an absolute claim for the organisation of the church. 'One might imagine as a future development a Christian community of some five hundred members, committed Christians in an entirely secularised community, with a bishop as their chief pastor and a presbytery of perhaps a dozen priests functioning with the bishop as a corporate body, and perhaps the bishop as the only full-time minister,

---

63. For an illuminating discussion see the work of the Australian theologian Geoffrey Lilburne, *A Sense of Place: A Christian Theology of the Land* (Nashville: Abingdon, 1989), especially chapter 4, 'The Poetics of Space: Place and Space in the Western Tradition'. See also John Inge, *A Christian Theology of Place* (Aldershot: Ashgate, 2003).
64. I am indebted to a late friend and mentor, RP McDermott, for this discussion of territoriality. It was ahead of its time in the late 1960s. See his, 'An Anglican's Reflections on Priesthood', in *The Christian Priesthood*, edited by N Lash and J Rhymer (London: Darton, Longman and Todd, 1970), 141–61 and this quotation, 158.
65. *Ibid*, 159.
66. *Ibid*.

and all the rest earning their living in some ordinary occupation'.[67] These words, penned over three decades ago, certainly envisaged a more flexible approach to the organisation of the church. It has resonances with a much earlier 'minister model' with a strong orientation on mission and resourcing the people of God.

More recent developments point to a future 'mission shaped church' which will have to be responsive to new forms of community. The church might have a more 'liquid' feel with greater flexibility in its structuring and linkages within and across communities of faith. Minimally the idea of territoriality will have to be rethought in more dynamic terms. This might require a new sense of place for the church in which geography, human interactions and mobility, and patterns of communication combine in diverse ways to redefine what 'local' in relation to universal church actually looks like. It may also help to recover a dynamic of movement between a hub or focus outwards and more dispersed communities of faith as well as the complex of networks between different communities that are only indirectly linked to the centre.

The correlate of an emerging church is an emerging episcopate able to faithfully fulfil its vows. It is difficult to conceive how this can occur without a more intentionally grounded episcopate that functions at less of a distance from the church for which it provides an appropriate guardianship and oversight. The natural and/or optimal 'episcopal reach' may have to be thought. The 'order that orders' requires a more than purely formal relationship with the ministries of the baptised. Rather, the episcopal order has to be dynamically related to the 'ordered ministries'. The theory of delegation of authority and ministry is fine *in theory*. But delegation ought not to be a means by which dysfunctional relations between the ministries are maintained. In other words, episcopal oversight has to be real and concrete, that is, grounded, not presumed nor simply imagined. In the future we might be able to talk about a 'natural episcopacy' related to a variety of factors and criteria, but undergirded by a priority on facilitation of face-to-face relations, high quality interpersonal life, and the embedding of episcope in the local church with an orientation and

67. *Ibid.*

impulse that expands the interconnections between different locales. To effect this the episcopate may need to be re-placed.[68]

In the complexities of a post-modern environment—in which the search for 'primal spirituality' continues unabated and the particular (bordering on tribalism) has priority over the universal—the life of the church and its mission has to be reconstructed from 'below'. An ecclesiology from the ground up is not one that begins entirely new and without the impress of the past. Rather, out of that very inheritance such a church begins to think again about its place and how the ancient ministries of word, sacrament and care might be reconstituted. This points to an ecclesiology of wholeness and its structural form looks very different from the modern Anglican diocese. In some respects no one knows exactly what may emerge—in this we are joined with Ignatius, Tertullian, Irenaeus, Clement and the early church in a gnostic world. But it is critical for the well-being and wholeness of the community of faith that there is an episcope that is generous in its presence. In this way the dynamics of the episcopate can follow the generosity of the triune God's holy and faithful presence in Jesus and the Spirit.

An old chestnut: parity of orders

This involves a rethinking of the relations between the traditional orders and their diaconal foundations. This is particularly urgent for the relationship between priest and bishop. The fact is that the office of a bishop is highly mobile and fluid with respect to territory covered, communities encountered, public spaces addressed. The 'apostolic' nature of episcopal life is a feature of the diocesan structure. Increasingly the bishop functions more like a 'visitor'.[69] This 'peripatetic' ministry of visitation, of encouraging existing communities, networking and reconnecting communities, assisting in the founding of new ones has a decidedly ancient and Celtic lineage. The idea of a 'missionary bishop' enriches the exercise of episcope and suggests that the more 'settled' episcope of the priest of a local church does have an inescapable episcopal dimension.

68. See above footnote 21.

69. Duncan Reid proposes a 'visitor' model for episcopacy as more culturally relevant in an Australian context which is suspicious of notions of 'oversight' and associated tones of authority. See *Episcopacy*, edited by Cadwallader, 302f.

The traditional argument for delegation of such an episcope requires a more honest reappraisal. It is not simply a question of parity of orders or stratification. There is a dynamic relation between the two orders, as clearly evidenced from the long history of the tradition that stretches back to the early Medieval church. Smaller dioceses make for a more embedded episcopate within the life of the many eucharistic communities. Yet a more open relation between priest and bishop, where the accent is on the exercise of mutual episcope—as a balance to delegation *of* and sharing *in* the bishop's episcope—can enrich and model a form of episcope for the whole people of God. It also addresses the overtones of romanticism underlying a desire to return to the ancient Ignatian model, wherein the bishop presided over the local eucharistic community. In a modified territorial model (as discussed above), the bishop is both apostolic visitor and overseer but this episcope is dynamically related to the episcope of the priest /presbyter of the micro eucharistic community. This form of relation and differentiation of functions makes for that generosity of presence so vital for the life of the church.[70] It is not difficult to see how such an approach would orientate traditional orders to a genuinely collaborative ministry and represent organisationally a 'top down' influence with positive effect for the ministries of the whole church.

The great advantage of Anglicanism is that it already has a strong doctrine of the church catholic and interconnectedness between the many local churches. An ecclesiology from below is one which reconceives territoriality in such a way that the particular and the universal continue to be held in dynamic interplay, but only as the ecclesia is nurtured from the micro local. *The church may be the one form of human community that can meet the post-modern on its own terms*

---

70. It also lends strength to the ancient tradition of the parity of orders in which the critical differentiation was one of jurisdiction and associated authority to ordain. With the emphasis clearly on the shared episcope of the whole church the 'parity' argument cannot be so easily dismissed. Compare *The Porvoo Common Statement*: 'The bishop gathers together those who are ordained to share the tasks of ministry and to represent the concerns of the community'. *The Porvoo Common Statement: Conversations Between The British and Irish Anglican Churches and the Nordic and Baltic Lutheran Churches* (London: Council for Christian Unity of the General Synod of the Church of England, 1993), paragraph 44.

without being seduced by the lure of the tribe. Clearly in such a conception the communion of the churches appears fragile and embryonic, a work in progress from a new location. This increases the responsibility of the bishop as the symbol and sign of the church's unity through time and space. But the sign is a fragile one and points the episcopate and the church to the priority of trusts given and received, lived out of and lived into. Trust is at the heart of the baptismal calling and the one thing needful in our fragmented times.[71]

Catholicity from below

Such structural changes not only modify traditional approaches to space and territory, and relations between the orders, they also imply a reappraisal of the church's catholicity. Concomitant to diocesan downsizing is a reconfiguring of catholicity from below. Rather than claim the 'guarantee' and security of catholicity through the episcopal sign, the church can rediscover what the catholicity of the church, symbolised through the episcopate, actually means for the local church. It not only means the unity Anglicanism has with the church universal. It also involves recognition and experience of the wholeness of the church in any particular place and the need for this to be expressed in the wholeness of an ordered ministry. Yet the episcopal sign is a fractured sign and has been so for centuries. Catholicity has been partial at best; it too is fractured. Downsizing offers an opportunity for recovery of the wholeness of the episcopal sign of catholicity.

It is not clear what the shape might be of a reconfigured catholicity. But it will certainly be an enriched catholicity because smaller diocesan communities provide the basis for much closer working relationship with other churches in a local community, whether we like it, tolerate it or despise it. This interdependence is never an end in itself but for serving the *missio dei.* This entails the search for wisdom to discern the presence of the sacred and embody the gospel in faith and life. This is precisely the way in which the gains of recent decades in ecumenism might be furthered. For it is in the overlaps and intersections of different ministries of the churches that it is possible to recover a deeper sense of shared episcope for the church of Jesus Christ.

---

71. See Anthony Giddens' discussion of trust in the modern world, *The Consequences of Modernity* (Cambridge: Polity Press, 1990), chapter 3.

Overcoming distance between the churches through a re-formed catholicity (at the local level) might be the next stage for Anglican ecumenism and strengthen the episcopal sign in the midst of the churches. It may be part of the Anglican brief to re-build the episcopal sign of catholicity from and through the local church. In this way episcopacy may be able to make its own particular contribution to the nurture of a missionary ecclesiology combining strong roots in local communities and a global vision of the coming kingdom. In such a new context faithfulness to the Anglican episcopal tradition in the gospel remains at best partial until it is shared among men and women. There are no simple solutions to a fractured catholicity but this is one thing that Australian Anglicans ought to be able to do that would make for the healing of the wounds of the church. Though even such an episcopal ointment may have an initial sting.

Deeper into baptism: the mark of the episcopate

It would be an understatement to suggest that re-form of the church was difficult. Changing outlooks and changing structures has to be achieved against the backdrop of powerful 'attractors'—those enduring stories of an organisation that shape its present constitution and function negatively to thwart change.[72] Most organisations are in the grip of attractors that skew the organisation in certain predetermined directions, functions and forms. Attractors function as systemic sources of chaos in an organisation. As such, attractors orientate an organisation back into repetitive patterns of behaviour and practices that block permissions, and prevent healthy changes that arise through the embrace of creative developments. Personnel may come and go, reviews and reorganisation may occur but creative change may prove elusive. 'Feedback loops' become fixed and unresponsive to new situations and 'iterations continue to flow throughout the system to support a set of fixed responses'.[73]

The secret powers of an organisation lie in the way attractors exert influence within the organisation, more often at subliminal levels. This chapter has drawn attention to the operation of some 'attractors'. They

72. See F David Peat, *From Certainty to Uncertainty: The Story of Science and Ideas in the Twentieth Century* (Washington DC: Joseph Henry Press, 2002), 146–9.

73. *Ibid*, 148.

subsist in stories about episcopal identity formed through mechanical means (unbroken succession in the episcopate); stories that fund a self-constituting autonomy poorly related to the wider episcope of the church (excessive hierarchy and unjustified hubris in the ecumenical sphere); stories about previous experiences of ruptured identity and recovery based on exclusion (whether through an Act of Uniformity from 1662 or over contemporary issues of gender). The problem with such attractors is that they thwart initiatives for change; all change becomes 'attracted' to the underlying organisation history which serves to nullify change. Attractors contribute to significant organisation dysfunction which may lead people to feel that the organisation 'isn't going anywhere'. Because attractors operate at subliminal levels the chaotic system can never move into new forms of order and harmony. In such environments 'agents can appear as passive recipients caught in the endless stream of their heritage'.[74] The power of such attractors becomes evident in times of change and transition when there are emerging powers based on newly forming stories—shared episcope, collaborative ministry, cooperative ventures.

The above proposals require a significant change in attitudes towards the exercise of power. It is simplistic to claim that bishops have too much power or that other more 'invisible' people or groups exert power or even that structural imbalances in power need attention. These claims may be conceded immediately; the circuits of power can be uncovered. Beyond this there is the power of the stories that we are unable to forget, of pasts that determine present dispositions. How is the power of such stories broken or exorcised? Re-forming episcopacy will involve a revisitation, a remembering of the identity-shaping pasts that hold us. Episcopal memory carries a host of stories that may need to be re-membered, put back together in another way; in short, allowed to die so that they might be reconstituted.[75] What emerges will depend entirely upon where the

74. RC Holb, *Jurgen Habermas: Critique in the Public Sphere* (New York Routledge, 1991), 66.

75. Duncan Reid concludes his examination of bishops as an ecumenical problem thus: 'Churches may be called to give up, in an act of Christlike self-emptying, something precious that has been received'. Importantly Reid notes: 'It is not necessarily the most obvious—in this case the historic episcopate . . . It may be the administrative authority we tend to invest in bishops, which frequently stands in the way of their exploring the diaconal elements of their own Christian episcope. It is certainly the

gaze is set, its orientation and the company kept. The argument of this chapter is that re-membering has to generate a 'grounded episcopate' more closely woven into the pastoral and missionary dimensions of the ministries of the local church. This requires a giving up as well as a taking on of new challenges. But this kind of remembering involves *metanoia* and renewal. It is the baptismal gift. The possibility of fulfilling episcopal vows is rooted in Christian baptism, of giving up, being reconstituted and re-formed in Christ through the Spirit. Luther's statement is as relevant to the episcopate as any Christian; 'we all crawl towards our baptism'. It is as relevant to the community of faith as it is to its office bearers. The reason is clear. It is only as the ecclesia as a whole reappropriates the baptismal gift through the development of new forms of polity that a re-formed episcopate can make its vows in trust to God.

---

tunnel-vision that has prevented us in the past from seeing genuine episcope manifested in non-episcopal churches', in *Episcopacy*, edited by Cadwallader, 305.

7

Hand Dances And Waltzes: Reclaiming Common Worship For The Twenty-First Century

Jane Foulcher

Once upon a time . . .

Once it was simple (or so it seemed). We were a church defined by our praxis, and at the core of our practice was worship, and ordering that worship was a book: the Book of Common Prayer. Our worship was central to our sense of being church, and we had a wonderful primer that kept us on track.

As Anglicans we have regularly reminded ourselves, because we are forgetful, that we are not a confessional church. We refrain from defining ourselves in relation to a particular expression of Christian doctrine. This was a hard won position in a period of history where in the West most churches were narrowing their beliefs and practices.[1] Neither do we insist on a particular, requisite experience of the faith, such as 'baptism in the Spirit' or 'being born again'.[2] Instead we marvel at the range of expressions of the work of the Spirit. Neither do we define ourselves by defining others out—and this was an important step in the wake of the question that dogged much of the Reformation period: 'what is the true church?' It remains an important principle. Instead our origins were pragmatic (the desire of Henry VIII for a male heir) and led directly to the core question which we have continued to ask ourselves, which, as Paul Marshall suggests, is 'We

1. WP Haugaard, 'From the Reformation to the Eighteenth Century', in *The Study of Anglicanism*, edited by S Sykes and J Booty (London: SPCK, 1988), 14.
2. P Marshall, 'Anglican Spirituality', in *Protestant Spiritual Traditions*, edited by F Senn (New York: Paulist Press, 1986), 125.

are responsible to be the church, so how should we act?'[3] A certain pragmatism remains central to our being.

Historically, after Henry VIII, the 'how should we act' question unravelled alarmingly as the English church lurched from one extreme to another in a shocking web of politics and dogma. Peace, when it finally came in the form of the Elizabethan Settlement, enabled us to be the church by focussing on common worship rather than on dogmatic differences. What Elizabeth claimed on our behalf was a level of freedom to continue in the apostolic tradition to simply be the church. Underpinning that way of being was a shared way of worship mediated by the Book of Common Prayer.

It is important, of course, not to read the past nostalgically. There is no golden past time when the Anglican Church didn't feel the strain of holding together diverse views. Because we have constructed our identity through shared praxis it is in the area of worship we often see our differences played out. This has ever been so. Anthony Trollope's fictional *Barchester Towers*, with its conflict between High and Low Church parties, still resonates. It is in the context of worship, from the cathedral pulpit, that the newly arrived Low Churchman, Mr Slope, launches his attack on the 'high and dry' practices of the clergy of the diocese, their conduct of worship, the use of chant and the 'undue preponderance' of music. For Slope and his party there was no place for 'feeling' or 'mystery' in worship. Rather 'inward conviction was everything' while 'each word of the minister's lips should fall intelligibly into the listener's heart'. In *Barchester Towers* the words of the script are not being contested—both parties are committed to the Book of Common Prayer. The conflict is focussed on how that script is enacted.[4] The practice of worship signals the underlying ecclesiology. Having said this it remains true that the Book of Common Prayer set parameters that helped us in a practical way to get on with being the church.

---

3. Marshall, 126.
4. 'The words of our morning service, how beautiful, how apposite, how intelligible they were, when read with simple and distinct decorum! but how much of the meaning of the words was lost when they were produced with all the meretricious charms of melody!' So says Mr Slope in the very presence of the makers of melody seated in the cathedral. A Trollope, *Barchester Towers* (London: Penguin, (1857), 1987), 45.

The future is here

The Book of Common Prayer was birthed in a particular national context, in a pre-industrial world, but was successfully spread around the globe on the back of British colonialism. This world is no more. The context in which we now find ourselves is almost unrecognisable.

By the beginning of the twenty-first century the cultural influence of the Anglican Church has receded rapidly, and not just in Australia. Once, the King James Bible and the Book of Common Prayer underpinned English, particularly literary, culture. We know that this is no longer true and saw this revealed with utter clarity in the media reports prior to the wedding of Prince Charles and Camilla Parker Bowles. The inclusion of the General Confession, clothed in its 1662 form, as part of the service of blessing for the marriage was regarded as newsworthy and somehow interpreted by the media as a particular inclusion for the formerly adulterous couple. A whole generation of reporters is entirely ignorant of the practice of regular, corporate confession in the Anglican tradition. We have *all* 'strayed like lost sheep': Charles and Camilla are not alone in this. In fact prayers of penitence are a standard element of the Order for Prayer and Dedication of a Civil Marriage in Common Worship, the Church of England's latest supplement to the Book of Common Prayer. But none of this is now common knowledge. This revealing moment brings home vividly what we have known for some time: we live in a post-Christian culture. We have lost the 'common' from the Book of Common Prayer.

The world which we now inhabit has been mapped extensively in the course of this collection of essays. We live in a post-modern age amidst the remnants of modernity, and in a post-colonial era amidst the remnants of colonialism. In the unravelling of the British Empire we have witnessed the emergence of Indigenous churches—independence often being marked by the adoption of a new prayer book (the publication of *An Australian Prayer Book* in 1978 was a significant coming of age for the Anglican Church of Australia). Add to this the liturgical reform movement and ecumenical convergence over the last quarter of the twentieth century, and the common worship that once held us together seems barely recognisable. The world has become a veritable spiritual supermarket, carried along by a tide of individualism. We now have little, if any, positional authority: integrity issues, especially over sexual abuse, have undermined our capacity to be heard on moral matters. The growing power of fundamentalist views within Christianity completes the complex situation in which we are called to be the church. No wonder that we often feel lost!

These are not merely theoretical matters. This context, not unique to Australian Anglicans of course, is the one in which we have to make sense of what we are doing. In the context in which I've worked for the last seven years, 'the people of God' need to know what it means to be the Anglican Church in Coffs Harbour. In this rapidly expanding coastal region of New South Wales there are, at last count, twenty-five different denominational churches, most of a pentecostal or evangelical flavour. What does it mean to be Anglican here?

'We'll all be doomed'

There is an alarming amount of panic abroad in our church, much of which is counterproductive. It is possible to be serious about our call to be church in the contemporary world without lurching from one fix-all solution to the next. A core task is the careful distillation of our heritage, enabling us to discern what we need to take with us to create the future Anglican Church. This is particularly crucial in our consideration of the relationship of church and worship.

If once it was simple—we were essentially a church defined by our worship—our current, protracted identity crisis has much to do with our confusion about worship. Take this statement produced in a recent diocesan strategic review process:

> Worship is now less likely to be regarded as a strategy for mission, in which we work hard to attract people from outside our church community to attend our contemporary worship, but more likely to be regarded as a spiritual undergirding for our mission, in which we are motivated and enabled to participate actively in God's mission in the world. Of course, worship remains as the recognised manner in which we offer ourselves to God in love and praise.

From worship as 'strategy for mission' to worship as 'undergirding for our mission'. Whilst the intention of this statement might have been to relieve us of the phenomenon of the perpetual 'altar call' that is the hall mark of much ill conceived 'contemporary' services of worship, there is a more dangerous edge to this comment. You can almost sense the relief in this shift from 'mission' to 'spiritual undergirding': we worked hard (didn't we) to make our worship attractive and contemporary, but it didn't really work (bring in the young people, boost our numbers). Now we can give up that fruitless project and concentrate on equipping ourselves. No more battling over 'modern' music, no need to compete with the warehouse performances of the Pentecostals down the road, no need to worry about the language of our liturgy. We are on a mission, and it is out there 'in the world', so let's close the doors and have a good feed before we set out.

There is potentially a terrible loss here that has to do with our origins, the Book of Common Prayer and the heritage of Anglican ecclesiology.

Worship without walls

One of the key planks of the reform of the English church in the sixteenth century was its reclamation of the church *for the people*. Worship was to be in the common tongue. It was public worship. Nothing was to be done secretively, 'behind closed doors'. Worship was seen as fundamentally communal, not the preserve of an elite, clerical caste. All this is reflected in the provisions of the Book of Common Prayer.

Similarly Anglicanism has never been sectarian. As Bruce Kaye argues in *A Church without Walls*:

> Anglicanism is essentially a 'church in society' tradition. This quality could also be called 'incarnational' because it is the ecclesial expression of the Anglican emphasis on the presence of God in the world and in human society as the background for the claim that Jesus came as the Son of God in the fullness of time . . .

Kaye continues:

> We have often been tempted to give up this 'church in society' tradition for a sectarian citadel. But to yield to such a temptation would be to separate ourselves from the profound strength in our Anglican tradition of our

> emphasis on the Incarnation as God's presence in the world.[5]

It is, indeed, 'a church without walls'. The temptation we face now to withdraw arises because we perceive that *society* has withdrawn from the equation: how can we be church in society, when our society doesn't appear to care if we exist or not? This is a crucial issue in situating ourselves in a post-Christian world. It is possible, of course, to respond to this challenge by reminding ourselves if God is present in the world, then *we are* the church in society whether or not we are publicly acknowledged. But the issue won't easily disappear. You can only whistle in the dark for so long.

Still, I'm doubtful whether our worship ought to be 'behind closed doors', conceived as a weekly filling station to equip us for mission 'out there'. I don't want to give up our historically well-trod path of being a church in society, whatever that might mean, into our future. Nor do I want to give up on the notion of common, communal prayer. Maybe a church *without walls* can only truly *worship without walls*.

Church as rehearsal space

In his recent book on Christian spirituality, *Facets of Faith*, Paul Jones helpfully places Christian worship in its ecclesial (and soteriological) frame. Christianity tells a story, he says, and this story is told in the context of the church, in all its glorious, inadequate forms. It is in the rehearsal of that story that we are formed and re-formed along the way. We are, Jones vividly suggests, players in a drama (life) in which our role is 'to discover the identity of the playwright'. In this drama 'worship is the Play within the play', 'the microcosm within the macrocosm, the distillation of the whole'. In case you are imagining that such an activity must be of a different order to your experience of church, Jones goes on:

> In the face of a world in frightening disorder, the function of Christian worship is to provide such an ordering that on Sunday morning, in an insignificant building across the street from McDonalds, we can participate for one hour in the plot that floods all of

---

5. B Kaye, *A Church without Walls: Being Anglican in Australia* (North Blackburn: Dove, 1995), 7.

> space and time with its primal meaning. Worship is a play about promises, and about the Playwright who keeps them.[6]

Somehow I find this helpful looking across from our sanctuary at St John's to the Formula One Motel on a Sunday morning as we sing and pray our way through the liturgy. I like the audacious idea that something resembling the performance of an amateur musical has cosmic significance! (And we trust that our heavenly audience will accept 'our sacrifice of praise and thanksgiving' with all its ragged edges).

Jones continues:

> Worship is the primal rehearsal in memory and hope of the big picture, the vision that makes all of life sacred . . . In spite of popular thinking, the focus of public worship is not upon personal problems, nor upon energizing persons for the jaded week ahead. The purpose is to reconstitute each worshipper in particular and the community as a whole—by drawing us into losing ourselves with the defining rhythm of the whole.[7]

Here is a theology of church and worship that is genuinely liveable: it makes practical sense, it can be lived into in a way that makes sense of what we do and who were are becoming. Paul Jones was a United Methodist minister for more than forty years before becoming a Trappist monk and Roman Catholic priest, but the picture he paints of church and worship resonates strongly with Anglican understandings. Our emphasis on communal, liturgical worship is our way of remembering-in-the-present who we are in the story of God. We are both formed and re-formed in the context of our common worship.

Maybe we had forgotten this amidst the array of changes and challenges that we faced by end of the twentieth century, but the centrality of corporate anamnesis is there in our history. The Book of

---

6. W Paul Jones, *Facets of Faith: Living the Dimensions of Christian Spirituality* (Cambridge, Massachusetts: Cowley Publications), 20.
7. Jones, *Facets of Faith*, 23–4.

Common Prayer, particularly the Services of Morning and Evening Prayer, were formative for whole generations of Anglicans because they invited people to situate their own experience (both individual and communal) in the larger frame of the story of God. Through the recitation of canticles, psalms and scripture readings we remembered God's faithful presence in the past and consequently looked for the same in the present. The canticles and psalms in particular were cherished not because of their poetic language (although this helped): but because they had the capacity to read the reader. The *Magnificat* is the song of every lowly handmaiden; the *Nunc Dimittis* the prayer of everyone longing for a peaceful end where all is completed; the psalms an affirmation of 'all sorts of conditions of men.' The repetition of these elements facilitated this process.

We probably need to get intentional about this process again. The power of remembering-in-the-present was brought powerfully home when I attended the Sunday morning Eucharist in Redfern in the week following the 2004 riot on the Block which followed the tragic and accidental death of a fifteen year Aboriginal boy, T J Hickey. We heard the hope-filled story of how further violence had been averted through the work of elders and Indigenous Christian pastors. Then, as part of the intercessions, the parish's Aboriginal pastor sang a song based on Psalm 125:

> Those who trust in the Lord
> are like Mount Zion
> which shall never be removed
> and shall remain for ever.
>
> As the mountains are about
> are about Jerusalem,
> so the Lord is 'round about' round about his people here.
>
> Peace be on Israel
> peace be on Israel
> peace be on Israel
> now and for ever more.

Peace be on Redfern
peace be on Redfern
peace be on Redfern
now and for ever more.
Alleluia . . .

Here was a remarkable (because we rarely expect it now) instance of praying the psalms, a powerful process of anamnesis—remembering who we are in the present. Invoking not just 'peace on Israel', but 'peace on Redfern' placed the struggle for justice and peace in this urban Indigenous community squarely into the unfolding story of God. I felt immensely proud, and humbled, to have been there, witnessing the deeply felt prayer of thanks and intercession that arose from this numerically tiny Anglican parish in a problematic corner of Sydney. Here was a wonderful rehearsal of the Gospel. It was an act that was powerfully identity forming: we knew who we were as church because we were living the story—the story that we believe underpins our existence.

Rehearsal is, I think, a helpful way of imagining our gathering as church—because we never get it right. Our clay feet are always peeking out from our freshly laundered white robes: the presider stumbles over a word in the collect, the crucifer takes off in the wrong direction, someone has a turn in the back pew and the ambulance has to be called. From this perspective, this side of heaven, we will only ever participate in rehearsals. But we know that sometimes the best performances occur at the rehearsal.

Take, for instance, the Sunday the power went off in the midst of our 9 am Eucharist. Bereft of microphones and keyboard, and left with only two candles lighting the suddenly dimmed interior, I invited everyone to gather closer around the altar. As we began the dialogue of the Great Thanksgiving the energy of the whole congregation seemed to be focussed in a palpable way, like one giant concelebration, taking us literally out of the ordinary and into the sacred. We still remember with joy 'the day the power went off'.

Similarly, the metaphor of rehearsal has a helpful modesty about it and gives us permission to try some things out. And, we understand that over the course of many rehearsals, a motley band of individuals is gradually formed into a company: worship forms us as the 'people of God'. We are becoming the church.

But the question remains, is anyone today interested in the play?

Living in an alien land[8]

Graham Hughes, in a striking contribution to liturgical theology, *Worship as Meaning*, unpacks the various strategies that have emerged in response to the 'disenchantment' of modern and post-modern cultures. How can worship be construed as meaningful in a world cut loose from the 'sacred canopy',[9] where there is no shared grand narrative? Where we've lost the common from common prayer? How can we worship in an alien land?[10] The gap between Sunday and Monday, between church and world, has never seemed bigger. Indeed you only need to stroll into the local shopping mall *after* gathering for Sunday worship to experience the radical dissonance between the thought world inhabited by the church and, it seems, the rest of the universe. In fact there is no Sunday anymore.

Hughes suggests that there have been three basic responses to this situation. While his focus is on liturgical theology—and in particular the key question 'how can worship be meaningful in late modernity?'—each response implies a different way of conceiving church, a different ecclesiology. A short excursus here may be helpful.

Hughes describes his first category as 'church theology'. He includes here much of the theology that arises from the Roman Catholic tradition.[11] Here the key shared assumption is that 'the church's traditional liturgical formulations . . . when joined to an appropriate performance of them, may confidently be relied upon to effect their own meanings'.[12] The effect simply (or perhaps more

8. The title for this section is drawn from G Hughes, *Worship as Meaning: A Liturgical Theology for Late Modernity* (Cambridge: Cambridge University Press, 2003). Part III is entitled 'As in an alien land: making sense of God in a disenchanted age'. Living in an alien land is, of course, a recurrent biblical theme.
9. P Berger, *The Sacred Canopy: Elements of a Sociological Theory of Religion* (New York: Doubleday, 1967).
10. We are not the first to express this concern. This is the same question powerfully asked in Psalm 137 by the people of Israel in exile: 'How can we sing the Lord's song in a foreign land?' This experience of living in an alien land reshapes their telling of their foundational stories and their worship.
11. Liturgical theologians such as Aiden Kavanagh and Robert Taft, as well as Geoffrey Wainwright (Methodist) and Alexander Schmemann (Orthodox).
12. Hughes, *Worship as Meaning*, 222.

accurately, graciously) happens, as an epiphany or gift. Christ *is* encountered in word and sacrament, in the words of Scripture, the words of the liturgy, in the bread and wine at the altar, in the gathering of Christ's body, the church.

For Hughes this is too optimistic. The recipients of the liturgical symbols and actions—the worshippers—are given insufficient attention in this picture: the receiver must have the capacity to tune in to the signals (and this is precisely what has been lost in our culture). Otherwise, to use our other metaphor, the players cannot enact their part in the script. You cannot, says Hughes, simply wish away modernity: 'the recipients of liturgical signs are inhabitants of this modern culture and complete their meanings from within it'.[13] Worshippers, we need to remember, shop at the local mall too! Our congregations (including our clergy) are, as Hughes says, 'both inhabitants and products' of late modernity.

The second strategy Hughes labels 'evangelical'. He uses this term to designate 'the diverse conservative Protestant groups who regard the scriptures as an inerrant Word of God.' We may wish to argue with his use of the term 'evangelical' here, but the paradigm is easily recognisable. The scriptures become an 'a-cultural, a-historical theological datum', a fixed reference point against which the world is kept at a safe distance. This is, as Hughes points out, in Richard Niebuhr's classic scheme, a clear case of 'Christ against Culture'.[14] Much has been said about the attraction of such an expression of religious faith in the context of a pluralist world: it offers a level of clarity and simplicity in its well-trod path of personal conversion and discipleship. However, the paradox in this position, as Hughes sees it, is that Protestant evangelicalism is itself a clear product of modernity and survives through a form of symbiosis with it. So, for example, many of its core features are paralleled in the secular world: the priesthood of all believers mirrors the rise of democracy and egalitarianism; the

---

13. Hughes, *Worship as Meaning*, 253. Hughes helpfully quotes Langdon Gilkey: 'Any current theology . . . that does not recognize and seek reflectively to deal with this presence of secularity, of doubt, of scepticism, and so of a sense of meaninglessness of religious language inside the church as well as outside, and so inside the theologian and believer, is so far irrelevant to our present situation.' See LB Gilkey, *Naming the Whirlwind: The Renewal of God-language* (Indianapolis: Bobbs-Merrill, 1969), 10.

14. Hughes, *Worship as Meaning*, 223.

focus on individual salvation parallels the centrality of the individual in modernity; the emphasis on accessibility and the vernacular reflects the triumph of popular over high culture. It is not hard to recognise the style:

> Strict demarcations between ordained and lay leaders are imperceptible; the dominant idiom is informality—of dress, of personal manner, or forms of communication. Worship spaces are deliberately chosen or constructed to be 'irreligious'—ie, as unlike traditional 'church' buildings—as they can be; and musical idioms are directly continuous with their secular counterparts.[15]

This odd relationship with modernity (claiming separateness from the modern world and yet in its use of cultural forms strongly identified with it) is, Hughes argues, both the source of evangelicalism's strength, and potentially its greatest weakness. The boundaries between the sacred and the ordinary are virtually erased. In evangelical worship there is an almost total reliance on words as the medium for expressing the 'otherness' or 'transcendence' of God. In the Australian context we might see this most spectacularly in the Hillsong phenomenon, where there seems to be little to distinguish a worship service from popular entertainment. The words are just about the only clue. This dependence on language, Hughes suggests, is ultimately precarious. And in rejecting liturgical worship, and its use of ritual and sacred space, this strand puts itself outside the mainstream of two thousand years of Christian tradition.

Hughes' final category is what he calls mainstream Protestantism. Here the strategy has been to construct meaning from within modern culture. In its classic Protestant liberal form, the perceived continuity between God and world allowed for a bold embrace of the 'modern spirit' together with an identification of social progress with the unfolding Kingdom of God.[16] The early optimism of liberal Protestantism was severely dinted by the experience of two world wars during the first half of the twentieth century. It remains the case, however, that contemporary theologies emerging out of this tradition

15. Hughes, *Worship as Meaning*, 242.
16. Hughes, *Worship as Meaning*, 224.

(such as contextual, liberation, feminist and ecological theologies) continue to focus almost exclusively on God's immanence. God is to be sought and found in the midst of daily life. In worship this is often reflected in an emphasis on God's presence in the day to day[17] or on social service as the arena of true worship.

Anglicanism (not surprisingly) is barely mentioned by Hughes. What would he make of us? Certainly in his three categories we can easily discern elements of the varying historical stands of Anglicanism (including their shadow selves): from the optimistic liturgical practice of Anglo-Catholicism, through the emphasis on words in the Evangelical wing to the seamless world-embrace of the Liberals. Whilst Hughes deliberately sharpens each of his categories his analysis gives us some helpful clues for unpacking our current difficulties around worship and church. What is more significant for our purpose though is his mapping of a more fruitful way forward and its implications for re-imagining a 'church without walls'. It is to this we now turn.

Dancing at the edge of the known

Returning then to Hughes' basic question: how can worship be meaningful in late modernity? Hughes suggests a two-staged approach.[18] The first stage consists of recognising the places where we are most likely, as inhabitants of the modern world, to notice our contingency: 'at the edge of the known'. The second stage is about naming this experience in terms of our Christian faith. We make (liturgical) meaning in the context of a dialectic between identity and difference, that is, in the engagement between universal human experience (the place where we 'identify' with others, the common ground) and the naming of this experience from within the Christian

---

17. Some of John Bell's lyrics spring to mind here. For example: 'Jesus Christ is waiting,/ Waiting in the streets;/ No one is his neighbour,/ All alone he eats./ Listen, Lord Jesus, / I am lonely too./ Make me, friend or stranger,/ Fit to wait on you.' J Bell and G Maule, *Enemy of Apathy* (Glasgow: Wild Goose Publications, 1988), 87.
18. Hughes, *Worship as Meaning*, 255–260. I am aware here of the potential of doing Hughes an injustice by over simplifying his carefully nuanced thesis. Note too that Hughes acknowledges that he is not unique in proposing a two-staged approach. Both Langdon Gilkey and David Tracy suggest somewhat similar strategies.

faith (the place of 'difference'). Attending to this dialectic will help us, Hughes suggests, avoid the pitfalls of the three responses previously mapped. The 'church theology' advocates and evangelicals stress difference at the expense of a genuine engagement with modern culture, while the mainline Protestant stream assimilates or over identifies at the expense of difference or the otherness of God. Hughes' dialectical approach endeavours to find a place where we, inhabitants of late modernity, can encounter and name God.

In some ways this sort of approach is natural territory for Anglicans: it certainly resonates with the 'three-fold cord' of Scripture, Tradition and Reason. We have never been afraid to engage with contemporary thought. But we are less confident when it comes to the working through the consequences for our worship. It is as though we make brave forays into the modern world and then return to the relative safety of the known.

It is worth unpacking the notion of 'edge' a little more because, if Hughes is correct, this is where we will find common ground on which to build common prayer.

Modernity, as Hughes suggests, 'is a cultural phenomenon dedicated to the achievement of human autonomy'.[19] Everything can be mastered, we believe, given time, effort and freedom. This basic assumption underpins our political, economic and social systems. It is a key dynamic in the demand for more and more access to life-prolonging technologies. It is a player in our failure to grasp the consequences of our abuse of the environment. We conduct ourselves as if we are 'masters of the universe'.

But of course, there are limits. It is just that our lives are constructed to avoid or deny them. Imagine, Hughes invites:

> . . . that the meanings we manage to construct form a vast platform on which we find ourselves able—more or less successfully—to live and to communicate with each other. The modernity of which I speak, then, in its endless promotion among us of our own self-sustainability, encourages at every opportunity 'forgetfulness' of the platform's dangerous 'edge'—the fact that there are limits to our human forms of existence—and a consequent preoccupation with our

19. Hughes, *Worship as Meaning*, 260.

> own 'centre', the place in which the various technologies lend an illusion of safety and permanence.[20]

It is at the 'edge' that we experience our contingency. Ultimately, regardless of our multiple avoidance strategies, we all find ourselves there. The experience of limit is common ground for all of us. These edge or limit moments come in many different ways—sometimes invited, sometimes uninvited—but they all share the same quality of taking us outside the everyday into a more intense, vulnerable space. Sometimes we take ourselves to the edge as a sort of test of our own limits just to see if we can push a bit further: abseiling over a cliff or living in a foreign culture. Other times we are taken to the edge by things that happen *to* us: the death of a loved one, a debilitating illness, the birth of a child, an unexpected win, a shocking accident, a natural disaster. Sometimes we are taken there by others who have dared to look over the edge: the stretch of the imagination when reading a poem or viewing a painting, for example. In each of these experiences we are faced with the more than strong possibility that we don't know it all and that we are not as perfectly in control as we thought: we find ourselves 'at the edge of the known'.

Edge or limit experiences share a number of characteristics. First there is an intensification of emotions (anxiety, doubt, joy, elation) often to an almost unbearable degree. Second, the experience has a potentially religious quality—awe, or wonder, or horror—akin to Rudolph Otto's *mysterium fascinans tremendum*.[21] Third, the experience renders the person more vulnerable or open to 'depths and possibilities'.

This is the common ground we share as human beings. It is also the place where our worship plays.[22]

---

20. Hughes, *Worship as Meaning*, 262–3.
21. Although as Hughes points out we'd rather have the *mysterium* without the terror thanks very much. *Worship as Meaning*, 275.
22. In Aidan Kavanagh's words, 'liturgy leads regularly to the edge of chaos, and from this regular flirt with doom comes a theology different from any other.' Quoted in Hughes, *Worship as Meaning*, 275. This is overly optimistic of course in terms of our actual practice, but he's right about the potential.

> Worship . . . belongs with the sorts of daunting-but-thrilling adventures which turn outward from the safe centre towards the scary perimeter. For that is where worship—has long learned to find its health, its sources of strength and its wisdom.[23]

It is a place of health and life because as we come to our own end we are met by *the* Other. Jesus, of course, regularly inhabited this place and encouraged his disciples to join him: 'those who lose their life for my sake, and for the sake of the gospel, will save it'.[24] It is, in a very real way, 'the way of the cross'. Indeed the central ground of our Christian faith is that in Jesus we encounter the shape of this Other, the One we name as God. And it is in remembering (in that deep sense of anamnesis) his death and resurrection that we find a surprising and graced capacity to dance with him on the edge.

Onto the verandah

In fact as Anglicans we have been good at this engagement with the edge for much of our history. Most obviously the provisions in our prayer books for the rites of passage—birth, marriage, death—have enabled us to meet countless people at these particular limit moments of their lives. Post-Christendom we are no longer routinely invited to stand with people at these edges. We need to carefully embrace the times when we are. We need to again become a church of the edge.

Hughes has made, I believe, a significant contribution to our understanding of the construction of meaning in worship at the beginning of the twenty-first century. But for Anglicans the next questions will always be pragmatic. How does this look on the ground? How do we create spaces for exploring 'the edge of the known'?

Such a space might look very much like the verandah described by Stephen Pickard:

> The verandah represents that life in-between. On the verandah one exists at the point of intersection. This involves openness to the beyond, safety and protection and a good place in which to dwell. Architecturally it

23. Hughes, *Worship as Meaning*, 301.
24. Mark 8:35.

> is the place of mediation between different worlds — inside the house and beyond the home base, a launch pad for further exploration and engagement, a solace from the unknown, from fears and dangers that threaten to extinguish life.[25]

The verandah faces the edge, but furnishes a buffer. It creates a space where the edge can be considered, contemplated. For Pickard the verandah is hospitable space, a breeze–way where we are met by the God of the 'in–between'.

The metaphor of verandah furnishes us with a vision of the church as a sanctuary which is an 'open and inviting place offering safety, nourishment and energy for the work'. At its best it can become the place where the dialectic of similarity and difference is played out, the place where the experience of limit or edge and our Christian understanding of God might encounter each other.

It is important here not to carelessly mix metaphors. Hughes explicitly uses the metaphor of the raft with its dangerous edge as an image for our construction of day-to-day meaning. Pickard's verandah is an ecclesiological vision of the church as a particular type of sanctuary. The common thread though is the notion of an edge. For Hughes' raft, the edge represents the limits to the everyday construction of meaning, the place where we find ourselves alternately experiencing exhilaration and panic. For Pickard the edge is a boundary between church and world and place for dialogue and negotiation.

The verandah is a seductive image—one that has us dreaming all sorts of possible ways in which we can construct church as 'open and inviting space'—but unless we have the edge in view our schemes are unlikely to connect very deeply with the people we invite onto our verandahs. Indeed we tend to behave as though we own and, therefore, control the verandah. We like to conduct things in our terms, on our turf.[26] Yet we also know, with Nicodemus, that 'the wind

---

25. S Pickard, 'The view from the verandah: gospel and spirituality in an Australian setting', *St Mark's Review*, Winter (1998): 9.
26. In the 1970s, for example, we constructed 'Coffee Shops', and more recently, 'Café Church'—mostly on our physical turf—often without real clarity about what we thought we were doing, beyond an attempt at

(spirit) blows where it chooses'.[27] In his secret, night-time visit to Jesus he experienced the limits of his own understanding and experienced the vertigo of the edge.

The verandah is not simply a place for tea parties or barbeques. Some years ago Janet Gaden told the story of being put out to sleep on the verandah as a small child.[28] This was during World War 11. The house faced the sea. There were gun emplacements nearby and regular aerial patrols. The rest of the household slept safely behind the blackout curtains. This was a fiercely shocking experience as she was exposed to the terror of the dark night—the 'imagined' sea of enemies cloaked in the blackness focussed solely on her. One of the things that must mark us as a church is our willingness to stand with each other, facing the terror of the edge. We must be people who dare.

Identifying the edge or limit experience is not simply about identifying subject matter for the task of apologetics. It is about finding our common ground, the places where we find ourselves standing together as (modern) human beings. What we do with this common ground is crucial.

Reclaiming the common

So here's the challenge. Finding the common ground, the edge, where we can begin to make common prayer. Bringing our Christian tradition, our naming of the Other, to the edge so that we can pray with each other. These two movements need to dance together.

It may sound like a truism but the reality is that we are on a journey and we don't yet know the destination. Our *Book of Common Prayer* identity was not easily forged and was, perhaps, never as stable as we now imagine. But what we can offer, as Anglicans, is a method, a practical way of being the church. We understand that worship and ecclesiology are related (that's why we argue so vigorously in this arena). We immerse ourselves in Scripture (sometimes, it seems, we are positively drowning in it!—few denominations have such a strong commitment to the public reading of such significant portions of the

being 'relevant'. Much more interesting are the bolder experiments, the ones that take us out of the safety of the parish grounds.

27. John 3:8.

28. The story was told in the context of a talk entitled 'Remember that you were slaves in Egypt' at The Third National Feminist Theology Conference, Melbourne, 1993.

Bible) and in this we are listening for God's word for us now. We have a deep commitment to the treasure house of our tradition, stretching back through the Reformation to Patristic times. We have been known to imaginatively rework that tradition (the Book of Common Prayer is our most clear example). We take seriously our relationship to the culture in which we find ourselves. We are committed to the use of the common tongue, that is, we have a commitment to communication. We face the world. Our worship is not intended for a clerical (or even lay) elite. And we do this together. It is a corporate, communal exercise.

A contemporary quest to reclaim common prayer will need, I think, to be conducted within this framework and with the sorts of additional processes we have explored in this chapter. We need a more creative engagement with the process of corporate anamnesis, that is, the telling of our stories within the large frame of the story of God (though our liturgy can stray into the opposite territory so that it can feel like corporate amnesia, a place of forgetting rather than a place for reconstituting or remaking our often difficult lives in the context of the story of salvation). We need a level of modesty also about what we do as well as the courage to experiment: the notion of worship as rehearsal will be helpful here. Above all we need to encourage dancing on the edge, with whoever we find there. Playing it safe won't do.

Postlude: rehearsals on the verandah

This is an exciting time to be part of the church. Verandahs are being constructed everywhere! There are rehearsals being conducted, often creatively reshaping old scripts (Bell Shakespeare doesn't have a monopoly here!). Every contemporary Anglican community will have a range of verandah stories, which tell of the ways in which we are learning anew to dance on the edge. Here are a few from my recent experience.

Fortnightly on Thursdays there is a gathering in the lounge room of St John's House (once the rectory, now our offices) in Coffs Harbour. We've called the gathering 'Friends for Lunch'. It has a simple pattern: we sing (with great gusto and our best efforts at tunefulness) the favourite hymns and songs of those gathered (we always sing *Amazing Grace* for Jemma); we read the Gospel that will be read next Sunday; we talk about what it might be saying to us; we pray, especially remembering those who are struggling; we give God thanks for the food; we set the table and share the food; then we return to our homes or business.

Around the table on any one day you might find elderly widows, people with Down's Syndrome or other intellectual disabilities, folk struggling with addictions, sole parents (connected to the parish through an Anglicare project) and folk who just happen to be around the parish that day (cleaning, mowing, or just dropping by). Everyone there knows about the edge: about falling over, about watching your child struggle with a disability, about exclusion or marginalisation. The space was particularly conceived out of a need to develop a more hospitable space for those who live with disabilities, but is evolving into something much better: a verandah where you can simply 'come as you are'.

Good, healing things happen. Like the day John told us that 'I feel safe here'. Or when Sarah told us how frightened she was when the train was delayed on her way home from the Snowy trip because 'my Mum and Dad might not be there to pick me up'. She was hugged and comforted by Priscilla who knows such terror too. That day I began to glimpse a different world and honour the amazing courage it must take to live independently. There have been hand dances and waltzes and the laying on of hands—each led by those who have lived all their lives on the edge, fully aware of their limits, and who are showing the rest of us the way of Jesus. All this happened because we cleared a space and built a 'verandah' where we could meet on equal ground. And if the shape of this verandah sounds like the shape of our Sunday Eucharistic gatherings who am I to say what the Spirit is doing at 'Friends for Lunch'?[29]

Another verandah. One of the great deficits in our culture concerns the loss of rites of passage. Our mission in Anglican schools gives us an opportunity to creatively meet students and their families as they travel the journey through the school years. These are verandah spaces *par excellence*.

---

29. One of the interesting things that I observed in relation to 'Friends for Lunch' was how it began to transform our Sunday Eucharist in subtle, spontaneous ways. The confident participation at 'Friends' overflowed into more confident, relaxed ownership of Sunday worship. For example, Lorraine, who has an intellectual disability, would remind everyone (if I forgot) when 'Friends for Lunch' was on.

In the local Anglican school in Coffs Harbour we developed particular rites of passage for the end of Year 6 as students prepare for a new phase of their journey in secondary school, and a range of rites for Year 12 students as they prepare to leave school. As part of a weekend retreat Year 12 students participate in a liturgy of reconciliation. This is how it looked last year.

Students gather in a space they have earlier helped to create: footprints traced from their own feet, candles, bowls of scented oil, a chair, piles of paper ties. A single candle is lit as they enter. Music is playing to create an atmosphere of reflection. Students light the candles around the space then sit in a large circle. The process is explained, so that students will know what is ahead.

We read the story of Lazarus, bound in his tomb and imagine ourselves in it. Then we ask: what are the things that are binding us? What are the things that are cutting us off from life? What prevents us from moving confidently into the future? One student, the scapegoat (we've explained that idea), sits on the chair and the students are invited to bind him/her with the paper ties. The ties stand for the things that keep us bound to old and dysfunctional habits, the things we want to say goodbye to. When this is done the scapegoat is well and truly bound, and someone prays the words of the confession. Then we read the rest of the Lazarus story, imagine the stone of the tomb being removed and Jesus calling us to freedom. A priest proclaims the absolution: 'God forgives you, forgive others, forgive yourself . . . ' and then, together, the students remove the bindings.

One more thing: we cannot be truly free until we are reconciled with each other. So, we offer peace to each other. 'Don't leave with regrets. Is there someone here that you have hurt? Is there someone who you have kept bound?' Slowly at first, journeys are made across the room, words and hugs, touch and words. We give this time, and then we share some words of hope about life beyond the familiar (the resurrected Jesus sharing breakfast with his friends) and talk about how to share the bread. We pray for peace in the world and pray one last time the prayer that they've dragged through at chapel over the years (the Lord's Prayer). And then the blessing . . . made tangible by fragrant oil as everyone participates. I am anointed by a girl that gave me a hard time in my first year as a chaplain—it smelled like pure nard! 'The Liturgy' is always deemed the highlight of the retreat. It's a creative verandah piece, drawing deeply on the wisdom of our tradition, a scattering of seed into the lives of the students. Who knows when and where the seeds will sprout and grow?

A final note of hope. Recently, in the midst of the readjustment phase of a major move, the stresses and strains were beginning to show in our household. Reflecting on 'what helps', my husband immediately named daily prayer—held each morning with staff in his new Anglican school community—as the key sanity factor. It is a space that 'helps you reclaim the big picture', 'get a perspective on things'. And it builds community, as we risk knowing each other in holy space. Designed as inclusive, hospitable space (not all staff would identify as Christian) the nudges of the Spirit are already evident in this practice. And my arrival at a different St John's has coincided with the formation of a student community house which also has a commitment to daily prayer each morning, transforming what would once have been a largely clerical commitment to the Daily Office.

None of these are unusual stories. Nor are they new. All have their roots strongly in our tradition of liturgical worship: the reclamation of daily (liturgical) prayer, with its conscious sanctification of our daily lives; the recreation of rites of passage and the provision of processes for reconciliation; the opening up of Eucharistic hospitality as common ground. All of this has the effect of transforming the way we experience and think about church, that is, how we locate the church and express an ecclesiology. We can, if we choose, dance on the edge in good company—with the wisdom of 'a great cloud of witnesses' present and past. It is shaping up to be an exhilarating journey!

8

Anglicanism, Post-Modernity And A Habitat For Giftedness

Scott Cowdell

The contributions to this collection cover a range of issues to do with Anglican faith and practice. My brief in this essay is to reflect on 'gifts' from an Anglican perspective, by which is meant 'gifts for ministry'.

But describing them thus is already to display a prejudice, seeing 'gifts' in the context of the church's ministry and, hence, understanding them against the whole backdrop of God's nature and God's purposes in the world. The increasingly widespread alternative, of course, is to see 'gifts' primarily in terms of the individual Christian's personal 'giftedness', as attributes innate to the religious self rather than *charismata* given by God to serve the church's overarching mission. Such an attitude reflects an individualistic worldview, and its frequent concomitant is the rhetoric of personal rights. A 'gift' implies the right to exercise it, appealing to deeply held beliefs about individual prerogatives and religious freedom in today's West, and to widespread expectations that self-development and self-actualisation are necessary and worthwhile religious goals. Thus 'gift' implies rights to express that gift, the denial of which risks personal diminishment and a threat to wellbeing.

Hence a phenomenon that every parish priest, examining chaplain, theological college principal and bishop is familiar with: individual Christians demanding the right to exercise a ministry based on their assessment of their own 'giftedness'. Whether this is a lay congregant claiming rights to a particular role in the parish, or a would-be priest forever unreconciled with the church's refusal to accept them as an ordination candidate, there is the unwelcome discovery that personal assessment of 'gift' is not enough to secure a ministry role without a wider process of discernment, recognising a broader context for 'giftedness'.

Yet, having said that, a sense of individual 'giftedness' remains highly significant. Fewer and fewer Christians and congregations are convinced by abstract appeals to authority and official position in the church where these are unsupported by evidence of personal 'gift' and calling. So clergy everywhere are increasingly unable to fall back on the clericalism that secures their right to adjudicate the potential contributions of others while remaining beyond criticism themselves. Today's church, everywhere more 'charismatic', is open to potentially significant contributions from all members, refusing to see God's influence constrained by ecclesial tradition, structure or hierarchy.

Further, there are times when demanding the expression of one's personal 'giftedness' has proved not only appropriate but also significant and Godly, contributing to a rethinking of ministry in the church. I refer to insistent claims from women over recent decades and, increasingly today, from gay and lesbian Christians, for inclusion in the ordained ministry on the basis of obvious 'gifts' and a personal sense of calling. In this debate the deployment of rights language has not primarily sought personal gain, so much as given personal witness to the new thing many believed God to be doing. This Godly activism has led the church in many places to revisit its habits of discernment.

So while individualism and the rhetoric linking 'gifts' and rights needs tempering by a more collective and purposive understanding of Christian vocation, a sense of individual 'giftedness' is also essential for the church's discernment of that vocation. Here we see something of the tension between individualism and collectivism characteristic of post-modern culture—on the one hand, individuals insisting on their own version of reality; on the other, a newfound awareness of collective forces shaping individuals and determining what range of expression is possible to them. A word about this tension.

The individual and the collective

Following the impetus of modernity in the West, individual rights and the triumph of material consumption in defining the human have blossomed into the deregulated hyper-individualism of post-modernity. The prevailing cultural imperative is to 'look good, feel good and make good', without a strong countervailing sense that individuals abide in wider collectives that define meaning and impose a proper constraint. Postmodern hyper-individualism is thus the inevitable concomitant of postmodern pluralism—a world of individuals decoupled from objective truth, from the many givens and tacit assumptions woven into communal solidarity, and from all moral constraint, bar that of material consumption which is under the sway of the one remaining authority of global market forces. Truth according to post-modernity thus becomes the realm of Nietzsche's 'will to power', where contending versions of reality provide the raw material for everyone's 'personal philosophy'. Consequently, meaning becomes privatised.

But if it is true in gambling that 'the house always wins', so in a world of the imagination dominated by late-capitalist, global economic forces, the culture always wins. The extent of choice in meaning making is subtly controlled. The culture has a stake in maintaining an off-balance, dissatisfied individualism, so we will be sure to 'keep spending', in search of a satisfaction we are in fact being programmatically denied. This pushy, insistent individualism can be present in the church, manifest in the way 'giftedness' presses its claims.

For all of today's rampant individualism, then, culture and context still profoundly shape what individuals can become, and the meaning they can make. This is also true of traditions. Anthropology, sociology, linguistics and cultural studies teach that our place in human networks of relationship and language shapes the way we experience and order the world. Marx and Nietzsche taught that power relations, including economic ones, determined the range of what was thinkable.

Here we see something of a reversal of modernity's suspicion of tradition. The Enlightenment gave us the modern individual, to be sure (now volatilised as its post-modern successor), but it also gave us a sustained critique of tradition—a critique for which post-modernity has shown far less interest. The post-modern individual is, paradoxically, the product of tradition, community and context. Even if life is a pastiche of various culturally-formed and traditionally-mediated lifestyle options, nevertheless such individual choice is dependent upon the perseverance of coherent traditio-cultural alternatives from which individuals can 'pic 'n mix' (we choose it but we don't *occupy* it). Choosing a particular tradition or identifying with a particular community, even a strict one, is thus a real post-modern option. Even Nietzsche's Zarathustra showed his leanings back to modernity, by setting the goal of an entirely original radicality beyond all established options. But the true post-modern, for all her hyper-individuality, for all the smorgasbord nature of his imaginative environment, is willing and able to identify with and inhabit a particular truth, a particular path—modernism's contempt for tradition, and for the past more generally, is now a thing of the past.

My point here is that individualism, on the one hand, and commitment to tradition and community, on the other, can go together in post-modernity. And so the tension I am identifying in the church, particularly in its attitude to 'gifts' and their expression, is explicable —assimilable—at the level of culture. I also want to argue that it is explicable from the perspective of Anglican tradition. Individual 'giftedness' brings rights within Anglicanism, but only within a tradition and a community where persons and their 'gifts' are caught up in a bigger picture. It is a bigger picture that *situates* individuals and 'gifts'—by no means accepting every claim on its own terms—but which also mandates affirmation of individuals and 'gifts'. This is a church able to accommodate diversity according to its own particular tradition, holding individual 'giftedness' and community roles (ministries) together. It is a church, too, that recognises a critical role for ordained leaders in the context of a 'whole people of God' ecclesiology, in a way that potentially takes us beyond both clericalism and congregationalism—the Scylla and Charybdis of classical Anglican divinity. So not only is a balanced Christian ecclesiology of 'gifts' accessible from post-modern culture, but it is also characteristic of a spiritually healthy Anglicanism. Let me now explore some aspects of this realisation.

Diversity is a gift

It is widely recognised that Anglicanism can tolerate internal diversity better than many Christian traditions. Apart from increasingly militant Anglican minorities seeking a church every bit as monochrome as other current conservative Christian groups, both Roman Catholic and Protestant, nevertheless there remains broad tolerance within mainstream Anglicanism for a range of positions and practices concerning faith and order. Perhaps this reflects the tolerant mood of the Enlightenment, which made such decisive inroads into English religious sensibility at the expense of doctrinal precision and pastoral zeal? Perhaps it goes further back, to the uneasy terms of England's Elizabethan Settlement? There, religious unity at the level of worship and church order was imposed by fiat, while allowing significant room for individuals to stake out widely varying personal positions within a loose, structural conformity. This was a church that could, in principle, accommodate both Puritan and Catholic within its wide and generous embrace, as long as they both used the Prayer Book and respected the established Episcopal hierarchy. Queen Elizabeth herself had no desire to 'make a window into men's souls', provided external obedience was maintained. So, within an overarching order that (to some extent) inevitably limited diversity of practice, nevertheless significant diversity of thought and action remained as a foundational Anglican possibility.

Consequently, mainstream Anglicanism imposes no rigorous dogmatic tests, recognises no Reformation-style confession of faith, and resists strict doctrinal conformity. Anglican theology naturally tends to take place within the praying life, and very often (though not always) within the ministerial commission. The principle of *lex orandi, lex credendi* lends a personal, spiritual cast to the theological enterprise that in other hands tends in more rationalistic and speculative directions. So Anglican divinity is less hedged about by rules, and less driven to self-definition in terms of content (though, as a consequence of these tendencies, its theological method can claim to be distinctive). A church that can incorporate a present day spectrum of writers—from Don Cupitt (radical protestant) to Peter Jensen (another type of radical protestant); from John Shelby Spong (liberal Protestant) and Richard Holloway (liberal Catholic) to John Milbank and Catherine Pickstock (Radical Orthodox)—is a church with plenty of room for diversity. All this means that a measure of freedom for conscience is enshrined in Anglican sensibility, because God is seen to be known and served best if not over-defined and over-regulated.

Another aspect of that diversity is seen in the Anglican conception of vocation. The clergy loom large in Anglican formularies, as in the classic sixteenth century Anglican liturgies, as the most active participants in worship, offering leadership for the people of God. However, the English Reformation brought a complementary understanding of lay vocation. The laity were expected to worship, pray, live holy and gracious lives, contract fruitful and faithful marriages, obey the Sovereign's laws and generally contribute to building-up the Tudor Commonwealth in the way they lived—all of which is evident from the liturgies they participated in.[1] Broad principles such as this

1. Fredrica Harris Thompsett, 'The Laity', in *The Study of Anglicanism*, edited by Stephen Sykes and John Booty (London: SPCK, 1988), 245–60.

set a pattern for each to serve God in the estate of life to which they were called. The role of clergy was different to the extent that leadership in the church, by teaching, pastoral care and personal example, was required—though sharing in the common life of all Christians was to be the basis of the clergy's personal example, including sharing in the estate of marriage.[2] Here we see a theology of complementary vocations each contributing to the quality of life in Christendom.

Nowadays we live in a more differentiated world. Political economy shapes nations now, whereas pre-modern states like Tudor England demonstrated (and needed) a far more unified and intentional conception of faith and life, of spiritual and practical ends. Still, the same Anglican instinct for lay participation in the spiritual goal of maintaining a certain sort of national life remains in the undeniably public nature of much Anglican focus. We are not typically a sect-type church that withdraws from the world in search of meaning (of course, with notable exceptions). Instead, many Anglicans find the outworking of their Christian calling in the commitments of life in work, home and community, and in the embrace of public causes. The chief goal is not so much salvation for fallen sinners as the striving after a vision of God's justice and peace in the life of the world. While there are Anglican expressions that are chiefly soteriological in their motivation, I suggest that mainstream Anglican instincts are primarily doxological, seeking the praise and glorification of God not only in worship but also in life.

But what about the life of the church, apart from the wider society? The priestly monologue of Tudor worship is now a thing of the past, and with it the structural exclusion of laity from ministry in the church. There always was a role for laity in church governance within the Anglican vision, with England's Parliament effectively constituting the first synod, and the Sovereign—a layperson—as Supreme Governor of the Church of England. That instinct for incorporating lay authority has been retained with the now universal reach of synodical government within the Anglican Communion. But it is also present more generally in the collaborative attitude to ministry between clergy and laity that has grown up in the second half of the twentieth century, and which is reflected in newer Anglican liturgies. This has

2. See the comprehensive discussion in Muriel Porter, *Sex, Marriage and the Church: Patterns of Change* (Melbourne: Dove, 1996).

partly followed the biblical theology movement and the ecumenical movement, both helping to recover a 'whole people of God' ecclesiology, and the charismatic movement, with its emphasis on personal inspiration by the Holy Spirit of God. However the conviction arose, it is now a commonplace of Anglican teaching everywhere that all God's people are chosen, called and gifted, and that here we see the truest nature of the church.

Such a conception comprises the baptismal paradigm, as Paul Avis calls it, seen as presenting a truer reflection of the church's identity and continuity than either 'the Erastian paradigm' or 'the apostolic paradigm', both of which have been appealed to by Anglicans in the past—the one seeking identity in an ordering of things consistent with the pre-modern monarchical state; the other seeking identity and continuity in modern secular surroundings by the unbroken succession of Episcopally ordained ministry originating with the first Apostles.[3] The latter is a highly structural and depersonalised conception, but one that nevertheless served to critique the Erastian paradigm in the hands of nineteenth century Anglo-Catholics. But, nowadays, apostolic succession has proved inadequate to account for the calling of all God's people and their collective empowerment on the basis of baptism—Episcopal confirmation can no longer claim to be the preferred conduit of God's Holy Spirit into the lives of lay people (might I add that this is one reason its significance has declined, as more and more people realise that while God's blessings are structurally and communally named, celebrated and worked out, nevertheless they are not structurally and clerically mediated at the expense of direct encounter with God in person and in the community as a whole). For this reason, clericalism—a key mark of what we might call 'the institutional captivity of the Spirit'—is increasingly no longer tolerated in Anglican circles, as the passivity and impersonality of certain earlier conceptions of God's presence and action refuse to commend themselves to a new, critically-aware, spiritually-seeking and experientially-oriented generation.

The truest wellspring of a 'whole people of God' ecclesiology is of course the Pauline epistles. In particular 1 Corinthians, over which Bruce Kaye enthuses as the charter for a renewed Anglican witness.

---

3. Paul Avis, *The Anglican Understanding of the Church: An Introduction* (London: SPCK, 2000), 15–29.

He writes of Paul's brainwave in the face of the Corinthian church's incorrigible diversity—a melting pot of racial types, personal circumstances and ministry agendas. Paul's goal was to convince the Corinthian Christians of their calling together in Christ for the purpose of witness. The breakthrough insight was that their diversity represented more than a sociological fact. It was actually a gift from God, with complementary 'gifts' working together like body parts, contributing to the life of the whole. Kaye echoes Avis on the preeminent attractiveness and timeliness of this conception, but goes further. Chief among Kaye's burdens is to commend the further uptake of this collective vision. While we know that top-down models of God's action and their clericalist manifestations are on the wane, nevertheless this can't happen fast enough for Bruce Kaye, who pursues a networked, relational, post-institutional Anglicanism in which all are crew, none are passengers—a path along which we have come some way, but not far enough.[4]

Here, of course, the problem is not so much the pressing of 'gifts' by individuals as the very opposite: the failure to appreciate the fact of our individual 'giftedness' and the concomitant call to ministry. To a discussion of this issue, and more generally to considering 'gifts' in their wider context, I now turn.

'Gifts' and their ownership

Paul's theology of 'gifts' and 'giftedness', in his classic discussion through 1 Corinthians, Chapter 12, is entirely God-focussed, christological, ecclesiological and missiological. It is not primarily the theology of the human person he starts with in understanding individual 'giftedness', but it is the purposes of God in Christ for the life of the world that give rise to the church and its ministry. The 'gifts' of individuals are understood to come from God, in that mystical chemistry linking the individual Christian with the risen life of Jesus Christ guiding and building up the church by his Spirit. 'Gifts' are given 'in Christ', for the sake of expressing his life and furthering his mission for the glory of God. The ministry is Christ's, the individual Christian having a share in it. The aim of this ministry is building up

4. Bruce Kaye, *Reinventing Anglicanism: A Vision of Confidence, Community and Engagement in Anglican Christianity* (Adelaide: OpenBook, 2003).

the body of Christ, and giving the world an embodied expression of the heart and mind and will of God.

Consequently, there is little warrant here for approaching 'gifts' in terms of rights and individual fulfilment. In a very real sense we do not own our 'gifts', to boast of them or dispose of them however we choose. In the same way Paul argues that our bodies are not our own, seeing our embodied life as given to us by God and owed to God in obedience. This could not be more different from today's rhetoric of our bodies as personal possessions, to do with as we choose. And here is the imaginative basis of Paul's sexual ethic, which begins by re-imagining the nature and goal of our embodied life. Accordingly, sexual license is not so much objectively immoral as imaginatively impoverished.[5]

In the same way, 'gifts' are not ours, and our rights to use them are better understood as obligations to use them, from God. And also, of course, to recognise and not despise the 'giftedness' of others. Paul's teaching on 'gifts' is about the building up of the body, and the Corinthian problem was very often a failure to appreciate the diversity of 'gifts' on offer in that church.[6]

But while the 'gifts' are not our own property, and must not be used as evidence in a debate about personal rights without tearing the Pauline logic of Christian 'giftedness', nevertheless neither are we dumb vehicles of God's action through these 'gifts'. The Christian individual retains responsibility for these 'gifts' and their use. The ordinal asks the deacon, under examination by the bishop immediately prior to ordination as priest: 'Will you constantly stir up the gift of God which is in you?',[7] just as Paul urges those with particular 'gifts'

5. Following the logic of Stephen Fowle on the inappropriateness of stealing, according to the logic of paranetic passages in Ephesians—not so much for its objective wrongness as for its inconceivability in the face of a robust Christian self understanding. See his essay 'Making Stealing Possible: Criminal Thoughts on Building an Ecclesial Common Life', in *Engaging Scripture: A Model for Theological Interpretation* (Oxford: Blackwell, 1998), 161–77.
6. 1 Corinthians 12:19–26; see also Romans 12:4–5, also Ephesians 4:14–16.
7. See for example, 'The Ordination of Priests (also called Presbyters)', in *A Prayer Book for Australia* (Sydney: Broughton Books, 1995), 795.

to use them for the common good according to their nature. The same big picture context of Christian 'giftedness' that removes 'gifts' from the realm of the ego also mandates their use, for a purpose. And of course this also means accepting the fact of our 'giftedness'—that God has equipped us for ministry, and that those 'gifts' call for discernment and expression. Bruce Kaye is far from alone in associating Anglican renewal with the full flowering of 'giftedness' among all the Anglican faithful.

There need be no contradiction between the sort of claims being made here: on the one hand, the shift of 'gift' from the realm of individual to collective; on the other hand, the requirement that individuals recognise and employ their 'gifts'. Individuals are of absolute value to Christ, and each one is an indispensably gifted part of the whole.[8] We might say that an individual finding their identity and 'giftedness' fulfilled in Christ and his mission finds a more secure identity and a higher sense of worth and purpose than would be accessible in a me-centred approach to the world, where identity is forever sought, needing endless defence against encroachment by others. Such agonistic striving for self-definition, which is carried out under pressure from a commodifying late-capitalist culture, is unreliable by comparison with the gift of identity and purpose from Christ, as part of which personal 'gifts' find their truest meaning.

The big picture here, precisely because it is a Christ-formed big picture, is friendlier to the individual than the alternative vision of life provided by post-modern pluralism and late-capitalist commodific-ation. Moreover, it is a big picture that ensures individual 'gifts' are deployed, in no way seeking to thwart them. Indeed, precisely because it is Christ's ministry, being carried out through his members, there can be a version of the rights argument (to exercise one's 'gift') that is in no way individualistic, but grounded rather in the imperative of Christ himself. The plea of Paul for Christians to recognise and respect a diversity of 'gifts' requires those in positions of church leadership to take the 'gifts' of clergy and laity seriously, for to thwart the expression of 'gifts' is to dishonour Christ who gives them. Thus we sense a way beyond the tension between individual and collective in the matter of individual Christian 'giftedness'—individual 'gifts' come from Christ, manifesting our belonging together to his life and his ministry, and precisely as such they demand both recognition and

8. 1 Corinthians 12:12–26.

expression. What is the correct environment for the recognition and development of those 'gifts'?

'Gifts' require a habitat

We have seen that 'gifts' emerge in Christians from their origin in Christ and are ecclesially defined. The church is the context and seedbed of individual Christian 'giftedness'. For Anglicans the primary context of individual formation is through worship in the common prayer tradition, nowadays primarily taking a Eucharistic form. Worship is the primary context of faith formation and empowerment for mission. Mission for most Anglicans is less about saving individuals from the world and more about living a vision of the Kingdom of God in the midst of the world—a vision of life under God nurtured in worship. This connection between church and world, sacred and secular, is an Anglican instinct rooted in an incarnational vision of the church, and strengthened through English history by the continual interpenetration of church and state, reaching back long before the English Reformation and the Elizabethan Settlement. It is in this tradition of worship, faith and practice interwoven in a commitment to the life of the world, that Anglicanism understands 'gifts' for ministry in individual Christians. This 'habitat' of Christian formation elicits and develops 'giftedness'.

One of the ways it does this is through what we might call 'the politics of recognition'. Individual 'gifts' are named, interpreted and shaped by the community and its characteristic agenda. Individuals thus discern their own 'giftedness' with the help of teaching and recognition and encouragement from others. The sense of calling and 'giftedness' in individuals is tested by the church against its best understanding of how Christ operates. And the individual finds the right expression of these 'gifts' in conversation with the faith and order—the understanding of what it is to be a church in the world—characteristic of Anglicanism.

This means, for instance, that personal qualities, a sense of 'giftedness' and calling, are put to the test when people seek ordination. Does the presenting individual have the manner, qualities and spiritual perspective to lead the actual church in its life with the world God loves? Characteristically, firebrands and sectarians will not get far along this path, as a typically Anglican approach to the identity and role of the church guides the politics of recognition. Alternatively, attributes that might mark Christians of other stamps for certain ministries will be differently deployed in Anglicanism. We tend not to see ordained ministry or consecration in religious life as necessarily the highest of callings, for instance, and many lay Anglicans with 'gifts' exercise them in entirely secular callings, or through lay ministries in the church.

But, as I have mentioned, there is a further dimension to the politics of recognition. Urgent agendas for change in Anglican ministry have emerged out of groups formerly excluded from that ministry, with the result that Anglicanism everywhere has experienced a sea change. Women's ministry is widely (though not universally) seen as a valid development of the understanding of priesthood, and the theological arguments for this are widely known. But it is not the case that sober reflection on theological ideas in the abstract provided the sole impetus for change. Rather, real flesh and blood Christian women with obvious 'gifts' for ministry and a sense of calling pressed their claim.

While there was a lot of rights language used, particularly in the home of civil rights, the United States, on the path to women's ordination within Anglicanism, nevertheless the debate was not entirely along these lines. The plain 'giftedness' of women, and the case they championed for the rights of Christ to be represented by both the genders made in God's image, provided equally prominent lines of argument. While women were regularly told that it was unchristian to press their case, and that they should let the male hierarchy sort the matter out in the fullness of time, nevertheless such patriarchal talk is readily deconstructed as no less potentially ego serving than the feminist insistence it purported to criticise.[9] So although it is the case that the church's habitat of faith influences the recognition, development and expression of 'gifts', it is again the case that the

9. See for example the unsparing discussion by Monica Furlong of the Episcopal Ministry Act of the 1993 Church of England General Synod in her 'Introduction' to *Act of Synod—Act of Folly*, edited by Monica Furlong (London: SCM, 1998), 1–13. Those opposed to women's ordination in England insisted on and got their own way, while Movement for the Ordination of Women members had long been told to be patient and not press their case.

demand for a right to the expression of 'gifts', for sound and compelling reasons, also profoundly influences the habitat of faith.

The next instalment of this pattern in Anglicanism is that of gay and lesbian people claiming a right to be ordained. This right is not being pressed in the name of individual rights to equity or to personal fulfilment by all its advocates (though of course it is by some). And, as the Godliness of the case continues to commend itself, we can anticipate a further widespread shift in Anglican sensibility to embrace the change.[10] Hence the politics of recognition is both affirming and transforming of the tradition—on the one hand ensuring that 'gifts' are in keeping with the Anglican vision; on the other hand contributing to the evolution of that tradition as a vehicle for God's work through the Anglican Church.

In all of this there is a strong nexus between 'gift' and role. A 'gift' does not necessarily warrant a role, yet no role is appropriate without a 'gift'. 'Gifts' in Anglicanism are essential precursors for a role in ministry, but the role is not granted—the change in status of the individual is not effected—without that 'gift' being acknowledged and affirmed by the community. Here I want to suggest that 'gift' and acknowledgement, which together make a ministry in the Anglican Church, are best understood in terms of a role in the church's ministry—either 'internally' or in the wider, secular world. Ministry is a role, an identity in the body, conveying status, distinction, marking out difference, honouring diversity, while not sundering the overarching unity of the one ministry of Christ distributed throughout his members.

John Macquarrie gives a good example of this in his discussion of priestly character. This is a traditional catholic doctrine asserting that ordination conveys character, effecting an ontological change—an alteration in the fundamental being or fabric of a person. This notion, linked to the objective reliability of a priest's sacramental ministrations regardless of the personal morality of the priest, was seen as a

---

10. See my discussion of this point in 'Anglican Moral Theology and the Challenge of Same-Sex Unions', in *Faithfulness in Fellowship: Reflections on Homosexuality and the Church* (Melbourne: John Garratt, 2001), 141–60, especially 145–7. This follows Luke Timothy Johnson, *Scripture and Discernment: Decision Making In The Church* (Nashville: Abingdon, 1983), 147.

manifestation of God's faithfulness, not abandoning the work of God's hands. Macquarrie realises that such an image sounds magical and sub-personal nowadays, rightly insisting that God's presence and action through a person cannot be independent of that person's choices. After all, we have seen that 'gifts' from God nevertheless need to be 'stirred up' by those who hold them. So Macquarrie maintains the traditional teaching together with a more personalist contemporary understanding, linking priestly character with role in the network of relationships forming the community.[11]

As our role in a group changes, so we change. Who we are is influenced by becoming a parent, taking a role of leadership or putting on the uniform of our country—not least in the way others' perceptions of us, and their way of relating to us, changes as a result, and as we grow into the new set of expectations. Our being, our ontology, changes as our role within a web of relationships changes. Ordination to the priesthood brings such a changed role—a changed identity in a network of relationships—and hence a changed person, whose priestly character emerges through faithful execution of the 'gift' in performance of the role, with the politics of recognition acting to affirm and encourage the priest in their role. Thus the Anglican conviction that ordination is not purely functional is held together with the equally strong conviction that it is not purely formal.

Certainly an emphasis on 'gifts' expressed in roles, with Christ ultimately the source of both, is an emphasis that saves elitism in the church, including clericalism. It is an organic conception that ideally prevents the egotistical annexation of ministry. 'Gifts' are seen less as personal attributes than manifestations of Christ's presence and glory for the building up of his body and for its ministry in the world. Particular ministry roles are seen as responses to his calling and as part of the working of his body, with no part of the body allowed to lord it over another or declare another unworthy. But is ordained ministry simply a manifestation of the body's own working? Is the special charism of pastoral leadership reducible to a function of the church, or need more be said?

11. John Macquarrie, 'The Church and the Ministry', in *Theology, Church and Ministry* (London: SCM, 1986), 167.

Ordination: beyond functionalism and sacerdotalism

It is a more recent development in Anglican theology to see the ministerial charism as arising from the whole church's priestly calling.[12] Yet Anglican liturgy continues to emphasise the ministry of the priest in terms of being sent to the church, rather than arising from it. While contemporary ordinals include the people of God among those interrogated concerning the fitness of candidates for ordination, including lay examining chaplains and representatives of congregations where would-be clergy have ministered as laypersons, nevertheless it is not the norm for ordained ministers to be raised up from particular congregations to assume positions of leadership in those congregations only. This is happening increasingly with 'distinctive' or 'vocational' deacons, but not with priests. In part this must reflect the Episcopal polity of Anglicanism, embracing a wider conception of the local church than merely the gathered congregation. Ergo, an order of priests finds its focus in the diocese rather than the local congregation, often serving a succession of parishes within a particular diocese across their period of fulltime ministry, if not further afield. In these circumstances, while it is true that everyone's 'giftedness for ministry' comes with their baptism and is nurtured in the bosom of the church, and that invitation and a sense of 'fit' regularly attends pastoral appointments, nevertheless who can doubt that these priests are also sent to these congregations?

Further, my role as a parish priest is not merely to serve and support but to lead, guide and challenge my parish. It is not clear to what extent I am automatically a part of it, as I came to it as a stranger and one day will leave it, while a lot of the lay people remain. I belong to the Anglican Church, and to its Australian manifestation, though not yet fully to my present diocese after only four years in it. It could be argued that I belong more properly to my former parish, or the one I left as a young adult and returned to as a curate, in both of which I am welcomed as a member of the family still. Perhaps we are sent, and only in time does our ministry begin to emerge from the context to which we are sent—that is to say, when eventually we are shaped by the new context, and our ministry is (hopefully) developed and

12. See for example Robin Greenwood, *Transforming Priesthood: A New Theology of Mission and Ministry* (London: SPCK, 1995).

matured by it. So only some while after being invited or sent to the particular community does our ministry come to be a manifestation of the life of that community, and only to the extent that we allow ourselves to be so influenced.

Also requiring consideration is the fact that clericalism and sacerdotalism in Anglican life are fully matched by a strongly contentious lay culture. The resultant mood is often one of 'us versus them', which has been a feature of church life in England since before the Reformation. This native English anticlericalism can be traced back to the fourteenth century Lollards,[13] and is alive and well throughout the Anglican world today. This tendency was confirmed at the Reformation and the Elizabethan Settlement by the insistence on aspects of both Catholic and Protestant order in the Reformed Church of England. The traditional prerogatives of priests and bishops were brought together with a new empowerment of the laity, while the separateness of clergy from laity in lifestyle and in their right of recourse to church courts was removed. Priest and layperson were thus brought together in one form of life, albeit with different callings.

This distinctive Anglican solution has evolved at its best into a truly groundbreaking collaborative vision of ministry where priests and lay people value one another's roles and identities, working together in a joint commitment to mission. Synodical government at its best reflects this state of affairs. But at its worst Anglican church life is an unresolved struggle for power between clergy and laity, the one frustrating the other. At our best, we offer a vision of catholic Christianity with a truly mature church order—the sort of thing many Roman Catholics glimpsed at Vatican II and have yearned for ever since. At our worst, however, we are paralysed—here, progressive clergy are locked in opposition with anxious, backward looking laity; there, progressive laity are thwarted in owning and developing their 'gifts' for ministry by reactionary, controlling clergy.

What can one say? We have an understanding of 'gifts' and ministries adequate to resolve this frequent impasse, and we have evolved a synodical system of government to embody it. Increasingly the rhetoric of ministry and church life is a rhetoric of collaborative leadership. This is as it should be. But will this 'best practice' find expression? Time will tell if we are confident enough to pursue our

---

13. Claire Cross, *Church and People 1450–1660: The Triumph of the Laity in the English Church* (London: Fontana, 1976).

best Anglican instincts in this matter, or else allow ourselves to be polarised by the strident currents that dominate other churches—Rome, with its inappropriately paternalistic control of the laity, and many Protestant churches where there is no structurally mediated prophetic authority from God to reign in whatever licence and disorder.

In this essay I have appealed to the Anglican instinct for creative tension, with particular reference to 'gifts' and the church's ministry in post–modern times. Discussing the recognition of 'giftedness', I have emphasised the appropriateness of seeking expression for 'gifts', though without the motive of self-assertive individualism. Instead the collective vision of life in Christ is seen both as the source of individual 'gifts' and as the context for their recognition, formation and deployment. This vision of ministry, beyond rights and individualism, is the very best guard against the predations of post-modern hyper-individualism and related identity-eroding cultural trappings of late-capitalism in the West more generally. An understanding of 'gifts' is developed in terms of roles within the body of Christ, serving both to protect the church from those who would enterprise it, and protect the individual from an inadequate sense of their own worth and dignity as 'gifted' ambassadors of Christ. In a related move, I have emphasised the feedback that accompanies this process: 'gifts' made manifest influence the church in its politics of recognition, so God's will emerges in an interplay between the individual and the collective.

Anglicanism at its best affirms individuality without individualism, and community without collectivism. It is a distinctive tradition, as we have seen, but it is a tradition not bound by traditionalism, and hence it is able to reinvent itself, as the women's ordination issue has demonstrated. It remains to be seen, however, if we Anglicans can remain true to our best instincts during our present extraordinary period of testing in the life of our Communion.

Part Three: Bridging

Part Three: Bridging

Introduction

The four chapters in this section deal with varying aspects of the institutional life of the church. Approaching the questions from very different angles, the authors examine aspects of the life of the church which cross boundaries of time and framework: governance, faithfulness to biblical principles, managing diversity and power relationships. These central ecclesiological issues are discussed in the context of Anglicanism in contemporary Australia.

Sarah Macneil grapples with some of the issues that arise as the church seeks to reinvent its ways of operating in order to fulfil its mission more effectively. Arguing for the theological significance of governance structures, she discusses the importance of theologically coherent decision-making for the integrity of the church and offers a conceptual framework for ecclesiological discussion by decision-makers involved in effecting change to its structures and processes.

Mark Thompson contends that the Anglican Church in Australia is at serious risk of losing its way. If it is to have a future as an institution it needs significant reorientation to the character and purposes of God. There needs to be a wholesale return to biblical truth and to the patterns of behaviour which flow out of the gospel. Critical to this will be a realisation that the local congregations are the church of God on earth and the denomination a service organisation.

In his examination of Anglican diversity and conflict, using the lens of a current debate between three prominent Anglican churchmen (Kevin Giles, Peter Jensen and Peter Carnley), Duncan Reid highlights the fragmentedness of Australian Anglicanism at the dawn of the third millennium. The difficult challenge facing Australian Anglicans is to manage this diversity and to determine its tolerable limits.

Alan Cadwallader conducts a painstaking examination of the complex and constantly changing character of the relationships between Anglican Church leaders, church members and society, arguing that the dynamics of power and authority vary markedly when seen from differing angles. Using the concept of triangulation as a conceptual framework for his discussion, he argues that the most fruitful mode of discourse between the three (leaders, members and society) is a non-authoritarian, horizontal approach.

This section shows very clearly the diversity of voice and approach characterising the Anglican Church in Australia today. Fundamental to each of these essays is, however, a passionate concern for the theological and institutional health of the Christian community.

9

Body Image: Ecclesiology And Governance In Changing Times

Sarah Macneil

> Where thinges have beene instituted, which being convenient and good at the first, do afterwares in processe of time waxe otherwise; we make no doubt but that they may be altered, yea, though councells or customes generall have receaved them.[1]

> The Church . . . must commit itself to each new day . . . afresh, accept the changes and transformations of history and human life, and constantly be willing to reform, to renew, to rethink.[2]

> Your body image is how you perceive, think and feel about your body. This may have no bearing at all on your actual appearance . . . A distorted body image can lead to self-destructive behaviour.[3]

Body image? At first blush, it might seem a little odd to link this deeply physical concept with theological discourse. However, in this chapter I will be arguing that accurate understanding of our empirical ecclesial reality, of our body as church, is just as important to

1. Richard Hooker, *Of the Lawes of Ecclesiastical Polity, Book 4.14.5*, in *The Folger Library Edition of The Works of Richard Hooker*, volume 1, edited by G Edelen (Cambridge, Massachusetts: Belknap Press, (1977) 1995), 340.
2. Hans Küng, *The Church* (London: Burns & Oates, 1967), 14.
3. Better Health Channel quoted on http://www.healthinsite.-gov.au/-topics/Body_Image, accessed 18 February 2006.

ecclesiological discussion as an accurate body image is to our physical health. As Australian Anglicans respond to a new environment and implement structural transformation, we need to be aware of the way in which our structures shape us and articulate understandings about the nature of God and of humanity. We are the body of Christ—how do Australian Anglicans live that reality today and how do we want to live it in the future?

In this chapter, I will argue that the particular situation in which the Anglican Church of Australia currently finds itself is such that institutional change at a profound level is imminent. This change will inevitably involve altering the governance structures of the church. Such changes are theologically significant and have identity implications. To push my analogy, they will affect our body. It is important, therefore, that they are made in an intentional and theologically coherent way, rather than as a set of haphazard responses to particular crises.

For our religious life to be faithful to its calling, it is imperative that we seek to respond in a godly way to the opportunities and challenges opening up before us, genuinely seeking God's will for the church and acting in a way which is consistent with the teachings of Jesus. We should be embarking on a profoundly theological enterprise, grounded in careful hermeneutics, prayer, institutional awareness and rigorous discussion.

Moreover, the decision-making structures of the Anglican Church of Australia are such that it is important that this ecclesiological conversation happens at a grass roots level and in a way which is widely accessible.

The synodical system offers, at least in principle, a sharing of decision-making power among the membership of the church. In his chapter on authority and power Alan Cadwallader has graphically described the risks of dysfunctionality in these processes. I take an optimistic view, namely that a genuine, broad-based discourse can take place and be the basis for theologically coherent decision-making. For this to happen, however, it is essential that the ecclesiological conversation is framed in a way which clearly connects the reality of the life of the church with the life of faith and God's calling to the church.

I have entered this discourse essentially as a practitioner, rather than as a theoretician. Praxis and theory belong together, of course. Praxis which is not informed by theory risks incoherence and meaninglessness. Theory which is not informed by praxis risks irrelevance. As we seek to put in place new governance mechanisms we face an enormous challenge to hold praxis and theory in productive dialogue.

In this chapter I will begin by discussing the reality of change in our society and some of the particular challenges facing the Anglican communion. This will lead into a discussion of the institutional response to those challenges and the governance implications. The ecclesiological significance of governance, both as an expression of theological understandings and as formative of ecclesial identity will then be considered. The importance of theological input to the governance change process is affirmed. The final section of the chapter critiques the current academic theological discourse, suggesting it operates at too abstract a level, and proposes an 'intermediate' theological conversation, connecting the ecclesial ideal and the empirical reality.

The reality of change in our society

It has become a truism, and one I do not wish to challenge, that we live in an age of exponential change. Stephen Pattison draws attention to the consequences of this for business organisations:

> There is, of course, nothing new about change in itself. Every individual or institution changes gradually, often imperceptibly, over time. It is the volume, rapidity, radicality and discontinuity of the changes which are presently occurring which is new and which requires managing. In response to rapid technological, competitive and other changes, business organisations are changing shape, changing their fundamental *raison d'être*, changing their ways of doing business, changing patterns of ownership, downsizing and changing their culture.[4]

---

4. Stephen Pattison, *The Faith of the Managers* (London: Cassell, 1997), 120.

In doing this, these organisations are reflecting what is happening generally throughout our society. The industrial society has given way to the technology-driven information society.

Large movements of people throughout the nineteenth and twentieth centuries, through both voluntary and involuntary migration, coupled with the information revolution, have brought increased awareness of cultural and religious diversity. In Australia, ethnically homogeneous communities have given way to multicultural communities and a Christian monoculture has been displaced by religious plurality.

These changes have been accompanied by a reconfiguring of social organisation at the most fundamental level: that of the family. In 1969, 7.1% of families with dependent children were lone parent families. By 2003, that proportion had risen to 22.3%. In 1976, 64.5% of the population aged over fifteen were married. In 2001, that figure had dropped to only 54.6%. Over the same period, living together without getting married has become increasingly common, both as a temporary phase before marriage and as a long term choice.[5]

There is also mounting pressure on organisations and institutions to change. Moreover, the rate of change within our society means that the trend is towards lean, focussed organisations with quick decision-making processes and quick outcome delivery times.

Changes in the wider society have been accompanied by change within the church. Over the last fifty years, the face of Anglicanism in Australia has changed considerably. To name but a few developments: new liturgies have found their ways into regular usage, women have been ordained as deacons and priests in most dioceses, people who have been divorced are able to be remarried in church, low fee Anglican schools have been established and Anglican dioceses have become partners with government in the provision of professional welfare services through Anglicare agencies. The institution continues to change under our feet.

It seems to me, however, that we are entering a significant new phase of institutional change, one in which we will be examining the very heart of our institutional structures and decision-making processes. Rather than tinkering at the edges, adapting in a piecemeal

---

5. A Nevile, 'What do Australian Families Look like Today', in *State of the Family 2005*, edited by S Leppert (Canberra: Anglicare Australia, 2005), 7–12.

fashion to the changes that are occurring, the next decades will see fundamental changes in the way in which we structure the institution of which we are a part. Some of the most basic patterns of our lives together are being opened for debate and change. The predominance of the parish as the core grass roots community within which people gather to worship, and the synodical process based on formal parliamentary practice are but two of the fundamental church structures which are being increasingly scrutinised. Indeed, in many places basic structural change has already begun.[6]

These changes are occurring in response to the particular challenges facing Anglicanism at the start of the new millennium. In the next section I will examine some of those challenges and then consider the response to those challenges. This will lead us into a discussion of the institutional changes that will be needed to give effect to that response.

Two challenges facing the Anglican Communion

In this section I wish to consider two major challenges facing both the Anglican communion internationally and the member dioceses of the Anglican Church of Australia. The first of these challenges is the perceived decline of the Anglican Church within Western society, a phenomenon closely linked to religious pluralism. The second challenge is of a different nature, and is essentially endogenous: the entrenched divisions within Anglicanism, both internationally and in Australia.

It has become a commonplace to reflect on pluralism within Western culture and on the challenges that it poses for our church. As it has become an increasingly important feature of our society, there has been a parallel decline in the significance of the denomination and in its influence in the society. After the ecclesiastical boom times of the 1950s and early 1960s, the later decades of the twentieth century have been characterised by this sense of decline through much of Western

6. For example, the Governance Ordinance 2000 of the Diocese of Canberra and Goulburn provided for non-parish ministry units to be established and be part of the decision-making structures of the diocese.

Anglicanism, including the Anglican Church of Australia.[7] David Hilliard comments:

> At the end of the twentieth century Australian Anglicanism was a less confident and a less unified body than it had been thirty years earlier. Like other old-established religious institutions, it was finding it difficult to engage with a pluralist and multicultural society.[8]

The divisions which have long permeated the Anglican communion worldwide have also been increasingly evident in recent years. The Anglican principle of episcopal leadership and synodical government has been locally enculturated wherever Anglicanism has taken root. This has given strength and cultural relevance to member churches. It has also inevitably led to diversity and adaptability. The gospel speaks in each place and each time and each responds as it is able. However, the cultural and hermeneutic differences within worldwide Anglicanism are now so great that it is naïve to think we can walk together in some sort of simple uniformity. Diversity within the Anglican communion has brought it to the point of crisis. This crisis is, however, not simply a crisis of the international Anglican communion. It also exists within Australian Anglicanism with relationships between dioceses strained almost to breaking point over issues such as the ordination of women, both as priests and bishops, the role of practising homosexuals within the life of the church and lay presidency of the eucharist.

These controversies reflect deep differences of hermeneutical approach and theological conclusions, not least in the area of ecclesiology. These differences have recently been explicit in an ongoing dialogue between the former Primate of the Anglican Church of Australia, Dr Peter Carnley, and the Archbishop of Sydney, Dr Peter

---

7. For a detailed examination of the various factors at work in Australian Anglicanism during this period, see David Hilliard's chapter 'Pluralism and New Alignments in Society and Church', in *Anglicanism in Australia*, edited by B Kaye (Melbourne: Melbourne University Press, 2002), 124–48.
8. *Ibid*, 147.

Jensen. This dialogue is discussed in greater depth in Duncan Reid's chapter on diversity.

It is clear that Anglicanism is at best the home of a vigorous diversity and at worst a denomination divided. It could be argued that this has always been the case,[9] but the critical question in our time is whether the divisions are such that the denomination itself will actually split along one or more of the fault lines which have become increasingly evident.

Concerns about this situation at international level have prompted a number of attempts to foster greater unity within the communion. The proposals of the Windsor Report are, of course, the most recent of these. It remains to be seen whether there will be any move to greater unity or whether the centrifugal forces driving the communion apart are too strong to resist.

So central are these questions of pluralism and declining attendance on the one hand, and internal division on the other, that the first four issues of the *Journal of Anglican Studies* were dominated by discussions of the challenges of diversity, both within Anglicanism itself and in the cultures of which we are a part.

The institutional response: a focus on mission

In a response to the phenomenon of pluralism and declining attendance, there has been within Anglicanism a renewed focus on actively seeking new membership through mission. This focus takes seriously the Biblical command to 'make disciples of all nations' (Matthew 28:19) and recaptures the missionary roots of the church. Moreover, it serves both to recruit new members and to unify in a common purpose those who are already members. The power of an external focus in bringing previously divided people together should not be underestimated. The response of so many around the world to the tsunami crisis in early 2005 is an excellent example of normal

9. In his article 'Has the Anglican General Synod Turned the Corner?', *St Mark's Review*, number 186, (2001): 23–30, Bruce Kaye argues this point cogently in relation to the Anglican Church of Australia.

obstacles and divisions being overridden in the face of an external need.[10]

In the space of a decade the Church of England produced two reports dealing with the theology and the practical issues surrounding active, outward-looking mission. The first 'Breaking New Ground: Church Planting in the Church of England' was published in 1994.[11] The second, 'Mission-shaped Church: Church Planting and Fresh Expressions of Church in a Changing Context' followed in 2004.[12]

The Anglican Church in Australia is also intentionally positioning itself to respond to the challenges of our times. The Diocese of Sydney has long been seeking to find ways of spreading the gospel. It states its Diocesan mission in the following terms: 'To glorify God by proclaiming our saviour the Lord Jesus Christ in prayerful dependence on the Holy Spirit, so that everyone will hear his call to repent, trust and serve Christ in love, and be established in the fellowship of his disciples while they await his return.' The Diocese has now adopted a goal of seeing ten per cent of the people of Sydney in Bible-based churches in ten years.[13]

The Anglican Diocese of Canberra and Goulburn has appointed an Assistant Bishop with particular episcopal responsibility for developing and implementing a missional strategy within the diocese. The three neighbouring dioceses of Riverina, Bathurst and Canberra and Goulburn, which cover more than two thirds of NSW, worked together in Lent 2005 on a program of events designed to encourage a missional focus in the dioceses.

The October 2004 General Synod of the Anglican Church of Australia identified the need for a missional focus and the March 2005

---

10. Alistair Mant, in his book *Intelligent Leadership* develops the concept of ternary focus. In discussing leadership he argues that a good leader will encourage people to look beyond themselves and their own concerns to the particular task in hand—to take a ternary approach. Alistair Mant, *Intelligent Leadership*, (St Leonards, NSW: Allen and Unwin, 1997), 5–17.

11. Church of England House of Bishops, *Breaking New Ground* (London: Church House Publishing, 1994).

12. Church of England Mission and Public Affairs Council, *Mission-shaped Church* (London: Church House Publishing, 1994).

13. Mission statement and goal from the Diocese of Sydney's home page: www.sydneyanglican.asn.au .

meeting of the Standing Committee started the process of determining and implementing strategies to assist the national church in this area.

As we change institutional structures to facilitate this focus on mission, what are the issues we need to consider? Many of the strategies proposed involve the creation of new communities of faith which do not fit the traditional parish structure. Finding ways of providing theological and administrative oversight for these comm.-unities will involve changes to the governance arrangements of our dioceses.

Also on the restructuring agenda are the governance arrangements linking quasi-autonomous Anglican entities such as schools, and social justice and welfare agencies to Diocesan structures. In his chapter in this book, Ray Cleary has highlighted a number of issues concerning the nexus between the life of the gathered Christian community and the delivery of welfare programs and social critique.

The proliferation of non-traditional Anglican faith communities also raises important questions of synodical representation. How are these faith communities to be included in the decision-making processes of the denomination?

As we grapple with these issues, an important question to ask is whether changes to governance arrangements have any significance. In the next section I will argue that the answer to that question is an emphatic yes. Changes to governance arrangements are in no way neutral. They carry theological significance and have implications for Anglican identity: they need to be soundly based and theologically coherent.

The significance of governance

It could be argued that the governance mechanisms of religious institutions are merely tools and of little significance. If we were to take the 1962 Constitution of the Anglican Church of Australia as our example, such an argument might suggest that in agreeing to the 1962 Constitution, Australian Anglicans have done no more than agree to a certain set of ground rules by which they will conduct their business together. It could be posited that these ground rules are simply instruments designed to enable members of the Anglican Church of Australia to cooperate on matters of mutual interest. Just as the rules of the game are not the game itself but rather enable the game to be played, so the Constitution is not the Anglican Church in Australia. It could be argued, therefore, that governance mechanisms are of no great importance and, indeed, not an appropriate subject of theological discourse or concern.

This somewhat disingenuous interpretation of the role of governance in general, and of the 1962 Constitution in the life of Australian Anglicanism in particular, does not stand up to closer examination. Institutional governance mechanisms formalise the distribution of power, set roles and codify relationships. The particular arrangements in each institution reflect certain understandings about the roles of various groups within the institution, about the importance of certain activities and about the core business of the institution. It is also the case that the structures and processes that human beings create to order their relationships are expressions of their beliefs about the nature of humanity. They carry within them statements about the nature of relationship. The very existence of institutions presupposes human relationship. Their existence speaks of both an ability and a desire to meet and work together for common ends. In providing mechanisms for the resolution of disagreement, institutional structures acknowledge the inherent tendency for that cooperative desire to break down and for relationship to be impaired. Such mechanisms also point to a desire for reconciliation and harmony.

The quality of the relationships expressed in the organisational structures will vary according to the type of organisation. In religious institutions, quality of relationship is explicitly linked to an understanding of the nature of God and of the relationship between God and humanity. The way in which this relationship is expressed in the structures and processes of the institution has, therefore, profound theological significance. Not only do the structures and processes speak of the nature of the relationship between humans, but also of the relationship between God and humanity.

Governance cannot, therefore, be seen as theologically neutral. The 1997 Virginia Report expresses the link between structure and theology in the following terms:

> in the way [the structures of the Church] are ordered as well as in the way they inter-relate and function they are to reflect and embody the fundamental reality

> of the Church's life—its communion in the life and love of God, Father, Son and Holy Spirit.[14]

One of the primary tasks of theology is to evaluate and critique the life of the community of faith. If, as Colin Gunton has asserted, 'the Church is called to be the kind of reality at a finite level that God is in eternity',[15] then the actual embodiment of that reality is an appropriate subject for theological discourse. This call for coherence between the eternal divine presence and the finite ecclesial community confronts us with a dual challenge: firstly, to understand as best we might the nature of God, and secondly, to determine whether the church is, in its empirical, finite manifestations, reflecting that reality.

One of the ways in which that reality is embodied is through the governance mechanisms of the particular community of faith. The various structures and processes by which we govern ourselves, in any field, can be understood as codified relationships. Governance at its simplest can be expressed in the formula: 'Who decides what and how'. The governance mechanisms of religious institutions embody, either explicitly or implicitly, positions on the balance between diversity and unity and on the nature of the relationship between the divine and the human. They have, therefore, an inescapable theological dimension. Moreover, their theological significance lies not just in the fact that they reify the abstract but also in the manner in which the abstract is reified.

This is true at all levels of our ecclesial life, from the most local to the most universal. What we do in Parish Council and how we do it expresses something of our understanding of God—it matters theologically. How Anglican churches from around the world respond structurally to the challenges facing the Anglican communion matters.

---

14. *The Virginia Report: The Report of the Inter-Anglican Theological and Doctrinal Commission 1997,* section 5.3: http://www.anglican-communion.org/documents/virginia/english/index.html .
15. Colin Gunton, 'The Church on Earth: The Roots of Community' in *On Being the Church*, edited by Colin Gunton and Dan Hardy (Edinburgh: T&T Clark, 1989), 78.

Anglicanism in Australia: governance and identity

The particular structure of Anglicanism has important consequences for the manner in which ecclesiological discourse is undertaken. Anglicanism has successfully enculturated itself across much of the globe, adapting the general principle of episcopal leadership and synodical government to local circumstance. Because of this there is much local diversity, as we have noted earlier in this chapter.

Individuals' experience of Anglicanism is mediated through local particularity. Anglicans in Australia today are formed as people of God through the mediating structures of the Anglican Church of Australia. These mediating structures, which include the governance arrangements of the church, both bear and contribute to a sense of ecclesial identity for Australian Anglicans. This is not to say, however, that the international Anglican communion, with its shared history and areas of cooperation, is irrelevant to Australian Anglicans' sense of identity as Anglicans. Indeed, as Australian Anglicans form their identity as people of God, the context in which they do so is one of local particularity which nonetheless links in to a global network, a network within which the local particularity has been and continues to be shaped. Anglican identity draws on a perichoretic dance of the global and the particular.

In the second part of this chapter I will argue that this has consequences for the nature of ecclesiogical discourse within Australian Anglicanism, critique the academic discourse and offer an 'intermediate' theological narrative. The directness of the language may jar theologians and, indeed, seem imprecise. But what I am attempting here is to start a conversation, rather than carefully tie up all the loose ends. Moreover, I write from the point of view of somebody whose life is spent dealing with the practical questions which arise, both at diocesan and at parish level, when groups of people wrestle with institutional change in the church. How do we have the conversations which help us to decide what are the appropriate changes to make? What language, what theological concepts help us winnow the ecclesial wheat from the chaff as we attempt to retain the essentials and respond to what we believe is God's call to us now?

Ecclesiology and governance in Australian Anglicanism: the case for a broadly based discourse

A detailed analysis of the theological principles embedded in our governance structures would take more space than we have available here. However, as we have noted earlier, two of the governance mechanisms under current scrutiny are the parish and the synodical process. As we consider alternative structures and processes, it is important that we are aware of the theological principles embedded in these existing mechanisms.

In Anglicanism, the fundamental building block of decision-making is the synodical process. Indeed, the principle of lay and clerical participation in ecclesiastical decision-making was articulated by Richard Hooker in the seventeenth century: 'we are to hold it a thing most consonant with equitie and reason that no *Ecclesiasticall* lawe be made in a *Christian Commonwealth* without consent as well of the laitie as of the Clergie'.[16] In Australia, little power is vested in the national church body, the General Synod, and it is the diocesan synod which is the engine-house of change. The decisions which will be taken to effect institutional change in the Anglican Church in Australia will, for the most part, be taken in diocesan synods.

These synods bring together both clergy and laity in a broad-based body representing the ecclesial life of the diocese and making decisions that will affect the life of the church in that diocese. Although the development of diocesan synods in Australia has created a situation where local conditions have produced local solutions,[17] there is a fundamental ecclesiological principle they hold in common. As Bruce Kaye has noted, 'because of the way in which they emerged in the middle of the nineteenth century they also institutionalised a way of settling questions which involved the whole church community'.[18] Indeed, former Primate, Archbishop Peter Carnley, has referred to

16. Hooker, *Lawes*, Book 8.6.7, in *The Folger Library Edition of the Works of Richard Hooker*, volume III, edited by P Stanwood (Cambridge, Massachusetts: Harvard, 1981), 404 (emphasis retained).
17. Bruce Kaye outlines this development in 'The Strange Birth of Anglican Synods in Australia and the 1850 Bishops' Conference', *Journal of Religious History*, 27/2 (2003): 177–97.
18. *Ibid*, 196.

synods as 'the living voice of the church'.[19] The synodical system speaks of interdependence, the sharing of power and, ideally, of mutual respect. No one person or group has a monopoly of power, nor of the knowledge of the will of God for the dioceses.

This mutuality and interdependence of the whole people of God is reflected within parish governance. The decision-making processes of clergy, wardens and parish council speak of shared responsibility within the faith community. Both the clerical incumbent and the lay members of the parish carry responsibility for appointing wardens and councillors, underlining the basic principle that neither the clerical nor the lay voice should predominate in the governance of the community of faith.

This is not to deny the potential for dysfunction, nor for corruption of process within the system. It does, however, point to an ideal of shared power and mutual interdependence.

It may be, as suggested earlier, that these governance structures of synods and parishes need to be changed or adapted. The quick decision times of today's society suggest that annual synods and even monthly or bi-monthly meetings of the Standing Committees of the synod are ineffective governance mechanisms when dealing with the intersection of diocese and secular society. At national level this institutional sluggishness is even more startling. Justice Keith Mason has commented:

> The Constitution of the national Church now called the Anglican Church of Australia which came into effect in 1962 has so many checks and balances that it makes the United States Constitution look like a unitary dictatorship.[20]

The technologically driven changing face of human groupings suggests that non-geographically based worshipping communities will increasingly become part of the life of the church. As we develop new governance arrangements for these changing circumstances, the

---

19. Peter Carnley, interview with author, 13 November 2000.
20. K Mason, *Controlling Conscience: The Role of Law in the Struggle for Women's Ordination*, Theological College Occasional Paper, number 1, (Brisbane: St Francis' Theological College), 11.

theological import of the existing mechanisms and of the proposed innovations must be part of the discourse.

Given the broadly based decision-making structures of Anglicanism in Australia, it is important that as we consider institutional change and ponder the meaning of 'things necessary' and 'things indifferent' for our time, the theological discourse happens on as broad a base as possible, involving as many members of the church as possible.

Abstract discussion of the nature of God must be linked with the empirical reality of the structures of the church and in a way which is accessible to a group wider than academic theologians. Much academic theology is obscure to the average reader and its insights tend not to be part of the everyday discussions of church members, whether those discussions happen in parish councils, over a bottle of wine at dinner or in diocesan councils.

The academic discourse: the trinitarian paradigm

As theologians over the centuries have reflected on the nature of the church, the doctrine of the Trinity has proven to be a rich seam to mine:

> Christian community is God-centred or it is nothing . . . The church that satisfies postmoderns in their search for real spirituality will allow God to be himself—the giant and glorious Trinitarian mystery, never properly encompassed, always unpredictable, and always available to be explored afresh.[21]

Current accounts of the church are usually based on this doctrine, seeing the relationships posited within the godhead as definitive of the ideal state for the church.[22] Varying understandings of the nature of those relationships lead inevitably to varying understandings of the

21. B Jackson, *Hope for the Church* (London: Church House Publishing, 2002), 185.
22. A useful overview is given by Anne Hunt, 'Trinity and Church: Explorations in Ecclesiology from a Trinitarian Perspective', *St Mark's Review*, number 198 (2005): 32–44.

distribution of power within the church. Implicit in this approach is the doctrine of the *imago dei*. If we human beings are made in the image of God, then the nature of our community, once redeemed by Christ from the disfigurements of sin, will reflect the nature of God.

> The Church is called in Christ and through the Spirit, to model or to be a sign of that *communion* which is the very being of God and the shape of his desire for the perfection of the cosmos. God's intention that creation and humanity should have at their heart the power and the will for mutual interrelatedness becomes the internal shape and the external witness and gospel of the Church.[23]

I wish to suggest, however, that this approach perhaps does not go far enough theologically. It speaks of an ideal situation, calling us to bridge the proleptic gap between the present and the eternal. This risks leaving us only able to lament the present, flawed, divided state of the church as a sinful disfigurement, with no conceptual framework to bridge the gap between the vision of the eternal reality and the empirical ecclesial reality within which we live.

Moreover, it offers an image of the life of the church which risks being seen as a static, self-contained model: the three persons of the Trinity are not subject to the constant change that is the lot of humanity. Co-eternal, the Trinity is as it was, is now and ever shall be, world without end. Humanity, on the other hand, lives in a constant cycle of birth and death, of decay and renewal. Linking the structures of the church too closely to a Trinitarian model could lead to an understanding of church structure as immutable.

It is also essentially a self-contained image, without an explicit linkage to anything beyond itself. Just as the Trinity can be described as a self-contained unity of three persons in one being, so could the church be thought to be sufficient unto itself, rather than deeply embedded in human society.

In the next section I will propose an intermediate account of the church which preserves the trinitarian insights of mutual interdependence and love and yet speaks more clearly of linkages between the nature of God and the realities of human society. This account is based

---

23. Robin Greenwood, *Practising Community* (London: SPCK 1996), 48.

on the two great commandments and on the Pauline image of the body of Christ. It is, I believe, a potentially more fruitful basis on which to build theological discussions about institutional change. It is also more immediate, more concrete, and, I believe, more readily understood by those who are not schooled in academic theology.[24] We need to question the accessibility of the Trinitarian paradigm when stated in ideal form and its usefulness in a wide-ranging discourse. In some irritation and frustration, a parishioner commented, 'I don't find it particularly useful when someone attempts to explain the mystery of the nature of God by offering another mystery, the Trinity.' I suspect he is not alone. The Trinity is essentially a mystery and the nature of the relationship between the three members of the Trinity is a matter of supposition and conjecture on our part.

The body of Christ and the two great commandments

The powerful Pauline analogy of the Christian community as the body of Christ (developed at length in 1 Corinthians 12) provides a readily accessible theological image of great depth. It is an image which holds within it the notion of the Christian community as an enfleshed reality and also as a foretaste of the community of the godhead.

As members of the body of Christ, each Chritstian is differentiated, with individual particularity, just as arms, legs, eyes and ears are different from each other. Each member contains the imprint of God throughout their being, just as every part of our physical body carries our DNA. Each member is, however, dependent on the others and unable as an individual to reflect the nature of the whole.

And yet each member, as well as being an individual, is part of a organic whole, and that organic whole mirrors both the divinity and th humanity of Jesus in a way that the individual members do no Inasmuch as the church does this, then it can be thought to participate i some measure in the Trinity. As community, we are drawn by Chris into the very heart of the godhead.

The image of the church as the body of Christ is essentially a static image—a description of the community as a whole and of the way in which the component parts are linked in a symbiotic relationship.

24. This view has been confirmed, albeit on a small scale, through conversations held with ministry students and with parishioners.

However, just as the trinitarian paradigm of the church is open to varying readings, particularly of the power relationships that operate within the godhead, so too does the image of the body of Christ carry interpretative ambivalence. Although the text contains within it the statement 'the members of the body that seem to be weaker are indispensable' (1 Corinthians 12:22), and stresses the interdependence of the members, a very literal reading of the metaphor could well lead to the elaboration of a hierarchy of importance based on the human body. How tempting to see oneself as the heart, or at least a major organ, and your opponent as the appendix!

It is here that the practical, ethical instruction of the two great commandments can be applied as the yardstick by which relationships within the body of Christ are measured:

> One of the scribes came near and heard them disputing with one another, and seeing that he answered them well, he asked him, 'Which commandment is the first of all?' Jesus answered, 'The first is, "Hear, O Israel: the Lord our God, the Lord is one; you shall love the Lord your God with all your heart, and with all your soul, and with all your mind, and with all your strength." The second is this, "You shall love your neighbour as yourself". There is no other commandment greater than these.' [25]

The imperative to live in loving relationship with God, with others and with oneself applies the corrective to any tendency to assert one's dominance over another. Moreover, the clear instruction that we are to love our neighbours as ourselves applies not just within church communities, but takes us beyond the walls of the church to the societies within which we live.

A productive dialogue

Having argued for this mediating ecclesiological discourse, it remains for me to suggest how it can be brought to bear on the actual questions facing us. At the decision-making level, whether it be local, diocesan, or national, the ecclesiological questions should be consciously before

25. Mark 12:28–31 (NRSV).

us. The questions will vary, depending on the issues involved, but they might well look something like this:

1) How does what we are proposing to do, whatever it might be, embody the ecclesiological principles of interconnectedness, interdependence and mutual respect?
2) Do the power relationships express a mutuality of responsibility?
3) Do the roles and functions in our organisation (parish, welfare agency, diocese and others) allow the members of the body of Christ to use their gifts for the benefit of the organisation?
4) Do the goals of our organisation reflect love of God and love of neighbour?

There is, of course, nothing distinctively Anglican about these questions, which flow from the Biblical texts I have offered as paradigmatic. There are further questions which can help locate the discourse within the frameworks of Anglicanism:

5) Is there anything in Anglican tradition which might serve as a template?
6) Are the 'bottom lines' of Anglicanism[26] honoured in ways which also enable positive responses to be given to the first four questions?

---

26. The 'bottom lines' of Anglicanism are usually understood to be those embodied in the 1888 Lambeth Quadrilateral which identifies four 'absolutely essential features of the Anglican position': the holy Scriptures of the Old and New Testaments, the Apostles' and Nicene Creeds, the two dominical sacraments (baptism and eucharist), and the historic episcopate. William Reed Huntington, cited in Paul Avis, *Anglicanism and the Christian Church* (Edinburgh: T&T Clark, 1989), 305. More recent texts use the phrase 'episcopally led and synodically governed' to describe the commonality of the members of the Anglican communion. See for example Appendix One of the Windsor Report: http://www.anglicancommunion.org/windsor2004/downloads/windsor2004c.pdf (accessed 18 February 2006).

These questions are not intended to be prescriptive; they are simply 'interface questions', indicative of the way in which the productive dialogue between theory and praxis might be formulated.

Conclusion

I can think of no time in my life when it has been more important to engage in theological discussion at grassroots level. The opportunities and challenges faced by Anglicanism in the new millennium have a direct impact on how we meet together as church. This is true at all levels of our church life: locally, at diocesan level and nationally. The structural changes we will make as we respond to these opportunities and challenges are theologically loaded. In a complex set of interactions the structures and processes both speak of and help form our beliefs about who we are as disciples of Jesus Christ and members of the Anglican Church. The responses we make to the environment in which we live, move and have our being, will have an impact on the shape of the church in the years to come and on the way in which our successors will understand who they are as Christians and who they are as Anglicans. The stakes are high.

In this chapter I have argued that the changes we make will best serve the future church if they are informed by a constructive ecclesiological conversation that engages all those involved in the decision-making processes, whether they be clergy or lay, academic theologians, synod representatives or parish councillors. This conversation must, moreover, be grounded in the empirical ecclesial reality of Australian Anglicanism, at parish, diocesan and national level.

I have made some suggestions about how this conversation might happen and look forward to the debate continuing.

In the midst of it all, however, may we never lose sight of the fact that the institutional life of the church exists solely to be of service to God and to the people of God. As the English theologian, Janet Morley, has written:

> Holy God,
> whose presence is known
> in the structures we build,
> and also in their collapse;

establish in us a community of hope,
not to contain your mystery
but to be led beyond security
into your sacred space,
through Jesus Christ, Amen. [27]

27. Janet Morley, *All Desires Known* (London: SPCK, 1992). Collect for Epiphany 4, 8

10

The Church Of God And The Anglican Church of Australia

Mark D Thompson

It is often argued that Anglican evangelicals are strong on the gospel but weak on the church. In other words, Anglican evangelicals are said to have neglected ecclesiology in their concern for individual soteriology. The result, we are told, is an idiosyncratic—in some cases strident—individualism which leads to congregationalism and denominational disengagement. This caricature has persisted despite a constant stream of articles and books on the nature, function and future of the church from the pens of Anglican evangelical scholars and churchmen.[1] It has also persisted despite repeated protests from

1. See for example: JC Ryle, 'The Church', in *Knots Untied* (1871, thirty-first edition), (London: James Clarke, 1954), 157–74; DWB Robinson, 'The Church in the New Testament', *St Mark's Review*, 17 (1959): 4–14; DWB Robinson, *The Church of God: Its Form and Unity* (Punchbowl, NSW: Jordan, 1965); DWB Robinson, 'The Doctrine of the Church and its Implications for Evangelism', *Interchange*, 15 (1974): 156–62; DWB Robinson, ' "The Church" Revisited: An Autobiographical Fragment', *Reformed Theological Review*, 48 (1989): 4–14; AM Stibbs, *God's Church: A Study in the Biblical Doctrine of the People of God* (London: IVF, 1959); AM Stibbs, *The Unity that Matters* (Marcham Manor, 1968); WJ Dumbrell, 'The Meaning and Use of Ekklesia in the New Testament with Special Reference to its Old Testament Background' (Unpublished MTh Thesis, University of London, 1966); DB Knox, 'Demythologizing the Church', *Reformed Theological Review*, 32 (1973): 48–55; DB Knox, 'The Biblical Concept of Fellowship', in *Explorations 2: Church, Worship and the Local Congregation*, edited by BG Webb (Homebush West, NSW: Lancer, 1987), 59–82; DB Knox, 'The Church, the Churches and the Denominations of the Churches', *Reformed Theological Review*, 48 (1989): 15–25; JI Packer, *A Kind of*

evangelicals that the disengagement which has occurred is generated, not by a neglect of biblical ecclesiology on the part of evangelicals but by a departure from orthodox theology and practice on the part of key denominational bodies and leaders. At present the Anglican communion is in crisis, not because of a lack of ecclesiological reflection—Anglican theologians sometimes seem to write on little else—but because significant sections of this association of church networks have proposed innovations which entail a repudiation of biblical authority on a range of doctrines and ethical issues.

Evangelical reflection upon the nature and function of the churches and the denominations is demonstrably rich and productive. In particular, evangelical theologians and biblical scholars in the diocese of Sydney have been involved in serious and extensive discussion of the biblical doctrine of the church and the role of denominational structures throughout the second half of the twentieth century. Most notably the biblical studies of Donald Robinson (Vice-Principal of Moore College, 1959–75; Archbishop of Sydney, 1982–93) and the theological reflection of Broughton Knox (Principal of Moore College, 1959–85) raised the profile of evangelical Anglican ecclesiology in many quarters. This contribution has itself been misunderstood and caricatured. Its deeply theological character is strangely and persistently overlooked while the charge is made that it is based upon a narrow word study of εκκλησια. One noted British author is said to have told his students that the understanding of the church presented by Knox and Robinson is unbiblical and unanglican (without justifying

---

Noah's Ark: The Anglican Commitment to Comprehensiveness (Oxford: Latimer House, 1981); LL Morris, *What's a Nice Church Like Ours Doing in a World Like This?* (Sydney: Anglican Information Office, 1983); GA Cole, 'The Doctrine of the Church: Towards Conceptual Clarification', in *Explorations 2: Church, Worship and the Local Congregation*, edited by BG Webb (Homebush West, NSW: Lancer, 1987), 3–17; PT O'Brien, 'The Church as a Heavenly and Eschatological Entity', in *The Church in the Bible and the World*, edited by DA Carson (Exeter/Grand Rapids: Paternoster/Baker, 1987), 88–119; MD Thompson, 'Does the Local Church Have a Mission?', in *Explorations 7: Exploring the Missionary Church*, edited by BG Webb (Homebush West, NSW: Lancer, 1994), 1–25; JRW Stott, *Calling Christian Leaders: Biblical Models of Church, Gospel and Ministry* (Leicester: IVP, 2002); JW Woodhouse, *Unity that Helps and Unity that Hinders* (Sheffield: REFORM, 2002).

either claim). Yet such an understanding is in fact a vital corrective to sterile institutionalism and self-indulgent individualism. It emphasises both the Christian's corporate responsibilities and the true location of authority and allegiance in the person and work of the One who is building a church against which the gates of hell will not prevail.

This paper will argue that an evangelical doctrine of the church, grounded as it is in the gospel purposes of God in Christ, lives in creative tension with the institutionalising tendencies of the denominations in general and features of worldwide Anglicanism in particular. Furthermore, it will become clear why this tension is heightened at moments of institutional deviation from the teaching of Scripture such as that represented by recent episcopal denial of the bodily resurrection of Jesus,[2] the uniqueness of Christ and the 'lostness' of the world outside of Christ,[3] the penal and substitutionary nature of the atonement,[4] as well as the episcopal endorsement of homosexual behaviour

---

2. Most notoriously Bishop David Jenkins' comments on the BBC program *Credo* following his appointment as Bishop of Durham in 1984. See also Peter Carnley, 'The rising of the Son', *The Bulletin*, 118/6221 (25 April 2000), 40–3 and *Reflections in Glass: Trends and Tensions in the Contemporary Anglican Church* (Sydney: HarperCollins, 2004), 115–28. Bishop John Spong of Newark's 'Twelve Theses' includes this as number 7: 'Resurrection is an action of God, who raised Jesus into the meaning of God. It therefore cannot be a physical resuscitation occurring inside human history.' See JS Spong, *Here I Stand: My Struggle for a Christianity of Integrity, Love, & Equality* (San Francisco: Harper Collins, 2000), 453. The failures in understanding biblical theology by all three of these men are legion. In contrast, note the comment from Professor TF Torrance of Edinburgh: 'Everything depends on the resurrection of the body, otherwise all we have is a ghost for a saviour'. See TF Torrance, *Space, Time and Resurrection* (Edinburgh: Handsel, 1976), 87.
3. Bishop Michael Ingham of New Westminster: 'It's time for Christians to drop the idea that Christ is the one sure way to salvation'. See *Ottawa Citizen*, September 26, 1997. His ideas are developed more fully in *Mansions of the Spirit: The Gospel in a Multifaith World* (Toronto: Anglican Book Centre, 1997).
4. Peter Carnley, 'Theory of Atonement makes God look cruel', *Anglican Messenger*, (July 1991): 12–13. See also Peter Carnley, 'King on a Cross', *The Bulletin*, 119/6270 (17 April 2001): 32–5; *Reflections*, 128–55.

as acceptable to God and therefore no hindrance to ministry in the churches,[5] and synodical decisions to ordain women to the presbyterate.[6] In such cases individuals, congregations and even dioceses find themselves in conflict with an institution which claims too much and believes too little. Their own efforts to proclaim Christ and adorn his gospel with godly living are undermined, ridiculed and sometimes aggressively checked by those who ought to be rejoicing at their vigour, thanking God for their faithfulness and providing every possible resource for the expansion of their ministry. Attempts to assert institutional authority in such circumstances and to stifle dissent are bound to be seen as the dying gasp of a structure out of touch with reality and with no future of its own, or else as a kind of bullying which is completely out of step with the character and purposes of God.[7]

---

5. As witnessed by Bishop Richard Harries of Oxford's advocacy of Jeffrey John for the office of Bishop of Reading in 2003 and the installation of the same man as Dean of St Albans in 2004. Most notoriously, the election, confirmation and consecration of Gene Robinson as Bishop of New Hampshire in the Episcopal Church of the USA in November 2003 and various statements of support from the Presiding Bishop, Frank Griswold and other bishops in the Anglican communion that both preceded and followed it. One should note, however, the strong dissent voiced by the orthodox bishops of the Global South. See also the comments of Peter Carnley in *The Bulletin*, 22 May 2001.
6. General Synod of the Church of England, 26 February 1987 and 11 November 1992; General Synod of the Anglican Church of Australia, 7 July 1992.
7. The examples are numerous but internationally some of the most prominent cases have been: action against the parish of St Martin's, North Vancouver by the Bishop of New Westminster in September 2003, when he replaced two church wardens and ordered the locks on the doors of the church changed (http://www.anglican-mainstream.net/news/news90.asp); pressure applied to the Diocese of Fort Worth by the General Convention of ECUSA which resulted in a letter of protest from the diocese to the Archbishop of Canterbury in July 2005 (http://www.fwepiscopal.org/news/AppealCover.html); deprivation on 13 July 2005 of the minister of St John's Church in Bristol, Connecticut for speaking out against the consecration of Gene Robinson and other deviations from orthodox doctrine and practice in ECUSA and so distancing themselves from the diocesan bishop (http://www.ctdiocese.org/news/press.shtml); and the deposition of Bishop Cavalcanti of

The Anglican Church of Australia is in fact a case in point. Public confidence in the denomination has been eroded by a number of high profile scandals. Prevarication in the face of the moral and judicial failure of some of its leaders has led to further disenchantment in the community. As a national public entity, all that seems left is sacerdotal posturing and empty rhetoric. At a regional level, the level of the dioceses, the picture is more varied, with pockets of spectacular growth, many more examples of stagnation, and far too many undeniable signs of rapid decline. Yet internally, as an institution, the Anglican Church of Australia is deeply and bitterly divided and increasingly ineffectual. It is hardly an exaggeration to suggest that the Anglican Church of Australia is on the verge of fragmentation and collapse. Yet once again all this is not because insufficient attention has been given to the doctrine of the church. Though undoubtedly there are larger social and cultural factors at work in the decline in national influence and the rapid downhill slide in attendance figures, the internal—seemingly terminal—haemorrhage is undeniably the result of a failure to maintain biblical priorities and perspectives, though many of the recent innovations in teaching and practice are presented in pious language and with an air of theological sophistication. Institutional responses to evangelical dissent have included the slandering of individuals and groups as heretical despite international respected testimony to their orthodoxy[8] and more coercive measures besides.

There is a present, urgent need for Anglicanism worldwide to recover a biblical perspective on the nature of the church and of Christian service (or 'ministry'). Current attempts to hold the institution together by institutional means seem doomed to failure because they fail to address the underlying cause of the fractures that

---

Recife and thirty-two of his clergy by the Archbishop of Brazil (http://www.anglican-mainstream.net/Dec05/missioncrisis.html). To this list should be added the statements and actions leading to the valid but irregular ordination in Southwark in November 2005 and the subsequent removal of the licence of a leading critic of the diocesan bishop (http://www.co-mission.org/ordination.php).

8. Carnley, *Reflections*, 232–41; see also: PF Carnley, 'TC Hammond and the Theological Roots of Sydney Arianism', *St Mark's Review*, 198 (2005): 5–10; DF Wright, 'Dr Carnley on TC Hammond and Arianism', *St Mark's Review*, 199 (2005): 46–8 (48).

have appeared in recent years.[9] Only if a reorientation to the character and purposes of God takes place within Anglican structures is there any long-term future for the denomination in Australia and elsewhere. What follows is one attempt to draw attention to the biblical and theological resources which need fresh appropriation in this process of reorientation.

The gathering purposes of God

Fellowship is something in which God himself has a deep and personal investment. Despite growing disquiet about the grandiose claims of contemporary trinitarian theology,[10] particularly the more detailed accounts of intratrinitarian life, we can affirm with orthodox Christian theology over the last two thousand years that God's dealings with humanity in the economy of creation and redemption arise from his own character and being. The decision to create human beings 'in his own image' (Genesis 1:27), to commit himself to their welfare (Genesis 1:28), to persist with some of the rebellious race after the Fall (Genesis 3:21; 5:24; 12:1; Exodus 19:3–6; Jeremiah 31:31–34; John 3:16 and others), to redeem and reconcile to himself those men and women he has chosen—all this finds its ultimate source in the eternal, uninterrupted and perfect fellowship which God enjoys in his own triune being. As one contemporary Anglican writer puts it, 'The Father wills that *ex nihilo* there should come into being a creaturely counterpart to the fellowship of love which is the inner life of the Holy Trinity'.[11]

---

9. See for example: *To Mend the Net: Anglican Faith and Order for Renewed Mission*, edited by DW Gomez and MW Sinclair (Carrollton, Texas: Ekklesia Society, 2001); The Lambeth Commission on Communion, *The Windsor Report 2004* (London: Anglican Communion Office, 2004).
10. RM Fermer, 'The Limits of Trinitarian Theology as a Methodological Paradigm', *Neu Zeitschrift für Systematische Theologie*, 41 (1999): 158–86; Wright, 'Arianism', 48.
11. JB Webster, 'On Evangelical Ecclesiology', *Ecclesiology*, 1 (2004): 9–35 (9). It remains important, of course, to insist upon the freedom of this decision on God's part. There can be no suggestion that creation or redemption is necessary to complete some 'lack' in God. He wills and establishes creaturely life 'out of his own perfection' (13).

God draws people to himself to enjoy the ordered and yet mutual love which is his own eternal experience. Just as an unqualified unity and equality of being does not make the persons of the Trinity interchangeable (the Father is always the Father, the Son is always the Son of the Father, and the Spirit is always the Spirit of the Father and the Son) so those drawn into relationship with the living God remain his creatures and he remains their God. Mutual love, new life, even indeed a 'participation in the divine nature' (2 Peter 1:4), do not do away with this ineradicable element of reality. At this most basic level, it is clear that fellowship in the richest sense need not exclude notions of order or even structure.

Yet God does not simply gather individuals to himself, as if their relationship with him could be isolated from relationship with other human beings. Rather, being drawn into fellowship with the living God inevitably draws the Christian into fellowship with other Christians who have likewise been made his children by grace (1 John 1:3). Christian living is inescapably corporate in character. The first Christians were taught to pray '*Our* Father in heaven' (Matthew 6:9). The bulk of the epistolary material in the New Testament addresses its readers in the second person plural. The gifts of the Spirit are given 'for the common good' (1 Corinthians 12:7). Any attempt to live the Christian life in isolation from others is rightly seen as a distortion of the good that God has for his people. By the same gospel with which he calls men and women from darkness to light and from death to life, God calls us to each other.[12]

Here lies the theological significance of local assemblies of God's people. God gathers his people to himself and with each other. He brings people together before him. Indeed this notion of physical gathering is one of the chief signs of God's blessing throughout the Old Testament, just as the opposite, scattering (among the nations), is a critical indication of God's judgment against his rebellious people (Deuteronomy 28:64).[13] The assembly of God's people at the rock of

---

12. Broughton Knox used to gloss the Westminster Shorter Catechism's first answer to reflect this truth: 'Q. What is the chief end of man? A. Man's chief end is to glorify God and to enjoy him *in the company of his people* forever'.
13. Deeper still we must reckon with the fragmentation of the race as a consequence of the Fall and of the way God's ultimate purposes involve

Horeb (that is, Mount Sinai) is archetypical. God's redemptive activity had constituted, not individuals redeemed without any reference to others, but a 'holy nation' (Exodus 19:3–6). The spiritual victory of Yahweh in the Exodus (Exodus 14–15) is manifested physically by the assembly at the base of the mountain (Exodus 19). Later, the physical assembly of God's people at the time of the dedication of the Temple (1 Kings 8) and upon the return from exile (Nehemiah 8) further establish the critical gathering element of God's redemptive purposes.

Though there are significant changes when we come to the New Testament, not least the rejection of national Israel and the gospel mission to the nations, the gathering purposes of God have not been abandoned. Indeed, the New Testament ends with the vision of 'a great multitude that no one could count, from every nation, tribe, people and language standing before the throne and in front of the Lamb' (Revelation 7:9). Yet even before that wonderful vision is presented, it is clear that gathering and corporate life remain at the centre of God's purposes. This is demonstrable just from Jesus' own ministry. As his public ministry began in earnest, he called his earliest followers into a fellowship (Mark 3:13–19). He spoke often about the responsibilities they had to each other and the attitude of service which should characterise their relationships (for example, Mark 10:35–45). However, the twelve were merely the inner core of a wider group. Jesus spoke of himself as the good shepherd who calls and leads his sheep and brings other sheep 'that are not of this sheep pen' so that 'there will be one flock and one shepherd' (John 10:14–16). The mission to the nations which is on view in Jesus' last great commission (Matthew 28:16–20), may on the surface appear to involve a scattering which runs counter to this wider biblical concern with gathering, but it is a going out into all the nations in order to gather disciples there. Jesus is about building an assembly, a church, which will withstand the assault of even the ancient enemy of God and his purposes. No charge will be admitted against those in that august assembly. No harm shall come to them. Instead they rejoice together in the victory finally consummated and enjoy the fellowship of the Son with the Father in the Spirit. This heavenly and eschatological reality remains the passion of the Son in his mission of bringing glory to the Father. The day will come when he will present to himself those assembled

---

the tearing down of barriers between people as well as those between each individual and the living God (Genesis 3, 11; Ephesians 2).

around the throne and heaven will be filled with praise of the manifest wisdom of God (Ephesians 5:25–27; 3:10–11). The original disciples and their heirs participate in that same great mission, indeed they are the agents by which that mission proceeds down through the ages, as men and women are called out from the nations to repent and believe and find life in the One sent as the saviour of the world.

As we are gathered to Christ in the gospel we are brought into the great fellowship which Hebrews describes as 'the church of the firstborn'. The deep spiritual reality of our membership of this heavenly congregation is explained with reference to the assembly at Mount Sinai after the exodus. It is not so much a goal as a present reality which cannot remain unexpressed in our earthly situation:

> You *have come* to Mount Zion, to the heavenly Jerusalem, the city of the living God. You *have come* to thousands upon thousands of angels in joyful assembly to the church of the firstborn, whose names are written in heaven. You *have come* to God, the judge of all men, to the spirits of righteous men made perfect, to Jesus the mediator of new covenant, and to the sprinkled blood that speaks a better word than the blood of Abel (Hebrews 12:22–24).

This has all happened. It is part and parcel of being united to Christ by faith. Furthermore, the writer to the Hebrews does not leave the implications of our new situation unexpressed. As earlier he urged his readers not to neglect meeting together for encouragement and edification (Hebrews 10:24–25) so he goes on to speak of worshipping God acceptably with reverence and awe, of loving each other as brothers, and of remembering those leaders 'who spoke the word of God to you' (Hebrews 12:28; 13:1, 7).

To be united to Jesus necessarily involves being united to others who have also been united to Jesus. This, as we have said, is a relation that cannot go unexpressed since it goes to the core of our new identity as Christians. Another way of saying this is to say that the common possession of the Spirit of Christ draws people together to express the fact that they belong to Christ and to each other.[14] In this way, membership of a local congregation is a necessary expression of the fellowship we now have with Christ and with each other, our membership of the heavenly assembly around the throne of God and the Lamb.[15] To refuse such membership, to attempt to live as an independent Christian, is to deny a critical aspect of what has happened to us when we were converted. Christian living must not be self-centred, precisely because Christ was not self-centred. Just as we cannot have the mind of Christ and fail to recognise the world outside of Christ is lost and desperately needs to hear the message of forgiveness secured and life freely given, so we cannot ignore the preciousness of those others he has already rescued from that awful condition. We cannot grow in Christlikeness and remain unconcerned either for the salvation of men and women or for their growth to Christian maturity. The gospel overturns the catastrophic bias towards self-legislation, self-protection and self-promotion which is Adam's legacy to us all. In the words of Luther, it frees us to live 'in God by faith and in our neighbour by love'.[16]

It is not at all surprising, then, that local congregations sprang up throughout the ancient world in the wake of the gospel mission to the nations. This was not simply the emulation of Jewish synagogue practice. It reflected the new reality brought about by the gospel of Jesus Christ. Christian congregations are gospel entities. And yet, as John Webster reminds us, 'gospel and church exist in a strict and irreversible order, one in which the gospel precedes and the church follows'.[17] We will need to return to this vitally important point. However, for the moment what is critical is a recognition that gospel and church are not rivals. To return to Broughton Knox:

---

14. 'So why go to church? The reason is that we are drawn into each other's company by the Holy Spirit who dwells within us. We are drawn together to give expression to the reality that we are all in Christ's presence.' Knox, 'The Biblical concept of Fellowship', 75.
15. Knox, 'The Biblical Concept of Fellowship', 78.
16. M Luther, 'The Freedom of a Christian' (1521), translated by WA Lambert, revised by HJ Grimm, in *Luther's Works*, edited by HT Lehmann and J Pelikan (Philadelphia: Fortress, 1957), XXXI, 371.
17. Webster, On Evangelical Ecclesiology, 10.

> Congregations are part of the gospel. Wherever the gospel is preached congregations form, reflecting and expressing the spiritual and very real relationship between the believer and Christ and one another.[18]

Relationships cannot exist simply in theory, abstracted in some way from actual personal engagement. It is only with the most severe qualification that we can speak of a relationship with someone we have never met, spoken to, or corresponded with. Just so, Christian fellow-ship requires some measure of propinquity.[19] A church needs to gather if it is to be a church, a physical expression of the spiritual relationship we share in the presence of Christ. As it meets, with Christ present through his word and Spirit just as he promised (Matthew 18:20; 28:20; John 14:18; Ephesians 3:17), faith is nourished, mutual love and service are freely given and the faces of all are turned towards the world that is lost without Christ and needs to hear of him.[20] In other words, the centrepiece of God's work in the world is the local congregation rather than larger structures which, with all the best will in the world, never actually meet and are in fact unable to meet except in a purely representative way. This does not, of course, dismiss these larger entities as unnecessary or unimportant. They may indeed have a very significant role to play. However, there is conceptual and terminological slippage in the traditional practice of referring to such entities as 'the church'.[21]

As we have seen, genuine personal relationships in general and Christian fellowship in particular does not exclude notions of order or structure. Recognition of these realities is found even within the pages of the New Testament. What is critical, though, is that the structures that emerge serve the fellowship and not the other way around. In fact,

---

18. DB Knox, 'Notes on Authority in the Church', reproduced in *D Broughton Knox: Selected Works. Volume II: Church and Ministry*, edited by Kirsten Birkett (Kingsford: Matthias Media, 2003), 101.
19. '. . . fellowship which is not expressed in propinquity and common action does not exist', in Knox, 'The Biblical Concept of Fellowship', 80. See also Knox, 'Demythologizing the Church', 54.
20. Thompson, 'Does the Local Church Have a Mission?', 24.
21. Knox, 'The Church, the Churches and the Denominations of the Churches', 24.

revision of these structures takes place where they hinder the effective service of each other in the name of Christ. This, it would appear, is what happened in the young Jerusalem church of Acts 6. Existing structures and ways of doing things gave at least the impression of injustice and so a new structure was put in place. The Christian fellowship generates its own structure which is intended to foster both faith and love. This accounts for what seems to be some variety in congregational structure even within the Pauline sphere of operations (compare Paul's instructions regarding qualities for overseers [εκκλησια] and deacons [διακονοι] in 1 Timothy 3, and similar material about elders [πρεσβυτεροι] in Titus 1). To quote Knox again:

> The church is a fellowship, and if we reflect on the nature of fellowship we will see that all fellowships create structures through which they express themselves and which assist them in being fellowships. The great danger is the ever present tendency to regard the structures as important in themselves, especially as they are more visible than is fellowship, which is personal and invisible though the real thing . . . The test of any church structure is whether it assists the fellowship of the Spirit and aids the Spirit-given ministries of the members.[22]

The gathering and the gospel

The gospel which generates congregational life is the gospel concerning God's Son (Romans 1:3) and specifically his death and resurrection to secure our freedom from condemnation, corruption and enslavement to sin (Romans 3–4). It is an announcement about the fulfilment of God's ancient promises (Romans 1:2; 3:21), his victory over the principalities and powers (Colossians 2:15), and the installation of Jesus as both judge and king (Acts 17:30–31; Hebrews 1:1–4). Gospel proclamation requires an explicit focus upon Jesus. It is also

22. DB Knox, 'The Spirit, the Church and the Denomination', *Protestant Faith Radio Broadcast*, 7 March 1976, reproduced in *D Broughton Knox Selected Works: Volume II: Church and Ministry*, edited by Kirsten Birkett (Kingsford, NSW: Matthias, 2003), 34. See also: 'The Christian faith is thus ecclesial because it is evangelical', in Webster, 'On Evangelical Ecclesiology', 10.

inescapably concerned with the human sin problem and its resolution in the atoning death and glorious resurrection of Jesus. In practical terms this means that while congregational life is an indispensable consequence of gospel proclamation, it must not itself become the focus of that proclamation. Christian congregations, even more so, associations of Christian congregations (denominations), echo the words of the apostle Paul: 'we do not preach ourselves but Jesus Christ as Lord' (2 Corinthians 4:5). In other words, the church arises out of the gospel; it is not in itself the gospel. The Christian gathering finds its centre in the presence of Christ by his word and through his Spirit.[23] He is the head of the church and the loyalty of its members is rightly directed to him alone. While those who teach his word in the congregations are worthy of honour—double honour to be sure (1 Timothy 5:17)—they are not to be treated as sources of a more particular identity or foci for personal allegiance (1 Corinthians 1:10–17).

The priority of gospel rather than church, without any diminution of the significance of church, explains the critical value placed upon truth and its behavioural corollary, personal and corporate integrity.[24] The Christian congregation is not the product of a powerful myth but of a proclamation of the truth about Jesus and his saving work. Everything depends upon the truthfulness of this proclamation. The apostle Paul's telling words about the resurrection make this point emphatically: 'If Christ has not been raised your faith is futile; you are still in your sins' (1 Corinthians 15:17). The truth matters and it makes a difference. Lies are the stock in trade of the enemy of God (John 8:44) and teaching error is in fact an assault upon the life of the congregation. The evil one is persistent in his desire to distract and derail believers by enticing alternatives to the truth. It is, after all, a strategy that worked remarkably well in the Garden of Eden. Error is not neutral but harmful and error about God and his purposes is most harmful of all. Equally, integrity of life, appropriate behaviour in the light of the salvation that is ours in Christ, matters to the Christian

23. For an important, though somewhat neglected, meditation on the presence of Christ see D Ritschl, *Memory and Hope: An Inquiry into the Presence of Christ* (New York: Macmillan, 1967).

24. Here we return to the observation of John Webster mentioned above and its implications.

congregation. The ethical injunctions of much of the New Testament make the point explicitly that failure in the area of personal and social morality critically compromises the life of the Christian congregation (eg Col 3:5–6). It not only undermines the witness of the congregation to the world—tied as it is to a distinctiveness in both message and lifestyle —it corrupts those who are directly involved and the wider community as well. The seriousness with which the apostles took such failure is seen at various points in the New Testament (for example: Acts 5:1–11; 1 Corinthians 5), as is the constant availability of forgiveness for the sinner who repents (for example: 2 Corinthians 2:5–11; 1 John 1:82:2).

The elders of the Christian congregation have a particular responsibility, not only to teach the truth but to combat error in both the doctrinal and moral sphere. The critical resource in this ongoing task is the inspired Scripture (2 Timothy 3:16–17). Departure from the teaching of Scripture is so serious that Christians personally and corporately are charged to disassociate themselves from those who persist in it. The teaching of Scripture, whether, say, on the nature of Christ's person and work or the appropriate expression of Christian sexuality, is not to be regarded as a culturally conditioned artefact of previous generations. It is not something any congregation or individual has the right to ignore or overturn according to the wisdom of their own time. The words of Scripture are to be treated in the way Jesus treated Scripture: as the authoritative word of God which is inviolable and which directs the intellectual framework and behavioural commitments of those God has redeemed. Any suggestion that we do not have a clear word from God on such matters is to be seen for what it is, namely the same sophistry which led to the primeval Fall into sin (Genesis 3:1). Christian teachers are to cherish the faith that was once for all entrusted to the saints; they are to carry it to the rest of the congregation. Yet they are also to contend for it, to defend it from assault on all sides (Jude 3).

The New Testament expects defection from within the churches as well as persecution from without. We are told to expect that false teachers will arise and even that they will shipwreck the faith of many (for example: Matthew 24:4–5; Acts 20:29–31; 2 Peter 2:1–22; 2 Timothy 3:1–9). Yet we are also told how we should respond to this phenomenon, one sadly familiar within worldwide Anglicanism. False teachers and the lies they peddle are to be exposed, they are to be resisted, they are to be removed from any position of possible influence. Their contradiction of the teaching of the Scriptures is to be made known as clearly and as boldly as possible. Generosity, mercy and open-hearted acceptance are most certainly the appropriate stance with respect to the repentant sinner or false teacher. Yet there is to be no generosity, no toleration and certainly no acceptance of the errors they have taught or the immorality they have practiced. With confidence borne of a deep acquaintance with the word of God written, Christian teachers are to say 'No' as well as 'Yes': 'this is the truth of God' and 'that most definitely is not'. In the centuries that followed the completion of the New Testament, creeds were developed which both expounded significant areas of the truth and effectively excluded heretical deviations.[25] It has proved to be more difficult for the congregations and associations of congregations to practice church discipline in a manner consistent with the gospel.

Structure on the larger scale

So far we have concentrated on that real and physical expression of the heavenly fellowship, the local congregation of believers on earth. Along the way we have noted the simple fact that order and structure emerge within the reality which we call fellowship and are not necessarily inimical to it. The act of serving each other, especially as this extends over time, generates patterns and structures which facilitate that service and which are subject to review where they are found to hinder fellowship rather than promote it.[26] However, as Broughton Knox observed:

---

25. The most obvious example is the Chalcedonian Definition of AD 381 with the line: ' . . . one and the same Christ, Son, Lord, Only-begotten, to be acknowledged in two natures, without confusion, without change (excluding Eutychianism), without division, without separation (excluding Nestorianism) . . . '

26. This is akin to that phenomenon sociologists label 'institutionalization': 'institutionalization occurs whenever there is a reciprocal typification of habitualized actions by types of actors', in P Berger and T Luckmann, *The Social Construction of Reality: A Treatise in the Sociology of Knowledge* (New York: Doubleday, 1966), 51. Put more simply, 'institutions are continuing patterns of relationship between people and/or things', in BN Kaye, *Reinventing Anglicanism: A Vision of Confidence, Community and Engagement in Anglican Christianity*

> Christian fellowship is not restricted within the local congregation; the congregation is the expression of the fellowship which is the church of Christ. The latter will overleap the limits of geography to create fellowship between congregations.[27]

Christian living is characterised by service and interdependence. For this reason, strident individualism is utterly inappropriate. We are bound to meet with others to serve them with the gifts the Spirit has given for the common good. In meeting with them we express the union we have with them as members of the heavenly church gathered around Christ. The gospel brings us together as it brings us to Christ. Just so, Christian congregations do not exist in isolation from one another and even within the pages of the New Testament there is evidence of relationships and responsibilities which stretch across geographical boundaries.[28] This association of churches is intended to serve the fellowship which exists in each congregation, a fellowship which, as we have seen, gives a critical place to biblical truth and integrity at a personal and corporate level. It provides encouragement to remain faithful to the gospel, resources to those in need, and

---

(Adelaide, SA: Open Book, 2003), 182. See also: T Parsons, *On Institutions and Social Evolution: Selected Writings*, edited by LH Mayhew (Chicago: University of Chicago Press, 1982); B Holmberg, *Sociology and the New Testament* (Minneapolis: Fortress, 1990). However, attempts to apply sociological categories to the development of churches and associations between churches seem remarkably procrustean. Christian churches are at root a supernatural rather than a natural phenomenon. They challenge prevailing patterns of relating in corporate settings. So Colin Gunton, following Harnack, has traced the difficulties caused by thinking of church structures in terms a neo-platonic hierarchy of being or by analogy from the legal–political conception of an earthly empire. CE Gunton, 'The Community: The Trinity and the Being of the Church', in *The Promise of Trinitarian Theology*, second edition (London: T&T Clark, 1997), 56–61.

27. Knox, 'Demythologizing the Church', 55.
28. 'An independent congregation of Christ is a contradiction in terms. Inter-dependence, not independence is the principle on which the world has been created, for inter-dependence is the principle within the Trinity itself, who is ultimate reality.' Knox, 'The Biblical Concept of Fellowship', 81.

support in a common mission to honour God by proclaiming Christ to the world.

It is true that over time different associations have formed. The reasons for creating new associations and withdrawing from old ones have been varied, some right and proper, others less so. However, the contemporary phenomenon of denominationalism, in this sense of a variety of associations which link Christian congregations and facilitate their life and mission, need not be viewed with suspicion or contempt. At their best a multiplicity of such associations or denominations provide room for freedom of conscience on matters about which the Bible is silent or has little to say and they allow for different cultural and social distinctives. In a sinful world there remains, of course, the danger of partisanship, of looking down on other denominations as somehow deficient or deviant. There have also been muddle-headed attempts to amalgamate denominations out of a sense that the unity that the New Testament speaks about can only be realised when there is one single institutional structure embracing all earthly congregations. Yet, when members of different associations treat each other as brothers and rejoice in the rich variety amongst God's people that multiple denominations preserve, we can concern ourselves with the more important matters of faithful living and believing in the light of the gospel and in our own particular context.

Being Anglican is not the only way of being Christian but its Reformation heritage is something worth understanding, rejoicing in and preserving in a contemporary setting. At the time of the Reformation, the Church of England generated new structures and resources to assist the realignment of its various congregations to the biblical gospel and away from both superstition and sacerdotalism. Chief amongst these were *ex animo* subscription to the *Thirty-Nine Articles of Religion*, uniform use of a radically revised liturgy in the Book of Common Prayer and periodic recourse to the *First and Second Books of Homilies*. These were supported by various royal injunctions and acts of the English parliament. For our present purposes we might leave aside the problems associated with an attempt to bring about reformation by legal and other coercive measures, though we should note that the legacy this has bequeathed to contemporary Anglicanism is far from helpful at many points. What is more significant is the way it signalled that at the heart of the national association of Christian congregations which called itself the Church of England, there was to be a common commitment to biblical doctrine and personal godliness which reflects the priority of the gospel in corporate and individual Christian living. These Reformation formularies insisted that truth mattered and behaviour at both an individual and congregational level was not simply an issue of personal preference. This association of churches was to be, at least as Latimer, Ridley, Cranmer and the other English Reformers envisaged it, confessional in the very best sense. The formularies and structures were to assist in keeping it so.

We have already hinted at the danger that, at the congregational level, it is always possible to prize the structures, which have been generated to facilitate fellowship, above the fellowship itself. In the same way, it has proven all too easy to elevate the structures built up around inter–congregational fellowship in a way which threatens the reality they were meant to serve. It did not take too long in the history of the Christian churches before the inter-congregational organisation became more conspicuous than the local congregation.[29] The Roman hierarchy, with the extraordinary honour accorded the Pope and his curia, is a case in point. So too, in Elizabethan England, the Queen's use of 'her' bishops to enforce uniformity of religion throughout the realm in effect taught that fellowship in the congregation was to be subservient to other external factors. Almost inevitably this led some to identify themselves in terms of these structures and to give an inappropriate allegiance to them. Moving forward some 450 years, it is remarkable that today some Anglicans, even in Australia, should talk about the Archbishop of Canterbury, the Primates' Meeting, the Lambeth Conference and the Anglican Consultative Council as 'instruments of unity'.[30] Similarly, the prominence given to 'full communion with the see of Canterbury' is rather disturbing. It is hard to reconcile this focus on institutional structures and office bearers with the theological realities we have explored in this paper. When the

29. Knox, 'Demythologizing the Church', 55.
30. In reality these structures preserve the appearance of organisational cohesion where real unity in the truth of the gospel has been compromised by a range of decisions, pronouncements, and actions. This problem is reflected at a national level in Australia by the General Synod of the Anglican Church of Australia which pretends to hold together major and irreconcilable differences on critical matters of faith and practice.

structures supporting inter-congregational fellowship become a focus of loyalty we have moved a long way away from biblical ecclesiology.

The tension between local fellowship and larger institutional structure need not be destructive and is present even within the pages of the New Testament itself. Nevertheless, it has tended to become destructive in the face of the claims of larger organisational entities such as the papacy or modern denominations. 'Fellowship and compulsion do not mix'[31] but in too many parts of the world compulsion is used by institutional bodies and office bearers against those congregations and individuals who protest in the name of biblical truth against their 'official and agreed' innovations. High profile cases in New Westminster, Texas and Brazil are just the tip of the iceberg.[32]

When the survival of the institutional structures becomes an end in itself, when, for instance, the integrity of episcopal jurisdiction becomes a more serious matter than the fact that some bishops have in effect abandoned the faith and indulge in behaviour the Bible condemns as perverse and unnatural (Romans 1:26–32), survival is in fact the last thing it can expect. That which the structures were created to protect has been compromised. It has been said that in some quarters inclusiveness or comprehensiveness has become the new Anglican gospel. No one can be excluded, no behaviour can be condemned, no theological innovation can be dismissed, or even evaluated, against the teaching of Scripture. All who will may come. Yet the reality behind the rhetoric is that those judged less inclusive (for example, those who on biblical grounds oppose the ordination of women to the presbyterate or the consecration of a homosexual bishop) become targets for vilification and exclusion from the institution. There have been cases of just such coercive behaviour by bishops within the Anglican Church of Australia in recent years.

Denominational structures were intended to preserve gospel truth, protect and resource those who would preach Christ faithfully and fearlessly, and pre-eminently to assist the genuine Christian fellowship of the churches, that is, the local congregations. Denominational structures of various kinds are, in and of themselves, part of God's kind provision in the age until Jesus returns. The manifest failure of

31. Knox, 'The Biblical Concept of Fellowship', 81.
32. See the details above in footnote 7.

Anglican structures to preserve doctrinal faithfulness and moral integrity at all levels might lead some Christian men and women, congregations and even dioceses to throw up their hands and completely disengage from the wider institution. However this response, though understandable, neglects one simple truth.

Hope for the future

The remarkable thing is that despite the contemporary compromises of institutional Anglicanism, the church of God remains unscathed. Christ continues to build his church and it is impregnable. God's purposes cannot but triumph. Institutions and structures come and go but the gospel and the church, which arises out of it, remain. That day will surely come when 'a great multitude that no one can count from every nation, tribe, people and language' will stand before the throne and in front of the Lamb proclaiming to the entire created order the wonder of the salvation that has been accomplished by God through his Son (Revelation 7:9–10). Faithful Christian congregations—and individuals—have no need to despair as they hear regular stories of the betrayal of biblical truth and standards of behaviour by Anglican leaders. Christ has sat down at the right hand of the Father in heaven, the day of judgment is fixed, and the complete and utter vindication of Jesus' faithful disciples is assured.

What is more, even a cursory glance at church history makes clear that we have been here before. Athanasius watched as the entire world appeared to embrace the Arian heresy. Wycliffe and his followers were hunted down with such ferocity that the great man's bones were exhumed on the orders of a church council so that he could be burnt at the stake as a heretic. Luther stood alone against the church and empire at Worms. Cranmer watched his friends, Latimer and Ridley, burnt at the stake before suffering the same fate. Grindal was placed under house arrest. Whitefield was ridiculed, and Charles Simeon was locked out of his church for a time.

There are indeed great signs of life and faithfulness in Anglican congregations all over Australia. There are many godly leaders in the denomination who seek to proclaim Christ boldly and honour him with a personal moral integrity of the highest order. It is not at all a picture of unmitigated darkness and betrayal. Christian faith survives in Anglican churches, often oblivious to the actions, decisions and pronouncements of denominational functionaries. Furthermore, there are many godly and learned men and women who work within the various councils, committees, commissions and synods of the denomination to promote gospel truth and to protest at the departures from orthodoxy and godliness. Yet if the Anglican Church of Australia as an institution is to have a future it needs serious reorientation to the character and purposes of God. There needs to be a wholesale return to biblical truth and to the patterns of behaviour which flow out of the gospel. Critical to this will be a recognition that the denomination serves the gospel fellowship and mission of the local congregations and it does this by itself embracing without reservation the plain teaching of Scripture.[33] The denomination is a service organisation but the local congregations are the church of God on earth.

33. For a reasoned defence of the clarity of Scripture see MD Thompson, *A Clear and Present Word: The Clarity of Scripture* (Leicester: IVP, 2006).

11

Anglican Diversity And Conflict: A Case Study On God, Gender And Authority

Duncan Reid

The recent publications of three polemical works by Australian Anglicans, Kevin Giles,[1] Peter Jensen[2] and Peter Carnley,[3] have highlighted what every casual newspaper reader in Australia knows well: that the Anglican church in this country is fragmented. For example, this report was to be found in the Melbourne *Age* of 29 June 2003:

> The Anglican Church is an institution that Australians, of all faiths and none, have grown used to regarding as part of the cultural background. It arrived in this country with the first white settlers and has been a substantial presence in national life ever since. In the past few weeks, however, many people have been surprised to learn that this institution whose existence they have always taken for granted is in danger of disintegrating.

The fragmentedness of Australian Anglicanism comes as a shock not only to Australian Anglicans and those members of the wider public who may seldom attend church but who feel the need for a

---

1. Kevin Giles, *The Trinity and Subordinationism: The Doctrine of God & the Contemporary Gender Debate* (Downers Grove: InterVarsity Press, 2002).
2. Peter Jensen, *The Revelation of God: Contours of Christian Theology* (Leicester: InterVarsity Press, 2002).
3. Peter Carnley, *Reflections in Glass: Trends andTtensions in the Contemporary Anglican Church* (Sydney: Harper Collins, 2004).

stable church to 'make up for the instabilities of modern life'.[4] It is also out of keeping with Anglicanism's historical character. Did not Anglicanism in its early modern form start as an attempt to hold together in one church the religiously varied sensibilities of the whole English nation? And have not Anglicans been at the forefront of the ecumenical movement, with its aim of bringing together separated Christians?

There are at least two markers of identity that have functioned in the past for Australian Anglicans. The first is a sort of religious tribalism linked with ethnicity and social class. Anglicans in Australia were ethnically people from English (rather than Irish, Scottish or Welsh) backgrounds, or else middle class or with middle-class aspirations. England—not the United Kingdom, note—continued to be, if no longer 'home', then certainly the 'mother country'. It was possible to be working-class and Anglican if you were of English background. A great many post-war English migrants fit this category; these people even now continuing to form the backbone of many suburban Anglican parishes. It was also possible to be middle or upper class and non-Anglican. And of course, it was relatively easy for individuals to change denominational allegiance—especially among non-Roman Catholics—through marriage, or simply because of the availability or non-availability of somewhere to worship or send children to school. And though—with the possible exception of the earliest convict settlements—Anglicanism was never the established religious denomination in Australia, it long remained (and in some minds still has pretensions to remain) quasi-established. Local parish churches in the 1950s still displayed the national flag and, often as not, the Union Jack; and the iconography of Anglican churches still includes an imposing presence of brass plaques celebrating the donations and benefactions of past public worthies. All these functioned as signifiers of substance, stability, and identification with nation and Empire. They gave Anglican worshippers a powerful sense of belonging, of identity, that somehow transcended the immediate context of the alien Australian landscape and the ethnically and religiously mixed Australian populace.

There is a second form of past Anglican identity that we could call a common outlook, or even a common aesthetic. This is the worldview,

4. Jürgen Moltmann, *Theology Today: Two Contributions Towards Making Theology Present* (London: SCM/ Philadelpha: TPI, 1988), 8.

and the aesthetic sensibility, formed by the Book of Common Prayer. Until the early 1970s, all Anglicans—not only in Australia, but world-wide—had this formation in common. Anglican theology certainly, and arguably Anglican aesthetic taste as well, were formed by a particular text, a text that made clear and frequent reference to the Bible in its 1611 English translation and the Coverdale Psalms, and which in turn inspired a whole range of literary offshoots. Anglican clergy read the offices of morning and evening prayer daily, and Anglican lay people frequently knew large sections of the prayer book off by heart. This was not necessarily the result of a conscious decision, but simply through the familiarity that comes from frequent, intensive hearing of the text read. If Anglican 'tribal' identity was at least in part an external, publicly recognisable marker of identity, this second marker of identity was largely internal, assuring Anglicans of an inner bond of understanding and outlook that they had in common with other Anglicans, and also, it has to be said, with a great many other English-speaking Protestants. Neither the Authorised Version of the Bible nor the Book of Common Prayer were ever the sole possessions, or intended to be the sole possessions, of Anglicans, and so in one sense this 'Anglican' identity was always open-ended.

The current situation is that both these markers of Anglican identity, external and internal, have become things of the past. Few Australians, even Anglican Australians, nowadays want to be associated with England or Englishness, and legal ties with the United Kingdom—where, at least in England, Anglicanism continues to be established—are slowly melting away.[5] The Book of Common Prayer has gradually disappeared from public worship in Australia since 1978, when *An Australian Prayer Book* was introduced throughout the country. The process, which started earlier in some places, now means that familiarity with the Book of Common Prayer is a rarity except among older generation Anglicans, and even they in most cases have not heard the old prayer book in regular use for almost a quarter of a century. Neither of these changes is to be regretted. They both have come about slowly and in an orderly 'Anglican' way for all sorts of

5. A recent Australian High Court ruling, for example, establishes that British subjects who are not Australian citizens may now be deported as aliens (*The Age*, 10 December 2003: 1). Britain is now, and arguably has been for some decades, a foreign country.

good reasons. But they do pose the question: how are contemporary Australian Anglicans (and non-Anglicans, for that matter) to understand Anglican identity?

Kathryn Tanner suggests that identity resides in a sense of 'style',[6] an intangible feel for which practices may be appropriate and which not. Different styles will themselves be proper in different contexts. Every community has its own sense of style, and it is this, according to Tanner, that gives communities their identities. Beliefs and practices are embodied in style, and come to expression in it, but the community cannot be reduced to matters of belief and practice. If I were to try to describe the Anglican style, and the qualities I find in Anglicanism that continue to keep me within this community, the list would be something like this: an understated conviction that does not shy away from naming evil for what it is and engaging it vigorously when necessary; a dignity that can smile at its own attempts at seriousness; a circumspection that refrains from probing too deeply into the minds of others; a modesty that does not advertise its own good works; an urbane graciousness that can live with disagreement; a generosity that delights in otherness when it encounters it and also, out of gratitude for what it has itself received, shares the good. These qualities, furthermore, are nurtured in a church whose polity balances the democratic impulse with the personalism of episcopal care and oversight, and the personalism of *episcope* with the democratic safeguard of synodical governance.[7] These are not the qualities of all Anglicans or all Anglican communities, nor are they the sole possession of Anglicans. They are not dramatic or eye-catching characteristics, and they are not necessarily successful according to the expectations of the world at large, but they endure through time and across space, and they characterise Anglicanism at its best.

---

6. Kathryn Tanner, *Theories of Culture: A New Agenda for Theology* (Minneapolis: Fortresss, 1997), 144.

7. A proper Anglican understanding of *episcope* is, I believe, personal rather than hierarchical. See: Keith Rayner, 'The Bishop in the Anglican Church Today', in *Common Ground: Covenanting for Mutual Recognition and Reconciliation Between the Anglican Church of Australia and the Lutheran Church of Australia; A Report from the Anglican–Lutheran Dialogue in Australia* (Adelaide: 2001), 35–9; also *Episcopacy: Views from the Antipodes*, edited by Alan Cadwallader, (Adelaide: Anglican Board of Christian Education, 1994).

The Anglican Church of Australia is divided on at least three practical questions. There are different views with regard to the leadership of women in the church, to lay presidency at (or administration of) the eucharist, and to homosexuality. From the late 1970s to the early 1990s the internal Anglican debate focussed on the ordination of women, especially to the priesthood. This was resolved in most Australian Anglican dioceses during the 1980s with the ordinations of women to the diaconate, and in 1992 with the first ordinations of women priests. In 2006 there remain some dioceses that continue to oppose the ordination of women and even seek to reverse the decisions of the previous decades. The consecration of women to the episcopate continues to be a matter of debate in Australia. With regard to the second issue, the Sydney Diocese for some time argued that ordination to the priesthood should not be a condition for celebrants at the eucharist. For most Anglicans, this argument called in question the meaning of ordination, and its connection with eucharistic worship. However, in general the focus of the ordination debate has shifted from the issues of gender and lay presidency to that of sexuality, and specifically to the ordination of practicing homosexuals. Media attention has been brought to bear on this issue in other parts of the Anglican communion, the United Kingdom and the United States, with strong reactions from some third world members of the communion. During 2003 the Archbishop of Sydney recommended a withdrawal of recognition of a particular overseas diocese on this issue,[8] pointing, not without some justification, to the cross-cultural problems occasioned by the proposal, especially in parts of the third world where some of the most vigorous Anglican churches have their homes. While culture should not determine theology, it is worth noting that the stance of the Sydney Diocese on all these matters of practice is in opposition to the majority opinion among the Australian public, and a great many Australian Anglicans find no particular conflict between majority public opinion in this area and their own faith.

There may be a cultural factor to this divergence. If we can take Anglicanism as a style of intellectual life and then apply John Docker's analysis of the differing styles of intellectual life in Sydney and Melbourne, for example, an interesting regional contrast suggests

8. *The Age*, 3 October 2003.

itself.[9] Docker argues that intellectuals in Melbourne have historically felt themselves more in harmony with the surrounding popular culture, and so have taken their place more comfortably and confidently within it. Sydney intellectuals, by contrast, have felt themselves to be outside of the surrounding culture, and this has led to a split between a reclusive or bohemian intellectual life either escapist from the surrounding popular culture or assertively contemptuous of it. In terms of Moltmann's[10] dialectic of relevance and identity, Sydney intellectuals have had identity—as intellectuals—but have stood outside of and been ignored by their social context, where Melbourne intellectuals as a group have enjoyed relevance but have felt no great impulse to develop or provide for themselves a radical alternative to the larger society in which they live. Applied to the Anglican Church, if such an application be permissible, this might explain the greater integration of Melbourne Anglicanism with the society in which it finds itself and the stronger identity of Sydney Anglicanism as a cohesive group that stands over against, and in opposition to, many aspects of the wider culture. These differing styles are not necessarily self-chosen: there may be differences in the histories of these two cities, to say nothing of the other Australian state capitals, and the contexts in which Anglicanism has found itself, which have compelled these differing developments in self-understanding. These different views have come to expression also in differing understandings of trinitarian doctrine, especially on the question of hierarchy and subordinationism within the Trinity. Closely related are the issues of theological method and the question of authority.

The books by Giles and Carnley, authors of the very different theological perspectives, attest, among other things, to the theological dimensions of the fragmentedness of Australian Anglican identity. Jensen's book, when set beside them, highlights the methodological aspects of this fragmentedness, and the role of authority. For this reason the three books will serve as the focus for this discussion. Giles and Carnley focus on what they see as theological aberrations of the official theology of the Anglican Diocese of Sydney. It is hard to

9. John Docker, *Australian Cultural Elites: Intellectual Traditions in Sydney and Melbourne* (Sydney: Angus and Robertson, 1974).

10. Jürgen Moltmann, *The Crucified God: The Cross of Christ as the Foundation and Criticism of Christian Theology* (London: SCM Press, 1974), 7–28.

review these books without appearing unduly critical of Sydney Anglicans. That is not my intention. Sydney Diocese is by no means uniform in its theological outlook. The problem is that, from the outside, it appears to be—and this appearance is underscored by what often seems to be the monocultural official stance of that Diocese. Sydney Diocese does not appear, at least from the outside, to encourage diversity. There appear to be, in the words of one of the colleagues who read the first draft of this chapter, two kinds of Christianity in Australia both claiming the name 'Anglican'. Both Giles and Carnley offer critiques of the official theology of the Sydney Diocese, or what might be better called after its source, 'Moore College theology'. Jensen, whose book is dedicated to his colleagues of Moore College faculty, by contrast writes as an apologist for and exponent of this theology. What theological principle, then, divides these two kinds of Christianity?

In 1999 the Doctrine Commission of the Diocese of Sydney issued a report on Trinity critiquing the contemporary egalitarian interpretation of trinitarian doctrine and arguing instead for an eternal inner-trinitarian subordination of the Son to the Father. This subordination was then extended to justify the permanent subordination of women in the church and the home. Kevin Giles offers an extended critique of the Sydney Doctrine Commission interpretation of trinitarian doctrine. He begins by pointing to the prolonged and painful debate that took place in the early church to establish the contours of the doctrine of the Trinity. In this debate all hierarchical ordering in the Trinity was rejected. It was agreed that Father, Son and Holy Spirit were one in being and act. However, Giles observes, across the centuries, time and time again, subordinationist teaching has reappeared. In our own time the argument that the Son is subordinated—eternally, not simply during his time in the flesh—to the Father has reemerged in conservative evangelical circles, notably within the Anglican Diocese of Sydney, as an argument to justify the ongoing subordination of women.

Giles documents the contemporary conservative evangelical arguments for the eternal subordination of the Son and then refutes them by appeal to the historical sources and the best of recent treatments of the Trinity. Giles applies his fundamentally egalitarian model in a powerful refutation of the subordinationist thinking of some of his fellow evangelical Anglicans. Giles' particular target is the trinitarian argument in much conservative evangelical theology for subordinating women to the 'headship' of men. He notes that in this literature, the term 'difference' functions as a code word for inequality, and the term 'equality' is assumed to mean sameness. The very point of the trinitarian doctrine of God, as Giles points out, is that real difference and real equality can go together, and to confuse equality with sameness, or difference with inequality, are category mistakes.

In the second half of the book Giles evaluates the other arguments used by contemporary conservative evangelicals to subordinate women, and finds them both novel and unconvincing. Advocates of gender subordination (including those who propose the innocent-sounding 'difference of roles' theory) are demonstrated to be just as selective in their readings of the biblical texts and the tradition, and on the basis of considerably less evidence, as were the nineteenth century evangelical and reformed advocates of racial subordination that justified slavery. Giles' historical work on slavery is alarming: it shows how good Christians, with the best of intentions, can misinterpret the Bible to serve their own ends. Giles concludes by offering three methodological rules for formulating a theology of gender equality: one based in the differentiated equality expressed in Genesis 1: 26–8; a second in the priority of an eschatological perspective over any 'orders of creation' theology; and a third rule, based on the relationships seen in the co-equal Trinity, for interpreting the texts that tend to be cited in the gender debate.[11]

A common theme in the recent upsurge in scholarly and popular discussions of the Trinity is the level of agreement about the practicality of the trinitarian approach to God. If even twenty years ago one might have heard the Trinity dismissed as having no implications for everyday life, this opinion itself now sounds quaintly old-fashioned. The Trinity has returned to being—in reality, not just in theory—one of the central non-negotiables for Christians. So it is hardly surprising that, given the wide diversity of opinions among Christians as to how real, practical Christian life is to be lived, it has now, again, become a matter of some consequence what sort of trinitarian God one professes. In Kevin Giles' book a particular version of the Trinity is forcefully advocated and another version just as forcefully refuted, and both in relation to an immensely practical ethical question, that of hegemony and subordination. More

11. Giles, 202–3, 268.

specifically, this relates to the official Sydney Anglican position on the hegemony of one gender and the subordination of the other. Giles' passionate advocacy of the historic orthodox position thus finds concrete expression in opposing the tendency to subordinate women on the basis of a supposedly hierarchical ordering of persons within the Trinity. Peter Carnley has more recently tackled the Sydney Anglican phenomenon. Significantly subtitled 'trends and tensions in the contemporary Anglican church', his book sets out to 'clarify some of the issues that surfaced among Australian Anglicans in April 2000'.[12] The reference is to the author's feeling of having been misinterpreted and attacked, especially in the media of the Sydney Diocese, for an Easter reflection he published that year, shortly before he was installed as primate of the Anglican Church of Australia. It is written in the belief, he continues, 'that the resolution of the conflict of ideas can only be achieved by the grace of God in generosity of spirit through reasoned conversation and debate'. This methodological presupposition continues through to the book's concluding call to engagement in dialogue rather than the modern secularist reduction of all matters of faith to the private sphere, and for believers to 'retreat into a cool and liberal-minded tolerance bordering on indifference'.[13] The Christian imperative to 'speak the truth in love' (Ephesians 4:15), cited in justification of the attack on the author's Easter reflection, is in reality a call to 'us all to careful listening in a spirit of attentiveness to the views of the other'.[14] Carnley thus turns the weapon of attack back on those who had wielded them.

Carnley's twin opponents are post-Enlightenment liberalism and what he sees as its product and mirror-image, the rationalistic and largely propositional official theology of the Anglican Diocese of Sydney.[15] It was the representatives of this theology that in Carnley's estimation so seriously failed to understand his Easter reflection, a failure that has provoked his book-length response and attempt at clarification. Chapter one is an extended critique of liberalism (a theme to which Carnley later returns) from the viewpoint of his own arguably more post-modern 'progressive orthodox' position, allowing

---

12. Carnley, 13.
13. Carnley, 312.
14. Carnley, 19.
15. Carnley, 6.

scope for communal—rather than merely individual—experience. Liberalism, which belongs to classical modernity, emphasises the rights and freedoms of the individual. It is this individualistic ideology, according to Carnley, that lies at the root of Sydney's departure from the shared, common wisdom of the Anglican (and wider Christian) tradition.

It appears at the outset that Carnley lays the blame for the aberration of 'Sydney Anglicans'—he puts the term in quote marks[16] to indicate it is the official theology of Sydney Diocese he has in mind, not the faith of all Anglicans who happen to live in Sydney—on a particular theory of atonement, the Anselmian or 'penal substitutionary theory'.[17] Certainly it is a major problem—not confined to Anglicans—if salvation is understood purely or even largely in penal substitutionary terms. This theory is, as Carnley correctly points out, extra-biblical and belongs to the history of doctrine.[18] Sydney's advocacy of it seems out of keeping with the insistence that the Bible should be the sole source of doctrine.

But the problem is more complex than just one atonement theory. There is also the understanding of 'revelation as a body of information of a propositional kind'[19] and both the propositional–cognitivist understanding of doctrine that flows from such an approach to revelation and the naïve 'plain meaning of scripture'[20] approach to the hermeneutics that informs it. These are connected of course. Only if there is a plain unambiguous meaning of scripture is it possible hold a coherent understanding of doctrine as unambiguous propositions.

Peter Jensen champions such a view of revelation. Jensen's focus is on theological method: on how we do theology, and before that, on how we know God. There are two basic themes: revelation is fundamentally propositional, and the proper attitude of the Christian believer is one of obedience to revelation. But neither of these themes

16. Carnley, 14.
17. Carnley here follows Gustav Aulen's, *Christus Victor: An historical Study of the Thee Main Types of the Idea of the Atonement* (London: SPCK, 1970) classic typology of atonement theories.
18. Carnley, 155.
19. Carnley, 14. The reference is to George Lindbeck's *The Nature of Doctrine: Religion and Theology in a Postliberal Age* (Philadelphia: Westminster, 1984).
20. Carnley, 105–9.

is developed in an unsophisticated way as such a bald summary might suggest. Jensen at the outset nuances this propositionalist view of revelation.[21] Biblical revelation is the revelation of a person, Jesus Christ, and is a matter of trust or faith. But this revelation is encompassed in words, and the words of the Bible are to be identified with God's revelation.[22] 'The revelation is not the proper nouns "Jesus Christ", but the proposition "Jesus is the Christ, the Lord".'[23] The words of scripture are thus the words of God in a 'direct and revelatory sense'.[24] And yet this revelation is not mere information; it is information that provokes an existential response.[25] No distinction is to be made between propositional knowledge and personal knowing.[26] It is the words that give rise to personal intimacy, not—as in most human experience—the existential and initially unarticulated sense of trust that may or may not then lead to words, words that in turn show a person to be either trustworthy or untrustworthy. The existential response of the believer is what endorses revelation—in this propositional sense—to be revelation, and this existential response must be one of obedience,[27] or subservience.[28]

There is, at first glance, much to commend in Jensen's viewpoint. There is an emphasis on eschatology;[29] the quest for a relational knowledge of God,[30] the living God.[31] He rejects a natural theology in favour of a theology of nature.[32] He rejects individualism,[33] and its concomitant privatisation of religious belief, as a legacy of the Enlightenment.

---

21. Jensen, 18–19.
22. Jensen, 22.
23. Jensen, 49.
24. Jensen, 26, 273.
25. Jensen, 61.
26. Jensen, 88.
27. Jensen, 269.
28. Jensen, 151, 161.
29. Jensen, 52–3.
30. Jensen, 65.
31. Jensen, 260.
32. Jensen, 116.
33. Jensen, 145–6.

The problems arise at closer examination. What is the real meaning of Jensen's 'theology of nature'? Creation is effected by a divine word of *command*[34]—not, as other contemporary theologians of creation have argued, the divine permission that invites creation to come into being. 'The covenantal Scripture is the instrument by which the Lord Jesus rules over his covenant people',[35] and we in turn 'are made in the image of God to rule the world he has made'.[36] The scriptures 'rule';[37] the gospel is to be 'obeyed'.[38] If the gospel is good news, might we not say it is to be received? The teachings of the Bible are to be obeyed.[39] Again, my question is: are teachings 'obeyed' or are they assimilated, followed, heeded; even critically evaluated? Christian freedom for Jensen is not to be found in autonomy.[40] Well yes, but are autonomy or subservience the only alternatives? 'We are not only the Lord's servants,' states Jensen, 'but also his slaves, bound to please him in all things'.[41] 'Authentic faith involves the capacity to trust and obey words, sentences and paragraphs'.[42] Words like obedience, submis-sion, and subservience occur several times on almost every page of Jensen's book.

Here we see the methodological underpinnings of the 1999 Report with its reintroduction of trinitarian subordination. Like Carnley, but drawing very different theological conclusions, Peter Jensen has set his face against the Enlightenment as the source of the ills of contemporary society and church. For Jensen, the problem is that the liberation theme of the Enlightenment has 'entered the Christian soul'.[43] But what if the Enlightenment theme of liberation is a message latent in the gospel itself, waiting for the right social conditions to allow it to emerge? What if it is something Enlightenment Europe may have learnt from Christianity? Where Carnley seeks to go beyond the Enlightenment, Jensen seems to want to return to the pre-

34. Jensen, 72–73.
35. Jensen, 161.
36. Jensen, 174; see also, 243.
37. Jensen, 178.
38. Jensen, 90. Reception comes only later, 91.
39. Jensen, 269.
40. Jensen, 151.
41. Jensen, 72.
42. Jensen, 83.
43. Jensen, 92; see also: 145–6, 147, 149, 176.

Enlightenment hierarchical world.[44] Methodologically Jensen posits a 'biblical theology'[45] that minimises the diversity of scripture. There is no post-modern or post-colonial hearkening here to the dissonances, the spaces between the words, or the minority voices in the text. The naming of God as 'Father' or 'Lord' is apparently quite unproblematic for Jensen. This is not mere innocence of recent contributions to biblical criticism and theology. Jensen's book has its quite intentional polemical edge: 'the word of God does not help me to decide whether to choose fish or pork for dinner. Instead it tells me that I am free from any religion interested in such worldly concern . . .'[46] Jensen is by no means so naïve as to be unaware of the implications of such a line with regard to fasting as a religious practice, and many Christians, to say nothing of Jews or Muslims, might feel some cause to take offence.

The books by Giles and Carnley both seek to answer this style of theology. Carnley identifies a gnostic element in the Sydney reliance on revelation as entirely propositional information, and it is this that leads him to identify another insight about the difference between Moore College theology and the wider Anglican tradition. He contrasts this gnosticism with a sort of theological agnosticism, an unknowing of God. Christianity is agnostic in its historic opposition to ways of secret knowledge that supposedly function as passwords through the heavens. Carnley overstates his case at this point. His proper objection to gnosticism leads him, for example, to endorse the position of HL Mansel in his great nineteenth century debate with FD Maurice. I think it would be arguable that it was Maurice who held a proper dialectical tension between God's economic revelation of God, and the hiddenness of God in Godself. To oppose gnosticism we do not have to follow Mansel's particular theology of divine unknowability over against Maurice's, to my mind more helpful, dialectic of known and yet unknown, unknown and yet known. Carnley is justified in his concern that a propositional understanding of revelation as information once given tends to gnosticism, and this in turn leads to the arrogant assumption that one's own knowledge is right and everyone else must therefore be wrong. Such a stance closes dialogue. Conversation can only be replaced by conversion—or its

44. Jensen, 147–8.

45. Jensen, 225.

46. Jensen, 265.

opposite, isolation. Even so, Carnley also slips into generalisation at times, as when he speaks of the 'gnostic and defensive tendencies of much evangelical theory'.[47] Although he does not say it outright, this statement seems provocatively close to suggesting that all evangelical theology is tarred with the same brush. But it is only fair to distinguish between the authentic evangelical theology that arose out of the spiritual revivals of the eighteenth century and the retreat into Protestant scholasticism that Carnley discerns in the official line of Sydney Diocese. The evangelical revivals were precisely reactions against the scholastic staidness of the previous century. However, given the understanding of revelation we have noted in Jensen's book, in which words are certainly the starting point but personal discipleship the intended outcome, we have to ask if the Sydney approach to the knowledge of God is quite as unambiguously propositional as Carnley suggests.

Carnley notices another evidently long-standing feature of official Sydney Anglican theology: its dissociation of the spiritual from the material. As long ago as 1956, in a revealing anecdote related in his book, Broughton Knox advised the then archbishop of Sydney that a cross placed in the sanctuary of a church might lead to superstition. Idolatry was defined to include the worship of the true God 'by the aid of unauthorised sensuous media'.[48] Carnley quite rightly discerns in this statement not only 'a paradigm statement of the propositionalist–descriptivist approach to faith and doctrine', in which 'faith is an intellectual assent to abstract doctrinal truths', but also—more importantly in my opinion—'an alarming dualism in Dr Knox's statements insofar as he draws an unfortunate gnostic dichotomy between the spiritual and the material'.[49] For if we accept this dichotomy, we deny the possibility of the spiritual revealing itself through matter. Christian discourse about the Word's becoming flesh, God's bodily participation in the world, would then be transformed from a radical claim into a pious myth, a mere manner of speech with no real content. This of course has connections with the trinitarian subordination of the Son to the Father that Giles discerns. If the eternal Word were somehow on a lower ontological level than God the Father, eternally subordinate, then his being in the world would be something

47. Carnley, 153.
48. Carnley, 69.
49. Carnley, 69–70.

less than God incarnate. And if Jesus were something less than God incarnate, then his eternal subordination to the Father would be a matter of no real consequence. The social and indeed political consequences about the legitimacy of subordinating one group of human beings to another (whether it be women to men, or black people to white people—the two examples Giles gives) could then go safely unchallenged.

So I suspect this dualism that Carnley discerns in Sydney Anglicanism may be the crux of the matter. Such a dualism will see no fundamental problem in subordinating some people to others, nor in a cavalier approach to the sacraments,[50] but will fear the power of sense experience, whether this be in the form of charismatic spiritual experience or the aesthetic experience of the creative arts. Such an outlook betrays an attitude that can only be described as fundamentally anti-incarnational, and therefore anti-trinitarian. This methodological tendency strikes me as closer to the heart of things than a particular stance on sexuality, or the ecclesiastical–political matter of ordination of women, or a particular understanding of salvation exclusively in terms of penal substitution. These other things, on the other hand, will surely follow from a questionable theology of incarnation and Trinity. The truly alarming thing to my mind is that so much time has passed since the quoted statement of Broughton Knox. It seems to me the real question that Australian Anglicans need to explore as a matter of urgency, the question on which other, penultimate questions will be decided, is this: who is the one triune God, whose eternal Word became flesh, and what is the relationship between this God and the created universe into which God has entered in the flesh, as a human child? If we can find agreement on these questions—real, searching agreement, not simply reiteration of traditional doctrinal formulas—then I am confident other agreements will follow, even though these may be agreements about where to disagree. But without agreement on these questions, the only possible way forward for Anglicans would be to slouch quietly off in separate

50. See Jensen, 269, for his dismissal of the Eucharistic revival as 'a sign of weakness' in the contemporary church: 'A growth in interest in expounding and obeying the Scriptures would indicate a recovery of strength'.

directions, preferably with as little mutual recrimination and ill feeling as possible.

Kevin Giles argues that a theological divergence appears to have arisen out of the perceived need to justify a divergence in pastoral practice and church order. At the time of writing, however, there is reason to hope that Giles' call to his fellow evangelicals in Sydney may have been heeded. The Sydney bishops themselves placed the question on the agenda for the Australian Anglican bishops' meeting in March 2004, and have also directed the Sydney Diocesan Doctrine Commission to review the 1999 Report. Carnley writes from a very different theological background from Giles—the two have conducted a public debate in print,[51] and Carnley takes issue with Giles' approach to hermeneutics in this book.[52] Yet both find the official Sydney line theologically inadequate and indeed objectionable. Giles' book is largely a single-issue response to Sydney, arguing that a particular political issue, Sydney's rejection of the leadership of women, has led Sydney Diocese to conform its theology to this political agenda, and that this in turn has in effect led Sydney Anglican theology beyond the limits of Christian orthodoxy. Carnley's book is a multi-issue response to Sydney, covering a range of questions on which the author feels Sydney Diocese is mistaken. Carnley's chapters cover the theological themes of revelation, doctrine, hermeneutics, atonement, ministry, leadership, gender, ethics and dialogue across and between religious communities. But both Giles and Carnley, from their differing viewpoints are agreed that Sydney Anglicanism has

---

51. On the question of subordination and hierarchy see *Common Theology: A Quarterly Journal for Australians*, 1.1,2,3 (2002). Carnley is more guarded in his statements in this book than in the earlier articles, which did indeed leave him open to Giles' criticisms. The point of orthodox trinitarianism is precisely that origin does not necessarily convey pre-eminence—herein lies the fundamental radicalism of trinitarian Christianity's historical challenge to the patriarchy inherent in ancient Roman law.

52. Carnley, 236. Giles' statement that scripture can be trusted to 'accurately reveal the full truth about the whole triune God' offends Carnley's sense of God's unknowability. But it does serve to establish Giles' bonafides as an evangelical Anglican, and, in any case, Carnley may be less troubled by this claim if his paradigmatic 'Demean' theologian were Maurice instead of Mansel. Giles in any case sets out clearly his own interpretative rules (Giles, 202–3).

taken trinitarian theology 'beyond the parameters of Christian orthodoxy'.[53] But both are also wary of name-calling, because both know that it is this above all that cuts off the possibility of ongoing dialogue. Both books contain a hard, prophetic message for Sydney Anglicanism to hear. Kevin Giles claims it was a good eighteen months after publication of his book before he received a considered reply from the representatives of the theology he calls in question, with Peter Carnley's critique addressed in the same article.[54] Both authors name the sense of hostility they claim to have experienced, not only for their theological opinions, but towards themselves personally. In doing so, they give voice to something that many Anglicans—to say nothing of non-Anglican Christians—have often experienced when confronted by the official theological positions of the Diocese of Sydney.

What are the theological issues at stake here? According to Kevin Giles, a theological agenda is being driven by a political agenda, to continue the subordination of women in the home and the church. The Trinity, he argues, is redefined to support the exclusion of women from priestly and episcopal ministries. But this leads him to ask the question: are the formulators of the official theology of the Anglican Diocese of Sydney really being faithful to scripture as it has been understood by the best of theologians from the past and to the creeds and Reformation confessions of faith that they so strongly claim to uphold? According to Carnley, the basic theological problem is the elevation of a matter of theological opinion, the Anselmian atonement theory, to the status of unquestionable dogma. This leads them into a range of other, more complex theological problems. I have suggested that perhaps the fundamental question is whether God's presence can be mediated by material realities. The anecdote about Broughton Knox's advice is most revealing in this regard. If the presence of God cannot be so mediated, then any presence of God in this material world is called in question. Sacraments would no longer be conveyers of God's presence, and all artistic creativity would become immediately suspect. But more importantly, God's presence in the incarnation would become fundamentally unreal, fundamentally

53. Carnley, 241; see also: 233, 234–5.

54. Mark Baddeley, 'Heretics at heart? Sydney goes on trial', in *Southern Cross*, April 2004, online edition.

docetic. And the Son would also be understood as fundamentally subordinate, in eternity, to the one God the Father.

The practical question that arises in each of these interrelated debates is: which practices, and which beliefs underlying them, are matters of doctrine (first order), and which are *theologoumena*, or to be considered matters of opinion (second order)? In other words, where are the boundaries of the church to be drawn? May one diocese withdraw recognition from another, or suspend communion with another, and if so, on what grounds? And if recognition were to be withdrawn, or communion to be suspended, would there be a basis for retaliation against the more scrupulous party on the grounds that its own position may be contestable on another point of practice or doctrine? The current tendency to fragmentation in Australian Anglicanism reflects a problem of identity, of two diverging ways of describing Anglican identity in the Australia at the beginning of the twenty-first century.

Christian identity is, according to Kathryn Tanner, 'essentially relational'.[55] This means that 'Christian identity cannot be secured by sharp cultural boundaries', and that 'the practices that mark a boundary need not be good indicators of what is required to maintain Christian identity'.[56] Markers of identity are contextually determined, and what is a decisive marker of identity in one era or context may disappear entirely, or almost entirely, in another context. As an example we could mention the early Christian custom, so universal that it was itself a Christian badge of identity, of facing east for prayer. Christians do not differ culturally from their non-Christian neighbours, but reshape the existing cultural material. Hierarchy may be adopted, for example, but with its significance reversed (the first last, and the last first). 'Christian practices', writes Tanner, 'are always the practices of others made odd'[57]—not only phenomenologically, but for good theological reasons. Thus, 'one should not try, for example, to purify Christian practices from outside influences out of

55. Tanner, 108.

56. Tanner (109) gives the example of the freedom to eat beef as a boundary marker that identifies Christians in largely Hindu India, but nowhere else in the world.

57. Tanner, 113.

fear of their possibly corrupting influences', because God's grace meets us—as the saying goes—where we are.[58]

Tanner's argument is of direct relevance to some of the divisive debates within Australian Anglicanism at present. Her statement, 'the propriety of a new use . . . is not apparent before it actually emerges and there has been some public effort to establish whether it works',[59] means that there can be no pre-emptory rejection of a proposal to change Christian practice. Each proposal must be considered anew. This applies equally to the introduction of lay presidency at the eucharist as to ordination of practicing homosexuals. There needs to be argument and testing of these proposed changes in practice. Any premature condemnation is theologically problematic. For Tanner, this situation becomes a demand for the maintaining of communication, and communion. 'Because one's point of view is invariably inadequate, it makes sense to keep in touch with those who have formed other conclusions: one might conceivably be corrected by them'.[60] The latter wry remark is a reference, of course, to the possibility of a radical change in one's perspective; to the possibility of conversion.[61] But this is not to say there has to be a winner to the argument: quite the contrary. 'The purpose of engaging in argument with others cannot be . . . to bring about conformity with the account of the object one brings to the debate'.[62] Rather, the object is to maintain a 'fellowship of mutual concern and admonition',[63] in which debate with other Christians is to be expected as the norm, and 'Christian agreements' when they do occur, 'are agreements about how to have an argument'.[64] This may appear a bleak prospect, except that it is this reality that maintains openness to God's future, to the new thing God is always doing in our midst. It is a warning against any attempt at

58. Tanner, 113.
59. Tanner, 79.
60. Tanner, 127.
61. Elsewhere Tanner remarks: 'For this reason theological arguments are often bad arguments, if understood in purely logical terms', because they work not by persuasion but by demanding a change in perspective—they 'transpose the grounds of argument as they proceed' (Tanner, 117).
62. Tanner, 128.
63. Tanner, 178.
64. Tanner, 174.

closure through 'deeming some things out of bounds',[65] or any hasty exclusion of another from Christian fellowship. 'The beliefs and actions that are to make Christian practice uniform must be ones that all parties, and not just some, come to agree upon', writes Tanner, and this agreement should 'be looked for with the utmost patience'.[66] Christianity's reliance on God's grace lies behind Tanner's wise advocacy of utmost patience and the transcendence of rules. It is an encouragement to live joyously with difference and not to be disheartened or defeated by it. Style will reflect beliefs and practices, but need not be fundamentally divisive. From this perspective, there are very few questions that could be considered first order or non-negotiable. How these are to be identified will still, of course, be a matter for debate.

But style on its own is not enough: it must embody beliefs and practices. The substantive theological issues of the current debate concern how we know God and how we relate to God. Is our knowledge of God essentially propositional, and is our relating to God essentially one of obedience? It is here that a coherent alternative needs to be stated clearly and unambiguously: the gospel imperative towards liberation, and the egalitarian social implications of orthodox trinitarianism.[67]

God's church—including the Anglican attempt to be God's church—is the community that meets in memory of and participation in a broken body, around a piece of broken, fragmented bread and a cup of poured-out wine. It is hardly surprising that it should itself be a broken community, a broken body. But diversity, though a feature of Christianity, need not mean fragmentation. Michael Kinnamon remarks that the diversity of the New Testament church 'opens us to the possibility of a unity that (following scripture) is richly diverse and oriented toward the future leading of the Spirit'.[68] This insight applies as much to the Anglican Church, and the particularities of the

65. Tanner, 174. This is my main reason for objecting to the Archbishop of Sydney's advocacy of 'withdrawal of fellowship': it closes the conversation.

66. Tanner, 172.

67. See my short article 'Trinity and Personhood', *St Mark's Review*, 1/198, 2005: 29–31.

68. Michael Kinnamon, *Truth and Community: Diversity and its Limits in the Ecumenical Movement* (Grand Rapids: Eerdmans, 1988), 3.

Anglican expression of the Christian common life in Australia, as it does to the church of God as a whole.

To say this is not to underestimate the seriousness of the current situation. The books surveyed here are warnings about Australian Anglicanism's fragmenting identity. I do not want in any way to minimise this danger. There are grounds for genuine doubt about the extent to which Australian Anglicans hold common beliefs and values. The issue becomes one of how we are to manage our diversity. In practice this means: what are the limits of acceptable diversity? Various guidelines have been suggested for this, but tend to generalities that are hard to implement in practice. There will always be different understandings as to what constitutes those things we agree are unacceptable. It is a principle of ecumenical theology that truth must be sought in community, and this is as true of intra-Anglican differences as it is in the broader ecumenical context.[69] It is in keeping with the Anglican liturgical principle that prayer—and therefore our relationship with God—is something done in common, communally.

It could be that the Anglican Church in Australia is only beginning to find its own true identity, as a church of the southern hemisphere.[70] The old identity has had to fragment to allow this new, more authentic identity to begin to emerge. This new identity will be unlike the old in more ways than one: it cannot be a monocultural identity, but pluriform. It must be porous to surrounding cultures—including the predominantly secular Australian culture—while making these cultures odd, shaping them to convey the good news of Jesus Christ. It is this blending that will give Australian Anglicanism its own sense of style, its own relevance and its own identity.

---

69. Kinnamon, 11, 29ff.

70. *The Age*, 17 January 2004, 13, Philip Huggins interview by Barney Zwartz. This emerging redefinition of Anglican identity is by no means simply an Australian phenomenon: see *Beyond Colonial Anglicanism: The Anglican Communion in the Twenty-First Century*, edited by IT Douglas and K Pui-lan (New York: Church Publishing, 2001).

12

Authority And Power In A Voluntarist Church

Alan Cadwallader

A retrospective introduction

Aphrodisias was a modest city of Hellenistic foundation south-west of Colossae and Laodiceia across the craggy divide of the Taurus mountains of Asia Minor, modern-day Turkey. Like Eumeneia and other towns of the Roman provinces of Phrygia and Caria, it has yielded some curious indications of Christian life at the ordinary levels of the general populace. In 1993, Charlotte Roueché published a number of inscriptions from Aphrodisias dated to the later Roman period. One funerary inscription honours a man who raised bulls. Roueché interprets the inscription in the context of the entertainment that delighted the crowds who gathered in Aphrodisias' large (and well-preserved) stadium.[1] This specialist husbandry was geared towards one of the essential elements in the maintenance of the spectacles that were regularly staged in the city. Whether gladiatorial contests or re-enactments of culture-defining military contests, animals needed to be provided for the agonistic battles of the arena. At one stage in the social life of Aphrodisias, this man had made his living satisfying that demand.

The inscription is approximately coincident with the time when the intellectual leadership of the church was inveighing against the theatre, the stadium, the entertainment of the masses that were a staple of social and cultural life. Tertullian castigated those Christians who ventured an involvement in the tiers of poisonous spectacles;[2] he

1. C Roueché, *Performers and Partisans at Aphrodisias* (London: Society for the Promotion of Roman Studies, 1993), paragraph 44.
2. Tertullian, *On the Spectacles*, 27 (translation from the ANCL series).

festooned his full rhetorical flourishing with a forecast of the glorious ring-side seat he will occupy for the advent judgment of Christ:

> I shall have a better opportunity then of hearing the tragedians, louder-voiced in their own calamity; of viewing the play-actors, much more dissolute in the dissolving flame; of looking upon the charioteer, all glowing in his chariot of fire; of witnessing the wrestlers not in their gymnasia, but tossing in the fiery billows . . . [3]

This was hardly an isolated utterance from Tertullian[4] nor an orphaned outburst from the intelligentsia of the church. Especially in the pre-Constantinian period, the intellectual leadership of the church promoted the church as an alternate society disengaged from the potential pollutions of political and cultural life.[5] Even after the Constantinian settlement ecclesial heavyweights would reformulate the antagonism whenever they considered that the state was abrogating direction of church matters (temporal or spiritual) to itself.[6]

Here surfaces the irony: the aforementioned Aphrodisian inscription begins with a cross. Although Roueché provides no discussion of the significance, it appears that our 'bull-raiser' was a Christian.[7] A concentration on the elite textual parameters set forth by the literati might raise doubts about his religious adherence, even as they vilified his practice, but this is unwarrantedly to privilege one section of the church above another. It would promote history as nothing other than an uncritical repetition of ancient texts with perhaps the veiled agenda of a desire to reinforce doctrinal and ethical orthodoxy in a

3. *Ibid*, 30.
4. See also, for example, his *On Idolatry* 2.4.
5. See Origen, *Against Celsus* 3.30, 8.75, and the anonymous *Epistle to Diognetius* 5.5, 9.
6. So for example John Chrysostom; see also JL González, *The Story of Christianity* (New York: HarperSanFrancisco, 1988), 1, paragraph 198–9.
7. Although some dispute remains about the significance of the presence of a cross on earlier finds, by the third century little doubt is entertained. Certainly, Sir William Ramsay sees the presence of a cross as a clear indication of a Christian: *Cities and Bishoprics of Phrygia*, 2 volumes (Oxford: Clarendon Press, 1895), 561.

contemporary period. Peter Brown's succession of writings on the patristic and Byzantine church has taught us to be reserved in applying the multiple texts and rulings of a minority to the actual lives of the majority of Christians.[8] Gary Johnson's collection of epitaphs from Anatolia, for example, reveals Christians as *agonothetes* (financiers and supervisors of games and entertainments), hunters, and athletes.[9] Anthony Sheppard concludes that the Christians of third and fourth century Phrygian Eumeneia, as revealed not by preserved ecclesiastical writings but the survival of local and semi-public inscriptions, display 'a desire to conform with society's demands' rather than stand against them.[10]

This is merely a snapshot of some of the evidence that has begun to cause a substantial reconsideration of the early centuries of Christianity.[11] The church was not in fact a counter-cultural sect fired by oppositional dynamics to forge its self-definition. At the popular, majority, non-elite level, the church was not merely given to assimilatory patterns of life to ensure its survival (a strategic accommodation to the surrounding society), its members were integrated culturally and socially to many if not most of the mores that characterised their local situation. In the second century, this could even be turned to apologetic advantage: 'Christians are distinguished from the rest of humanity neither by land, nor language nor customs' (*Epistle to Diognetus* 5:1), though the writer was also at pains to paint Christians, in spite of this paradox, as quite singular. In general however, especially as the church increased its influence in society, whatever distinctive injunctions issued from intellectual theologians and ecclesiastical councils, Christians outside of such privileged

8. See, for example, G Johnson, *The Body and Society: Men, Women and Sexual Renunciation in Early Christianity* (London: Faber & Faber, 1990), 24, 250, 428–31.
9. GJ Johnson, *Early Christian Epitaphs from Anatolia* (Atlanta, GA: Scholars Press, 1995), paragraphs 3.1, 3.8, 3.4.
10. ARR Sheppard 'RECAM Notes and Studies number 6: Jews, Christians and heretics in Acmonia and Eumeneia', *Anatolian Studies*, 29 (1979): 171.
11. See especially, PA Harland, *Associations, Synagogues and Congregations: Claiming a Place in Ancient Mediterranean Society* (Minneapolis: Fortress, 2003).

groups more or less cheerfully engaged the patterns of life of their non-Christian neighbours, and, in later triumphal Christian dominance, preserved various repudiated practices through a variety of accommodating and tolerant revisions. The danger of a concentration on the written texts transmitted under church and imperial patronage is that these early transmitted and repeated writings become further re-inscribed by later commentators and are forced to perform as history though they were written as rhetoric. Certainly these juridical and rhetorical texts had some impact beyond the literati especially under imperial patronage, but they cannot be compelled, without other evidence, to indicate the beliefs and practices of ordinary Christians, even though they presume to speak for them.

Using the distant past to bring perspective on the present

The advantage of such a distant historical awareness is that the limited evidence and removed personal interest can carve broad heuristic lines for the interpretation of the source, direction and invigoration of power and authority in the church in a more recent period. The usual bi-polar construct of 'church and society' or 'church and state' is capable of greater definition. The operative actants from this brief dip into early Christianity in western Asia Minor can be triangulated as society—ordinary Christian membership—church leadership. Each one of these elements interacts in a complex tensile relationship with both of the others and the dynamics of any single line of connection affects the other. Recognising this enables an important caveat to be placed on the often legalistic, frequently technical descriptions of how power and authority operate in the Anglican Church of Australia. The tendency is to concentrate on the intellectual analyses that blend description and prescription and draw on constitutional frameworks and theological ideologies,[12] even should it be condescendingly acknowledged that ordinary Christians provide the key building

12. Whilst all texts, defined broadly, are ideological, here there is a recognition that theology frequently operates as oblique servant of ecclesiastical structures and practices providing an ideational rationale. Frequently such theology adopts the stance of an 'obvious' metaphysical proposition, a form of ideology that Pierre Bourdieu distinguishes as 'symbolic domination'. On the varieties of ideology, see P Bourdieu and T Eagleton, 'Doxa and Common Life: An Interview', in *Mapping Ideology*,edited by S Zizek (London/New York: Verso, 1994), 265–77.

blocks for the church, that they are all ministers of the church and that they provide the visible face of the church within the community. This finds particular focus in such analyses with the extolling of the role of synods in the legislative, structural and policy dimensions of church polity, precisely because these synods are populated by the laity, the traditional equation with the 'voluntary', non-stipended membership of the church.

Theological analysis of authority and power within the church then becomes, on the one hand, emaciated both conceptually and operationally because of a failure to acknowledge the important role ordinary Christians play in negotiating society on their own terms. On the other hand, it becomes surreptitiously embroiled in its own power dynamics because of the assumption that such elite, and often institutional, analyses speak (and are meant to speak) for the whole church. For an Anglican Church that has trumpeted its own Protestant distrust of a magisterial imposition of uniformity, it has merely turned to other sources of magisterial control, dislodging one locus of control and replacing it with another that usefully serves a limited cartel within its walls. If nothing else, the failure of Lambeth Resolutions to control its members' reading material (Resolution #63, 1897) and birth control practices (Resolution #68, 1920) raises the suspicion that the ordinary 'volunteer' in its membership neither thinks nor acts necessarily as the official church leadership and its theological script writers 'resolve'. Sometimes this operates at the level of silent resistance (or blissful ignorance). At other times, regardless of official decisions at episcopal, council or diocesan levels, the resistance bursts into active protest. She (and membership figures require that this be the dominant pronoun for the ordinary member) operates from considerations frequently at variance with the pronouncements of doctrine commissions, synod resolutions and even canon law.

Efforts either to overcome the subversion by ordinary members of the power and authority (the authoritarian approach) or to absorb their interests, practices and understandings into the so-called higher levels of office and thought (the populist appeal) become an important indicator that, whatever may be said of power and authority in more official or recognised pronouncements,[13] there is at least a residual,

13. See for example, Stephen Sykes, *Unashamed Anglicanism* (London: DLT, 1995), 140ff where the unfolding of the discussion rests on the

resistant power and authority that lies beyond these. The *vox/lex populi* is a significant component of the power and authority of the church. But that voice is as much informed by the ideas operating within the society in which that voice is produced as it is by ideas that emanate from the dragomen of scripture and tradition. This is the more pronounced in the Anglican Church which, whether by law (as in England) or by nostalgia (as in Australia), understands its boundaries in part as society in general, not as its own particular society.[14]

Similarly, in spite of the overt claim to handle scripture and tradition as the source of its authority (if not its power), the clerisy is equally indebted to the power and structures of the social fabric to enforce its claims and eminence, and it provides a powerful return on that investment.[15] The sometimes necessary reference to civic authority to establish its constitutional and disciplinary frameworks that belong to the foundation of Anglican polity in Australia has proved so resilient that it has become a mark of Anglican practice. Official structures of the church make recourse to the law courts (as in the women's ordination test-case of *Scandrett v Dowling*)[16] and to civil

---

distinction between the decision-making processes of the Anglican communion and what he designates as the 'theological topic of "authority" '. Sykes bumps against sociological categories when he adds 'as it is articulated and reflected upon in the common stock of experiences shared by the Anglican family' but the constant reference to published theological argumentation shows the select pool he draws from when it comes to doing 'theology'.

14. This is not merely or even primarily a missionary stance: see B Kaye, *A Church without Walls: Being Anglican in Australia* (Melbourne: Dove, 1995).

15. 'Clerisy' is the term used by the social analyst, Ernest Gellner, for the seemingly independent group which provides the wisdom that justifies existing inequalities in access and influence in human affairs, and the policing that enforces those inequalities. See my 'Swords into Ploughshares: The End of War? (Q/Luke 9:62)', in *The Earth Story in the New Testament*, edited by N Habel and V Balabanski, volume 5 (London: Sheffield University Press, 2002), 57–60 (and the references there cited).

16. See generally Justice Keith Mason, 'Believers in Court: Sydney Anglicans Going to Law', The Kenneth Cable Lecture, 9 September 2005.

government (as in the coverage of internal reports on sexual abuse cases with the blanket of parliamentary privilege) both in an effort to resolve internal theological debates that ideologise actual or proposed ecclesial practice or to deal with infringements of state law. The pronouncement of the death of Christendom that has infatuated many hopefuls in recent decades has been found to be considerably premature as the clerisy works to regain its integrated position and recognised standing in wider society, after the dents of recent organisational, financial and reputational crises. The growing power, influence and moral positioning of the media has only expanded the connections that some within the church court with it so that the church may participate in the very characteristics that define the complex role of media in society.[17]

The state is not without its own interests in both these groups—the ordinary or voluntary member of the church and the more recognisable clerisy, especially as it portrays itself as both the micro-organism and also the arbiter for society. The courting of a recognisable electoral force in the *Hillsong* connection, that the current Australian Treasurer (amongst a number) indulges, is but one pragmatic political posture designed to secure the power of a ruling elite and, in the adoption of resonant discursive devices, to appropriate a linguistic range to justify decisions, policies and even budget rationales in pseudo-theological terms.[18] The exchange of language is part of the mechanism by which the stability of society is politically managed and dissent discredited, marginalised and thereby controlled. On the one hand, appeals to family, care, order, even prosperity and border protection, can be given a Christian gloss and on the other hand, criticism (such as of poker machines and industrial deregulation) can be emasculated into band-aid remedies for

17. On the rise of the media as moralising watchdog and weapon of control, see *Do Not Disturb: is the media failing Australia?*, edited by R Manne (Melbourne: Black Inc Agenda, 2005) and *Remote Control: New Media, New Ethics*, edited by C Lumby and E Probyn, (Cambridge/Port Melbourne: Cambridge University Press, 2003).

18. See generally M Maddox, *God Under Howard: The Rise of the Religious Right in Australian Politics* (Crows Nest, NSW: Allen & Unwin, 2005).

occasional, unfortunate and 'unintended' extreme consequences of state policies.[19]

The triangulation then of society—ordinary Christian membership —church leadership can provide a useful heuristic tool to negotiate and hopefully extend understanding of the dynamics of authority and power within a church that is described in some measure as 'voluntarist'. Each of these key terms, 'authority', 'power', 'voluntary' will shift in meaning and focus according to the originating apex of this triangulation. In what follows, nothing more than a beginning is made and will constantly interchange historico-theological, sociological and political perspectives. In part, this derives from the demand of the parameters established for this essay; in part also it questions the value and truthfulness of singular foundations.

The triangulation of church leadership—ordinary Christian membership—society

In an introduction to a collection of essays on the church and democracy published in 1992, James Provost and Knut Walf had suggested that the evidence of past and recent history was that 'democratisation is incompatible with the essence of the church'.[20] The backdrop for their writing is the Church of Rome, but the emphasis on hierarchical structures within other churches suggests that any differences between churches are likely to be in degree rather than in kind.

For the Anglican Church of Australia the general observations on the relationships between the three apices of the triangulation have been particularly focussed on the decision-making structure of 'synod'. Authority becomes defined in terms of the synodal process and results with particular accent on the supposed Anglican virtue of the dispersion of authority amongst different entities. A general theological wash has been applied across the Anglican communion, provinces, dioceses and to some extent even parishes, that seeks to make the temporal expression of church dependent on the range of authoritative contributions to theology. The voluminous definition in a report of a Committee of 1948 Lambeth Conference is worth quoting,

19. See J Paget-Wilkes, *Poverty, Revolution and the Church* (Exeter: Paternoster, 1981).
20. J Provost and Knut Walf, editors, 'The Tabu of Democracy within the Church', *Concilium*, 5 (1992): vii.

not because of the specific elements within its content but because of its clear intent to provide a theological grounding for the realities of the expression of Anglican polity:

> Authority, as inherited by the Anglican Communion from the undivided Church of the earlier centuries of the Christian era, is single in that it is derived from a single Divine source, and reflects within itself the richness and historicity of the divine Revelation, the authority of the eternal Father, the incarnate Son, and the life-giving Spirit. It is distributed among Scripture, Tradition, Creeds, the Ministry of the Word and Sacraments, the witness of saints, and the *consensus fidelium*, which is the continuing experience of the Holy Spirit through his faithful people in the Church. It is thus a dispersed rather than a centralised authority having many elements which combine, interact with, and check each other; these elements together contributing by a process of mutual support, mutual checking, and redressing of errors or exaggerations to the many-sided fullness of the authority which Christ has committed to His Church. Where this authority of Christ is to be found mediated not in one mode but in several we recognise in this multiplicity God's loving provision against the temptations to tyranny and the dangers of unchecked power.[21]

With exemplary Anglican politeness, the euphemism of 'tyranny and . . . unchecked power' is used as an oblique reference to 'Romish' authoritarianism against which much of what is 'inherited by the Anglican communion' is defined.

This has received two particular accents in partially apologetic defences of synodal government. On the one hand, Keith Chittleborough situates synodal government at the heart of Anglican order: it provides the structural expression to the application of 'dispersed

21. *The Lambeth Conference, 1948: The Encyclical Letter from the Bishops; together with Resolutions and Reports* (London: SPCK, 1948), 81–94 and here 84, 85.

authority' in the fundamental historically inherited (and providentially bequeathed?) ecclesiastical unit called the diocese.[22] As such, he sought to provide a theological justification for the evolved reality of historical and political contexts, episcopal styles and constitutional mimesis, a justification that accented the organic rather than the hierarchical mode of being church. This is particularly significant, for even though some theological argument had accompanied the nineteenth century debates about the movement towards synodal structures, these were neither definitive nor determinative. However, the nineteenth century legacy of the Cambridge triumvirate (BF Westcott, JB Lightfoot and FJA Hort)—that theological reflection *follows* historical (and textual) recognition[23]—justified Chittleborough's approach,[24] provided that there could be some affirmation that the historical given of synodal development was also 'providential'.

This was precisely the affirmation made in a second treatment of the development of synodal government in the Anglican Church of

---

22. KS Chittleborough, 'Toward a Theology and Practice of the Bishop-in-Synod', *St Mark's Review*, 109 (1982): 27–33, reprinted with minor revisions in *Authority in the Anglican Communion: Essays Presented to Bishop John Howe*, edited by SW Sykes (Toronto: Anglican Book Centre, 1987), 144–62.
23. See G Treloar, *Lightfoot the Historian: The Nature and Role of History in the Life and Thought of JB Lightfoot (1828–1889) as Churchman and Scholar* (Tübingen: Mohr Siebeck, 1998): 90ff, and see also generally, Duncan Forbes, *The Liberal Anglican Idea of History* (Cambridge: Cambridge University Press, 1952).
24. The influence of the three on Australian Anglicanism has never been explored. Not only were their ideas heavily circulated through the colonial purveying of the Macmillan publishing company but they were carried in person by a succession of at least thirty of their protégés in clerical and episcopal dress (source: unpublished index of nineteenth century Australian clergy collated by the late Professor K Cable). From the wharf perambulations of the mildly socialist Tasmanian bishop (Mercer), to the development of the bush brotherhoods by the Durham priest, GD Halford, their mark was openly acknowledged. See G Stephens, *The Anglican Church in Tasmania: A Diocesan History to Mark the Sesquicentenary: 1992* (Hobart: Trustees of the Diocese, 1991): 144; RHH Philps, 'Steel All Through: The Church of England in Central Queensland—Transplantation and Adaptation, 1892–1942', PhD Thesis, Central Queensland University (2002): 88–117.

Australia by Bruce Kaye.[25] He probed the detail of the birth of synods in Australia and demonstrated that the theological arguments privately and publicly espoused by the bishops, and recast at a later period by church historians, were not the prime motivators for the development of synods. Rather, a politically informed and/or motivated laity is credited with this advance, informed that is by developments in the civic sphere. Although Kaye does not argue for it in this essay, it is clear that this is but one reiteration of the Anglican understanding, going back to Richard Hooker, that no ecclesial structure is sacrosanct. At face value, this indicates that the distinction sometimes made between theocracy and democracy is artificial. Theocracy is often touted as the metaphysical justification for hierarchical structures—the bishop being espoused as the visible sign of an invisible authority, with derivative delegations passing through to local expressions of the church. But if these structures derive from a pragmatic base rather than a metaphysical dispensation then different constructions and validations are possible. This last is precisely what is argued by Kaye: firstly, in recognition that reliance on legislative support for the establishment of synods, as in Melbourne, or on a 'consensual compact' (albeit affirmed in its authenticity by English lawyers), as in Adelaide, made little difference to the outcome; and secondly, in the hermeneutical question he raises as to whether the historical context and political realities of contemporary Australian Anglicanism warrant further changes to the church's polity. Accordingly, 'voluntary' is roughly equated with the laity, 'authority' with synodal constitutionality and 'power', in significant measure, derived from both these elements.

However, both treatments fail to recognise that, whether synodal government be justified by contemporary theological rhetoric or historical drives for enfranchisement, there are certain mystifications that obscure the reality that synodal government is not a laicisation or even democratisation of the church. Rather, a *part* of the voluntary membership of the church is drawn into the support of existing power arrangements which later themselves adapt in order to maintain their hegemony. Kaye's emphasis on Bishop Short's pragmatic negotiation

---

25. BN Kaye, 'The Strange Birth of Anglican Synods in Australia and the 1850 Bishops' Conference', *Journal of Religious History*, 27 (2003): 196.

of lay demands completely accords with this (especially when coupled with the problems of finances that the church was confronting in the 1850s). Even though the nineteenth century witnessed considerable changes in enfranchisement, the pre-eminent encapsulation of the overall movement, Lord Russell's 1832 (English) Reform Act, is increasingly interpreted as an adroit concession to a limited (male) section of the broader contending alliance.[26] Not only did the accession successfully divide the suffrage movement but it secured from the newly enfranchised, upwardly mobile members, support for ruling interests. Kaye recognises the influence of English political ideas of the time. He does not mention that the *strategies* adopted in negotiation of the dispute also are reflected in the Australian context, albeit local factors having some nuisance value. The emphasis on the 'property qualification' for parochial membership in synods and the granting of extended representation based on the number of clergy supported (both of which remain in force in many dioceses), are clear indications that the clerisy did not yield power to the voluntary members of the church but merely changed the appearance of authority under which a temporal church operated.

Moreover, there is a development in synodal practice that has crept unheralded into the *realpolitick* of church governance, namely the aggregation of power by diocesan councils through delegated authority from synods (as, for example, by resolution), through the initiation and 'guidance' of measures through synod and through their sometimes conflictual relationships with bishops. Kaye's astute linkage of the development of synodal government with the general socio-political expansion of the franchise in the nineteenth century remains true today, albeit morphed towards the increased emphasis on *executive* decision-making in contemporary western democracies. A further caveat on the argument that synodal government represents the authority of the lay or voluntary members of the church is the crisis of faith in the synodal process that sometimes is delivered by the silent resistance apparent in the ignoring of financial or attendance obligations and which sometimes surfaces in open expression. A

26. See, for example, C Behagg, 'An Alliance with the Middle Class: the Birmingham Political Union and Early Chartism', in *The Chartist Experience: Studies in Working-Class Radicalism and Culture 1830–1860*, edited by J Epstein and D Thompson (Exeter: Macmillan, 1982), 59–86.

student of mine, the late Anne Roder, offered a satirical variation on the apostle Paul's 'sufferings of the sage' based on a lay person's experience of synod:

> But whatever anyone dares to boast of—I am speaking as a fool—I also dare to boast of that. Are they Anglican? So am I. Are they Synod members? So am I. Are they debaters? I am talking like a madman—I am a better one: with far greater interjections, far more Episcopal glares, with countless floggings, and often near death. Five times I have received from the President the forty glares less one. Three times I have been beaten by procedural motions. Once I received a reprimand. Three times I was heckled; for two days and two nights I was adrift in motions, or frequent amendments; in danger from ordinances, danger from budgets, danger from my own people, danger from Archdeacons, danger in the Executive and Finance, danger in Diocesan Council, danger at Synod, danger from Archbishop; in toil and hardship, through many a sleepless night, hungry and thirsty, often without spiritual food, cold and forsaken . . .

Here the synod is no longer part of the system of which the volunteer is a part but rather the conflictual element against which one defines oneself. The authority cultivated by constitutional arrangements and due procedure is under severe strain precisely because power is not perceived as derived from its processes, except in contrastive terms. Satirical parody it may be, but perhaps no more than Paul's own adoption of a familiar philosophical topos.[27]

From an Anglican perspective, Bradbury puts the sharp edge to Kaye's question, 'as society loses all deference for authority what decision-making structures will work best for the churches of post-

27. See AT Lincoln, 'Paul the Visionary: the Setting and Significance of the Rapture to Paradise in II Corinthians 12:1–10', *NTS*, 25 (1979): 204–20.

Christendom'.[28] The contemporary threat of the fragmentation of the Anglican communion and the West's enforced confrontation with terror has worked to promote in some quarters,[29] a retreat into increased hierarchical forms, under the veil of leadership, efficiency and, the ultimate ideological appeal, 'unity'. Dennis Oakman provides a telling summation of the alternative facing voluntary elements: 'Elites depend on normative interpretations of cultural forms to promote docile and tractable underlings. Non-elites reinterpret the great traditions in order to meet their own social needs.'[30] To the second, in the form of the apex of the voluntary church I now turn.

The triangulation of ordinary Christian membership—society—church leadership

Australian Anglicans have long been caught in the complex historical inheritance of conceptualising society and culture as a providential accompaniment to faith. A more Protestant take might visualise the providence as an evangelistic opportunity; a more catholic approach might visualise it as the arena for Christian expression. These two visualisations have manifold varieties but one necessary consequence is to acknowledge the social and societal existence of the members of a voluntary church. Moreover, the involvement of those members within the wider society creates networks of social alliances and ideational transference that frequently claim as much, if not more, of the attention of those 'volunteers'. In other words, voluntarist activity is not necessarily confined to the church; indeed such activity may well become negligible, such as to qualify them for Jack Spong's 'church alumni' tag. Regardless of their place in the spectrum of church allegiance, the Anglican Church of Australia has been loath to dismiss any of these volunteers from some sort of membership—a sort of charitable assumption of connection until proven otherwise. Even the

---

28. N Bradbury, 'Ecclesiology and Pastoral Theology', in *The Blackwell Reader in Pastoral and Practical Theology*, edited by J Woodward and S Pattison (Oxford: Blackwell, 2000), 179.
29. See P Carnley, *The Yellow Wallpaper and other Sermons* (Australia: HarperCollins, 2001), 199–206; and *Reflections in Glass: Trends and Tensions in the Contemporary Anglican Church* (Pymble, NSW: HarperCollins, 2004), 156–207.
30. D Oakman, 'Culture, Society and Embedded Religion in Antiquity', *Biblical Theology Bulletin*, 35 (2005): 10.

Constitution of the Anglican Church of Australia adopts a quite minimalist notion of membership: baptism, attendance (with no frequency specified) and indication of belonging (also broadly defined) (§74.1).[31] It means that of all churches, the Anglican Church has probably been the most dissatisfied with the *National Church Life Surveys* as expressing what its life actually is (both in the census questions and in the collated results), even as it faces the interrogation of reported statistical decline.

A significant issue, however, flows from a recognition of the breadth of types of allegiance amongst those who accrue no financial benefit from church membership yet who may be accorded a variety of recognised connections with the church (everything from a naming on the planned giving list to a regulated office for the organization of the local parish).[32] The 'volunteer's' personal locus of authority under which she engages with the church at whatever level may be informed by an array of stimulations and relationships, most of which are not provided by the church of which she is a member. Almost inevitably this personal locus of authority will at some points enter into conflict with the sources of authority that the church itself promotes (a representative list is quoted above).

In an open church this might be accommodated and made the energy of creative development. But, as Paul Avis argues, traditionally the church of whatever brand has not been open, but rather closed, dominated by an authoritarian consciousness which, when its authority is not recognised, reverts to a raw exercise of power over those who have displayed an 'aberrant' faith or life-style.[33] This flies in the face of the recommended engagement of volunteers in non-ecclesial societal groups. Such recommendations are, for example:

---

31. In fact, the constitutional definition appears even more minimalist than the elements of a 'consensual compact' exposited by JA Priestley, in *Scandrett v Dowling*, *NSWLR*, 27 (1992), 483, 512, 534–64, especially at 554 and 557–8.
32. State Parliament legislation proposed for South Australia (in late 2005) may add a significant variation on the meaning and import of church 'volunteer', by providing a specific and broad-ranging legal definition that will encompass many church members.
33. P Avis, *Authority, Leadership and Conflict in the Church* (London: Mowbray, 1992), 39, 85 *et passim*.

> The mission and priorities of the organisation are framed in terms of the problem or issue the organisation is addressing, not its short-range institutional concern . . . There is an openness to change, an eagerness to improve performance and conscious, organised efforts to learn from and about volunteers' experiences in the organization . . . Volunteers are seen as valuable human resources that can directly contribute to achievement of the organisation's mission, not primarily as a means to obtaining financial or other material resources.[34]

Whatever the desire for connection with and in the Anglican Church, the preferred avoidance of confrontation with authoritarianism has bred a silent resistance to conformity of thought, guarded disclosures of personal behaviours and an increasing nominalism and/or consumerism (of belief and action). Kierkegaard's rueful comment rings uncannily true a hundred and fifty years later:

> In the magnificent cathedral the Honourable and Right Reverend Geheime-General-Ober-Hof-Prädikant . . . appears before an elect company and preaches with emotion upon the text he himself elected: 'God hath elected the base things of the world and the things that are despised.' And nobody laughs.[35]

Individual authority thus becomes forged out of resistance to, or at least translation or careful selection of what flows from, the positions of power. The examples of Lambeth Resolutions on prescribed/proscribed ecclesiastical history books and birth control measures are sufficiently distant in time to raise a smile today about the laity's lack of observance, but the phenomena remain, whether in the popularity of Jack Spong's books (in spite of the pronouncements emanating from the official church media organs), in the variations on 'acceptable'

---

34. Katie N Campbell, 'Changing the Paradigm Project', *Australian Volunteer*, 7 (1993): 8.
35. Søren Kierkegaard, *Attack upon Christendom*, translated by W Lowrie, in *A Kierkegaard Anthology*, edited by R Bretall (NY: The Modern Library, 1974), 448.

practices of sexuality amongst ordinary church members, or other unrelated matters.

The assertion of individual power to exercise this authority, which is deliberately or unknowingly vested in a person especially in a Western context that avowedly privileges the autonomy of the self, may then extend to a re-allocation of relational connections to enable the cultivation of and reflection upon such authority. When this is a deliberate choice, the influences upon that cultivation and reflection are more likely to be a positive enhancement of the individual's own growth in understanding and contribution to the well-being of the world, though this cannot be guaranteed. So also, there is no guarantee that it will occur within the larger institution against which authority is asserted. The growth of house churches, base Christian communities and spirituality centres that maintain a detached connection with mainline Christianity, reflect the desire to retain a God-focus and a disdain for the requirements of conformity (from finances to morality) often associated with the institutional church. The power to think differently is thus fostered in open but limited surrounding supports. It makes possible an interior sense of the authority to believe and behave differently even as the larger entity continues to be engaged; occasionally, it fosters the development of sufficient momentum to bring change in a larger entity that has become so routinised into its own preservation that tolerance of difference and dissent has expired. As Robbins curtly observes:

> The scene surveyed from an episcopal bench looks very different from the church choir. Perhaps too much 'church history' has been from the standpoint of the shepherds and too little from that of the flock.[36]

Elsewhere, I have sought to explore the importance of the non-elite community in the recognition and execution of truth.[37] What is occasionally affirmed in scripture texts under the communal category

---

36. K Robbins, 'Institutions and Illusions: The Dilemma of the Modern Ecclesiastical Historian', *Studies in Church History*, 11 (1975): 359.
37. A Cadwallader, 'Enscribing Peter as Follower, Listener and Friend (John 21)', in *Episcopacy: Views from the Antipodes*, edited by AH Cadwallader with D Richardson (Adelaide: ABCE, 1994), 339.

of 'we' (such as John 21:24b; and see also Mark 4:30), and rigorously asserted in general socio-linguistic understanding, is that the recipient (individual or community) is a crucial component of any communication event.[38] There is no communication until what is communicated is appropriated. Power therefore lies in the volunteer, the unofficial handler of the tradition, in the way of listening and enacting. What is asserted in scripture is that this position is one that is authorised. For those Anglicans who see the boundaries of the community of faith narrowly drawn, there is a greater opportunity for influence, education and control of interpretation. For those who see the boundaries of Anglicanism as at least porous, if not invisible, such an opportunity is less possible and a range of influences enter upon the volunteer connected with the voluntarist church.

The danger however in this scenario is that one aspiring, if not actual, authoritarian control identified as/with the church institution will be replaced by another less identified and identifiable power, frequently more pervasive and confident in handling the means of influence on popular thinking and interpretation. Surreptitiously, the individual or small community can become prey to other masters rather than cultivating her/its own authority. The adoption of religious terminology and blatant religious appeals by Western leaders—such as the apocalyptic language of George Bush, the pseudo -ecological posture of Margaret Thatcher or the morally disturbed world constructed by John Howard—is not merely an attempt to align with a dominant religious group but a recognition that the disaffection of individuals, even with a vestige of a belief structure, renders those individuals more prone to influence in the absence of any substitute.

In this sense, there is nothing sacrosanct that necessarily flows from privileging the volunteer individual or community with autonomous authority. It is simply that this rarely happens overtly, given that state or church leadership continually usurp the volunteer's authority and power to speak, eager to pontificate for her, if not at her.

38. A Duranti, *Linguistic Anthropology* (Cambridge: Cambridge University Press, 1997), 218–44, 284–94.

The triangulation of society—ordinary Christian membership—church leadership

When the then premier of Victoria, Jeff Kennett criticised Tim Costello and other church leaders for their protests against a casino-led recovery for the state economy, he reminded the church that they should be concerned with spiritual matters not political activism.[39] Similar sentiments were expressed by the Australian Minister for Foreign Affairs, Alexander Downer, directed against the then Anglican Primate, Peter Carnley, for his criticism of Australia's obsequious pursuit of American foreign policy; Carnley was accused of a failure in Christian duty, which meant, according to Downer, 'comforting the victims and their families' and 'binding up the broken-hearted'.[40] Usually there is a dismissal of church concerns as ignorant and ill-informed, as in more recent reactions against church questioning of the intent and impact of the removal of protections for employees in the industrial arena.

Anglicans especially are placed in a quandary. The memory of English establishment has coloured much of the Anglican response to government and broader society. Its colonial foundation with an emphasis on civilisation, dutiful order and moral society, with the appointment of 'colonial' rather than 'missionary' bishops, has generated an uneasy relationship with radical protest and working-class interests. Anglican interpretation of the familiar biblical texts Mark 12:13–17 (taxes to Caesar), Romans 13:1–7 (obedience to government laws) and 1 Peter 2:13–14 (subjection to the emperor) has, almost without exception, promoted an acquiescent, conforming civic citizenship. One son of an Archbishop of Canterbury, Arthur Benson, provided the Victorian Anglican sentiment:

> If they are true to the spirituality of Christ, they have no concern with revolutionary concerns at all; Christ's own example teaches us to leave all that on one side,

39. See generally W Stewart, 'Crown of Thorns, Half Naked, Tits', *Zadok Papers*, 120A (Winter 2002).
40. 'The Sir Thomas Playford Annual Lecture', 27 August 2003.

> to conform to worldly instructions, to accept the framework of society . . .'[41]

It is no coincidence that the second book of Homilies enjoined to be read to the people by the Thirty-Fifth Article of Religion began with the 'right use of the Church' and climaxed with 'Against Rebellion'.[42]

General society and its various branches of government have had little interest in disagreeing with this attitude and seek to maintain a systemic place for the church in its overall operations and structures. The place of religious organizations in society has been a constant focus of analysis (as for example, by Max Weber and Emile Durkheim). Generally, religion within society has been seen at most as a cautious companion for reform (usually related to issues of morality) and more usually as an adjunct to honorific and celebratory rituals that enact the values of unity and order in society. State funerals orchestrated from Anglican cathedrals are a study in systemic reinforcement, just as welfare organizations become arms of government, most especially when they execute and administer state aims and objectives rather than develop advocacy programs for those who do not see that the state serves their interests. The church then is generally cultivated as an embedded member of society and all such embedding ultimately is designed to service the needs of the engulfing entity, just as the church looks to that entity for support.

The reflexively supportive relationship between church and society/state inevitably has implications at both a symbolic and practical level for ordinary church members. Not only are the ultimate values of church and state apparently blended, certain self-interested rhetoric notwithstanding, but the authority inspiring those values becomes understood as shared. Greater power frequently appears to rest with society and culture and the state that operates in and upon them; accordingly the church's espousal of a spiritualised understanding of power operates as a means of negotiating this reality and preserving its own identity within this larger reality. However, the sheer emulation of societal values and characteristics—everything

---

41. AC Benson, *From a College Window* (London: Smith, Elder & Co, 1906), 320.
42. The first Book of Homilies of Edward the Sixth, also recommended though not listed by Article 35, actually contained two such sermons: 'An Exhortation to Obedience' and 'Against Strife and Contention'.

from 'relevant' music in church services to managerial patterns of church organization and practice—carries with it the danger recognised by Richard Roberts, namely 'the corrupt, obfuscatory manipulation of others through the management of power at the most fundamental and insidious level, that is in the construction of the self-consciousness of the other'.[43]

Nevertheless, society is the place where the great bulk of Anglicans live the great bulk of their lives, believing in good measure that God may be found there also in good measure. Herein lies the unease in the relationship of church and state as it is played out in the lives of those who make up a substantial part of both. That they negotiate this tension (by and large) well is a cause of wonder and thanksgiving. That they can bring something of each to the other, however flawed according to the elites that operate in both spheres, is remarkable. As John Macquarrie commented, 'A few active and intelligent lay Christians involved in the political process are worth a thousand sententious utterances by bishops and synods'.[44] But at the same time, from the perspective of the society and state, their authority derives from their place within society; it is frequently a delegated authority rather than a mutual one and constantly subjected to the will to totalitarianism that governments of all persuasions rationalise. The current manipulative discourse on 'Australian values' is merely a more subtle variation on this drive. At its best, society can accept the diversity of microcosmic groups as a generative part of its own life rather than a threat, allowing that prophets probably contribute most when they are not absorbed into the court.

Conclusion: on the need for a horizontal triangulation

Where have we travelled and where have we arrived in this search for power and authority in a voluntarist church? In some ways, it is indeterminate and probably that is the way it has to be in the dynamics of the exchange between elements of a triangle that are themselves constantly changing both in themselves and in relation to

43. RH Roberts, *Religion, Theology and the Human Sciences* (Cambridge: Cambridge University Press, 2002), 159.
44. J Macquarrie, *Theology, Church and Ministry* (London: SCM, 1986), 201.

each other. This is not to be decried, except perhaps by those who desire to replace authority with authoritarianism. The dynamic unfolding nature of truth has been explored by the American post-theologian, Mark Taylor, who provides helpful analogies for how truth is negotiated in the contemporary world.[45] Just as most national currencies derive their value from constant interaction with other currencies (so that their value is constantly changing), just as the brain's neurological functioning is increasingly recognised as non-lineal in sequence, just as a computer's operations are ever-changing in its web of connections, so also the triangulation of the key elements in this analysis has not produced a rigid structural outcome but a diversity of perspectives. In this sense, perhaps the triangle needs to be flattened to a horizontal surface rather than imagined in an upright position with one or other apex asserting its hierarchical dominance. And perhaps in so doing, one might hear God's immanent sigh of relief.

45. MC Taylor, *About Religion: Economies of Faith in Virtual Culture* (Chicago / London: University of Chicago Press, 1999).

Part Four: Context

Part Four: Context

Introduction

The chapters in this section deal particularly with the context within which ecclesiology has been and continues to be shaped and created. Christians are called to live in the tension between heavenly vocation and the social and political context of our daily lives. That context presents the vital test of the integrity of our witness as a Christian community and thus is a touchstone for the value of our ecclesiology. These chapters grapple with that core ecclesiological challenge.

Peter Bolt' s reflection on Christian mission and Australian society urges us to make listening to the Scriptures our starting point in any missiological endeavours. Attempts to make society itself our starting point are misconceived and risk allowing the world to set the agenda, an agenda which is, in fact, God's. Geoff Smith argues a similar point, stating that for the church to be true to its calling it needs to be focussed on the kingdom of God. It is the model that Jesus offers of his own life, faith and ministry that so clearly provides a guide, a challenge and a vision for the church in Australia in the twenty-first century. This will involve a rethinking of structures, of focus and a willingness to let go of some comfortable habits.

David Cole and Ray Cleary write on the particular ecclesial issues facing Anglican schools and Anglican caring and community service organisations. David Cole considers how Anglican schools can both demonstrate their authenticity as worshipping Anglican communities in the way in which they go about their business and also promote the good news of Jesus Christ among students and families, and among staff. He argues that Anglican schools can provide the wider church with important insights into living and proclaiming the Christian message among young people and their families in contemporary Australia. Ray Cleary contends that the welfare and justice ministry are integral to the life and work of Anglican churches. He suggests that the trend towards locating these ministries in arms-length agencies carries the risk that congregations will become isolated from an important part of their Christian life.

Raewynne Whiteley examines the role of the church as public space. Charting the apparent transition of the Anglican Church in Australia, from a place at the heart of the public realm to a position at the margins of public life, she analyses the complex formal and informal relationships between the church and public space and the theological themes that underlie them. She concludes that the church remains a central contributor to public life in Australia, albeit one that owes more to its informal than its formal influences.

Far from it being possible to carve these areas out of the arena of ecclesiology they turn out to be central concerns and indispensable to the shaping of an Anglican ecclesiology.

13

Interpreting Australian Society For Christian Mission

Peter G Bolt

Observers of the earliest phase of Christian mission remarked that it was 'turning society upside down' (Acts 17:6).[1] This mission gradually transformed ancient society from the grass roots up, despite engaging in little direct confrontation with its structures.[2] Christian mission still has a place in contemporary Australia, but how can that first century revolution be duplicated in the twenty-first? Many would assume that society must be interpreted as a necessary prolegomena (roughly, 'prior thing to say') for Christian mission, but how is this interpretation properly done?

The impetus towards interpreting society

For success

Sometimes it is assumed that the 'success' or 'effectiveness' of Christian mission depends on this interpretation. Since the call to 'know thy mission field' is generally meant as a call to know via the methods of analysis found within the human sciences,[3] it has become

1. The Greek word used here, often translated 'world', signifies, not the cosmos (*kosmos*), but the organised world of human society (*oikoumene*).
2. See EA Judge, 'The Impact of Paul's Gospel on Ancient Society', in *The Gospel to the Nations: Perspectives on Paul's Mission: In Honour of Peter T O'Brien*, edited by PG Bolt and MD Thompson (Leicester: IVP, 2000), 297–308.
3. As one example drawn from the Diocese of Sydney, see Margaret Rodgers, 'Knowing our mission field', *Southern Cross* (July, 2003): 9. This article argued that churches should know material from the

almost axiomatic that such studies are frequently enlisted to mobilise churches for mission.

In October 2004, for example, General Synod heard that only four Australian dioceses showed increased church attendances from 1991 to 2001.[4] Recourse to the Australian Bureau of Statistics figures will show that even the growth of these four dioceses is behind that of the general population. The statistics speak a clear, twofold message: there are still plenty of Australians to be reached for Christ, and the Anglican Church is not really doing it.

The real power of these statistics is that they quantify what we already feel to be the case. There are a whole host of reasons why, when we think of the Christian mission, we already operate from a general feeling of failure. When statistical analysis is presented, it finds an already bloody wound in which to fester.

This particular issue is not raised here to be solved. It simply illustrates why the need for interpreting society is regarded as almost axiomatic. Such interpretation exposes the problems to be solved, if Christian mission is to be more successful, or effective. If we are better able to 'read' Australian society, then there will be a greater effectiveness ensuring a greater level of success. If we fail to read it properly, the decline will continue until there is no longer any Anglican witness in Australia. Interpreting Australian society is presented as a necessary step towards the recovery of that revolution caused by the earliest Christian movement.

For contextualisation

Why focus on *Australian* society? Moving beyond the trivial fact that Australia is the context for this publication, a more profound answer would appeal to the need for 'contextualisation' of the gospel. Given the many glaring mistakes made in the former days of 'foreign' missions, in which the missionaries themselves—let alone their recipients—often confused Christianity with Western culture, greater

---

Australian Bureau of Statistics, to 'underpin and strengthen the relevance and impact of their mission'.

4. Sydney (11%), Canberra–Goulburn (1%), Bunbury (4%), and Armidale (2%). See W Brighton, 'Attendance Statistics for the Anglican Church of Australia 1991–2001' (May, 2004): 17, table 4 at www.anglican.org.au/docs/2004–047ACAStatistics.pdf (accessed 9 February 2006).

sensitivity to the culture of the people receiving the gospel has properly been called for. This call has also been incorporated into thinking about 'internal' mission, that is, the spread of the gospel within, and not just beyond, the borders of a particular country.

It could be argued that these questions become particularly pertinent to Anglicanism in Australia. In 1788, representatives of what was the established church in England arrived when the British invaded the Great Southern Land to create a dumping ground for their convicts and yet another grand opportunity for colonial exploitation in the name of British commerce. For various reasons Anglicanism in Australia found it hard to break with English culture. Even as late as 1958, Bishop Stephen Neill could complain that all the Australian metropolitans were English and comment, 'it is greatly to be hoped that it may soon be found possible to elect an Australian archbishop'.[5] It is interesting that Neill apparently derived his desire for Australian-born bishops and archbishops from his missionary impulse, for he immediately adds (and well before any discussion of 'contextualisation'):

> For the Anglican Church of Australia is the largest and strongest of all the Christian denominations in the continent (about forty-four per cent of the population); and on it rests a heavy responsibility for the spiritual future of these great new lands.[6]

Our post-modern environment calls for even further specificity to the task of contextualisation. Not only do we live in a 'broken and divided' world, but (to extend the prayer book) in an almost totally fragmented and subdivided one. Any notion of 'humanity' is long-since destroyed. No doubt fed by Western individualism, pluralism and Australian multiculturalism, as well as by a consumerism in which the advertising industry continues to divide and conquer, people are now grouped according to their sub-cultures and tribes. To the post–modern world the symbol of community is the traffic jam:

5. S Neill, *Anglicanism* (Harmondsworth: Penguin, 1958, revised 1960), 312. His desire began to be fulfilled in the election of Marcus Loane as Archbishop of Sydney in 1966 (–1982).
6. Neill, *Anglicanism*, 313.

surrounded by people with whom you have no interaction, isolated in your own little space, feeling like you are pointing in a certain direction, but going absolutely nowhere. While Christian thinkers ask whether 'community' may be the key to mission,[7] the rhetoric of 'community' is becoming increasingly shrill, as the reality of genuine communion with others is rapidly disappearing.

This desire for greater success and the assumption of the necessity of contextualisation seems to lead inevitably to the question: if Christian mission is ever to create another revolution, is there not a great need to interpret Australian society for Christian mission?

Christian mission and Australian society

From the point of view of Australian society, Christian mission has a thoroughly legitimate place within it.

Christian mission in earliest Australian society

Christian mission has been a part of Australian society since its inception in 1788.[8] Whatever the unfortunate events that led up to this moment, when others viewed those 'victims of the overcrowding in the gaols', 'as exiles not only from their families and their country, but also from God,'[9] there were those both behind and within the colony that saw the great southland opening up new mission fields crying out for the gospel of Jesus Christ. The early chaplains were products of the evangelical revival and they brought their missionary impulse with them to the new colony,[10] as did other clergy who joined them later. A substantial body of free settlers, Anglican and otherwise—including prominent members of society at the highest level (such as Governors

7. For example, M McCoy, ' "Community": A Postmodern Mission Paradigm?', *JAS*, 1.1 (2003): 31–45.
8. This statement does not negate Aboriginal history before this date, but simply acknowledges that *Australian* society, as such, begins when the modern nation of Australia sprang into existence, with the arrival of the First Fleet.
9. CMH Clark, *A History of Australia I: From the Earliest Times to the Age of Macquarie* (Melbourne: Melbourne University Press, (1962) 1985), 72.
10. BH Fletcher, 'The Anglican Ascendancy 1788–1835', in BN Kaye, editor, *Anglicanism in Australia: A History* (Melbourne: Melbourne University Press, 2002), 7–30, here 14.

Hunter and Macquarie)—also added their energies to the gospel cause.[11]

In recent days, as the involvement in the political processes of the so-called 'religious right' have attracted public attention, questions have been raised about the appropriateness of 'the church' being involved in 'the state'. Some call for a strict understanding of church and state separation that would silence Christian opinion from public discourse altogether. In the early period of Australian history, of course, 'church' and 'state' were intertwined. The early chaplains acted as officials of the state in various capacities, and both Archdeacon Scott and then Bishop Broughton held a seat on Australia's first Legislative Council. When it came time for the state to deal with the variety of churches that had sprung up on Australian soil, rather than separating from them all, in the Church Act of 1836 the state *endorsed* them all. Fearing the worst, and perhaps with a great deal of prophetic insight, Bishop Broughton was most concerned that this further movement away from an established church may well lead to a completely secular Australian state. But, in fact, at the time it meant the state supported all denominations in the acquisition of land, the construction of buildings, the recruitment of clergy from overseas, the support of clergy already recruited, and the like.[12] Far from being an attempt to destroy or harm Christian churches, the Church Act 1836 was an attempt 'to extend institutional Christianity in the socially fragile colony'.[13] Even though state funds would eventually cease in 1862 (State Aid Re-Distribution Bill), it should be noted that as the colony was moving towards nationhood, the state assisted in laying firmer foundations for Christian mission. In other words, Christian mission was expressly given an important place in Australian society, by Australian society.

---

11. See BH Fletcher, 'Christianity and free society in New South Wales 1788–1840', *JRAHS*, 86.2 (2000): 93–113.
12. For further discussion, see P Curthoys, 'State Support for Churches 1836–1860', in Kaye, *Anglicanism in Australia*, 31–51.
13. K Cable, 'The Dioceses of Sydney and Newcastle', in *Colonial Tractarians: The Oxford Movement in Australia*, edited by B Porter, (Melbourne: Joint Board of Christian Education, 1989), 35–48, here 36.

Christian mission in contemporary Australian society

In more recent times this place has been secured even further. Australia's policy of multiculturalism ensures an environment in which Christianity may continue to be practised alongside other religions. Despite the fact that there have been some attempts to use anti-discrimination legislation to stifle freedom of speech and freedom to persuade, the Australian laws have, to date, upheld these freedoms.[14] In other words, contemporary Australian society has also expressly given a place to Christian mission.

Does Australian society have a place in Christian *mission?*

But if Australian society has given a place to Christian mission, is the reverse also true? Does Australian society have a place in Christian mission? That is, are the churches of Australia taking up the challenge of this mission within our society?

The figures presented to the 2004 General Synod of the Anglican Church of Australia, showing a severe decline in attendance figures, do not augur well for the future, if drastic action is not instituted. Perhaps the problem is not simply that we have a great need to better interpret society. We may even have to recover the Christian mission altogether.

Interpreting Australian society for Christian mission

To interpret Australian society for Christian mission is an enterprise of 'natural theology'. Natural theology has long been considered the central problem of foreign missions,[15] and as local mission becomes a more pressing concern, it becomes a problem in this domain too.

The quest for a point of contact

To simplify a very complex issue, the basic task of natural theology is to find a 'point of contact' between the unbeliever and the Christian gospel, from which the unbeliever might then be led by a series of

14. In 2005, when a (male) witch pressed charges against those running an Alpha course in a Victorian prison, on the grounds that the Bible was derogatory towards witchcraft, the court considered this vexatious, and outside the spirit of what the anti-discrimination and anti-vilification legislation was seeking to achieve.
15. See W Scott, *Karl Barth's Theology of Mission* (Downers Grove and Exeter, England: IVP and Paternoster, 1978), 13.

arguments towards a full-blown Christian commitment. Although 'classic' natural theology focussed upon 'argument' *per se*, in the current environment 'argument' does not have the appeal that it once had, either in society at large, or in Christian apologetics. It is perhaps legitimate, therefore, to speak of various *strategies* of natural theology. The 'point of contact' may consist of an argument, as in traditional argument-based apologetics, or it may be in the offer of a certain kind of experience. This may be the 'Sunday experience' of the church service, whether 'contemporary' liturgy, preaching and music, or the promise of the presence of God in a church ritual (such as the sacrament), or in a special experience (such as the charismatic speaking in tongues). The increasing number of church meetings being relocated from ecclesiastical buildings into more secular buildings—such as clubs, pubs, schools, and community halls—seems to assume that a point of contact can be established by a change of geography. Perhaps it might come from approximating the experience of the cultural group being reached, in terms of music, or worship styles, or hours of operation, and the like. It may be through social engagement in a way that the community can readily perceive the 'relevance' of what is being done—perhaps even back to the old characteristics of the established church: education, moral guidance and reform, charity work. The quest for the point of contact may also lead to a change of mode, away from 'word' to 'deed', or away from 'speaking' to 'listening', or away from 'proclamation' to 'presence' (interestingly, always away from 'word'!).

The recourse to human observation

Each of the various strategies of natural theology, whether relational (who we are connected with), vocational (what task we are connecting with), persuasional (what arguments we are using), ritual (what special rituals we are providing), requires some kind of interpretation of society as the prolegomena to mission. In order to acquire the necessary information, resort is usually made to human observation, whether through the anecdotes of individuals, or through the anecdote-collecting research of the social sciences.

This has several difficulties. Human judgments are always provisional, and often mistaken. Even such interpretation of society requires further interpretation! Given the dynamics of contemporary life, observations are almost out of date as soon as they are made, so there is a perpetual game of catch-up to be played. Such strategies open up more territory for human pride and arrogance, with the new breed of minister—the one known as 'the strategic thinker'—who is able to put the finger on the pulse of society, and pronounce that the church no longer has one!

More importantly, the observers and social commentators of this world do their work from a particular view of the world, with its attendant framework of thought, method, and manner of drawing conclusions. There may well be data that is 'neutral', but there will also be 'theory-laden' evaluative data, and the theory inscribed in the evaluation may also need theological critique. So, for example, elements of the Church Growth Movement can be criticised for the belief that its principles can grow churches, whatever the nature of these churches, or their message.[16] This commitment to 'technique' reflects one of the sorry results of the Enlightenment belief that reason is everything. As John Ralston Saul points out, reason is not enough, because it does not have purpose and morality, and over time it too easily degenerates into mere technology and becomes inhuman.[17] In an age in which many churches are declining, or stagnating, and church leaders begin to turn to mission largely due to some kind of survival instinct, it is all too easy to seek after magical techniques promising the Holy Grail of 'Growth'. By the same token, even in environments where churches seem 'strong'—because their attendance figures are higher (an equation that, in itself, should receive critique)—a focus on 'technique' can still be found with results that are just as inhuman as those achieved by other technocrats. The quest for numbers at all costs is hardly a Christian vision of mission.

Since all wisdom is God's wisdom, human observations of society will have their proper place, but they always need to be in their proper place:

---

16. PD Jensen, 'Obstacles and Opportunities', in *Ripe For Harvest: Christian Mission in the New Testament and in Our World*, edited by RJ Gibson (Explorations 12; Carlisle and Adelaide: Paternoster and Openbook, 1998), 89–105, here 96.

17. JR Saul, *Voltaire's Bastards: The Dictatorship of Reason in the West* (London: Penguin, 1993). For an application to the Church Growth Movement, see Jensen, 'Obstacles and Opportunities', 96.

> Because there is some truth in anthropology, even secular anthropology, we are easily seduced into thinking that the truth about contemporary mission is found there. However, truth lies not in the study of humanity, but in the truth of God.[18]

> We must not confuse 'scratching where they are itching' with the gospel. It is one thing to begin a talk with where people are at, but it is quite another to go out and ask what people are thinking in order to work out what we should say to them. Inevitably, if we are going to communicate, we will engage in anthropology, but it must be theological anthropology.[19]

Given such concerns, one Australian missiologist calls for missiology to be 'rescued from its captivity to the social sciences and returned to its proper moorings in biblical studies and Christian thought'.[20]

The world sets the agenda

As well as making Christian mission dependant upon the human sciences, the next most serious mistake in such strategies is that they tend to allow the world to set the agenda. Sure, there is a proper flexibility required from the preacher of the gospel, in order to be 'all things to all people' with the goal of 'saving some' (see 1 Corinthians 10:33), and there may even be good reasons to 'scratch where people are itching'. However, the Scriptures still warn against those whose itching ears will lead them away from God's 'sound teaching' towards teachers who say only what they want to hear (2 Timothy 4:3).

It is good to listen before we speak (see James 1:19), but our society may have more serious needs than those that are felt and articulated. The Epicurean may call for more opportunities to 'eat, drink, and be merry' (see 1 Corinthians 10:7 and 15:32), but it would be misguided

18. Jensen, 'Obstacles and Opportunities', 97.
19. Jensen, 'Obstacles and Opportunities', 101.
20. MD Raiter, ' "Sent for this purpose", "Mission" and "Missiology" and their Search for Meaning', in Gibson, *Ripe for Harvest*, 106–150, here 107.

for churches to cater for this whim. The gospel message of eternal life in Christ provides the answer to the deeper underlying problem, 'for tomorrow we die'. The materialistic consumers may eagerly run after what they eat and drink and wear, but this shouldn't be the motivation for opening more soup kitchens and op shops. The gospel message speaks of a Father in Heaven, who provides the answer to the deeper underlying problem of 'being anxious about tomorrow' (see Matthew 6:25–34). And we could go on.

The distinctiveness of the Christian *message is eroded*

The real danger inherent in the strategies of natural theology is that, by allowing the world to seize the initiative and set the agenda, the distinctiveness of the Christian message will be eroded. Interpreting Australian society along these lines *for the sake* of Christian mission can, in fact, lead to the *forsaking* of Christian mission.

There are, of course, many ways of evaluating a society, whether sociologically, historically, pragmatically, psychologically, and the like. However, if what is distinctive about our Christian calling is to be maintained, we need to evaluate society theologically, that is, in line with the historic Christian mission founded upon Christ and propagated by his apostles.

Interpreting Australian society by means of the Christian mission

The earliest Christian mission 'turned society upside down' (Acts 17:6). If this revolution is to be re-ignited, it appears to be a better question to ask, what was it about the Christian mission that caused this revolutionary effect on ancient society? In other words, our chief task ought to be to interpret Australian society *by means of* the Christian mission.

A mission that is of abiding relevance

It is a strange paradox that, in fact, the key to abiding relevance is for the Christian mission to continue to uphold its distinctiveness.[21] The strategies of natural theology are usually predicated upon the fairly

21. Barth argued this as part of his controversy with Brunner over the natural theology project; see *Church Dogmatics* 1.1, 29. When battling Arianism, the early church also needed distinctiveness from, not conformity to their world; see Rowan Williams, *Arius: Heresy and Tradition* (London: SCM, 2001), 237–8.

obvious claim that we are 'to communicate the gospel in a society that has changed dramatically over recent years'.[22] This claim is then followed by a second, namely, that this cultural change calls theology in general, or mission in particular, into question.[23] Whereas the usually unstated assumption is that this 'dramatic change' actually has significance, it is, in fact, possible (with Barth) to deny that there is any 'theological foundation for the assumed difference between our own and earlier times'.[24]

For this thinking makes at least two mistakes about time and change. The first is to assume that progress in time changes the basic facts of the human predicament addressed by the gospel. For sure, every new age has its particular context in which God's people must live and speak for Christ. But, on the other hand, as the ancient Preacher once said, 'there is nothing new under the sun. Vanity of vanities' (see Ecclesiastes 1.2–11). The gospel speaks both to the great 'liminal' moments (such as birth, coming of age, marriage, and death), and to the ordinary structures of life, such as relationships, good works, the need for wisdom, the nature of human sin and suffering. Just like its founder, it also proclaims a message of rescue for lost sinners (see Luke 19:10) who are facing the dreadful prospect of the wrath of God for our sins (see 1 Thessalonians 1:10). Certainly our proclamation of the gospel at these life borders and in the midst of these life issues needs to be clear and positive. But the issues themselves, like the poor, are 'always with us' (see Mark 14:7).

The second mistake is even more serious. This kind of thinking mistakenly includes the events of Jesus Christ and the subsequent apostolic witness as part of an old world that has now passed away. In fact, the coming of Jesus Christ into the world makes all of the

---

22. D Clark, 'Mission in a "Society without God" ', *Crucible* (April–July, 2004), 29–38, here 29, who argues that this new context requires 'a clear and persuasive model for the mission of the Church in a new era', and then seeks to develop it.
23. Even by his day Barth could say that it had become 'the customary procedure, followed with new zeal in modern work . . . to indicate the change in general cultural awareness and the general world-picture which has taken place in the last 300 years and called Theology as such in question', *Church Dogmatics*, 1.1, 26.
24. Barth, *Church Dogmatics*, 1.1, 28.

structures of this world (past, present and future) the 'old' that is passing away (see 1 Corinthians 7:21; 2 Peter 3; 1 John 2:17), and it is the gospel of Christ that brings what is perpetually new (2 Corinthians 5:17). In other words, the categories of 'old' and 'new' need to be understood, not temporally, but apocalyptically.[25]

The world has changed because the Son of God has come and we have now entered a new time (Mark 1:15). We now live beyond the fulfilment of God's plan, awaiting the final revelation of the Kingdom of God, brought near by the coming of Jesus Christ. The earliest movement that 'turned society upside down' sprang into existence because a man had risen from the dead, leaving his tomb emptied of the body that once lay in it (see Acts 2:29–32). The message of forgiveness of sins was proclaimed in the belief that this preaching was the final necessary activity before the end (Luke 24:45–47). These preachers were empowered by the last-days gift of the Spirit (Acts 2), to issue the world a final summons to repent (Acts 17:30–31), knowing that the one who will judge the world is the same one who has proven to be the world's Saviour (Acts 2:37–41; 10:34–43). When this message of the grace of God in Christ Jesus for everyone who believed (Acts 20:24, 32) was unleashed on the world, congregations sprang up in all kinds of localities. This powerful word about Jesus Christ is perpetually relevant and it is 'ever new' to this world at any period of history. At all our liminal moments, and in all our circumstances of life, it too, is 'always with us'.

The once–for–all point of contact

The gospel of Jesus Christ also means that there is no need to desperately seek after a potential point of contact between God and humanity. The central claim of the Christian message is that God has become flesh in Jesus of Nazareth; a claim that can be summarised in terms of his person, through him being named 'Emmanuel; God is with us' (see Matthew 1:23). But since the holy God cannot abide with

25. Or even in its existential form: 'The pivotal conception in Christianity, that which made all things new, is the fullness of time, but the fullness of time is the moment as the eternal and yet this eternal is also the future and the past', S Kierkegaard, *The Concept of Anxiety: A Simple Psychologically Orienting Deliberation on the Dogmatic Issue of Hereditary Sin*, edited and translated by R Thomte with AB Anderson (Princeton: Princeton University Press, 1980), 90.

sinful human beings, the message of the Emmanuel must also include Christ's work in dying for our sins, which can be summarised using his triumphant cry, 'It is finished!' (John 19:30).

But both the incarnation and the finished work of Christ on the cross have long been recognised as 'scandals' to human thinking. The recent burgeoning of discussions of the Trinity can be explained to some extent as arising from an endeavour to avoid the scandal found in Christology and atonement. But this is misguided, for the doctrine of the Trinity arises as an inevitable conclusion drawn from Christology and centres upon 'the crucified God'. Christ's Person and his work are inseparable. The one who died on the cross, only to rise bodily from the dead, is God become flesh. By means of his death on our behalf, he brings us to God (1 Peter 3:18), thus ensuring 'God with us'.

In Christ's person, God and humanity come together in hypostatic union. This is therefore a 'point of contact', which, once established, is never overcome, modified, or superseded. The fact that the Son of God, in his hypostatic union, experienced God-forsakenness on the cross in order to be a 'ransom for many' (Mark 10:45), shows that the 'point of contact' for we poor sinners is in the historical event of the crucifixion.[26] The incarnation and the atonement therefore show us that the various categories and subcategories into which human beings divide—only to be conquered—are irrelevant to the question of relating to God.

The uniqueness of Christ is not a problem to be avoided, or even to be solved, but it ought to be embraced. For standing face to face with the central scandals, at the most distinctive point of our faith, we can do the most good for the world, if only we continue to stand in this place (see 1 Corinthians 15:1–2).

In New Testament thought, the finished work of Christ is both the display of the righteousness of God and the provision for his people to be clothed in the righteousness of Christ (Romans 3:24–26). This is the doctrine of justification by faith which was at the heart of Reformation Anglicanism, and which provided the controlling truth for Cranmer's liturgies. When justification is understood against the backdrop of

---

26. For further exploration, see my *The Cross from a Distance: Atonement in Mark's Gospel* (NSBT 18), (Leicester: IVP, 2004).

God's righteousness as revealed in the prophetic material,[27] it is also the beginning of God re-establishing the order for which he originally created us. Sanctification can then be understood as the Spirit of God continuing to conform Christ's people to God's orderly way of life, to become the people they were originally meant to be. Thus, the distinctive message of Christianity leads to a distinctive morality, which springs from a changed heart, that is, from the depths of an individual's humanity.

To return to a familiar theme, because the gospel of justification in Christ is the 'power of God for salvation for everyone who believes' (Romans 1:16), it creates its own 'point of contact'.[28] The desperate search for a point of contact evident in so much contemporary church practice, really amounts not only to a shift away from the point of contact established in Jesus Christ by God himself, but also to a loss of confidence in the gospel as the power of God to transform its hearers. Sadly, whatever contact is made between churches and the world, if it entails the loss of this centre, then the loss is far too great and the world, in the end, will not be helped at all.

The mission of the Father in sending the Son

The most basic, fundamental, central, foundational, mission, which is at the core of the New Testament message and enshrined in the historic creeds, is God the Father sending his Son into the world.

The sending of the Son is from the pre-incarnate glory, which he shared with his Father, into the world as the incarnate Son of God, with a view to his death on the cross. The sending of the Son by the Father was not against the will of the Son. Because the Son embraced the will of the Father, his incarnate life climaxing in his death on the cross was the display of his obedience to his Father. In fact, Paul described his death as 'the one act of obedience' (see Romans 5:20). Drawing upon Isaiah's prophecy of the Servant of the Lord, in which the Servant is vindicated because of his willingness to die to justify the

---

27. See, for example, MA Seifrid, 'Righteousness Language in the Hebrew Scriptures and Early Judaism', in *Justification and Variegated Nomism*, edited by DA Carson, PT O'Brien and MA Seifrid, volume 1: *The Complexities of Second Temple Judaism* (Tübingen and Grand Rapids: Mohr Siebeck and Baker, 2001), 415–42.
28. Barth, *Church Dogmatics*, 1.1, 28. Dogmatics is 'not oriented to the contradiction of reason but to the declaration of revelation'.

many (see Isaiah 53:12), the New Testament consistently shows that it was because of the Son's obedience to death on the cross that he was raised from the dead and re-installed to his former glory (see Philippians 2:5–11).

His mission was salvific, that is, he was obedient to the point of death in order that by his sacrificial (that is, propitiatory) death he might 'justify many' (see Mark 10:45 and Isaiah 53:12; Romans 3:24–5). Ultimately his obedience was for the Father's glory and thus to be the agent of grace, for the Father is glorified through his amazing plan to rescue lost human beings through the obedient death of the Son. For this reason, as the risen Christ informed his bewildered disciples, it was necessary for the Christ to suffer before he entered into his glory (Luke 24:26). This necessity comes from the fact that this was the divine plan, as revealed by God in the prophetic Scriptures. This means, therefore, that the cross as the great moment of God's self-revelation and mission can be described as 'the increase of knowledge of God in the world'.[29]

The Church fathers recognised the Father to be the fount of Divinity. It is also proper to describe him as the fount of mission. He is the ultimate sender. As Aquinas put it: 'Since the Father is not from another, in no way can the verb "sent" apply to him, but only to the Son and to the Holy Spirit, to whom it belongs to be from another'.[30]

The mission of the Son: sent by the Father

If the Father is the Sender, the Son is the one who is the sent, the gift of the Father's mission. The Father sent the Son into the world as the clear demonstration of his love for a world in great need (John 3:16). The Son willingly embraced the Father's will, which led him to the cross where he demonstrated his love for the world through dealing with our sin and judgment. His resurrection from the dead then resulted in his installation to his present position as Lord and the guarantee that his salvific work has been achieved.

---

29. RC Doyle, 'Models of Mission and the Doctrine of the Spirit', in Gibson, *Ripe for Harvest*, 69–88, here 70.
30. Thomas Aquinas, *Summa Theologica*, volume 7, translated by TC O'Brien (London: Blackfriars, 1976), Q 43, article 4, 221.

The mission of the risen Son to the nations: through the Spirit

Exalted to heaven, the Risen Son then sends the Spirit on the day of Pentecost, thus launching his mission to the nations (Acts 2). Through the gift of his Spirit Jesus continues his mission, inviting the nations to hear the good news, to repent and to believe. This is an invitation to enter into fellowship with the Father, by incorporation into the Son, through the Spirit (see John 17:21–4).

The mission of the risen Son to the nations: through the apostolic witness

According to Jesus' 'High Priestly Prayer', this incorporation into the Godhead comes about when people believe in the apostolic word (John 17:20; see 15:26–7 and 16:12–15). The apostles therefore play a crucial role in Christ's mission to the nations. These men were the specially commissioned witnesses who form the foundation of the future mission.[31] As the group of people who were with Jesus from the beginning and saw his ministry, from John the Baptist days through to his resurrection and exaltation to heaven, they are the closed group whose word forms the essential control, the 'deposit' that is to be handed on to future generations. These men have a foundational role in the new missionary movement that sprang up after the reception of the Spirit on the day of Pentecost. The apostle Paul was then added to their ranks as the apostle to the Gentiles. The apostolic witness was the instrument by which churches were sustained in their growth and expansion, and this testimony is now embedded in the New Testament witness, and is proclaimed as the apostolic gospel. Through the missionary work of this group, and their co-workers, churches were established as centres of mission in their own regions.

Local churches and Christian mission

From the exposition so far, it would be true to say that the mission of Christ creates the churches. But how does Christ's mission continue through these local bodies?

Because of the importance of the apostolic word, it must be entrusted to faithful servants who can teach and pass it faithfully on for generation after generation (2 Timothy 2:2). For the first two centuries, according to Eusebius (*HE* III.37.2), the pattern of the historic

31. See further my 'Mission and Witness', in *Witness to the Gospel: The Theology of Acts*, edited by IH Marshall and DG Peterson (Carlisle: Paternoster, 1998), 191–214.

Christian mission was the same. As reflected in the Pastoral Epistles, the apostolic word would be taught by the apostolic delegates (such as Titus and Timothy), who then appointed elders in every place, so that the deposit of truth could be handed on further.

One view of mission current in contemporary Anglicanism stretches back to the early second century, namely, that the mission belongs to the bishop and others simply participate in the episcopal mission.[32] The bishop ought to be an evangelist, but this does not mean that the mission belongs to the bishop, for it remains the mission of the risen Christ. A second view, as in contemporary Pentecostal and Neo-Pentecostal circles, which also has very ancient roots, is that mission belongs to the Holy Spirit and so to all who are empowered by him.[33] Once again, according to the New Testament picture, the mission is that of the risen Christ, even if this is by the agency of the Holy Spirit empowering his witnesses (the apostles) and those after them who repeat their word.

Christ continues his mission through each one of his people. As the apostolic witness shaped the congregational life of the churches, the individuals within them were transformed and they continued Christ's mission in their local areas through the transformed speech that sprang from a transformed heart (2 Corinthians 4:13). This was speech that was directed to Christ, his saving work, and the hope that sprang from his resurrection (see 1 Thessalonians 1:5–10). This speech transformed individual and corporate life in a way unprecedented in the ancient world.

Technically, however, *the church* does not have a mission in and of itself. To be true to the New Testament portrait, the 'church' of God is the local assembly of believers, gathered around Christ in his word. This is reflected in the Anglican *Thirty-Nine Articles of Religion*, Article XIX, in which the church is the gathering of the faithful around the preaching in word and sacrament.[34] Now, on this view of church, it is fair to say that churches *as churches*, that is, as they gather together

---

32. See Doyle, 'Models of Mission', 70–7.
33. Doyle, 'Models of Mission', 71, 77–81.
34. This, of course, is held in common with other denominations in the Reformation tradition. See Barth, *Church Dogmatics*, 1.1, 281: 'The true Church exists in the act of hearing and proclaiming of God's Word by men'.

around Christ, have no direct responsibility for mission. It is the individual believers who constitute that gathering, who then go out into the world and seek to commend Christ to others in word and deed.

It may still be correct, however, to describe churches as 'centres of mission', in that the local congregation plays a crucial role in preparing its members for, and nurturing them in, their roles as instruments of Christ in the world. Local congregations can also commission and send their members into the various corners of Christ's harvest field. The congregation certainly ought to pray for these labourers, to recognise those called by the Spirit of God to enter the harvest field, and to stand in fellowship with them in terms of prayer and finance, and whatever other assistance may be possible.[35]

The historical Christian mission as the revelation of God

This historical Christian mission—stretching from the Father, through the Son, the Holy Spirit, the apostolic witnesses, the local elders, the ordinary believers (both then and now)—is the means by which God is revealed to the world.

When passing through Samaria, instead of instructing his followers to 'interpret' their society, Jesus called upon them to 'see': 'Lift up your eyes, and see that the fields are ripe for harvest' (John 4:35). The kind of seeing that Jesus called for is not simply empirical observation. It is the kind of seeing of which Paul would later speak, a seeing that does not regard anyone or anything 'according to the flesh' (see 2 Corinthians 5:16), or, to use Jesus' words to Peter, a seeing which thinks like God, rather than like human beings (Mark 8:33). This vision is apocalyptic, that is, it so depends upon a divine unveiling, that the world is seen from the perspective of God and his kingdom (see 2 Kings 6; or the visions of Daniel, or Revelation).

To see the world this way is not natural to human beings. It is a revelation from the Father, centering upon his Son (Matthew 11:25–30; 16:17). It comes through the preaching of the apostolic gospel, to hearts that are so illumined by the Spirit of God, that they hear the human words of the gospel message as the Word of God (1 Thessalonians 2:13, see 1:5; and John 10:4, 14–16). The revelation from the Father,

35. For this paragraph, see D Robinson, 'The Bible and the Authority of the Church', in *Works of Donald Robinson*, edited by PG Bolt and MD Thompson (forthcoming).

about the Son, comes by means of the apostolic word (John 17:20), illuminated by the Spirit (John 16:12–15). This revelation enables mere human beings to 'see' the world anew—from God's point of view.

Such revelation comes about as someone hears the gospel and is reconciled to God, in Christ.[36] Revelation is a reflex of reconciliation. And, in turn, the reflex of the revelation of Jesus Christ is that we also begin to understand the world and human society 'with God's eyes'. In other words, this revelation of God in Christ means that human society can now be 'interpreted' from God's point of view. Thus, true Christian mission must begin by listening to God's Word, so that society is properly 'seen'. *Seeing* things from the perspective of God's revelation then transforms a person's way of *being* in the world.[37] When a human being begins to 'see' things from God's point of view, they begin to experience a transformation of their existence in this world, so that they begin to live life according to God's kingdom.

In other words, seeing the world God's way leads to the overturning of human society.

The overturning of human society

To recover the revolutionary effects of the earliest phase of Christian mission, we therefore do not need to focus on Australian society, but on the mission of God in Christ, now at work through the apostolic gospel, illuminated by his Holy Spirit.

Interpreting society by recourse to human observation is not a necessary prolegomena for Christian mission, and it comes with inherent dangers. God's mission in Christ is of abiding relevance because when God became flesh the supreme point of contact between God and humanity was established for all time, and when the Son of God cried 'it is finished', he guaranteed that all people for all time could avail themselves of it through putting their faith in him. The Risen Christ commissioned the apostles as his witnesses and then poured out his Spirit upon them so that these great events could be

---

36. Barth, *Church Dogmatics*, 1.1, 34.
37. 'Scripture's literary genres generate not only ways of seeing but also ways of *being* in the world', KJ Vanhoozer, 'From Canon to Concept: "Same" and "Other" in the Relation between Biblical and Systematic Theology', *SBET*, 12 (1994): 96–124, here 123.

proclaimed throughout the nations for all generations, and human hearts powerfully changed, so that lives—and societies—would also be transformed.

The apostolic gospel works this revolution by bringing reconciliation and revelation. The world is now 'interpreted' by God himself, seen with eyes informed by the apocalyptic unveiling of reality. And, since revelation comes as a reflex of reconciliation, the gospel exposes our problem at exactly the same moment that it provides us with God's solution to it. Human beings have a problem at the core of their being, for their hearts are far away from God (Mark 7:1–23; Romans 1:21, 28), but while we were still sinners, Christ died for us (Romans 5:8–9). Humanity is lost, but Christ came to seek and to save (Luke 19:10). Human society, with all its power and attraction, is in the grip of the devil (Luke 4: 5–6), but the Son of God came to destroy the works of the devil (1 John 3:8). The whole world lies under the shadow of death (Matthew 4:12–17), forcing us all to battle with the struggles of our own mortality (Romans 8:10–11), but the Son of God has neutralised the one who holds us in slavery all our lives through the fear of death (Hebrews 2:14–15), for 'he is risen!' And we could go on.

If the older missions made the first mistake of confusing the donor culture with the gospel, the newer drive towards contextualisation can fall into the second mistake of glorifying the receptor culture. The gospel critiques all human culture. It does not address the various cultures, divisions, subcultures and tribes, which our post-modern world has turned to in the desperate quest for a sense of identity and community. Christ deals more broadly with humanity. His salvation does not stay on the surface of human life, but goes to its depths. His liberation is from judgment to salvation, from death to life, from the kingdoms and tribes of this world, into the glorious Kingdom of God. The enslaving features of human society are now cast aside to find the liberation that resides in Christ (see Mark 10:28–31; Acts 19:18–20; 1 Thessalonians 1:5–10; Philippians 3). For the first time ever, as human beings are renewed into the image of their Creator, they begin to live as they were created to live. Where there was death, now there is the hope of resurrection from the dead. And the hope of resurrection means perfect freedom (see Romans 8:18–23).

The first task of Christian mission is therefore to listen to the Scriptures. If there is no comfort found in the Scriptures, then we will lose our mission.[38] Are the churches who meet in the name of Christ, truly hearing the apostolic word as the Word of God (see 1 Thessalonians 2:13)? Are they still caught in the slavery of seeing the world through merely human eyes, or have they found the liberation of seeking to see things God's way? Does their proclamation conform to the revelation of God in Christ?[39] Heaven help Australia if our churches become so enamoured with human wisdom promising the Holy Grail of growth and success, that they lose the wisdom of God which centres on the scandal of the cross (1 Corinthians 1:17–2:5)!

The revelation of God in Christ is the Christian mission. 'It is finished' means that all nations can now know the transforming revolution that is found in the Risen Christ, the Emmanuel, 'God is with us'. Our task is quite simple. When this good news is proclaimed and believed, Australian society is interpreted in a fresh light: Australia is lost, but, Hallelujah! There is a Saviour.

Yet again, let the revolution begin.

---

38. K Barth, *God Here and Now*, translated by PM van Buren (London: Routledge, 2003), 61–3, 67–8, 71.
39. See: 'Dogmatic work stands or falls by whether the standard by which church proclamation is measured is the revelation attested in Holy Scripture and not a philosophical, ethical, psychological, or political theory' in Barth, *Church Dogmatics*, 1.1, 283. For the relevance of the Scriptures for mission, see *Church Dogmatics*, 1.1, 285.

14

The Mission Of The Church

Geoff Smith

What is the role of the church? What is our purpose? In other words, what is our mission?

These are questions at the forefront for many leaders and members of the Anglican Church of Australia. We have clearly moved from what has been called Christendom and the place of the church in our society has changed dramatically in the last fifty years. Our numbers as a percentage of the population continue to decline. The modern missionary era, which began in the late 1700s, is well and truly finished. Australia itself has become a very different place since World War 11. All of these factors naturally lead to a reconsideration of the role and purpose of the church in Australia for the twenty-first century.

My approach to this question has been profoundly influenced by my experience, particularly by the time I spent as a missionary in Papua New Guinea and by my four and a half years as National Director of the Anglican Board of Mission–Australia. In this latter role I was exposed to parts of the Anglican Church overseas that took 'kingdom action' very seriously. This meant that our fellow Anglicans were engaged in proclamation of the gospel by word, but also by their action. The Anglican Church in the Philippines and in South Korea were the most powerful examples of this. Much of what follows in this chapter has been born from reflection on the scriptures and on these experiences.

The mission of the church

Any consideration of the mission or purpose of the church, no matter what the era, must take into account the mission of Jesus. The mission of the church was and must be intimately connected with the mission of Jesus. It is clear from the gospel accounts that the church understood that the followers of Jesus would continue the process of what Jesus had been doing: announcing the kingdom.

There are a number of examples of the understanding that Jesus' followers would continue his mission. For instance, Jesus called people to follow him, and told some that they would be fishers of people not just people who caught fish (Matthew 4:19). In the course of his ministry Jesus sent out both the twelve recorded in Mark 6, and the seventy-two recorded in Luke 10. Both groups were sent out to do the kinds of things Jesus had been doing—'they went out and proclaimed that all should repent. They cast out many demons, and anointed with oil many who were sick and cured them' (Mark 6:12, 13).

Luke has the sending out of the seventy-two immediately following Jesus' request that they 'ask the Lord of the harvest to send out labourers into his harvest'. Among the instructions for the seventy-two are: 'whenever you enter a town and its people welcome you, eat what is set before you; cure the sick who are there and say to them, 'The kingdom of God has come near to you' (Luke 10:8, 9).

The four gospels also each record 'commissionings' of the disciples after Jesus' resurrection. Matthew has Jesus state:

> Go therefore and make disciples of all nations, baptizing them in the name of the Father and of the Son and of the Holy Spirit, and teaching them to obey everything that I have commanded you. And remember, I am with you always to the end of the age (Matthew 28:19, 20).

For Mark the disciples' commissioning is:

> Go into all the world and proclaim the good news to the whole creation. The one who believes and is baptised will be saved; but the one who does not believe will be condemned (Mark 16:15).

Luke's Gospel has a two-part commissioning beginning in Luke 24, which has Jesus saying:

> Thus it is written, that the Messiah is to suffer and to rise from the dead on the third day, and that repentance and forgiveness of sins is to be proclaimed in

> his name to all nations beginning from Jerusalem. You are witnesses of these things. And see, I am sending upon you what my Father promised; so stay here in the city until you have been clothed with power from on high (Luke 24:46–8).

This is continued in Acts 1:8, where the risen Christ says to the eleven:

> You will receive power when the Holy Spirit has come upon you; and you will be my witnesses in Jerusalem, and in all Judea and Samaria and to the ends of the earth.

John's gospel has the risen Christ saying to the disciples: 'As the father has sent me, so I send you'. 'If you forgive the sins of any, they are forgiven them; if you retain the sins of any, they are retained' (John 20:21–2).

The four 'commissionings' all focus on Jesus—making disciples of Jesus, proclaiming the good news which is Jesus, being witnesses for Jesus, being sent as Jesus was sent, continuing the mission of Jesus.

A vital task then in examining the mission of the church is to see what was Jesus' priority in his mission.

Jesus and the kingdom of God

According to the gospel writers, Jesus' own view was that he had come to announce the kingdom or reign of God (*basileia tou theou*). For instance: 'The time is fulfilled, and kingdom of God has come near; repent, and believe in the good news' (Mark1:15); and, 'I must proclaim the good news of the kingdom of God to the other cities also; for I was sent for this purpose', (Luke 4:43). Wright comments: 'We have substantial historical ground under our feet in saying that Jesus characteristic message was the announcement of the kingdom'.[1] Dych calls the reign of God 'the keynote of Jesus ministry'.[2] Fuellenbach is

---

1. NT Wright, *Jesus and the Victory of God* (London: SPCK, 1996), 227.
2. William Dych, *Thy Kingdom Come: Jesus and the Reign of God* (New York: Crossroad, 1999), 19.

even stronger when he says 'the most basic historical fact of Jesus life is the symbol which dominated all his preaching, the reality that gave meaning to all his activities, that is, *the kingdom of God*'.[3]

The phrase 'kingdom of God' is most commonly used in the synoptic gospels, but there are sufficient examples of its use in the other writings of the New Testament, to indicate that whilst it is not so common in those writings, the understanding of the reality of the kingdom formed a vital part of the theological background for the early church. It is as though the New Testament writers have Jesus proclaiming the kingdom, and the early church living with the coming and present kingdom a reality. For example, Acts 28:30–1, speaking of Paul, ' He lived there (Rome) two whole years at his own expense and welcomed all who came to him, proclaiming the kingdom of God and teaching about the Lord Jesus Christ with all boldness and without hindrance'; Romans 14:17, 'For the Kingdom of God is not food and drink but righteousness and peace and joy in the Holy Spirit'; 1 Corinthians 6:9, 'Do you not know that wrongdoers will not inherit the kingdom of God'; or James 2:5, 'Listen my beloved brothers and sisters. Has not God chosen the poor in the world to be rich in faith and to be heirs of the kingdom that he has promised to those who love him'.

Coming to grips with what exactly the kingdom of God was for Jesus is not a simple matter. Nowhere in the gospels is the kingdom defined. Instead the kingdom is spoken of and illustrated with parables and also powerful actions. It is clear from the gospel accounts that Jesus had come to announce the kingdom (Luke 4:43). The kingdom was obviously central to him, so his teaching needs to be seen in this context. His teaching was not some new philosophy, but announced the reality of the coming kingdom.[4] Jesus taught those who wished to follow him that the kingdom was *at hand* (Mark 15); how to

---

3. John Fuellenbach, *The Kingdom of God: The Message of Jesus Today* (New York: Orbis, 1995): 3.

4. R Song makes the point in *Jesus and the Reign of God* (Augsburg: Fortress Press, 1993), that the term 'kingdom of God' was not new and novel but was already in the religious vocabulary of Jesus' Jewish hearers (19). NT Wright also comments in *Jesus and the Victory of God*, that 'the kingdom of God' was already a familiar phrase to Jesus' Jewish hearers and was simply a Jewish way of talking about Israel's God becoming king. When this God became king, the whole world, the world of space and time would at last be put to rights (203).

prepare for the coming kingdom (Matthew 4:17; John 3:3, 5); what the kingdom is like (Matthew 13, Mark 4:26–9); and what it means to be members of the kingdom (Matthew 5, 6, 7; Luke 6). He did things which showed its reality already present and breaking into the old order (Luke 10:9). He taught people to pray for its coming (Matthew 6:10). Jesus taught by word and deed so that people could begin to come to grips with the new order of the kingdom, and be ready for its future fulfilment as well as live in its present reality.

Although now incomplete, when the kingdom comes into fullness it will be marked by a 'turning upside down' of many of the 'norms' of human society. This is illustrated by the canticle of praise Luke has Mary offer: 'he has brought down the powerful from their thrones, and lifted up the lowly; he has filled the hungry with good things, and sent the rich away empty' (Luke 1:52–53).[5] As the reality of the kingdom was lived out, humble service of others was applauded; forgiveness was to be without limit; prostitutes and tax collectors were entering the kingdom of God before the religious people; turning the other cheek was an appropriate response; relationships were to be faithful; 'other focussed' love was the key; the Holy Spirit was being poured out on all; ordinary people were filled with a new boldness to tell of the glories of God; death was ending; sickness was healed; the excluded were included; people imprisoned by sin, injustice and oppression were set free; a radical godliness was called for; and long established barriers between people were broken down.

The kingdom: word and deed

It is vitally important to recognise that the process of announcing the kingdom was not just one of words—teaching and preaching. Jesus' actions showed that the kingdom was 'breaking into' or invading the old order. They revealed what the kingdom of God would be like, and what life would be like for those who embraced the reality of the coming kingdom. In Luke 4, Jesus quotes from and changes slightly the words of the prophet Isaiah:

5. Song in *Jesus and the Reign of God*, 235, refers to the *Magnificat* as the 'song of God's reign'. He says 'it is the anthem of God's presence. It is the hymn of God's salvation'.

> The Spirit of the Lord is on me, because he has anointed me to preach good news to the poor. He has sent me to proclaim freedom for the prisoners and recovery of sight for the blind, to release the oppressed, to proclaim the year of the Lord's favour (Isaiah 61:1f; Luke 4:18–19).

Jesus then applies this to himself when he states: 'Today this scripture is fulfilled in your hearing' (Luke 4:21). When John the Baptist sent his disciples to Jesus to enquire whether Jesus was the 'one to come' (Matthew 11:3), Matthew has Jesus responding in terms of his actions—the blind receive their sight, the lame walk, the lepers are cleansed, the deaf hear, the dead are raised, and the poor have good news brought to them (Matthew 11:5). Certainly in his ministry Jesus' actions showed the in-breaking of the kingdom—the sick were healed, the dead were brought back to life, those oppressed by evil were set free.

The membership of the kingdom was also an issue both in terms of Jesus' teaching and actions. Jesus spent time with the poor and included the excluded and unclean, often healing the unclean and making them clean again, and so able to rejoin society.

Jesus' table fellowship with tax collectors and sinners provided a very potent example of the 'turning upside down' of normal conventions that will come and has come with the arrival of the kingdom in Jesus. A key to the gospel is grace, and Jesus' ministry, with people the religious leaders certainly would have thought were undeserving of God's love, spoke clearly of the kingdom Jesus had come to inaugurate.

Interestingly, it was Jesus' actions that often provided very potent opportunities for his teaching. Some examples of this are: the healing of the paralysed man recorded in Matthew 9 and Luke 5, where Jesus uses the situation of the paralysed man and his healing to declare his authority to forgive sins; and Jesus eating with tax collectors and sinners (Matthew 9:10–12). This incident provided an opportunity for the Pharisees to question Jesus' disciples about Jesus' choice of meal companions, and in response Jesus pointed to one the central features of the membership of the kingdom: he had come to call not the righteous but sinners. Another example is the healing of the demon-possessed man (Matthew 12:22ff), which again drew a challenge from the Pharisees and a response from Jesus stating his authority.

There are also examples of the lack of separation between teaching and actions: for instance, in Luke 4:32 the response of the people to Jesus' teaching is recorded as: 'they were astounded at his teaching because he spoke with authority'. Later, in the same encounter, Jesus ordered an evil spirit to leave a man (verse 35). The next verse comments: 'All the people were amazed and said to each other, "What is this teaching? With authority and power he gives orders to evil spirits and they come out!" ' In this incident it seems that the teaching and the action worked together to demonstrate Jesus authority and call forth a response.

There are also incidents which are recorded as having no teaching component at all; just the action is described. Examples of this include: the cleansing of the leper (Matthew 8:1–4); the healing of many people at Peter's house (Matthew 8:14–16); the healing of the sick (Matthew 14:14); the healing of many people (Matthew 15:29–31); the healing of a blind man at Bethesda (Mark 8:22–6); and the raising of the widow's son at Nain (Luke 7:11–15). This reality, the vital place of deed or action in the process of proclamation of the kingdom of God by Jesus, is a real challenge to much of the Western church which has separated word and deed, and often focusses on preaching and teaching in words as the most important or effective way to proclaim the kingdom. It is very significant that the early church obviously accepted the emphasis both on word and deed, and indicated this through the gospel accounts of Jesus' ministry. For the Jesus of the gospels both words and deeds of power or compassion, which demonstrated what the kingdom was and would be like, were an integral part of the process of announcing the kingdom. For his audience, Jesus' actions apparently gave his teaching even more authority and illustrated his words in ways that astounded, and at times caused scandal or drew responses of faith.

The kingdom and the role of the church

There is no doubt that in the mind of the early church community, as represented by the gospels, Jesus had 'sent' the church to continue the ministry of proclaiming in word and deed, in the power of the Holy Spirit, the present and coming kingdom. For Matthew the task was to make disciples, in other words, people who shared Jesus attitudes, priorities and theology. For Mark the task is to proclaim the 'good news'. Mark's gospel begins with: 'The beginning of the good news of Jesus Christ, the Son of God'. It proceeds to 'roll out' the ministry of Jesus—both word and deed, focussed on the kingdom of God. For Luke the followers of Jesus were to be 'witnesses', representing Jesus to those who had not seen him. For John, the disciples were 'sent as Jesus was sent'. In each case the 'commissioning' and the task the disciples is given focusses very much on Jesus, and his priorities.

It is clear that the gospels contain an expectation that the followers of Jesus will continue Jesus' ministry of announcing the kingdom of God in word and deed. What is particularly startling in both Jesus' ministry and his expectations for his followers is just how different the kingdom was to the normal expectations and rules of society. The kingdom was certainly 'good news for the poor', but also effectively tipped upside down the expectations especially of religious people. To respond to the kingdom requires therefore not only faith but also repentance (Mark 1:15).

The degree of challenge to the norm by Jesus was probably one of the reasons for the opposition which he and later his followers faced. Jesus was a challenge especially to those in power and particularly religious power, for whom the rules and customs of the community 'worked'.

The kingdom and the church today

So what does this mean for the church today?
Through history the understanding of the mission of the church has been influenced by the context in which it finds itself.[6] This is to be expected. Christianity is not a 'once for all' delivered in a prepackaged form and suitable in the same way for all time and times—Jesus was good news as he lived with people in their situation in Palestine. The incarnation is a central understanding of Christian theology, and the 'enfleshment' of the Son of God in the culture and the context of the day continues to be a vital part of our Christian understanding and mission.

This reality makes understanding the culture a vital part of answering the question: what is the purpose of the church today? It is plain that the kingdom of God has not yet come in its fullness, and that we continue to pray—'your kingdom come'. And the church does that

6. Stephen B Bevans and Roger P Schroeder, *Constants in Mission: A Theology of Mission for Today* (Maryknoll: Orbis Books, 2004), 396.

with hope. It is also plain that the church cannot build or extend the kingdom: the church does not pray 'let us realize your kingdom'; it prays rather 'may your kingdom come'.[7]

The church looks toward the kingdom of God, waits for it, proclaiming it to the world.[8] It is clear that the primary concern in Jesus' ministry was the kingdom of God. It is clear, as Kirk says, that 'there is good enough evidence for Jesus' belief that those whom he called to be with him would continue his mission of proclaiming and performing God's rule on earth'.[9]

Newbiggin comments that:

> Jesus manifestly did not intend to leave behind him simply a body of teaching. If that had been his intention he would surely have written a book and we should have something like the Koran instead of the book we have. What he did was to prepare a community chosen to be the bearer of the secret of the kingdom.[10]

The key for the church in these days is to see what it means for the church to be the bearer of this secret.

It is clear that the mission of the church is the kingdom of God. The task for the church is not to bring in the kingdom itself, since only God can do this. The challenging part of the equation is to work through what it means today to serve the kingdom of God. It is clear that the mission of the church is to proclaim the kingdom of God both in word and in deed, and to do so as a community of Jesus' disciples led, inspired and enabled by the Holy Spirit.

There will be observable signs as the church seeks to do this. The church will first of all have as its focus the kingdom of God. This will be the overarching norm: the present and coming kingdom of God. The church will have the role, to use Daniel Biles' expression, of

---

7. Hans Küng, *The Church*, (London: Search Press, 1968), 92.
8. Küng, *The Church*, 95.
9. Andrew J Kirk, *What is Mission?* (Minneapolis: Fortress Press, 2000), 52.
10. Leslie Newbiggin, *The Gospel in a Pluralist Society* (Grand Rapids: Eerdmans, 1989), 133.

'sighting, signalling, supporting and celebrating the kingdom of God'.[11] In its self-understanding the church will remember that it is not the church of God that has a mission in the world, but the God of mission who has a church in the world.[12]

In this it is important to remember the role of signalling the reality of the kingdom. The church is not just to proclaim the kingdom, but to live it, to be a foretaste of it, to be a tangible expression of the reality of the kingdom and, in the words of Snyder, 'a kingdom colony'.[13]

Challenges for the contemporary church in Australia

A key question therefore is how can we be a kingdom colony, how can we focus on the kingdom in the context in which we are in?

A major task right at the start is to help the church to see that the mission of the church is to focus on the kingdom-proclaiming it and witnessing to its reality. After centuries very much focussed on the people of the church in a pastoral model, any kind of very significant change will take a long time.

There are significant challenges to the Australian Anglican Church as it seeks to focus on the kingdom of God. The first challenge is the model of church organisation that constitutes much of the church in Australia, and that is the self-funding autonomous parish.

The whole issue of a congregation needing to pay its way—pay a clergy person, pay for the purchase construction or maintenance of buildings, pay a contribution to the diocese (because most of our dioceses are also self funding bodies), and pay running costs, for example—impacts on what the church needs to be in order to survive. The fact that parishes are defined as 'viable' by their ability to meet certain financial goals is a telling pointer to our priorities. In reality the model we use for much of our church life is like that of a small business.

---

11. Daniel V Biles, *Pursuing Excellence in Ministry* (Washington: The Alban Institute, 1998), 20.
12. Tim Dearborn, *Beyond Duty: a Passion for Christ, a Heart for Mission*, cited in Church of England Mission and Public Affairs Council, *Mission-Shaped Church* (London: Church House Publishing, 1994), 85.
13. Howard A Snyder, *Models of the Kingdom* (Nashville: Abingdon Press, 1991), 153, cited in Fuellenbach *The Kingdom of God*, 15.

This model makes focus on the kingdom of God very difficult. The focus becomes numerical growth and financial health of the congregation or parish and not necessarily the kingdom.

This focus on the church rather than on the kingdom also probably reflects the reality that most churches are small in number. Whilst there are some really huge churches, most congregations in Australia, for instance, are small—more than half have fewer than fifty people.[14] Instead of seeking to sight, signal, support and celebrate the kingdom—through evangelism, and worship, and the development of community relationships, active inclusion of the poor and work amongst the poor and outcast—the focus is really on church growth, or, in many cases, survival.

The focus is also strongly influenced by the clergy themselves whose sense of fulfilment, desire for promotion and call to higher offices (often outside parish life), very much depends on their ability to build a parish organisation. All of this impacts on what it is they and the church see as effective. In fact, the way most churches are set up and run in the West biases them away from the kingdom focus and toward a focus on the church itself. This is heightened in the Western context where the church is shrinking overall. The Western church has not experienced for many, many centuries life as a small or insignificant player in society. In the current situation of threat and fear, the pressure is huge to reverse the trend of decline, and church leaders whose parishes/churches do grow numerically are warmly encouraged.

This 'building the church' or 'attractional'[15] mode is firmly entrenched in the psyche of lay and ordained leaders as well as the organisation of the church. The problem is that it does not focus on the kingdom of God but on the church. Even where the parish is concerned to witness to the kingdom—and seek ways to include the excluded, reach out to the poor and bring justice and healing and wholeness to their community—the challenge of putting that into

---

14. Peter Kaldor, *Winds of Change: The Experience of Church in a Changing Australia* (Homebush: Lancer, 1994), ix.
15. Michael Frost and Alan Hirsch in *The Shaping of Things to Come: Innovation and Mission for the 21st Century Church* (Peabody: Hendrickson, 2003), 18, refer to the church as 'attractional' when it expects people to come to it and organises itself accordingly.

practice in the midst of the small business called the church, with limited financial and volunteer resources, is a very significant one.

In some parts of the Western church in recent times, as parishes either cannot afford to pay a clergy person, or a clergyperson is not available, experiments are happening with different forms of ministry. In some quarters these new models are being bemoaned as second best measures, whereas in fact they may be opportunities for freedom for the church which could, if embraced enthusiastically, provide more opportunity for the creation of a kingdom colony.

A second challenge to the way we are being church in Australia, is the biblical example of a holistic approach. It is clear that Jesus proclaimed the kingdom in words but also in action. Jesus' actions pointed in a very powerful way to the truth of the words he was speaking. For us in Australia however, proclamation of the gospel is mostly about words. Where action happens it does so almost as a second placed activity rather than an integral part of the process of announcing the good news of the kingdom of God.

The reality is that nowhere in the gospel records does Jesus compare or contrast the proclamation of the kingdom in words, with the deeds of the kingdom (healing the sick, freeing the oppressed, raising the dead, including the excluded, ministering to the poor). Nowhere in the gospel records does Jesus prioritise proclamation by word over any other part of his ministry.

Leslie Newbiggin offers a very helpful way to see the relationship between word and deed as the church seeks to continue the mission of Christ:

> It is clear that to set word and deed, preaching and action, against each other is absurd. The central reality is neither word nor act, but the total life of a community enabled by the spirit to live in Christ, sharing his passion and the power of his resurrection. Sometimes it is a word that pierces through layers of custom and opens up a new vision. Sometimes it is a deed which shakes a whole traditional plausibility structure. Second it is clear that action for Jesus in the world is not something which is secondary, marginal to the central task of evangelism. Rather it belongs to the heart of the matter. Jesus action in challenging the

> powers that rule the world was not marginal to his ministry: it was central to it.[16]

David Bosch puts the matter much more succinctly: 'The deed without the word is dumb; the word without the deed is empty'.[17]

Even when we agree for both word and deed, we tend to find difficulty in giving both equal importance and energy. As we strive to do so however, the way we organise ourselves as church must be impacted.

The tasks of genuinely being concerned for the poor who are usually not members of our congregations and of developing communities of faith which can actually include people of different racial and socio-economic backgrounds are very difficult.

The church of course does do an enormous amount to help the poor through its various welfare arms. And this is beneficial in itself. However, much of this work is done with government funding. Even though the church is the conduit, I wonder whether this is what Jesus really meant when he told the disciples that they were sent as he was sent. The picture of the early church we have in Acts seems to be the church sharing with radical generosity its own belongings rather than the resources of those outside the church.

Another significant area of effort in the Anglican Church of Australia is Anglican schools. Changes to government funding have meant that the church (and other groups) has access to significant government funding for schools. An important question needs to be asked and that is, how do these schools, which charge not insignificant fees and must be focussed on student numbers and income, witness to the kingdom of God? The schools themselves are businesses and in the competitive world of private schooling—where parents enrol their children not so much to participate in a radical experiment in kingdom living or for rigorous exposure to Christian teaching, but much more as an opportunity for a good education, in an environment of positive values and discipline. Indeed conversations with chaplains (where the schools can afford them because the government doesn't pay for chaplains) indicate how difficult their ministry is in the environment of

---

16. Leslie Newbiggin, *The Gospel in a Pluralist Society*, 137.
17. David J Bosch, *Transforming Mission: Paradigm Shifts in Theology of Mission* (New York: Maryknoll, 1991), 420.

the many demands of a school. This issue is dealt with in depth in David Cole's chapter in this volume.

The establishment of the schools themselves prompts questions of ecclesiology for a church that has seen the parish model as its primary example. With many schools having their own chaplains, the question of the relationship between an Anglican school and its local parish community naturally arises. Should the school develop its own worshipping community or should the school see itself as part of the life of the parish within whose boundaries it lies? There seems to be a wide range of answers to these questions but, in our context of rapid development of Anglican schools, the questions must be dealt with satisfactorily.

Conclusion

The focus on the kingdom of God is a significant challenge to the church today. This should not be surprising as Jesus' call to repentance and faith is as much addressed to the disciples as anyone else and therefore also the church. An honest assessment of the life and focus of the church in much of the world, certainly much of the church in the West, shows a church which is heavily involved with both wealth and power on one hand, and focussed on its numerical survival on the other. To speak and model the new order which Jesus inaugurated will involve a profound change for much of the church. The teaching of Jesus challenges not only the unbeliever to repentance and faith, but calls the church to the same thing. So much of church activity is focussed on the church itself. Evangelism, or more accurately church growth, is encouraged; otherwise, it is said, the church will cease to exist. Many congregations are more like religious clubs than disciples of Jesus. Huge amounts of money are spent on maintaining the church for the benefit mostly of its members. The priority often is on caring for the current members and seeking new like-minded members, with almost nothing which reflects Jesus' ministry to the poor and excluded. The church seems not to be good at demonstrating the new order of the kingdom. The kingdom after all is costly and discomforting. Perhaps that is why in some parts of the church there seems to have been a retreat into a focus on Bible teaching, which leads to great knowledge of the Bible, and a consequent drive for doctrinal purity, but little action of the kind that Jesus modelled. It is the model that Jesus offers of his own life, faith and ministry that so clearly provides a guide, a challenge and a vision for the church in Australia in the twenty-first century.

My own journey

As I reflect on my Christian journey so far, I am very conscious of a very significant shift in my own thinking on the subject of the mission of the church, especially over the past five years or so. I am a 'cradle Anglican' being raised as a member of the Anglican Church in Brisbane. I attended church regularly with my parents who were, and still are, committed Anglican Christians. After ordination I worked in the diocese of Grafton, mostly in rapidly growing coastal towns. In the midst of this my wife and I spent three years as missionaries in Papua New Guinea. I think it is true to say that my focus through this period was very much on church growth—how can we grow the church more effectively. There was, however, a nagging doubt that there was more to the mission of the church than we were doing. One cannot read the gospels and fail to notice the 'actions of the kingdom' that Jesus did as he spent time with not just the spiritually poor, but the physically poor and sick and marginalised as well. But that part of the mission of the church was not high in my priority. All my energy was taken up with leading the parish in the growth of the church; there was nothing much left for anything else.

The change for me came about through two factors. The first was preparing to write a thesis for a master's degree in philosophy entitled 'Being Effective Church in Rapidly Growing Coastal Communities'. As I read for this project, I discovered really for the first time, in a way that struck me powerfully and meaningfully, the concept of the kingdom of God. I began to realise that any notion of the mission of the church that neglected the expression of the kingdom of God was very poor. The other factor was that in this period I spent four and a half years as National Director of the Anglican Board of Mission–Australia. In this role I was exposed to parts of the Anglican Church overseas that took 'Kingdom action' very seriously. This meant that our fellow Anglicans were engaged in proclamation of the gospel by word, but also by their action. The church in the Philippines and in South Korea were the most powerful examples of this.

The Episcopal Church in the Philippines has an extensive ministry in community development as well as evangelism and church planting. Working with very poor rural people in both Northern and

Southern Philippines, the church is involved with projects which, for instance, bring clean water to isolated mountain villages; provide simple buildings in which rice farmers can store their crop; build large concrete slabs on which newly harvested rice can be dried safely (the alternative is to use the public road); and provide micro finance to enable poor rural people to borrow money without paying the outrageous interest charged by local 'loan sharks'. The aim for the church has been to combine both a spiritual outreach with very practical ministry which aims to help the lives of people who are poor and marginalised in very practical ways.

The Anglican Church of South Korea also works to help poor people, but more often those people are city dwellers rather than rural people. The economic development of South Korea in recent decades has been dramatic, but so has been the rise of urban poverty. The church has a wide range of social ministries most of which are run by local parishes. Projects include shelters for boys and girls who run away from home, community centres which provide after-school care and study space, and food banks which provide both cooked food and staples like rice for people in need.

One of the most significant features of these ministries is that generally they are not government funded. Some support does come from overseas partners, but very significant funding comes from the local church and, in the case of South Korea, businesses and the local community. This is in contrast to much of the social outreach by the church in Australia, in which the church is a channel for government funding.

The challenge for me, now that I am again serving as a parish priest, this time on the Gold Coast, is how to lead a church focussed on the kingdom of God. The Gold Coast is the sixth largest city in Australia with around 550,000 residents and only eight Anglican parishes. Once again I am the parish priest of a small business, and much (though certainly not all) of the desire for growth in the parish is focussed on securing its own future. The desire for numerical growth is very strong, and yet the breadth of the kingdom doesn't get much of a mention. My parish has a really excellent ministry to the poor and homeless of our community, and yet, despite the fact that a good number of parishioners volunteer at this service, there is little sense of the integration of the two parts of the parish—the welfare ministry and the 'church'.

I am convinced that proclamation of the kingdom by both word and action are integral to the mission of the church. My struggle is how to do both whilst keeping both in balance. And how to do both in the context of an urban parish, where the parish resources seem limited. I am sure we are called to be a 'kingdom colony'; the challenge is how to live that out in our current era.

15

The Ecclesial Nature Of Anglican Schools

David Cole

This chapter explores the 'churchliness' of Anglican schools in Australia, with a view to developing a clearer understanding of ways in which these schools do (or might) function as ecclesial communities and thereby contribute to the wider community that seeks to experience its life and express its faith by drawing upon Anglican heritage and sensibilities. Educational in their identity and orientation, they differ notably from other Anglican communities, and necessarily have their own compromises and tensions. Engaged in the fundamental task of both forming and informing young minds and hearts, each of these schools has the potential to experience and promote the good news of Jesus Christ among students and families, and among staff. Moreover, by working to ensure integrity of purpose and practice, these schools can demonstrate their authenticity as worshipping Anglican communities, and bear faithful witness to the Gospel. In doing so, Anglican schools can provide the wider church with important insights into living and proclaiming the Christian message among young people and their families in contemporary Australia.

'Anglican' schools

The Anglican Church has a long history of involvement in education. Today this may be observed in theological and university colleges, the educational programs of dioceses and church mission and service agencies, parish youth and children's ministry, the work in public schools of visiting religious education teachers, and in private schools affiliated with the Anglican church. This variety of approaches provides the church with the capacity to respond to a diversity of contexts and needs.

The role of the churches in providing religious education in public schools varies from state to state, and continues to evolve. It is important to remember that public schools are attended by many students whose families would describe themselves as 'Anglican' (whether or not they have an active involvement in parish life), though a direct consideration of the church's responsibility towards these students lies outside the scope of the present chapter.

Alongside the state schools are those of religious sponsorship, incorporating a wide range of religious perspectives and purposes. Anglican schools in Australia initially took their inspiration from the great English public schools and, while the ethos and character of such origins may continue to be discernible to the present time in some schools, others have moved on significantly.

Some of the Anglican church's educational programs listed above operate within an 'in-house' Anglican ethos, in which the mission of the church in the proclamation of the Gospel can operate as a plumbline: a reminder of core values when a corrective is required; theological colleges, diocesan education programs and parish ministry fall into this category. Such an 'in-house' ethos, however, does not necessarily apply in relation to institutions such as Anglican university colleges or schools. Where councils are composed of church non-attenders (or even agnostics or atheists),[1] and/or where non-Anglicans or even non-Christians participate as administrators, teachers or students, it might be difficult to find widespread acceptance of gospel-driven values as 'core'. In such a context, then, many influential players—including even those developing and implementing school policy—may have neither recourse to religious principles, nor any sense of the school's accountability to church authority or its place in a community of faith. Moreover, even where the Head of the school and others in senior positions *are* active in their personal faith, the pressures of curriculum, parental expectations, and the educational results of economic rationalism (with its attendant orientation to market values, a utilitarian core curriculum, and conformity to goals associated with higher productivity)[2] may interpose difficult barriers to an integrated expression of gospel values in the daily round

1. Ronald Noone, 'Facing the Future: Religious Education in Anglican Schools', *Interface*, 6/1 (May 2003): 57.
2. Brian Hill, *Exploring Religion in School* (Adelaide: Openbook, 2004), 12.

of school life. At the very least, for many participants the 'educational' (as distinct from 'religious' or 'spiritual') tasks might take overwhelming precedence, even though undertaken in an overall religious context.

It is, therefore, understandably difficult to find an adequate definition of an 'Anglican School', given the range of institutions embraced by this term. At one end of the spectrum are relatively new schools, some of which have been founded with a desire to keep fees as low as possible. At the other end are extremely well-resourced, high-profile schools with long histories and much higher fees. Some are fiercely independent, while others nestle closely with a local parish. A detailed description of this complex spectrum necessarily lies outside the scope of the current chapter.

The task of understanding what Anglican identity might mean in this context is further hampered by a lack of common expectations at many levels, in addition to those already mentioned. Despite the church's involvement in the provision of schools since colonial times, and the fact that these schools now constitute 'our Church's largest investment of resources in the educational field',[3] there is no national system of Anglican schools in Australia. Although a strong network exists among these schools, with principals and chaplains having the opportunity to meet regularly at a national level, and some organisational structures operating at diocesan level, it nevertheless remains that Anglican schools are perceived differently by those who attend them, those who send their children to them, those who teach in them, those who lead them, those who provide a chaplaincy ministry within them, and by the wider community looking in at them from the outside.

This differentiation in perception rests partly on a variety of expectations of what a school should be and do:

> The diocesan expectations are sometimes very different from the expectations of the school community—the parents, the school council, 'Friends' organisations and fundraisers. Even the teaching staff and the students

3. Bruce Kaye, 'Being an Anglican School', *Panorama*, 6/1 (Summer 1994).

> themselves have expectations of the school that they would think have nothing to do with religion.[4]

Moreover, there is further divergence in attitude between different Australian dioceses, each of which is independent and may have developed its own particular philosophical approach to the establishment and development of Anglican schools. Over time, some dioceses have favoured low-fee schools, some have encouraged more 'elitist' schools, while others have given particular support to 'parish' schools, or similar models.

In general, irrespective of diocesan differences, Anglican schools are typically not part of diocesan synod arrangements, though there are exceptions; while their chaplains may be members of synod, the schools usually do not report to it. Moreover, the schools may be regarded by the wider church as peripheral to it, or independent of it. Such a perception has some validity, especially given that diocesan involvement in the schools which bear the 'Anglican' title varies widely, from close monitoring to 'arm's length' observation. In addition, some Anglican schools particularly emphasise their independence, including independence from what might be considered 'too much' church influence; a few have gone so far as to remove references to 'Anglican' or 'Church of England' from their name and their publicity. It has been argued that such marginalisation of religion reflects a devaluing of it.[5] At the same time, other schools actively seek to strengthen their links with their diocese and the wider Anglican family. Those founded in conjunction with a parish (and which may even use the parish church as the school chapel, or vice versa) have a particularly close identification with the local community of faith.

Churchliness

The above factors serve to underscore the complexity of the task of determining the ecclesial nature, or 'churchliness' of such institutions: how they do (or have the potential to) display the 'marks' of a Christian community that is recognizably 'Anglican', and contribute to the mission of the church.

At a very basic level, a school may be perceived to be 'Anglican' on the basis of its foundation by a bishop or a diocese, (or, rather more

4. Noone, 'Facing the Future', 59.
5. Hill, *Exploring Religion in School*, 25.

superficially, because of a diocesan reference in its coat-of-arms, or religious connotations in its motto), or because there are clerical or diocesan representatives on its governing council. Such factors notwithstanding, the actual life of the school, and its commitment to Anglican values and identity, may vary enormously, from a whole-hearted embracing of them, to an embarrassed peripheralisation of them. Critics of established church schools note the potential for them, over time, to:

> lose their vision and integrity and [degenerate] into exclusive clubs which do a better job of preparing their students for the real world than do modern public schools.[6]

While such a criticism may be judged simplistic, it is nevertheless a reminder of the need to measure current practices and outcomes against founding principles, and of the necessity to review and freshly reinterpret the purposes of church schools in the light of contemporary theological and social priorities. As Wolterstorff argues:

> Christian schooling which is shaped by allegiance to God in Jesus Christ, by the Christian scriptures, by commitment to the Christian church, by formation in the Christian tradition, is as necessary as ever. But if it is to be relevant to these new times, it must be rethought and reconfigured.[7]

Measuring 'churchliness'

Anglican schools across Australia might consider it essential to appoint an Anglican deacon or priest as chaplain, to timetable regular worship, and to teach religious studies. On a deeper level, however, any investigation of a school's 'churchliness' raises important quest-ions as to the nature of the very institution itself, questions such as: To

---

6. Richard Edlin, *The Cause of Christian Education* (Blacktown: National Institute for Christian Education, 1999), 17.
7. Nicholas Wolterstorff, 'Introduction', in *The Crumbling Walls of Certainty: Towards a Christian Critique of Postmodernity and Education*, edited by I Lambert and S Mitchell (Sydney: Centre for the Study of Australian Christianity, 1997), 6.

what extent does the school live as a Christian community? How are the fruits of the Spirit evident in the curriculum, the organisational structure, the policies, the practices, and the everyday experience of students and staff? How central to staff, students, and parents is the awareness of the 'Anglican' identity of the school, its sense of 'belonging' within its diocesan family, and its consequent responsibilities?

A notable example of the development of criteria for measuring a school's relationship to its founding principles is the instrument for self-evaluation of Jesuit high schools in the USA.[8] This instrument identifies Catholic (and especially Jesuit) principles in secondary schooling, and then applies these principles in determining specific standards in relation to the day-to-day working of the school. The self-evaluation instrument is thorough and enables schools to monitor their own effectiveness as 'Jesuit' schools. In terms of 'Catholicity' the instrument includes the expectation that all students and families 'accept by their enrolment in the school a serious obligation to explore their religious life within, and commitment to the Catholic tradition'. It also expects that every member of the faculty will be 'a person whose religious convictions make him or her willing to share his or her religious experience with students and also to encourage their personal religious development'. It assumes the existence of a Religious Education department and a program which has the same degree of excellence, professional preparation, and resource materials as the other academic departments of the school. It regards it as necessary for each faculty member to be familiar with, and participate in the Ignatian *Spiritual Exercises* which lie at the heart of Jesuit rule-of-life. It holds to an imperative that justice is to be practised and understood in the pastoral, academic, and management aspects of the life of the school.

The instrument further establishes parallel principles, standards and questions in relation to academic matters, community and

---

8. C Melrose, editor, *Foundations* (Washington, DC: Jesuit Secondary Education Association, 1994). While some Anglican diocesan systems have developed their own evaluation instruments, the Jesuit model commends itself to further investigation, not least because of the objectivity it offers through its independence from any specific Australian Anglican context. The following quotations in the text are taken from 43–53.

spiritual life, and finances. The issues for consideration by the schools are clear and detailed, and include questioning whether administrators and teachers 'take care not to encourage false values in the school by excessively stressing grades, rank in class, or competition among the students . . .' Schools are to ask themselves about methods used 'to insure that the program of co-curricular and extra-curricular activities . . . is being administered in a manner that is congruent with the Christian environment of a Jesuit school'. The instrument asks whether 'the Trustees, the President, the Rector, the Development Officer, and the Treasurer [are] conversant with and convinced of the academic and spiritual goals and priorities of the school'. It further inquires whether in the daily running of the school and in the eyes of those outside the school, 'the quest for academic excellence and the responsibility for the total Christian growth of the students complement each other'. It requires schools to identify some of the signs 'that teachers are manifesting trust and cooperation among themselves and with their students', and seeks to know whether there is 'general agreement among the faculty that sarcasm, impatience, punishments which diminish the sense of worth of a student, and the like are not acceptable at the school'.

By employing this instrument, it would presumably be possible for a school that was Jesuit by foundation and name to ensure its continuing adherence to fundamental principles which the Jesuits themselves consider to be core to Jesuit identity. This would certainly provide an effective educational and spiritual plumbline.

Criteria for Anglican schools

The need for congruence of principles and practices in church schools, coupled with the necessity to ensure the kind of relevance advanced by Wolterstorff (above), may be observed in the development of Anglican Schools in Western Australia. Driven by the need to provide more affordable Anglican schools, the Anglican Schools Commission in Perth established six schools over seventeen years. In articulating the purposes and goals of this diocesan system, two documents are of particular interest. The first, prepared in consultation with the principals of Anglican Schools, describes the Christian purposes of these schools;[9] the second documents the distinctive Anglicanism of

9. Tom Wallace, editor, *The Christian Purposes of Anglican Schools in the Diocese of Perth* (Perth: Anglican Schools' Commission, WA, 1998).

these schools.[10] The desire is to develop schools whose life is distinctively Christian (and particularly Anglican), and where the integrity of this daily life can be monitored and reviewed.

Three Christian purposes are listed, which could be taken as fundamental to all Anglican schools: (i) to bear witness to God as Trinity, (ii) to offer students the opportunity to explore and develop faith, and (iii) to provide education 'founded upon Christian beliefs, values and attitudes in the context of a community of faith and worship'. In an endeavour to establish and maintain integrity in the daily realisation of such purposes in an integrated fashion in all aspects of a school's life, the 1998 document advocates several strategies, which may be summarised as follows:

1. The provision of meaningful Anglican worship in a chapel or sacred space, the responsibility for which rests with the chaplain.
2. The implementation of a religious studies program which is integral to the school, with a reasonable time and resource allocation, and taught by teachers who have themselves undertaken a course in Religious Education, and who have access to professional development opportunities.
3. An inclusive approach which affirms the dignity of all, recognises diversity, and in which values of justice, compassion and service inform relationships. A major goal is that decision-making processes, policies and structures be founded on Christian beliefs, values and attitudes. The endeavour is to 'create communities which are open to the possibility of human transformation and renewal by grace through word and sacrament'.
4. The provision of opportunities for Christian ministry and service.
5. Staff modelling of the Christian ethos; this to be achieved through the appointment of staff who are excellent teachers and committed Anglicans, and who have access to professional development in issues of faith and life.

10. Anglican Schools Commission, *What is it that Makes Anglican Schools Distinctive?* (Perth: Anglican Schools Commission, WA, www.wa.asc.edu.au, 2003).

6. Building collaborative relationships with parents and local parishes.
7. Establishing school councils with a majority of members who are practising Anglicans.

The second (2003) document identifies common aims. One is the provision of a well-rounded education of the whole person, to meet the students' 'spiritual, physical, intellectual, social emotional, aesthetic and moral needs'. This aim rests on the theological premise of each individual's inherent value, and the need to affirm the particularity of each student's God-given gifts and capacities. A further outcome is the high value each school is called upon to place on quality pastoral care, and the direction of substantial resources to the spiritual and moral dimensions of education.

Drawing on Anglicanism's valuing of both 'word' (with its rational emphasis) and 'sacrament' (with its more intuitive and affective emphasis) the Commission identifies as an important goal of each school to value both 'head' and 'heart'. This is interpreted as a concern to:

> encourage students to think and reason as well as to participate in the creative arts and to deepen relationships with others and the natural environment.

The Commission traces the Anglican openness to diversity to both its Catholic and its Protestant roots, and so identifies inclusiveness as a common goal: inclusiveness in terms not only of belief, but also student background, socio-economic status and ability.

Since Anglican schools seek to provide an excellent standard of education, they must maintain their capacity to be aware of, and respond to, educational initiatives from around the world. However, the Commission demonstrates the necessity to interpret such initiatives through the Anglican tradition:

> Anglicanism maintains continuity with the past in its liturgies, its adherence to the historic creeds, and its episcopal and synodical form of policy while retaining a capacity to be responsive to its cultural and contemporary context. In its school the church

> preserves what is good from the past while being thoughtfully responsive to education innovation.

Finally, the Commission identifies the importance of stability and reliability in leadership and teaching staff:

> Anglicanism by its very structure provides stability in leadership and a series of checks and balances in the decision-making processes which impact on its parishes and its agencies. No school or parish can operate in complete independence. There is a reasonable assurance to parents that a school's education policy and practice will not be overly influenced by any particular person or pressure group.

In 1985 the Diocese of Melbourne's Committee on Education produced a discussion paper on Anglican schools, the outcome of a decade of careful work. As a result of a process of revision at the Victorian provincial level, a draft document was produced in February 2004, and a final version endorsed by Archbishop in Council and published by the Diocese in November of that year.[11] While the document is clear in its purpose to provide guidelines rather than policy, it contains points which overlap with—and build upon—the Western Australian documents.

It notes that each Anglican school must 'make its way in a competitive market place where it needs to be responsive to the perceived goals for education on the part of the various sections of the community which it seeks to serve'. This acknowledges the reality of the strongly independent nature of most of the Anglican schools of the Province, and their need to operate in an educationally competitive environment.

The guidelines provide that each Anglican school have three particular identifiable qualities: (i) the opportunity for all students to hear and respond to the Gospel and its call for mission; (ii) a program of religious education/studies as part of the school's core curriculum; and (iii) the school's values be compatible with gospel values.

---

11. Anglican Schools' Committee of the Anglican Province of Victoria, *The Diocese of Melbourne and Anglican Schools: Guidelines*, November 2004.

In order to establish and maintain these qualities, the guidelines suggest *inter alia*:

> an educational vision concerned with the development of the whole person, evident across the curriculum; a perspective which encompasses dignity and sufficiency for all persons, and promotes respect for others; enrolment opportunities for disadvantaged students; that school council membership include active Anglicans; that the council to make adequate provision for the religious dimension; that the Head be a member of a church in communion with the Anglican Church of Australia; that an ordained Anglican chaplain be appointed; that religious education be regarded as 'core' at least up to Year 10, with a professionally-trained teaching staff; that there be opportunities for personal examination of the Christian faith; that regular worship be conducted; that a climate exist that is supportive of Christian students, staff and families; that the school be involved in social service activities; and that there be partnerships and links with Anglican parishes and agencies.

The above examples from Western Australia and Melbourne are by no means definitive, there being other diocesan statements and guidelines in existence. In all such developments we see the church endeavouring to assist schools to be authentically Anglican in policy-making and implementation.

Spiritual and educational leadership

A school's board and its principal exercise enormous influence over the school, determining priorities, emphases, and policies. A school which reflects Anglicanism's 'checks and balances' ought to have a mechanism to ensure that such influence is moderated by Anglican polity and tradition. This suggests the capacity for the governing body and the senior administration to regularly engage in disciplined theological reflection on their goals and outcomes.

Given the particular nature of the school as an Anglican community, the role of the spiritual leadership is an important consideration. While the school might have an ordained deacon or priest as its chaplain, overall leadership and responsibility resides with the principal. The principal has responsibility for every aspect of the school's life, including its spiritual direction. Much rests, therefore, on his/her spiritual maturity and commitment, and the way in which she/he exercises or shares that spiritual leadership. This is particularly so in relation to the chaplain, who must exercise his/her vocation in a very different way to that of a parish, where the priest has the pastoral and liturgical oversight. By her/his vocation and ordination, a priest is called and authorised by the church to exercise a ministry of servanthood leadership among the people of God. When a bishop licenses a deacon or priest to a school chaplaincy ministry, then some understanding must obtain as to the parameters of such leadership, and how that leadership will be incorporated in the overall leadership of the principal and other decision-makers within the school. This is not an easy task, given that there is no single model for the exercise of ordained ministry in Anglican schools. One vital consideration is that —unlike any other member of the staff—an ordained chaplain is accountable to both principal and bishop in very direct ways.

In some Anglican educational institutions chaplains serve on the governing council or board and have direct input into policy-making, bringing theological insights to bear on educational, financial and other determinations. In some cases the chaplain is regarded as a senior member of the staff, and might even work closely with the principal in day-to-day administrative matters. Again, here there is the possibility of the chaplain exercising a spiritual leadership, including the prophetic role: enabling theological reflection by the policy-makers in the community on issues of faith and justice. In other schools, the chaplain might be regarded as essentially a teacher employed with some responsibility to lead chapel services, or to respond to pastoral needs of students, staff and parents. Here the sense of prophetic spiritual leadership in the community is more limited.

In an address to heads of Anglican Secondary Schools in the United Kingdom, Archbishop Rowan Williams argues that:

> the religious basis of a school displays 'the management' as itself answerable to a wider world of moral reference; part—a crucial part—of the task of leader-

> ship in a religious school is to underline and develop that answerability and connectedness.[12]

A high level of such connectedness could be perceived when the place of faith is unarguably central: when a Christian worldview is recognised and honoured, when policy is formed in the light of gospel priorities and Anglican sensitivities, and when the chaplain has maximum capacity to exercise spiritual guidance and leadership. Matters of faith would be perceived to be integral rather than appended to the curriculum. In such a scenario, religious matters would arise in classroom discussion as well as chapel services, and in staff in-service sessions, and religious studies would reach well beyond comparative religion or historical studies, to engage students with issues of faith in daily life in their own situations.

'Anglican' marks

Additional criteria which would apply in relation to an Anglican understanding of the Christian life are outlined in Bruce Kaye's (1994) identification of the 'marks' of an Anglican school.[13]

Drawing on a deep historical and theological understanding of the tradition, Kaye argues that reason and understanding are important Anglican qualities in the life of a school, enabling it to foster a Christian learning environment that takes seriously its context in the wider world. This necessitates a range of epistemologies which extend beyond the rationalistic 'to include the aesthetic as well as the rational, the affective as well as the cognitive'. He takes a refreshing look at the important role of tradition in Anglican schools, noting how Anglican theology has sought (and continues to seek) ways of relating its heritage to the contemporary particularities. The role of tradition in a school, therefore, must be more than maintaining the past. Rather, for Kaye, tradition is 'walking in the footsteps of the heroes of the past in relating the past to the present for the benefit of the future'.

---

12. Rowan Williams, *A Culture of Hope? Priorities and Vision in Church Schools*, Association of Anglican Secondary School Heads Annual Conference, Exeter. (Lambeth Palace Press Office, http://www.archbishopofcanterbury.org/sermons_speeches/030911.htmn, September 2003).
13. Kaye, 'Being an Anglican School'. The following quotations are taken from 139–41.

In advocating incarnation as a mark of the Anglican school, Kaye argues that Anglican allegiance is 'not to a system, nor to a philosophy, but to the Son of God incarnate'. In an echo of the Jesuit self-evaluating instrument (see above), he suggests that the Anglican school ought constantly be asking of itself how the image of Christ is borne and demonstrated in its daily life.

Kaye's fourth mark is that of worship: an absolute necessity for an Anglican school. We might take it that worship is not to be regarded as peripheral to the healthy life of the school, but as central and fundamental to it. Anglican worship has a special function in the development and expression of Anglican theology. It is for this reason that any school which takes the name must engage in and be strongly committed to meaningful, engaging worship which is recognisably Anglican and connected to the wider curriculum.

Finally, Kaye underlines the need for Anglican schools to engage with the wider Australian society, drawing out the necessity to act on the priorities of the Gospel and to reach out beyond the borders of the school and even the local community, and experience the diversity of Australian society:

> . . . An Anglican school might . . . seek to develop an identity for all who have to live in a plural society, which is shaped by an open understanding of our Incarnational religion. Interactive, exploratory, persuasive rather than coercive, this method will produce more enduring results for our students and ourselves.

Distinctive communities

Despite the wider perception within the church of the peripherality of Anglican schools, when one begins to look for evidence of the life of faith within them, one is drawn to recognise that they are, indeed, communities: educational communities where faith ought to have an important place. Rowan Williams' *A Culture of Hope?* argues that the distinctively Christian community of a church school brings a vital dimension to the fundamental purpose of education. He makes the point that the current rhetoric of educational management in the UK seems to assume that the driving purpose of education is the imparting of knowledge and skills, with little recognition of the importance of what Williams calls 'the construction of a quality of mind in a collegial setting'; one is able to recognise parallel attitudes in contemporary Australia. For Williams, there can never be any sense of neutrality about the moral or spiritual ethos of a school; institutions which claim such neutrality are, in his view, 'generating an ethos of individualism, functionalism and ultimately fragmentation,' the assumption being that the students' spiritual and moral development will be dealt with by some other social influences in their lives.

In fact there is a long tradition that underscores the necessity that education be about the whole person. In the experience of many people, the very best teachers are those concerned with much more than the measurable educational outcomes of the curriculum; they know that in the formative years of a person's life one's learning extends beyond the functional model of education. We are formed as we integrate our academic and other skills with our developing understanding of who we are and how we relate to the world in which we live. The community in which we learn forms us in this process of integration; the point at issue here is nature of this formation. Given its moral and spiritual ethos, argues Williams, the church school attends to the whole person, taking it for granted that:

> the culture that needs developing has to include what many would call the single and most definitive factor in all human history up to and even including modernity: the beliefs and practices that express human relation to something more than the individual and the sum of contemporary individual experience, relation to what is holy, creative and unsurpassable.

As the Anglican Schools' Commission in Perth has noted (see above) an Anglican school might reasonably argue by its very *raison d'être* that it rightly does attend to the whole person in this way, and that there is no need for it to apologise for this. In fact, one might hope that this quality would stand out as one of the reasons why parents choose an Anglican school for their child. However, there are particular challenges and tensions here, not least in the nature of the Anglican school community itself.

Unlike a parish, where members of the congregation voluntarily identify with Anglicanism, our schools may have a diversity of faiths and denominational allegiances among both students and staff. Typically, membership of the Anglican Church is not a requirement for those who wish to study or teach at an Anglican school. In fact, members of the school community may be of any faith or none, though there will need to be a recognition and respect of the school's Anglican ethos. Respecting differences while maintaining a strong commitment to Anglican understanding and tradition, raises tensions for the school, which at their most creative will enable healthy dialogue and the exploration of Christian perspectives alongside others. This is most obviously so in schools where attendance at chapel services is compulsory. On the one hand, it is essential that Anglican worship be offered; on the other hand, respect must be maintained for those who are of a different religious persuasion, or none. While unashamedly proclaiming the Gospel in the context of Anglican liturgy, chapel services will need to be conducted mindful of the presence of non–Christians. At the same time, it is also vital to remember that regular church-going is not the norm for the majority of Australian students, and that their major (if not sole) experience of Christian community is their experience in the school. Of course, such an expression of 'ecclesia' requires a nuancing of Anglican worship, as well as the need for non-Anglican (and especially non-Christian) parents to have clear understanding of the school's expectations in this regard when they enrol their child. Fundamentals of authentic Anglican community remain: Anglican worship (including the Eucharist) regularly offered for staff, parents and students; baptism and confirmation preparation; pastoral ministry, including the conduct of marriages and funerals, as appropriate; and community service. While opportunities ought to be taken to build close links with local communities of faith where students and families would be welcomed into membership, one must nevertheless recognise that an Anglican school is a Christian community in its own right, and is not lesser than a parish in this regard. Rowan Williams argues that the rationale for the church school is the body of Christ. When Christians gather together to worship, when they form an educational community, when they live out their faith in a community context, then Williams' argument cannot be doubted. It is in such a community that we might find faith, hope and love as cherished qualities, experienced regularly, personally and systemically.

It would be unwise to assume that ideal conditions apply in Anglican schools across the country. One good example is provided by the Reverend Ted Witham, who records how, as a school chaplain, he visited various subject department/faculty meetings to explore the links between the subject discipline and the purposes of the school.

Having been well received by the Social Studies, English and Maths staff, he was surprised by his reception by the Science staff:

> There was immediate uproar. My visit was classed as unwanted and inappropriate 'inspection' by the school hierarchy. Science, they said, was pure discipline, and any interference challenged its integrity. I was threatening their academic freedom. My very visit implied that science had to yield to religious doctrine. I was given no opportunity to raise discussion. I was virtually dismissed with anger.[14]

Such a perception of the compartmentalization of the spiritual dimension to a place apart from curriculum, or even from policy, administration, and indeed any aspect of the school's life, restricts the school's capacity to continue to address the issues surrounding the nature of its faith community and its Anglican identity.

A culture of hope

Rowan Williams sees the church school as potentially demonstrating a culture of hope, 'not least in reminding the educational establishment of unfinished business when it drifts towards the narrowest kind of functionalism.' For him, the church school has the clearest possible rationale for offering students a corporate experience which intentionally forms socially active and responsible persons. This is especially important in a post-September 11 world which accords a ready linking of religious conviction and extremism and terrorist activities. Williams argues that Western sensitivities have been raised with regard to other religions, and especially Islam, and the importance of the study of comparative religions has increased. Moreover, the secularised First World has been reminded that religion continues to hold a very important place in the lives of many millions of people around the globe. Anglican schools can play an important role in helping their students understand the heritage of other religions, and, very importantly, the heritage of the Christian religion. An Anglican school, welcoming students of any faith or none, nevertheless rests firmly on Christian principles. As Williams explains:

---

14. Ted Witham, 'Do Anglican Schools Make Christians?', *Outlook* (August 1999).

> This is not in order to indoctrinate the unwilling; but there is a clear mission . . . which might be expressed by saying: 'You may or may not share these convictions; but you will at least have seen what a community looks like that works with these convictions, and you will have experienced some of the results.'

Integrity and congruence

It could be argued that the 'churchliness' of an Anglican school rests not so much on its organisational interaction with a diocesan synod or local church, but rather on the nature of its moral and spiritual ethos, and its capacity to point members of its community (staff, students and families alike) beyond themselves as individuals, and beyond the sum of contemporary human experience, and to enter into relationship with that which is 'holy, creative and unsurpassable'.[15]

The Jesuit self-evaluation instrument (see above) has been developed in the context of the clarity afforded by the culture of Roman magisterium and Ignatian regulation. Anglican culture exists in a very different environment, though it is just as vital for Anglican schools to be able to ensure their own integrity of purpose and congruent practice in order for them to be able to display the marks of a Christian community that is recognizably Anglican and to contribute to the mission of the church.

One approach in determining the 'churchliness' of an Anglican school would be to identify and compare two templates of its identity: 'explicit' and 'implicit'. Drawing on the Jesuit model, it would then be possible to identify a set of principles and standards, and produce a set of questions to provide schools with the necessary tools to measure their own integrity and congruence. The 'explicit' or educational identity is common to all schools, is value-laden, and is primarily geared to knowledge and skill-development, and therefore to the longterm material and intellectual wellbeing of students. It includes: the academic curriculum and programs, its content and outcomes; the co-curriculum; administrative policies and procedures; educational and administrative structures; and systems for decision-making.

---

15. Williams, *A Culture of Hope*, 2003.

The template of explicit outcomes would include the behaviours which flow from this identity, such as: the priorities of curriculum development and subject offerings; the pedagogical practices; the practices of student behaviour management; the exercise of discipline; the relationship of staff with their students, and with their colleagues; practices in determining the school's economic priorities, including the setting of fees and salary levels, and resource allocation; and the hiring and firing of staff.

The 'implicit identity' derives from the school's ecclesiastical foundation, which draws it beyond educational functionalism, and focusses it on the development of a 'quality of mind in a collegial setting'.[16] The implicit curriculum is concerned with the spiritual and moral wellbeing of the members of the school as a Christian community. This template might begin with fundamental qualities of faith, hope and love, or even the full list of the fruits of the Spirit: love, joy, peace, patience, kindness, goodness, faithfulness, self-control, and include marks of Anglican identity, such as:

> trinitarian witness; Christian values, beliefs and attitudes; a community of faith and worship; holistic education, both cognitive and affective; a dynamic tradition; and incarnational life.

The template of implicit outcomes would include the behaviours which flow from this identity, such as: worship as a priority, under the direction of a licensed chaplain; school boards which warmly embrace Christian values and Anglican practice; policies, systems, structures and behaviours which demonstrate faith, hope and love in design and operation; holistic education, both cognitive and affective; a prominent place for well-resourced religious education; well-trained religious education teachers, with opportunities for professional development; programs that interpret Anglican tradition in a contemporary context; and a focus on the image of Christ in daily interaction and social responsibility.

A superimposition of the two templates, and the questions derived from such a comparison, would permit a school to judge its own 'fit'

16. Stephen Prickett, *Education! Education! Education! Managerial Ethics and the Law of Unintended Consequences* (Thorverton: Imprint Academic, 2002). Quoted by Williams *A Culture of Hope?*.

and the way in which the outcomes of its explicit and implicit identities integrate or stand in tension. It would further enable the school to identify areas for its own growth and development as an Anglican institution.

Two–way contribution

In a recent address to Chairs of Boards of Anglican Schools in Australia, the distinguished social researcher and commentator, Hugh Mackay, argued the importance of taking into account the nature of the dominant modes of understanding of the present generation of students. Because these young people have particularly strong tribal needs, Mackay argues that schools must now provide an even richer social environment than ever before. 'They must now take the place of the parish church of the past'.[17] This suggestion points to the fact that Anglican schools at their very best can offer much to the church, not least a fresh view of what it means to be an authentic worshipping Anglican community, although this community may be expressed in ways very different from those of the parish. Anglican schools offer the church remarkable opportunities for mission, welcoming many thousands of young people who would otherwise have little contact with the church. These schools provide an environment where students can encounter Christian values and traditions, regular worship, biblical insights, and religious sensitivities as part of their formative process. Large numbers of staff, students and their families are ministered to through Anglican schools, with chaplains (responsible to both principal and bishop) taking the lead in a breadth of ministry from baptisms to funerals.

The wealth of the Anglican tradition brings enrichment to the educational endeavour, and at the same time provides a plumbline to enable schools to monitor their lives in the light of the Gospel. It is the responsibility of the schools to make the most of this resource, balancing it with their desire for educational and administrative independence.

Similarly, the schools are in a very strong position to make a vital contribution to the contemporary church, pointing to new ways of living the Christian message among young people and their families. In order to do this, however, it will be important for schools to develop

17. Hugh Mackay, unpublished address to Chairs of Boards, at the Australian Heads of Independent Schools Association Conference, 2004.

an authentic 'churchliness' in which their implicit identity, rich in the church's tradition, and focussed on the activity of the Christian Gospel in the daily life of individuals and the community, informs the development of the school's explicit educational identity. It is only in this way that a school can be authentically 'Anglican': in its very nature, in its daily life as well as in its name.

16

Our Worship Is Diminished If We Do Not Serve The Lord's Justice

Ray Cleary

> There is one way and one way only to save the drift and that is by giving the people of Australia a vision of the Christian faith recreating the social order in this new land; leaving behind the bitterness of the old world with its class hatreds and its international rivalries; establishing justice in economic fields and inspiring political action to great creative endeavours. The Christian faith did this once for Europe when it tamed barbarians and sustained a vision of unity for a whole continent. The Christian faith is still as vital and relevant to Australia as it ever was and is to Europe, but the churches must forget most of the things which now obsess them and be caught by a vision of the work to be done.[1]

The beginnings

Anglicans in Australia, since the time of the First Fleet, have played a significant role in outreach and ministry to those who, today, would be described as on the 'margins of society', the vulnerable, frail and 'at risk' members of the Australian community. Many who first arrived had criminal convictions for minor crimes and transportation to the

1. From an address on 4 July 1937, Burgmann papers, book 17, as quoted by Peter Hempenstall, 'An Anglican Strategy for Social Responsibility: the Burgmann Solution', in *Anglican Social Strategies from Burgmann to the Present*, edited by John Moses (St Lucia: Broughton Press 1989), 6.

new colony as their punishment. They left behind family and friends and arrived to be met by a new, and at times hostile, environment and the demands of their new masters. Many of the offences for which they were convicted were petty crimes, including stealing a loaf of bread to feed their families. They, themselves, were victims of poverty. Others were convicted of more serious crimes.

In sentencing men, women and children to the colonies, little, if any, attention was given to the social conditions which contributed to their crime. Poor wages, unemployment, lack of housing, education and health facilities were endemic among the working class. A lack of all contributed to crime as a way of life and survival.

Present debates about crime and poverty contain elements of the same claims. Many clients of Anglican welfare agencies today, also lack employment, housing, health care and an adequate income level. Like 200 years ago, critics of those in poverty still deny the link between poverty and crime.

The clergy of the new colony were expected to minister to the personal needs of the convicts and to maintain proper religious observances. In responding to these roles, they were both pastors and agents of government at the one time—a tension they themselves often recognised.

Ministry and service to the convicts of the first colony by the early clergy was the church's first response to the marginalised and disadvantaged. This ministry initially excluded contact with Indigenous Australians, although without doubt, as the new colony grew, this focus began to shift. The approach and attitude of the clergy was judgmental, a response to perceived wickedness and 'sin'. This is not to say that compassion was absent. Many free settlers and others offered comfort and hope, and there are many stories of friendships and newfound purposes. Those who responded this way saw it as their Christian duty and responsibility.

Today's engagement

Anglican welfare agencies today are in contact with the ten to fifteen per cent of Australians variously described as the poor, the unemployed, the dissident, the different and the difficult, and more recently, includes asylum seekers and refugees.[2] They come from all walks of life, from across the social, political and economic spectrum, and share many common experiences, including addictions to drugs both legal and illegal, unemployment, lack of income, homelessness, physical and mental health disorders, personal anguish, violence and ongoing pain. Life, for most, is a struggle for survival. Many have been ill-treated as children, raised in care and have benefited little from schooling. Many suffer ongoing ill health, while others are unable to find long-term employment with a sustainable level of income to provide for the basics of life, shelter, food, clothing and transport. Asylum seekers and refugees who form part of this group, are often victims of corrupt political regimes abroad, while others at home have suffered as a direct result of a change in social attitudes and economic reform. I remember vividly a response to a question asked of a young seventeen year old drug user as to why he continued to use a dangerous illegal drug of addiction. His response, 'because it is the only time I feel good about myself'.[3]

The children, young people and families who are supported by and engaged with Anglican agencies, do not experience a 'good life'. They are often victims of economic and social injustice, and of circumstances over which they may have limited or no control. Life is a constant struggle for survival, a reality often not understood by those who have not experienced such in their own lives or others who have overcome similar disadvantage. It is a salutary reminder that unemployed people do not create unemployment. Unemployment is a result of social and economic policy decisions made by governments and businesses. They are often made for ideological or long-term objectives with little expressed concern for their immediate impact on families or communities.

The church today

The church has a long tradition of justice, care and hospitality. Throughout the church's history, the response of faithful Christian

---

2. This represents a best effort description. It is based on the numbers seeking welfare support through agencies from data collected from Australian Council of Social Service (ACOSS).
3. A response by a participant in a youth focus group by the writer, conducted in 1998 in the western suburbs of Melbourne.

men and women has been witnessed, from the earliest monasteries providing hospitality and lodgings to the weary traveller, to hospices and programs for the care of the sick, emergency relief, shelter, housing, services for older people, emergency accommodation, foster care, children's homes, day care centres and pastoral care. Christian hospitality and a spirit of generosity towards one's neighbour have been guiding principles underlying this engagement, as has been the concern to bring individuals into a relationship with Christ. The parables of the good Samaritan and the prodigal son have underpinned this work.

The Anglican Church of Australia, along with the Salvation Army, Uniting and Roman Catholic Churches, is one of the largest providers of welfare services, known now as community services, to children and young people, the elderly, the unemployed, drug and alcohol users and those with a disability. These services are delivered through fifty large state or diocesan based agencies and hundreds of parish programs. This commitment is theology in action.

In the Anglican tradition in Australia, and across differing theological perspectives of the Australian church on the gospel imperative 'to love God and to love one's neighbour', churches and individuals undertake a vast and diverse ministry amongst, with, and to, those in need. In the early days those who participated in this ministry focussed their actions on helping those in need by offering shelter and relief, and in sharing the hope and good news in Christ. While this commitment may not have been expressed in either theological or mission language, it was driven by a strong belief in the centrality and place of God in all aspects of creation and human living, as well as a shared responsibility with the Creator to build a better world. It was modelled on the ministry of Jesus and the call to love God as we are loved by him.

Anglicans in Australia do not have an official '*Rerum Novarum*'[4] statement defining a set of principles of social and theological engagement with those in need, but rather have relied upon the insights and commitments of individuals who engage in welfare and justice ministry. This is not to say Anglican theology is devoid of any commitment to a theological basis for its engagement with the disadvantaged,

4. *Rerum Novarum: The Encyclical Letter of the late Pope Leo XIII on the Condition of Labour* (Melbourne: Australian Catholic Truth Society, 1891).

but rather to suggest an eclectic response to the mission task. During the nineteenth century in Australia, this response was understood in moral terms, focussing on the cause of disadvantage as an outcome of personal behaviour, expressed in notions of deserving and undeserving. Children were always deserving, as seen in early adoption practices. Parents were not. In the twentieth century a shift occurred, emerging from, and influenced to some degree by, the Christian Socialist movements in Europe and the writings of Tawney, Temple and others.[5]

While much of the early welfare work of Anglican agencies and churches was seen as worthy and supported, the majority of the initiatives stood outside the official diocesan and synod structures. Many are still today. Although welcomed and encouraged by bishops and others, they operated on the edge of diocesan life, and were often seen as an optional extra. They did not occupy a place of central importance.

Today, in many places, Anglican welfare and its place in mission, still remains a point of contention. Welfare agencies are not officially represented at General Synod, nor at many diocesan synods. Connections are kept alive by personal and agency relationships with their diocesan bishop and stakeholders. While formal recognition should not be seen as an end in itself, recognition gives both symbolic meaning and commitment to the welfare obligation of all Christians to contribute to the coming of God's kingdom, both here and in the future. Recent meetings of the General Synod Standing Committee have also suggested the need to connect more fully with the polis of welfare activity as part of the fullness of the church's mission.

Today's Anglican presence in community and justice work is substantial, innovative, and understood by those engaged in this ministry as integral to both the mission of the church and its interface with the community in which it exists. In many instances, the agencies represent the church's engagement with civil society. This approach continues an important tradition and way of being church for Anglicans and highlights the role of agencies and their leaders in influencing and shaping welfare provision and social security.

Today's engagement in the public arena and in the market place of ideas and discussions has always been central to Anglican mission.

---

5. For a full discussion, see A Wilkinson, *Christian Socialism: Scott Holland to Tony Blair* (London: SCM Press, 1998).

Anglicanism has always engaged with society and sought to influence its ways. Anglican welfare is no exception. This engagement continues and is valued by other churches and organisations with similar goals and vision to build a more just and compassionate Australia.

At the heart of today's engagement is the commitment to express, in both word and deed, servant leadership based on the pattern and ministry of Jesus himself. In practice, this involves washing the feet of the homeless, sharing a meal with the broken, speaking up for the voiceless, sharing our own resources with those who have none, and caring for the sick. It may, at times, mean silent witness when all else fails. Welfare service provision in this context is about personal change and social transformation. It is not a managerial response to manage those in need, but a theological and mission response, which recognises the church as a mediating agency of influence in the community. The church, like other associations, stands between the individual and the state, with the capacity to influence our sense of identity, reflecting values of a more just and humane society.

History of Anglican engagement

In Victoria, individual Christian citizens and philanthropists, such as the founders of the Sutherland Homes for Children, the Victorian Children's Aid Society, Hartnett House (now part of Melbourne Citymission), and the Brotherhood of St Laurence, provided land and buildings from their own personal estates. Many of these early philanthropists had a strong sense of Christian duty and often established services despite opposition or lack of interest from their church or governing body.

The beginnings of many church responses to meeting the needs of those in poverty were often linked to the evangelical goal to save souls. Poverty, drunkenness and idleness were understood as the outcome of individual moral decadence and irresponsibility. There was little recognition of structural or environmental poverty. Moral judgment, not human rights, was at the heart and centre of the church's response. Help or support was often given only after the individual had confessed their sins, acknowledged their depravity and sought forgiveness from Jesus. The principles of deserving and undeserving were pre-eminent: children deserving, women and men less so.

Many early responses and initiatives to those in need came from parishes, often led by women and mothers. They recognised the need to respond with compassion, as well as with a sense of moral concern. Many were generous givers and offered hospitality to the most disadvantaged. The legacy of this support is to be seen in the endowments of many agencies today.

Volunteerism was a key aspect of the work of these early charitable and parish initiatives. Women with wealthy husbands often saw it as their duty, not only to raise funds, but also to serve soup. Clergy wives were often the leaders of this charitable work and advocates in parish communities of this welfare task.

Volunteers were regarded as the practical expression of a faith commitment, and were the life-blood of many early agencies. Over time, volunteers became committees of management members as well as providing care on the streets and in the dormitories when needed. The staff employed were generally expected to be active Christians and to understand their work as a calling or vocation. Remuneration was minimal. Working conditions were often poor. Goodwill was highly valued and affirmed, while self-assessment and initiative was central. In many activities women raised the funds, while the men formed the boards of governance and decided how the money would be spent.

Len Tierney, in a paper presented in 1962 to the Victorian Council of Social Services, suggested that:

> Part of a stimulus to preach the Gospel came about as a reaction to a great deal of intemperance and degraded behaviour, which went hand in hand with great poverty, poor medical care and illiteracy.[6]

Early Anglican examples

Reading the histories of a number of Anglican welfare initiatives in the nineteenth century, a number of common themes can be identified. Many initiatives were started by entrepreneurial individuals, often by a single person. They attracted others to their cause, often financed them personally, and were established outside existing church government. In Tasmania in the 1890s, Bishop Henry Hutchinson, concerned

---

6. LJ Tierney, 'The Church and Social Welfare—The Historical Background', unpublished paper delivered to the Victorian Council of Churches Consultation on Social Welfare, 1962, 3.

about moral laxity and exploitation, believed that the test of real church work:

> lay in the attention paid to the lowest stratum of society, many of whom found themselves on the bottom rung of the social ladder simply as the victims of circumstances, and through very little fault of their own.[7]

He saw, 'prostitution, abandonment and appalling housing conditions, as constituting a huge problem'.[8]

In Melbourne, Bishop Perry and his wife, both strongly committed to works of philanthropy, called a public meeting in 1854 with the support of other churches in response to the increasing problem of homelessness. Six hundred residents of the new colony established the then Melbourne Citymission, one of the first ecumenical agencies, including Anglicans, in this country.

The origins of the Melbourne Citymission were grounded on both Christian theology and the realities of the day. 'Out of the turmoil threatening the citizens of gold rush Melbourne in 1854 came the comforting clear call for united endeavour to restore God to his people and order to society'.[9]

Throughout the history of the establishment of these new organisations, volunteers were the backbone of fundraising and management. Both men and women came together to do the Lord's work, often as a group of friends, sometimes as a parish outreach program, and on many occasions, responding to a spur of the moment initiative or crisis. Many formed associations, created organisations, and understood themselves as standing within the framework of the English Poorhouse Laws of the seventeenth century. The initiators of these acts of charity, and the establishment of agencies, did not necessarily see their work as becoming departments of Synod, the

---

7. G Stephens, *Clarendon a Century of Care*, published by the Board of Clarendon House, 1990, to mark the centenary, 3.
8. *Ibid*, 2.
9. R Otzen, 'Charity and Evangelisation: The Melbourne Citymission 1885–1914', PhD thesis, Department of History, University of Melbourne, 1986, 21.

governing body of the Diocese.[10] There is evidence to show that they assiduously guarded their independence, and especially their assets, from one another, and from synod.

Sister Kate, at the age of twenty-two, joined the community of the Sisters of the Church. Her first appointment was to an orphanage in Edgeware Road, London. In 1901, she arrived in Australia in Perth, with an entourage of child migrants. Two Perth institutions are today a reminder of her pioneering work: Perth College Mount Lawley and Parkerville Children's Home. Sister Kate, in 1903, purchased twenty acres at Parkerville for the 'League of Charity Home' for children. She introduced the concepts of cottage homes, and every child was given the opportunity to succeed in life. Sister Kate demonstrated the commitment of many Christian men and women who saw it as their vocation to assist those in need.

One outstanding contributor to an Anglican strategy of social responsibility and justice can be seen in the ministry of Bishop Ernest Burgmann, Bishop of Goulburn 1934–50, and Bishop of Canberra and Goulburn 1950–60. He exercised an active ministry in the fields of social and economic reform and the pursuit of a just society. Burgmann expressed a dream, a dream about a great Christian democracy evolving in Australia, which would give a lead to the rest of the world in consensus, cooperation and social justice.

Burgmann has been described as standing in the great tradition of Anglican social thinkers, including Bishop Frank Westin, and Archbishop William Temple. Critical enquiry embracing a whole of life approach was central to Burgmann's ministry and his engagement with others, although he was not himself directly involved in service provision other than his pastoral activities. Peter Hempenstall, in an article entitled, 'An Anglican Strategy for Social Responsibility: the Burgmann Solution' writes:

> He saw in present social conditions the continuation of Calvary. He further says, if comfortable Clergymen were to escape the guilt of participating in the daily

10. See B Dickey, *Giving a Hand: A History of Anglicare SA Since 1960*, (Adelaide: Anglicare SA and B Dickey, 2003) 1–8, for a detailed discussion on this topic.

> crucifixion of men and women, they must actively engage themselves in the process of social reform.[11]

Burgmann wrote letters to the editor, and published articles challenging and criticising capitalism as a distorted political economy. He also challenged the Anglican Church in its agenda, and was active in the public arena on many social and economic issues. He disturbed people's minds, and challenged their previous oppositions. Burgmann, in 1938, boldly told his colleagues:

> It is the business of the church to minister to sick and neurotic souls, [yet] it ends up far too often, with these fearful, neurotic souls in the saddle so far as the institution is concerned . . . The church has failed to bear witness to international justice as she has failed to bear witness to justice in inter-class relations. As her failure in the latter case produced communism, so her failure in the former has given us Nazism and Fascism . . . Churches are always a danger to religion. They get interested in themselves, in their own inground aggrandisement and power, and countless things that keep them too busy to live close to the life of the people . . . Churchmen get interested in the world beyond this world, largely to escape the trouble setting right for the wrongs that afflict the human race.[12]

Burgmann, along with Gerard Tucker, Geoffrey Sambell, Peter Hollingworth and David Scott, was influential in Victoria in shifting the role and place of Anglican charitable and welfare work into the new domain of social justice. Likewise in other states, the influence of the Australian Council of Social Services and local Councils of Social Services, often led by Anglicans, saw new ways of thinking about the church's engagement with society shift into a new role embracing biblical understandings of human rights and social justice. Sambell's influence in West Australia as Archbishop, and later Michael Challen, saw this agenda spread. During the 1980s, the General Synod's Social Responsibilities Committee, along with those in many of the dioceses,

---

11. Hempenstall, 'An Anglican Strategy for Social Responsibility', 3.
12. *Ibid*, 5.

established a new voice on Anglican involvement, along with a stronger advocacy role on public issues. The issuing of an annual ecumenical Social Justice Statement was one indication of this new and emerging role.

Throughout these years of engagement with civil society, emerged the flag for a more just and compassionate community, aligned with the Christian principles of justice and equality and resonating with themes associated with the Christian Socialist movement in England. This began a different approach for Anglican welfare, and in this process, aided by research and theological reflection, challenged much of the historical institutional work and responses to poverty. The idea of charity, often meaning giving money to charities, was replaced by principles of justice seen in the significant influence the Brotherhood of St Laurence and other Anglican agencies played in the 1972 Inquiry into Poverty in Australia. Today's emphasis on the place of community in addressing social inequality can be traced to these beginnings of the more pro-active engagement in social policy formation.

Today's response

Today's Anglican community and justice work, expressed through its agencies, has responded to changes in community thinking, new understandings of poverty and the impacts of social and economic policy. Building on the leaders of the past and influenced by new thinking on the need for changes in today's Australia, Anglican thinking has emerged as a significant contribution in the areas of child welfare, housing, community development and employment. In addition, changing attitudes by governments have provoked and initiated new debates, both within and outside the churches, on their role in today's multi-cultural, multi-faith society.

New challenges face Anglican welfare and justice ministries at this time. These include not only shifting social, economic and political thinking in the community, but also how the church itself understands its commitment to building a just and sustainable community for all.

Anglican welfare and justice today

I have already described briefly the background which saw a major shift take place in the role of Anglican welfare agencies in the late 1960s led by organisations such as the Brotherhood of St Laurence. This shift was, in part, influenced by Catholic social teaching, the Christian Socialist movement in England, and a new religious activism seen in Europe, experienced through the World Council of Churches. Many agencies began to see the need for social activism as an important adjunct to service delivery. Charity, by itself, was insufficient in addressing social inequality. Welfare was to be understood no longer as a moral response to those in need, but rather one embracing the principles of justice which argued that all citizens have the basic right to an adequate income, food, healthcare, education and shelter. It also embraced the principles of compassion, money, inclusiveness and forgiveness. Further, many saw it as reinforcing the values of Christian faith and the role faith and religion have in protecting human dignity in an increasing secular society. Here, the church through its agencies, was recognised at the cutting edge of the place of pain and suffering of many Australians. It made some in the church feel uncomfortable and nervous.

At the same time, a renewed interest in parish based welfare and justice ministries began to emerge, led by trained social workers and others interested in the interface between welfare and theology. In Victoria, David Chambers and Peter Burke led a new ministry in this area. Similar strategies were initiated in Sydney and other parts of the country, with the quest to integrate the work of welfare and justice with local faith communities. For a time, a network of people met from across the country to explore this approach further and many of the earlier NACON Conferences were designed to strengthen the network of Anglican organisations around parish-based initiatives.[13]

Around the same time, many agencies began to employ social work staff in key administrative and policy positions. Decision-making, which had been the domain and prerogative of ordained clergy and members of religious orders, was now under challenge from other professionals. Many of them were not members of the Anglican Church or of any Christian tradition. The broadening of staff employed in agencies occurred at the same time as major shifts in professionals occurred. Structural inequality was now seen as a major cause of poverty. New forms of service delivery were emerging. As a result of these changes, a number of children's homes and other institutions, operated by the Anglican Church across Australia, closed. Many shifted their focus to alternate forms of care or family support

---

13. NACON (National Anglican Caring Organisation Network) was formed in 1986 and was the predecessor to Anglicare Australia.

programs. The goal was to address the causes of poverty, deprivation and the need to remove children, rather than symptoms.

The emergence of social work, as well as professional training in youth work and the broader social sciences, challenged earlier responses to social need and the principles which undergirded it. Increasingly, the professionals who entered the field in the early 1970s brought more than a faith commitment as historically understood to their task. The establishment of the Action Resource Centre at the Brotherhood of St Laurence, the introduction of Careforce programs by St John's Homes for Boys and Girls in Victoria, New South Wales and Queensland, the closing of babies' homes by the Mission of St James and St John, the introduction of parish based partnerships by the Mission to Streets and Lanes in Melbourne, and the beginnings of Anglicare's new role in other cities and states including Sydney and Rockhampton surfaced as a result. Likewise, in South Australia initiatives began to reshape the face of Anglican welfare activity. Many of these initiatives were self-funded by the agencies themselves with the support of philanthropic trusts. Others were funded by the newly elected federal Labor Government in 1972.

The initial accommodation of new professional skills within an organisational framework inspired by religious values was seen, at the time, as complementary and non-threatening to agencies. Many saw the development as a natural extension and were enthusiastic about the new alliance. Their staff were both professional and many still had a religious commitment, although not church attendees or participants in institutional religion. It was thought ideal. The reality was, however, that with a changing society, less commitment to formal and institutional religion and greater professionalism, the impact of Christian values, and in particular the Anglican ethos and tradition, began to shift. The inspiration and values of the founders became less prevalent. Agencies which had a strong social action component, many of the Anglo–Catholic tradition, began to see their work literally 'taken over' and changed by others than those who professed faith. Governments also began to fund agencies to provide services, and the relationship between Anglican service providers and government shifted. As governments provided more funds, they demanded greater accountability and adherence to government policy. This opened the challenge to agencies to ensure their mission was not compromised, a challenge not recognised by some and ignored by others.

In June 1986, speaking to a meeting of Catholic Superiors in Victoria about the role and future of church based welfare agencies in a changing and challenging environment, I raised the question of how this emerging environment, where government was increasingly providing more funds, would affect agency thinking. Along with many of my colleagues in other agencies, I believed it was a time for some serious thinking on the subject. The charitable or welfare sector as it had been known, was changing dramatically. Poverty and generational family dysfunction were recognised as the major causes of why many children entered residential care. The growth of new services, including intensive family support, foster care, neighbourhood houses, and youth programs, to name a few, became the new agenda and the goal of a welfare system in transition. As such they were an outcome of the growing recognition of the importance of structural inequity in the community. Building on the strengths of the past, recognising the weaknesses and applying new knowledge, provided the framework for this development.

A way forward?

A ministry of social justice will respect the integrity of God's creation and the dignity of the human person. It acknowledges the centrality of God as the source of life and being. Why is the term social justice so difficult to define? Alan Nichols, in his book *Reluctant Conscience*, suggests two reasons.[14] First, there have been many moral traditions providing clearly defined attitudes to social justice throughout the history of Christian thought. Moral traditions saw poverty and oppression as a result of personal failure and lack of morality. Second, there has been insufficient attention to understanding the meaning of justice in the Old Testament and in the ministry of Jesus. I suggest a further reason. In Australia there has only been a slow, and then reluctant, understanding of the structural causes of poverty. Despite intensive education about poverty in Australia and its causes, only minimal advances have been made at both government and community levels, including the church.

A strategy for social justice rests on the assumption that we are able successfully to change people. It builds on charitable giving by asking questions of why and how. Seeking justice is the struggle to create an

14. A Nichols, *Reluctant Conscience* (Victoria: Dove Communications, 1984).

equitable and hospitable society for all, irrespective of wealth, skill or status. A justice agenda for the building of God's community or kingdom challenges each of us in our own lifestyle, work context and goals. It means giving to others from what we have ourselves. Justice embraces Isaiah's emphasis on being for others as suffering servants of God.

The principles of justice in the Christian tradition are recorded throughout the Hebrew Scriptures and New Testament. Both Matthew's Sermon on the Mount and Luke's Sermon on the Plain are clear examples of the Christian obligation to seek justice for all of God's creation. The church, in its full expression of God's mission is, therefore, to be a servant church, proclaiming in word and deed, the building blocks of God's kingdom. Our worship is diminished if we do not serve the Lord's justice.

Seeking justice for the poor and dispossessed is not a strategy to comfort one's own conscience or to provide immediate relief, but also a stategy to modify and influence the structures in our society which inflict pain, disadvantage and suffering. A commitment to a ministry of social justice involves dialogue with government, with community groups, as well as with the church. It is in this context that the struggle for justice means becoming political and engaged in the market place, if we are to be faithful and true Christian stewards of the gospel. Justice is about a vision—a vision of the kingdom or the realm of God. It is a call to the Christian noble vision for society. The church has this role.

A ministry of justice complements proclamation and adoration. A ministry of justice may take many forms. At the parish level, it may involve local outreach activities, workshops and education programs. It may include protests and demonstrations against governments, businesses, or even the institution of religion. At the agency level, it may involve social research and advocacy, and the provision of more specialist services. A ministry of justice listens to the community, affirming the dignity and purpose, not only of the human person, but of all creation. A ministry of justice is embedded in the biblical witness of God's encounter with the creation. This biblical witness tells of God's deep compassion for those in need and portrays a life with God enriched by the values of compassion, mercy, forgiveness and reconciliation.[15]

15. Micah 6:8; Isaiah 58:6–8; Romans 8:22–8; Acts 4:32, 34–5; Luke 1:46f

The principle of these encounters, this seeking after justice, is to be seen in the parable of the good Samaritan and in the story of the prodigal son. These stories, as examples of many others, encapsulate both Matthew's call to share the good news with everyone, and Isaiah's hope as told in Luke, of a vision for the church to build a just and compassionate community. Matthew's call to make disciples, is to be complemented by Luke's call to serve the poor. Jesus himself, as he announced at the beginning of his public ministry, his mission declaration, clearly understood the place and importance of justice in God's plan when he said:

> The Spirit of the Lord is upon me
> because he has chosen me to bring
> good news to the poor.
> He has sent me to proclaim liberty to the captives
> the recovery of sight to the blind
> to set free the oppressed
> and announce that the time has come
> when the Lord will save his people.[16]

Scripture affirms that Jesus practised what he preached. He sought out the rejected, engaged ordinary people, healed the sick and reminded the leaders of the day, both religious and political, not only of their responsibilities, but their obligation to the community. He dined with the prostitutes and tax collectors, engaging with them and sharing the good news of God's hospitality and desire for connection and relationship without compromising himself. He stands as the fulfilment of the prophetic tradition of Israel. He extended God's generosity and hospitality. This is also our task as church.

Principles of justice are not limited to those without an income. They apply to all who struggle to meet their potential. Nor does 'the poor' simply mean the poor in spirit, as some understand the writing of Matthew's Beatitudes. It also encompasses Luke's account embracing the disempowered, exploited and outcast. While the church's response to poverty may differ as to how, there should be no difference to the gospel imperative to action and to stand with the poor.

---

16. Luke 4:16.

The poor are the depressed, the frail, the oppressed, the homeless, the sick, the elderly, the traumatised and the widowed. Today's Australia is not without those in need. They are all around us. The prophets remind us of the responsibility we all have for those in need. They proclaim that to save the poor is the nature of God's justice and his generosity. It is our obligation. Christians are called to a ministry of social justice to save and to restore the covenant which the prophets, the law, the wisdom literature, Jesus and the gospel writers each sought to claim and restore in their own right.

The prophet Amos writes, 'But let justice roll down like waters, and righteousness like an ever flowing stream'.[17] Amos reminds us that we are to come to know God not because we have knowledge about him but in the very acts of compassion and justice. 'So long as the poor are with us, salvation will hinge on what we do for them, and with them. We enter the Kingdom of the least of the brothers.'[18]

In Acts we read:

> Now the whole group of those who believe were one heart and soul, and no one claimed private ownership of any possessions, but everything they owned was held in common. There was not a needy person among them, for as many who owned lands or houses sold them and brought the proceeds of what was sold. They laid it at the Apostles' feet and it was distributed to each as had need.[19]

Justice, from the Hebrew *Sedequah*, implies right relationships between the whole of creation and the creator and in particular the relationship between neighbour and neighbour. There is to be harmony in the covenant. *Sedequah* implies benevolence, generosity, kindness and hospitality. Justice in the context of righteousness is the observance of relationships. In our relationship with God righteousness implies a bias to the poor, a bias to restore those who have been oppressed and alienated from the creator. It is bias towards the victims of oppression.

---

17. Amos 5:24.
18. H Perkins, *Roots for Vision* (Singapore: WCC, 1986), 114.
19. Acts 4:32, 34–5.

A welfare and justice ministry expressed either at the parish, synod or agency level is, therefore, not an optional extra for Christians engaged in ministry and in their encounters with society. This justice obligation is integral to understanding God's mission in today's world. It provides a rationale, a theological underpinning and understanding for the urgent need by the Anglican Church of Australia to both affirm and commend welfare and justice ministry not as an optional extra or subsidiary to the mission task but integral to it. Connections to the organisational leadership of the church will enrich the relationship between agencies and the broader faith community, as well as signifying ownership of its task within the mission obligation.

External threats

In more recent times, in addition to the lack of commitment to Anglican welfare by the church itself, new threats and challenges have been emerging for agencies. The new competitive environment introduced in the early 1990s by governments throughout Australia, has threatened existing partnerships and created a different context for agencies and their role in serving those in need. While it is too simplistic to see these changes as merely grounded in the impacts of globalisation and the radical resurgence of market economics, they pose new challenges. Many church agencies express concern at being compromised when they have to report to government officials on individuals who fail to meet stringent tests for income benefit eligibility. Many agencies also feel outraged at the introduction of new social policies which discriminate against women, blame the victim for their current circumstances, and fail to recognise the structural impact of social and economic policies during periods of rapid global change. Others are not willing to accept the blame for bad past practices without government and communities sharing some of the responsibility.

This is not to suggest that all Anglican welfare and justice ministries agree on strategies or policies. Like our ecumenical partners, there is often tension on issues of policy and implementation of service delivery. Nor is it true to say that all agencies within the Anglican tradition are committed to social advocacy and justice. Some continue to provide emergency and short term responses without engagement with the causes of social disadvantage. Others continue to see welfare and justice as secondary to evangelism, while others confuse community involvement with social justice. There are still others willing to support government initiatives and programs yet hold serious reservations.

Likewise, the increasing political activities by some Anglican agencies and their leaders are not always welcomed by those in and outside the church. Sections of the church community have expressed concern at the agencies' involvement in what they describe as political matters. Archbishops and bishops have challenged their agencies on matters of faith, theology and morals. Individual government members have called for the church agency to be silent on public matters and to limit their role to spiritual and belief issues.

This suggests that Anglican agencies, in pursuing a mission of social justice and advocacy, and in the provision of services to the community, need to be vigilant in ensuring their theological reflection is strong, and public comment well researched. They need to be conscious of their role as spokespersons of the church and aware of the potential for challenge and discourse. Further, this requires an understanding that a ministry of social justice and service delivery will challenge the notion of charity, good works and the moral approach described earlier as the preferred model for Anglican welfare engagement. It is not that both charity and good works are wrong, but they are only part of the response necessary. It is how the church responds which is at the heart of its mission obligation.

Charity relieves symptoms. Social justice addresses and seeks solutions to issues of poverty, homelessness, abuse and lack of housing. Social justice involves both the giving of resources and oneself to the kingdom of God. Social justice is not just about welfare programs: it is about the building of community, respect for human dignity, human rights and self-worth, a fair share and distribution of resources, and the search for wholeness. It is about enabling individuals and communities to take charge of their own lives. Empowerment and compassion are two key elements. Welfare programs should be a means of achieving these goals. In his book entitled *Giving a Hand, a History of Anglicare South Australia since 1860,* Brian Dickey quotes the following:

> We are recapturing our vision of being an expression of the Gospel in action. We are a Christian Agency as affirmed in our value statements, seeking to serve the community. Our task for the next decade is to be an effective witness of God's total concern for his people.

> We must become an effective advocate for the disadvantaged in a society that is seeking increased polarisation between the haves and have nots.[20]
>
> We must be effective and innovative service delivers, developing low cost services in an environment where welfare is receiving few resources—increasing demands. We must also be an effective resource to the Anglican Church in South Australia.[21]

In defining a distinctive Christian and Anglican response to the social and economic ethical issues facing our community today and in the future, the challenge for all agencies and communities of faith, will be to engage in robust, rigorous and vigorous discourse, not only on the needs of the poor, but on the broader view of the future shape of Australian society and the role and place of the Anglican engagement. This should involve a declaration of intent from all sides of the church, that a ministry of justice is integral to its mission; a mission which is vigorous, vibrant and prophetic. Experience, scripture and theological reflection should underpin this involvement. Given the diversity within the Anglican Church in Australia, it is unlikely we will achieve consensus on all aspects of a ministry of justice, nor may this be desirable. However, as a minimum, a vision of ministry should recognise the following:

- the sacred and divine is grounded in our very being;
- love and service to others, as told in Scripture and proclaimed by Jesus, is to be our starting block and beginning;
- agencies and parishes are called to make a real difference to individuals and to their local communities by engaging in discourse and discussions that shape and influence community life;
- there is an obligation, if not an expectation, that followers of Jesus 'will act and do as he did' and that justice and welfare ministries are part of the mission of every faith community, and not to be regarded as an optional extra or add on;

---

20. Dickey, *Giving a Hand*, 3.
21. *Ibid*, 3.

- hope is what we have to offer—we are called to share the great act of reconciliation.

As Bruce Rumbold says:

> Within the community of faith, hope is to be directed beyond this world, which is understood to be in transition towards God's future. It is also directed towards the present, in that it is concerned with justice, love and service to the world.[22]

At the core of this understanding is the view expressed that personal salvation by itself is an insufficient response to Christian discipleship. A mature faith response involves a broader communal responsibility, including not only the human person, but the whole planet. To be created in the image of God, is to reflect in one's relationship with the whole of the created order, a deep respect and concern for all. To be created in the image of God, is to recognise the Christian's responsibility to share in God's love by a willingness to be active partners with God in fulfilling the divine plan for the community of God. This community is to be one of love, with respect, dignity, justice and mercy the cornerstones of all relationships.

The way forward

In responding to today's world and emerging needs, how should agencies engage in their mission as part of the worldwide Christian community, embracing peoples of all faiths or no faiths in the task? How can we build upon the ideas which have inspired those of the past and encourage the church of the future? The following are suggestions:

- Anglican motivation for involvement should not only be one of good works, charity and benevolence. Such attributes are important and admirable, but our response should not be to relieve symptoms but to challenge causes. Engaging with civil

---

22. B Rumbold, *Helplessness and Hope: Pastoral Care in Terminal Illness* (London: SCM Press, 1986), 58.

society on issues of life and death should not be an optional extra, but central to Christian discipleship.

- Anglican tradition acknowledges and affirms the presence of God in the world, and sees the presence of Christ in the community, the agencies and parishes. Our task is to engage and share the message of the gospel as authentic and relevant to the issues of the day. This should be a rational, intelligent and open approach allowing for the disturbing spirit of God to lead us to building his community. This includes not only the affluent and the successful, but also those who have been separated and alienated from mainstream society. The message is for life, hope and liberation, not despair and failure.
- As Christians, we are called to live on the edge, identifying and sharing in the pain and suffering of the world. This involves engagement with the community in which we live, participating in moral and ethical discourse, and acknowledging the divine in the midst of human suffering and pain. It means living and being for others.
- Wherever possible, Anglican welfare and justice work should be undertaken ecumenically, and in consultation and co-operation with others of a different faith or no faith. Service provision should be culturally relevant in an increasingly multi-cultural society. Mission in the community context should recognise the variety of gifts of ministry, but the one Spirit. While recognising the value and contribution of those who do not subscribe to the Christian faith, those who do should be encouraged to express their faith appropriately.
- A ministry of social justice should be open to the ongoing presence of the Spirit of God, and open to what God is doing in the world.

There are signs of hope in the work of Anglican welfare and justice ministries. The formation of Anglicare Australia, the increased activism of Anglican agencies and social justice committees give substance to this claim. But is this the church or the agencies alone?

The realisation of change that has taken place in Australian society provides a new offering of hope for agencies and the church in its mission to today's world. This will require more than a personal or individual response to emerging needs, but rather an acceptance by the broad church in all traditions, that the welfare and justice ministry are integral to the life and work of the Anglican Church in Australia. It is to be hoped that this leadership will be encouraged and exercised at the national, diocesan and parish level by engaging our congregations, communities and agencies in this broad mission task. It is ultimately an issue of ownership and the building of meaningful and resilient relationships between all parts of the communion. This ownership and our ongoing relationships will build on past engagement, yet offer new ways of being agency and church in today's world.

The challenge for the Anglican welfare agency is to ensure that its mission is not compromised and that it remains distinctly Christian and Anglican in its operation. It is my contention that the best way for this to be achieved is for Anglican welfare and justice to move closer to parish ministry and to integrate its own goals with the broader mission of the church. While the church needs to engage the agencies, likewise, many of the agencies need to reconnect with the church. Anglicare Australia offers one way to achieve this goal. Such an approach allows an engagement with local people where they are and in their own communities. It allows local communities to engage with other agencies and with government in bringing forward funds and resources to enable a building of a more just community. It allows the powerless to gain some power over their own agenda and to influence the church and its ministry in its response to others. Underlying all this is the belief that God is at work amongst his people, and relating this 'faith' to common experience at the grass roots level. This approach I know will not be popular with some. It will challenge agencies and their power base and also the exercise of influence which they have traditionally provided. Engaging with local communities may be just simply a new way of being the church in the twenty-first century. It shifts welfare from institution to community and offers a way of liberation and hope for the poor and dispossessed. Becoming truly part of the Anglican Church of Australia will challenge some agencies within the fold of the church with the need to rethink their own mission and goals. At the same time, they may also find new energy and ways of being church.

Leaders of agencies will need to be passionate about the Jesus story for themselves and others. They will also need to recognise the missionary task of the church as engaging with civil society, with the goal of creating the community of God where the values of our common humanity, exemplified in Jesus Christ, are embedded in all aspects of life.

This agenda of love and service as core mission objectives should over-ride internal divisions and reflect the never-ending heartache of God as the centre of the good news of the Christian faith.

17

Church In Public Space

Raewynne J Whiteley

Standing at the major crossroads of the city of Melbourne, directly opposite Flinders Street Station, St Paul's Cathedral demands attention from all who enter the city from the south. St Andrew's Cathedral jostles for attention beside the Sydney Town Hall; Christ Church Cathedral in Newcastle broods on the skyline, dominating the cityscape. These cathedrals, and many other churches like them around our country, occupy a dominant space in the Australian city landscape, and make their claim as central edifices of public life.

The relationship between the church and public space, as symbolised by these buildings, is complex and multi-faceted.[1] In this chapter, I will explore it in terms of four types of reality: embodied, symbolic (formal and informal), theological and practical. Each of these realities has implications for our ecclesiology.

Embodied reality: buildings and religious consciousness

> [St Paul's] stands at the ceremonial entry to Melbourne, at a landmark intersection, expressing both the life and the history of the city. The cathedral occupies one of the most noteworthy religious sites in Melbourne. It is a Melbourne icon and we must value and look after it.[2]

1. H Richard Niebuhr's classic book *Christ and Culture* (New York: Harper & Row, 1951) awakened Christians to the multiple modes of interaction between church and culture. Such relationships are not simply linear, but rather form part of the complex web of meaning in which we live our lives.
2. Victorian Premier Steve Bracks, in *The Australian*, 2 April 2004, http://www.theaustralian.news.com.au/common/story_page/0,5744,9165747%255E1702,00.html (accessed 5 April 2004).

In exploring the relationship between church and public space, what first comes to mind is the literal or physical manifestation of church buildings. For most people, regardless of how much we speak of church as the gathering of the faithful, what comes to mind when we speak of 'church' is the stone or wood or brick buildings in which we gather to worship God. These buildings have a physical relationship with other aspects of public life that more often than not embodies a particular ecclesiological perspective.

Traditionally, church buildings have been located in prominent places in a town or city. Building a church alongside the town hall or parliament building makes it both visible and accessible to the leaders of society and provides a convenient space for civic services. Building it on the main street or market place emphasises its accessibility to all people, encouraging them to enter, or at least pause as they pass by. Building it on the highest point of a town makes it a visible reminder of God, the 'city built on the hill'. Each of these reflects a slightly different ecclesiology; all three suggest a necessary engagement with the life of the wider society, whether by cooperation (collusion?) with societal leaders, involvement in the everyday life of citizens, or standing apart as a sign to wider society (the 'conscience of the nation').

But all assume a prominence in the public realm. Churches were not to be tucked away out of sight in the backstreets, but positioned at the centre of public life. They had a role to play beyond the individual and spiritual, engaging with community, society and world, as Sedgewick notes:

> The strength of Anglican polity was its determination to affect the whole of life, in each particular town or village, paying attention to the precise particularity of that location.[3]

But that traditional place has changed in recent years. Suburban development now sets churches in the middle of residential areas with little foot traffic; the decline of city and town centres as the primary focus of communal life has left our town-square churches on the

3. Peter Sedgewick, 'On Anglican Polity', in *Essentials of Christian Community*, edited by David F Ford and Dennis L Stamps (Edinburgh: T&T Clark, 1996), 199.

periphery of everyday life, more museums than community centres. Even where churches are built on new community corridors such as highways, there is little incentive for interaction between faith and everyday life. Church is compartmentalised, yet another of the many parts of life separated by car travel, to which we commute. Having lost its integral interface with society, it has slid from the public to the private world, identified with the personal and familial to the exclusions of the social and communal.

There are ways, of course, of attempting to increase the interaction between church and community. When St John's becomes a venue for community concerts, when All Saints holds a forum for political candidates, when St Andrew's hosts a pre-school, they become explicitly public spaces. This does not, however, necessarily mean that there will be any substantial interaction between faith and everyday life. It is possible for people to enter and leave these public spaces as if they are just neutral venues, without any identification of their distinctively religious purpose. Furthermore, where these activities are primarily entered in to with the purpose of attracting people to church and subsequently faith (that is, evangelism), their focus is again private and individual. Attempts to locate churches near new community focus points such as malls, risks cementing our identity as one service provider among many. As we contract to offer personal spiritual guidance or to provide an alternative form of entertainment, our members are transformed into clients or audience rather than the people of God—dual citizens of the kingdom of heaven and the kingdom on earth.

It is this dual identity that has been undermined as the church has become marginalised from the public realm. Both wider society and our own members begin to believe that the church has no business in the affairs of public life. And yet, alongside the de-sacralising of traditional religious space, we see the emergence of new sacred space: war memorials, sites of fatal car accidents marked with crosses and flowers, places where horrendous crimes have occurred. In New York, people gathered in silence around the rubble of the World Trade Centre. Although there were numerous church memorials, it was an on-site memorial, containing dirt and ashes from the site, that many families desperately desired. The vast majority of these local shrines have to do with death, in a culture that increasingly spends a significant amount of time and money trying to avoid, delay, or deny it. Clearly the urge to create a physical, tangible memorial remains strong in us, and depersonalised lawn cemeteries are not satisfying this need.

A second category of emerging sacred space comes through a new awareness of Aboriginal culture and its identification of the land as sacred, coupled with environmentalism and a renewed theology of creation. These three forces have served to reduce the emphasis on institutionally consecrated space, designated 'holy' because of its purpose or use,[4] in favour of a recognition of the innate holiness or sacredness of specific places by virtue of our histories and relationships with them. Here the holy has been encountered and is honoured, testimony to the integral relationship between God and creation.

What we see, therefore, is that while the suburbanisation of our culture has resulted in a weakening of the ties between faith and life, the emergence of local shrines and their holy creation redevelops that relationship, but outside the bounds of institutional faith. It is not so much that we have lost our sense of the holy as that our sense of the holy encompasses much more of the physical space that we inhabit. By the same token, our faith as personified by our buildings is less public and more associated with private faith and experience.

Theologically speaking, the Christian tradition carries within itself a tension between the God of place, most clearly exhibited in the Abrahamic covenant with its promise that intimately associates land, descendants and God, along with the dramatic embodiment of God's presence in cloud, fire, and temple, and a God of no place, exhibited in exilic assurances of the presence of God wherever the people of God are. The tension is ultimately resolved in favour of the God of place: the dream of the holy city of Zion to which all will return, to worship in the holy temple. But in Jesus, there is a shift; the embodied presence is no longer the temple in the holy city of Jerusalem but the temple of the body, and hence the person, of Christ. The fulfilment of God's

4. Hence Jean Corbon, *The Wellspring of Worship* (New York: Paulist Press, 1988) 131, where she argues: 'The church of stone or wood that we enter to share in the eternal liturgy is . . . set apart because it is space which the resurrection has burst open'; thus it is the purpose, the celebration of the resurrection, that identifies the space as holy. Often we experience a place as holy because of the use to which it has been put—the sense of holiness of a small country church, hallowed by decades of prayer.

promises, the fullness of God's blessing, rests not in a specific place but in the body of Christ.

But of course, Christ as resurrected is no longer tied to a specific place and time. It is this fact that gives impetus to the recognition that Christ may be encountered any- and everywhere. The awareness of such a spiritualised presence can result in a tendency to deny the concretisation of God in place and time in favour of affirming a God who is beyond both space and time. It must, however, be held in tension with the fact of Christ's incarnation, which (as Torrance notes) 'asserts the reality of space and time for God in the actuality of relations with us, and at the same time binds us to space and time in our relations with God'.[5]

Hence while all space is potentially the locus for divine communication, there is room for an explicit identification of particular spaces with the saving work of Christ. Indeed, this is essential. Human life is necessarily embodied. We reflect that embodiment when we set aside a tangible physical space which embodies the love of God in a specific and particular place, and facilitates our anamnesis of the saving work of Christ.

If, then, our encounter with God is necessarily embodied in space, then our churches in turn embody our own understanding of God's relationship with the world and of faith within our lives. Is faith primarily institutional, God and government drawing in the sand to delineate their respective spheres or lines of communication? Is it a matter of the individual and family, tucked away in suburbia? Whether we like it or not, our buildings form the understandings of both Christians and our wider culture alike, about the place and relevance of church in public space.

---

5. Thomas F Torrance, *Space, Time and Incarnation* (London: Oxford University Press, 1969), 107, cited in Susan J White, 'Can We Talk About a Theology of Sacred Space?' in *Searching for Sacred Space: Essays on Architecture and Liturgical Design in the Episcopal Church*, edited by John Ander Runkle (New York, NY: Church Publishing Inc, 2002), 28.

Symbolic reality: formal relationships of church and state

> Blessed be God, whose love it was
> To double-moat thee with his grace,
> And none but thee.[6]

If the embodied reality of church and public space is found in our buildings, the primary symbolic reality is found in the formal relationships of church and state. It is to these, albeit sometimes contentious, relationships, that our minds leap when we think of the relationship between church and public life.

When the Australian colony was founded in 1788, it was celebrated with the raising of the British flag and copious amounts of alcohol, rather than with prayer or religious symbolism. Yet it inherited a *de facto* establishment of the Church of England: the laws of the new colony were the laws of England, unless explicitly varied, and this included the Church's establishment.[7] The first chaplain to the colony, the Reverend Richard Johnson, was appointed by King George III and worked under the instruction of Governor Arthur Phillip, who ordered Johnson 'that you do by all proper methods enforce a due observance of religion and good order among the inhabitants of the new settlement, and that you do take such steps for the due celebration of publick worship as circumstances will permit'.[8]

The relationship between Johnson and Phillip was uneasy. Under the terms of his appointment Johnson was required to follow the orders of the governor 'according to the rules and discipline of war,' but received little support from the leaders of the colony. The church was granted land in the early days of the colony; however, no provision for church buildings was made, and by 1792, Johnson's frustration with this state of affairs, together with the insufficient rations for his household, is clear in his letters home.[9] These factors

6. George Herbert, 'The British Church', from *The Temple* (1633).
7. See chapter 2 of this volume for further exploration of the notion that the Church of England was effectively established in the early days of the New South Wales colony.
8. Historical Records of Australia, I. I, 14, in Jean Woolmington, *Religion in Early Australia* (Stanmore, NSW: Cassell, 1976), 1.
9. Letter from Port Jackson, 23 March 1792, in Iain Hamish Murray, *Australian Christian Life from 1788: An Introduction and an Anthology* (Edinburgh: Banner of Truth Trust, 1988), 16–17.

significantly inhibited his ministry. Although the colonial power supported the assumption of establishment, what was missing was consistent fiscal support.

Over subsequent years, support for chaplains improved. Civil boundaries were contiguous with parish boundaries, land grants were made to the church, governors were regularly active in church affairs, and chaplains served as magistrates. The Church of England was at the very least privileged, if not formally established. This was, however, a status that tended to serve the state better than it served the church.

As the colony developed, religious diversity became a reality to be addressed. Protestants were tolerated, as they shared common roots with the Church of England, and were not considered a political or doctrinal threat; the first Roman Catholic chaplain, however, was not appointed until 1820. The first significant move away from the Church of England's *de facto* establishment came with the Church Act of 1836.[10] This provided for financial support to all denominations from public funds for the provision of public worship and education. Governor Bourke had paved the way for this act in a letter to Lord Stanley, the colonial secretary, in 1833, in which he identified approximately one-fifth of the new colony as Roman Catholic, with substantial numbers of Presbyterians, and other 'Protestant Dissenters,' and argued for the three major denominations to be placed on an equitable financial footing.[11]

By early 1841, the Church Act had been in force for four years and funding had been allocated to Anglicans, Presbyterians, Wesleyans, Congregationalists and Roman Catholics to build churches, chapels, and parsonages. The number of clergy supported by the Crown had risen from thirty-two to eighty-four. Although the principles of funding were consistent for all denominations, funding was based on a matching formula. The Church of England, which counted among its members a greater proportion of the wealthier colonists, therefore

---

10. Although this applied only in New South Wales, similar measures were taken in Tasmania in 1836 and South Australia in 1846.
11. Bourke to Stanley, 30 September 1833. Historical Records of Australia, I, xvii, 224–30, in Woolmington, *Religion in Early Australia*, 94–5. Several smaller nonconformist denominations refused to apply for funding, being opposed to state aid to religion.

continued to receive a disproportionately large share of the funding. Established or not, it continued to cling to the mentality of establishment, upholding the social order of Britain and uncritically supporting existing colonial power structures.

However there was a groundswell against formal state support for religious activities, which came almost as much from the church, concerned at the level of government supervision and direction of its affairs, as from secularist pressures. In 1862, less than thirty years after its legislative institution, state aid for religion in New South Wales was withdrawn by the Grants for Public Worship Prohibition Act. It had been preceded by South Australia's 1852 withdrawal of public funding to religious bodies a mere six years after its institution[12] and was followed by Tasmania in 1869 (with a significant decrease in aid in 1862) and Victoria in the early 1870s. It was clear that any pretence of establishment must now be abandoned.

By the time of Federation in 1901, the Commonwealth was committed to a position that was not only detached from formal religion, but openly secular, albeit with a brief nod to God in the preamble to the Constitution. There was no Bill of Rights like that of the United States, but Section 116 of the Australian Constitution provided a limited guarantee of religious freedom, along with measures to prohibit the new Commonwealth from making any law that would establish any religion, impose any religious observance, prohibit any free exercise of any religion, or require a religious test as a qualification for any office or public trust under the Commonwealth. However, many still assumed a *de facto* establishment of the Church of England, or at least a favoured status, throughout the twentieth century.

Parallel to the relationship between church and state was the funding of education. In the early days of the colony of new South Wales, schools were founded by the government (the Male and Female Orphan Schools), private individuals, and the Church of England. The latter was also charged with the wider responsibility of providing religious instruction to all colonial children. With the 1836 Church Act, each denomination established its own schools. Limited resources meant that by the late 1840s, more than half of the colony's children did not have access to formal education; a new system, with parallel

---

12. With the exception of the official salary paid to the Colonial Chaplain until 1869.

denominational and secular elementary schools, was put in place. Meanwhile in Tasmania, the Church of England had had a monopoly on elementary/primary education until 1839 when the Board of Education assumed responsibility for many former church schools, creating an effectively secular system with no dominant denominational influence.

As the Church of England was edged out of its dominance in elementary/primary education, it moved into the provision of superior (elite) secondary education, which has remained the core of its educational provisions until the late twentieth century establishment of low fee schools. The debates over the role of the church also influenced the establishment of universities in the mid nineteenth century, when compromises between secular and religious concerns resulted in a division of roles. Education was secular, but affiliated residential colleges were—and largely remain today—denominationally affiliated enterprises.[13]

Although funding to churches was eliminated in the 1860s and 1870s and public schools took over much of the role of educating children, funding to church-sponsored schools has continued, albeit not unchallenged. A High Court case in the early 1980s ruled that the provisions of Section 116 of the Constitution did not prevent financial aid to church schools, because such aid does not constitute or recognise a particular religion (or branch of such) as a national institution. This distinction between support for services provided by religious bodies and the privileging of particular religions or denominations is crucial. The former is permitted, the latter proscribed. This permits religious organisations to offer education and social services using government funding and allows for special provisions in tax and equal opportunity law. Religious education in public schools is also permitted under this distinction—as long as equal provision is made for all religious groups represented in the school population.

However, two legal cases during the twentieth century underlined the continued complexity of formal church-state relationships. In 1944,

13. The recent addition of theology to the curricula of many universities, usually through affiliation with existing theological colleges, brings religion a credible place in education, but again, does not typically privilege a particular denomination.

a group of twenty-three laymen initiated action in the New South Wales Equity Court accusing Bishop Arnold Lomas Wylde of Bathurst of heresy for his authorisation of a devotional manual known as the 'Red Book'. The bishop's insistence that the evidence be taken on commission in England resulted in the charge being dropped. But in 1947 the laymen brought a charge under the New South Wales Church of England Property Trust Act (1917–23) of 'breach of trust of properties endowed for Church of England purposes'.[14] In 1948 a ruling was made in favour of the laymen, and an appeal to the High Court was dismissed.

The significance of this case was that property law, and hence civil courts, were being used to resolve what was essentially a theological conflict. The court rulings demonstrated that the church as a corporation had religious and economic interests that were intertwined; at the same time, the High Court ruling made clear that legal sanctions only covered issues of property. Matters of theology were outside the jurisdiction of civil courts.[15]

The second case was that of Scandrett and Others v Dowling and Others. On 23 December 1991, Bishop Owen Dowling of Canberra and Goulburn, frustrated by the impasse over the ordination of women, announced his intention to ordain eleven women deacons to the priesthood on 2 February 1992. In response, one layman and two priests commenced proceedings in the New South Wales Supreme Court, seeking an order restraining Bishop Dowling from proceeding with the ordination. Bishop Dowling refused to postpone the ordination pending the outcome of the case, so the plaintiffs sought to have a restraining order placed on him. That application was dismissed on 28 January 1992; however the plaintiffs went to the Court of Appeals and this time successfully obtained the restraining order. On 3 July of that same year, judgement was delivered and the case dismissed.[16] Again it was affirmed that only in property matters did

14. Ruth Teale, 'The "Red Book" Case', *Journal of Religious History*, 12/1 (June 1982): 74.

15. This provided significant impetus for the development of an adequate constitution for the Australian church with provisions for dealing with disputes of a theological nature.

16. A fuller discussion of this may be found in Tom Frame, *A Church for a Nation: A History of the Anglican Diocese of Canberra and Goulburn* (Alexandria: Hale & Iremonger, 2000), 312–13.

the courts have jurisdiction, and that such matters were not to be used as a surrogate for resolving theological disputes.

The relationship between church and state in Australia, at least until the early twentieth century, hinged on the assumption that the state could be understood as a unified entity committed to the ideals of Christendom. The continuing increase in diversity and the secular stance of the Commonwealth government gave new religious groups —both Christian and non-Christian—the same rights as those that had been present in the Australia from the founding of the colony. Pluralism has been built into our culture, both legally and practically, with the result that there is no enshrined ideological commitment, and neither a unitary state nor a unitary church between which to construct some hypothetical formal relationship or comprehensive theory.

This leaves the Anglican Church of the twenty-first century on the one hand bereft of our historical modes of operating, but on the other, freed from a simplistic model of church-state relations (based on some idealised reading of Romans 13) and ready to bring the divine demands for justice, order, ethics and compassion to the attention of our society in a new way. Therefore, we turn now to the informal relations of church and state.

Symbolic reality: informal shaping of culture

The role of the church in public space cannot be simply defined in terms of its physical and formal structural manifestations. Perhaps the most significant impact it has had in the history of colonised Australia is in its informal role in shaping culture. This informal role can be seen particularly clearly in three areas: power, ethics, and civil religion.

Power

> It may surprise some of you to know that an unusually high proportion of federal politicians on all sides are practising Christians who have a sense of faith and listen to what the churches tell us and the rest of the community. Imperfect as we all too obviously are, we're sincere about the faith that nurtured Western

> Civilisation. It's because of our beliefs that we tend to see public life as a vocation—a calling, not just a job.[17]

Alongside the formal relationships of church and state outlined above run informal power relationships. The Anglican Church might not be established, but it has always wielded significant power in government and the community through its members, and continues to do so. Bishop William Grant Broughton sat as an *ex officio* member of the Legislative Council until 1842 and the Executive Council until 1846 by virtue of his office. By the end of the nineteenth century, the power was less formal, but significant nonetheless. Novelist Anthony Trollope observed that:

> The bishops, deans and canons of the Church frequent Government House and are seen in the best society . . . They are intimate with the leading men of the colonies, who more generally belong to the Church of England than to other denominations, and thus, without intention, impress the minds of people with an idea of their ascendancy.[18]

During this period, it was considered advantageous to belong to the church associated with the British elite and the king. While wealth has interfered with Sunday observances (social brunches, holiday homes, and recreational activities seem inevitably to take precedence over worship), for many, the Anglican Church is still strongly associated with the establishment.

Of course, a simple matter of numbers. Anglicans were, until the census of 1986, the largest single denomination in Australia. In the earliest years of the colony they comprised as much as 60 per cent of the population. Although the percentage had dropped to just 39.7 per cent at the turn of the twentieth century, and by 2001 was a mere 20.9 per cent, Anglicans remain disproportionately represented in the echelons of power.

---

17. Alexander Downer, 'Sir Thomas Playford Annual Lecture of 2003', in *Church and Civil Society: A Theology of Engagement*, edited by Frances Sullivan and Sue Leppert (Adelaide: ATF Press, 2004), 14.
18. Anthony Trollope, *Australia and New Zealand* (Melbourne: Authorised Australian Edition, 1873), 505.

This must be at least in part a result of the Church of England's nineteenth century decision to concentrate its resources in the provision of elite secondary education, together with its continued sponsorship of denominationally affiliated university colleges. Brian Fletcher notes that 'the pages of the Australian Dictionary of Biography and other more detailed studies offer . . . insights into the ways in which many of those prominent in Australian life were influenced by Anglicanism'.[19] As a result, a significant number of leaders in our society are, if not themselves active churchgoers, at least affiliated with the Anglican church. Today, Anglicans continue to occupy prominent positions in politics, public service, the judiciary and the armed forces. Their faith inevitably shapes their leadership, and the values and priorities that shape them individually are expressed in the decisions they make.

Yet this association with power is a two-edged sword in a culture that has egalitarianism as a core value.[20] While it has allowed the Anglican Church to influence public policy, it also serves to continue the illusion that we are a church for the elite and well educated, rather than the poor and marginalised. This has the potential to limit our mission to those sectors of our society.

Ethics

When Australia was colonised, religion functioned as an essential form of social control over the 'dangerously amoral' convict and colonist population. Chaplains preached a strict moral code, and were often able to enforce it as magistrates. As the colonies developed and the 'law and order' function of chaplains diminished, the church's role in public morality continued, supporting the institution of marriage, upholding sabbatarian laws, opposing gambling and promoting restraint and even abstinence in alcohol consumption. Even when the institution of the church was weak, it had a strong voice as a guardian of morality, reaching a peak in the late nineteenth century. This, however, coincided with a privatisation of religion, focusing on the

---

19. Brian Fletcher, 'Anglicanism and the Shaping of Australian Society', in *Anglicanism in Australia: A History*, edited by Bruce Kaye (Carlton: Melbourne University Press, 2002), 314.

20. Gerard Brennan, 'Australian Values', in *Discerning the Australian Social Conscience* (Richmond: Jesuit Publications, 1999), 12.

family, which undermined the church's voice on anything other than private morality. Family, education, and moral instruction became the assumed concerns of the church—both in what it said and what it did. Religion was appealed to in issues of sexuality and relationships, the so-called 'family values'. It was not long before the clergy came to be regarded as 'wowsers', opposed to all manly pleasures.

This conception of the church as opposed to anything fun continued through the twentieth century. Churches were stereotyped (whether accurately or not) as opposing such innovations as the liberalisation of laws concerning pub hours, Sunday shopping, divorce and pornography. And yet there has also been an enduring assumption that the church would and should speak out on matters of morality. Both church members and the wider society expect that Christianity 'should provide the moral basis and conscience of the dominant social order'.[21]

Alexander Downer, Minister for Foreign Affairs, argued this strongly in the aftermath of the Bali bombing:

> without consistent moral teaching and example from bodies like the churches, how can most Australians be expected to behave selflessly or consider the common good and abide by any kind of social contract? . . . The greatest challenge today for leaders of all religions is to forego the opportunity to be amateur commentators on all manner of secular issues on which they inevitably lack expertise, and instead to find the spark of inspiration to give our lives greater moral and spiritual meaning.[22]

But the moral leadership envisioned by people like Alexander Downer is limited in scope. It is intended to encompass only matters of private morality. The wider areas of justice and ethics are contested ground, where religion and politics have the potential to meet head-on.

---

21. Ian Barns, 'Towards an Australian Post-Constantinian Public Theology', in David Neville and Philip Matthews, editors, *Faith and Freedom: Ethics in a Pluralist Culture,* (Adelaide: ATF Press, 2003), 176.
22. Downer, 'Sir Thomas Playford Annual Lecture of 2003', 15, 19–20.

Recent public policy debates in Australia have raised ethical and moral issues, but the association of political parties with particular positions has resulted in the church being accused of favouring partisanship over pastoral care when it attempts to participate in such debates. In 2004, Prime Minister John Howard argued that churches' primary responsibility was spiritual leadership, saying, 'I think church leaders should speak out on moral issues but there is a problem with that justification being actively translated into sounding very partisan'.[23]

What has emerged is a separation between the religious and the public, and in particular the political, a division of ethics into a public (political) realm administered by the government, and a spiritual realm administered by the church that harks back to the colony's early *de facto* establishment of the Church of England, wherein, as Rayner notes, 'the Church of England [was] understood as the spiritual side of the state under the common authority of the Crown'.[24]

It is deemed to be 'not the church's job' to enter into the political realm, to speak out in issues that manifest in party-political terms. The church is primarily there to give service and blessing rather than to confront in any meaningful way.

This has been complicated by the church's history of not only speaking about justice, but expressing its ethical imperatives in practical ways. Australian society has depended to a large extent on our provision of welfare services for those in need. Such work has been essential in undermining the accusations of wowserism and hypocrisy, as we match our words with actions. At the same time, there have also been failures that have seen the church perceived as not merely irrelevant but positively dangerous. The scandals of sexual abuse give our ethical statements a hollow ring. Our involvement in the (mis)treatment of Aborigines, albeit often well-intentioned, undercuts our pronouncements about justice.

Although the church has no intention of abandoning active ministries of social responsibility and justice, the tension between a Constantinian model of the church's engagement with public life, and

---

23. Reported in 'Keep quiet on politics', *The Advertiser*, 16 February 2004, http://www.cathnews.com/news/402/81.php, accessed 17 February 2004.
24. Keith Rayner, 'Australian Anglicanism and Global Anglicanism', in this volume.

resistance to it from a pluralistic society has led to a level of paralysis in our public theology.

In a post-Christendom world, a Constantinian model is not adequate justification. We can no longer make a claim (if we ever could) to a universal ethic grounded in Christianity. In a pluralistic world, we offer just one ethic among many. It is to this end that Ian Barns draws on the work of John Howard Yoder in developing a rationale for the church's involvement in public theology.[25] The church is a community defined by the gospel of Christ, and it is that gospel that provides a paradigm for the integral relationship between the spiritual and secular realms. The church's clear mission, as Geoff Smith suggests in his chapter, 'The Mission of the Church,' is to focus on the kingdom of God in both proclamation and witness, the clearest counter to such attacks (from both politicians and the general public) is the consistency of our words and actions, and the clarity of our articulation of the relationship between them and the coming kingdom of God

We do not rely on the power of an established position, formal or informal, but on our identity as a minority, one among many, with a voice that speaks to mainstream society as 'other'. As such, the church is free to speak independently, offering a critical voice arising from its own vision as a Christian community. Its vision and voice are based not in a generalised consensus on morality or values consensus but in our own distinctively Christian sources. Such a position may mean relinquishing our assumption that society should conform to 'Christian' values as a matter of right. On the other hand, it allows us to develop a clearer identity as a church and to reclaim the inherently spiritual foundation of our public policy, offering an ethical vision that arises out of our own faith, values and experience.

Civil religion

Although sixty-eight per cent of Australians identified themselves as Christian in the 2001 census, more than half never or rarely attend church, and only about five per cent are in church on any given Sunday.

---

25. Ian Barns, 'Towards an Australian Post-Constantinian Public Theology', in *Faith and Freedom: Ethics in a Pluralist Culture*, edited by David Neville and Philip Matthews (Adelaide: ATF Press, 2003), 175–94.

Yet there is still strong demand for the trappings of civil religion, People continue to call their local church to 'get the baby done' and for weddings and funerals; they continue to assume the participation of the church in major civic events and to give comfort at times of national disaster. Nowhere is this more prevalent than in Anzac Day celebrations. Clergy are invited to the local RSL or bowling club to say a prayer. Even in the far-flung reaches of overseas consulates, Australian clergy are called on to officiate at ceremonies of remembrance.[26] What is interesting about these events is that people often want a kind of idealised religion from the period of the participants' childhoods. Clergy have to use the traditional Lord's Prayer, not just because those are the words that people know, but because it brings back memories of a world with clear boundaries and shared ritual, a place of safety in times of trauma.

The danger is that the demands of civil religion are often burdensome and at times, threaten our peculiarly Christian identity. What people look for is often an affirmation of Australian myth, a ritual mateship of comradeship, ruggedness and service. They often resist any attempt to speak a distinctively Christian word. Our refusal to compromise our core beliefs, values and traditions may result in our rejection. But on the whole, the church is simply taken for granted, and called on at times of crisis. While that can be frustrating for those who are actively involved with church, it does have a positive aspect: church becomes a source of blessing to the Australian society beyond the faithful.

Theological reality

The relationships between the church and public space, both formal and informal, are complex, as are the theological understandings that underpin them. However three themes are particularly useful in this

26. It had been the dream of an Anglican priest, David Garland, for Anzac Day to be an occasion of spiritual reflection, a requiem for those who had died; his involvement in the campaign to establish April 25 as a day of remembrance was significant, although his hope for an exclusively devotional observance was not realised. John A Moses, 'Canon David John Garland and the ANZAC Tradition', *St Mark's Review*, 154 (Winter, 1993), 12–21.

exploration of the church's self-understanding in relation to public space: we are incarnational, redemptive, and communal.

Incarnational

> The world is charged with the grandeur of God.
> It will flame out, like shining from shook foil;
> It gathers to a greatness, like the ooze of oil
> Crushed. [27]

At the heart of our Christian faith is belief in a God who is manifested in Trinity. The God we know is not remote from the world, reaching out occasionally with a strong index finger to poke us into action, but a God who came and lived among us in the person of Jesus Christ, and who continues to live in and among us in the Holy Spirit. This triune God, the one who creates, redeems, and sustains all things, is intimately and inherently connected with our world. Because we as human beings can know only what is related to our realm of existence, our knowledge of this God is limited to the context of our world. As a result, part of the church's task is not only to worship and preach about God, but to seek out and to uncover the presence and activity of God in the world around us.[28]

With this understanding of God's, and the church's, involvement in the world, there can be no split between sacred and secular. As Christ is, in his body, human and divine united, so sacred and secular are united in our world, and cannot be separated one from the other. If our self-understanding is incarnational, we look to see the holy touching life at every point.

A natural consequence of the incarnational nature of the church is the notion of the church as embedded and embodied. That is to say, not only is the church inherently connected to the things of our world in a broad sense, but it takes distinct shape in relation to the realities of both the people who make up its membership and those who comprise the wider community in which it is situated. Part III of the Virginia Report notes that:

---

27. Gerard Manley Hopkins, 'God's Grandeur', in *Gerald Manley Hopkins*, edited by Catherine Phillips (Oxford: Oxford University Press, 1986).

28. For further exploration of this theme of incarnation, see Heather Thomson's chapter in this volume.

> The life and mission of the Church is at its most authentic and vibrant in a particular context . . . The Church is effective when it is embedded in a local place, challenging wrongs, healing relationships, standing with the vulnerable and marginalised, and opening up new possibilities for mutual service, respect and love. In such a context what the word 'church' stands for is a rich, many-sided reality embodying God's saving and reconciling presence within a particular context. It is a richly referential term, culturally resonant, and locked into an established symbolic system or network of meanings.[29]

The Anglican understanding of church-in-parish—that is, with an essential physical location—facilitates this embodiedness. This gives us a breadth of vision that cannot be confined to the internal but forces us to continually look outside ourselves into our communities, to seek how we might incarnate Christ among our peers.

If the church is indeed incarnational, embedded and embodied, there are clear implications for its place in the public realm. It cannot allow itself to be marginalised from public discourse, relegated to some realm of private morality. All of life is its concern, and it has a mission to bring God's perspective (such as we understand it) to the life of the world around us.

Redemptive

> The real battle just begun
> To claim the victory Jesus won
> On a Sunday, bloody Sunday[30]

The church is incarnational in character; however it is also redemptive. This second characteristic is once again rooted in the being and activity of God: God's commitment to the world is not only expressed in divine presence or sustenance but in the divine activity of redemption

29. *The Virginia Report: The Report Of The Inter-Anglican Theological And Doctrinal Commission*, http://www.anglicancommunion .org/documents /virginia/english/chapter4.html, paragraph 4.22.
30. U2, 'Sunday Bloody Sunday', from *War*.

through Jesus Christ. While there are many metaphors for this redemptive work of God, at the heart of them all is the notion that our God loved us so much that the God-incarnating Jesus Christ, who lived among us, was crucified for our sake for the forgiveness of our sins, removing the barrier that sin placed between humanity and God, opening the way for us to be friends with God. When on the third day Christ was raised, it was a sign, seal, and promise of that new-found relationship. We have peace with God through Jesus Christ. This is the gospel that we proclaim, the gospel that is the founding story of our identity as Christian. As people redeemed by our God, we ourselves cannot help but be in the business of redemption.

There are two dimensions to this redemptive character of the church. The first focuses on reconciliation with God. From its first days, the heart of the church's mission has been sharing that message of reconciliation with the world, as we are reminded in 2 Corinthians 5:18–19:

> All this is from God, who reconciled us to himself through Christ, and has given us the ministry of reconciliation; that is, in Christ God was reconciling the world to himself, not counting their trespasses against them, and entrusting the message of reconciliation to us.

Our proclamation of the redemptive work of God, our invitation to others to participate in that redemption and to enter a reconciled relationship with God and the peace that brings, is an essential part of who we are. We embody God's saving presence in the world.

But the story does not end there. Reconciliation with God can, indeed must, flow over into reconciliation with one another. The Lord's Prayer reminds us that we are called to forgive others just as God forgives us: the church is to be a place that is characterised by love, not just of and by God, but for one another. Hence we engage in ministries of reconciliation, fostering that forgiveness that we ourselves have received, not just among individuals but also among communities. The Virginia Report emphasises how important the church's mission is in healing relationships, bringing the reconciling love of God into the realm of human relationships.

If the church is redemptive in character, then our interactions with the public realm cannot be limited to the ethical. Our mission requires us to speak the language of redemption and reconciliation in our world. We cannot force others to participate in the redemptive work of God; we can, however, model reconciliation and facilitate that process in the wider society.

Communal

> The visible Church of Christ is a congregation of faithful men . . .[31]

The third theological characteristic of the church is that it is fundamentally communal. The church that Jesus instituted was never intended to be an individual thing; rather, it is about the calling of people into a community of faith, as we are reminded in 1 Peter 2:9: 'But you are a chosen race, a royal priesthood, a holy nation, God's own people, in order that you may proclaim the mighty acts of him who called you out of darkness into his marvellous light'.

This communal identity is grounded in the nature of God as Trinity, God-in-community, the model and source of our life. The Trinity is characterised by interdependence and love: we, through baptism, are welcomed into that community, participating in the divine nature. The Virginia Report reminds us that 'Communion with God and one another is both gift and divine expectation for the Church'.[32] The way we experience our participation in the divine community is in the community of the church; it is the earthly expression of that heavenly reality.

It is no wonder, then, that Paul uses the metaphor of the body for the church. No body part can exist on its own; each part is integrally related to every other one. Our faith is fundamentally about being in relation: with God, with one another, and, inevitably, with the wider world. And as such, we are characterised by our sense of responsibility and accountability. Our faith, and the ethical life that springs from it, are of necessity always oriented to the other. Our identity is fundamentally corporate.

---

31. Article XIX of the Thirty-Nine Articles.
32. *The Virginia Report: The Report Of The Inter-Anglican Theological And Doctrinal Commission*, http://www.anglicancommunion.org /documents /virginia/english/chapter2.html, paragraph 2.13.

The church as community constantly points to the importance of relationships, but this communal dimension is more than just a reiteration of our redemptive role. Our communal nature requires us to be aware of interests beyond the individual, to model a thoroughly unselfish mode of being, to constantly argue the value and dignity of every human being.

Practical reality: models of participation

The focus of much of this paper has been on formal and informal relationships between the church and public space and the theological themes that underlie them. This final section addresses two sometimes contentious areas of interaction between the church and public space and explores the ways in which those interactions occur and their contributions to our understanding of church.

Church as non-embodied icon of our time

It is not unusual today to find a web presence for dioceses and congregations. Websites include information about church beliefs, values, community and leadership, history, calendars, sermons, newsletters, photographs, and a myriad of other resources. Many people participate in diocesan, parish and other Christian e-mail lists, and e-mail has joined ordinary mail and the telephone as an essential means of communication. Technology has expanded the church's public space from the physical into the virtual realm.[33]

This expansion into virtual space raises the question of whether it is necessary to have a physical presence in order to be church. When, in early 2004, the Diocese of Oxford announced its plan to establish an internet-based church with no essential physical presence, it was greeted with both interest and scepticism. A year later, press interest had died down and the venture was well established.[34] I-church, as it is known, is 'a Christian community of the Church of England in the

33. An American survey found that twenty-five per cent of internet users have accessed religious or spiritual information online. Elena Larsen, 'Cyberfaith: How Americans pursue religion online', in *Religion Online: Finding Faith on the Internet*, edited by Lorne L Dawson and Douglas E Cowan (New York: Routledge, 2004), 17.

34. And it is not alone. Numerous religious groups, not only Christian, have ventured into the internet. See *Religion Online: Finding Faith on the Internet*, edited by Dawson and Cowan.

Diocese of Oxford. It is a web based community for those who wish to explore Christian discipleship, but who are not able, or do not wish, to join a local parish church'.[35] Its public space is a web-page; its congregation comprises individual members, who are just exploring, and community members who have made a greater commitment, including practical and financial support and adoption of a rule of life that includes prayer, study, and social action. Members gather online for worship at pre-arranged times; there is a regular newsletter, pastoral leaders who care for small groups, and requests for volunteers. In almost all respects, it resembles a regular congregation, with one central exception: there is no embodied gathering of the community.[36]

This is not necessarily a problem if I-church remains, as its founders intended, a support and supplement for the traditional church; however the vision of a fully functional internet-based church, albeit not the vision for I-church, remains. Margaret Wertheim takes up this idea in her provocative book, *The Pearly Gates of Cyberspace*, exploring the ways in which cyberspace has reawakened an alternative to the physical, lost when modern science and astronomy, with their exploration of the universe, effectively dismantled the physical soul-space of heaven and hence the soul-body dualism that had been foundational to Christian faith from the inception of the Christian church through the medieval period. Hence, she notes, cyberspace is being claimed as a new kind of spiritual space for the soul, providing both sensibility and transcendence.[37] This reaffirms a dualistic worldview in which the soul floats free in the new holiness (heaven?) of cyberspace while the physical is once again relegated to the non-physical world.

---

35. See: http://www.i-church.org (accessed 19 March 2004).
36. There are, of course, other criticisms. One, not unique to cyberchurch, but perhaps facilitated by its nature, is that internet-mediated groups allow the vast majority of members to remain passive, absorbing but not actively participating or contributing. See http://emergent.typepad.com/jasonclark/2004/02/public_space_an.html (accessed 9 June 2005).
37. Margaret Wertheim, *The Pearly Gates of Cyberspace: A History of Space from Dante to the Internet* (New York: WW Norton & Company, 1999), 255.

And that, from an Anglican perspective, is of course a fundamental criticism of cyberspace spirituality as fully functional church: it is not embodied. There is no room for incarnation here, no room to meet a Christ in human flesh, a God who makes a home in the holy temples of human bodies.

A second problem is that cyberspace spirituality is essentially individual: the very act of using a computer is, at least with current technology, something one does alone. This caters to those who want to be religious and/or spiritual on their own terms, to fashion their own faith; this freedom with its accompanying pluralism undermines the development of true community even while allowing for exponential numbers of relationships.[38]

Cyberspace's inability to be truly incarnational or communal undermines its ability to function as church. While at its best it may support individuals in their Christian life, and also support the church in places where embodied and communal life is difficult, what finally undermines it is the weakness of its mirror of our Trinitarian God, who is inherently incarnate, redemptive and communal. If the church is the earthly expression of a heavenly reality, it is a severely truncated view when limited to the perspective of cyberspace spirituality.

Prophetic speech

Our world has changed. The primary vehicle for mass communication is no longer the spoken or written word; instead, we turn to media, particularly television and the internet, to learn what is happening around us. Given this reality, there is a tendency in some parts of the church to declare that preaching is dead and to look for alternative means of communication.

Anyone who is a member of a church, however, knows that preaching is still alive and well. Sermons may limp along at times (often more as a result of preachers' loss of confidence than in lack of interest on the part of the listeners) but Sunday by Sunday, people sit in churches listening to hear if God might indeed have a word for them. If anything, new media has facilitated this growth, making sermons available to a wider audience on both television and the

38. For a more sustained discussion of this tension between freedom and community, see Lorne L Dawson and Jenna Hennebry, 'New Religions and the Internet: Recruiting in a New Public Space', in *Religion Online*, edited by Dawson and Cowan, 151–73.

internet. Sermons continue to be the primary way in which church communities are fed, are motivated, are invited to participate in the life of faith.

The reason that preaching is so important, so powerful, is that it is an echo of the word of God that calls us and forms us. We worship a God who speaks worlds into being, who spoke through the incarnate Word, who continues to speak in Scripture enlivened by the Spirit. Preaching draws on that power of speech to inform, and more importantly form, the people of God.

Part of the power of the sermon is its embodiment of the three theological themes identified above. Preaching is, at its best, incarnational, reflecting the God who is intimately connected with our world through Christ and knows the reality of human life. An essential part of the preaching task is to open the listeners' eyes to the presence of God, to see the continuities and connections between the God testified to in Scripture and the God experienced here in our world, to draw attention to the brooding Holy Spirit at work in creation. To do that, it is essential to engage with the public realm, because that is where God is at work. Preaching is redemptive. It is the place where we proclaim the good news of God in Christ, where we are able to articulate what the reconciliation of all things looks like, and how it may come about. This includes not just preaching about forgiveness, but also preaching about issues of justice and peace—anything that points to God's reconciling work in the world.

Preaching is communal. It arises from the community, as the church's life insinuates itself into preachers' minds as they prepare; it speaks to the community in the gathered assembly where the word is given voice; it speaks for the community, articulating its hopes and fears and dreams and passions.

Preaching that encompasses these themes is truly prophetic. There is a tendency to label anything that is *avant-garde* as prophetic, announcing new movements of the Spirit. However, that is only one aspect of prophetic preaching. Truly prophetic preaching "train[s] us in discerning the difference between the ways of the world and the ways of the Gospel, keeping us present to the Presence of God". It calls us to search out the divine in our world, to discern those things that are—and those that are not—of God, demanding that we engage with the public realm, prophetic speech that proclaims God's presence and work in our world in all its many facets.

Conclusion

In this chapter, I have identified four realities through which to explore the relationship between church and public space. The embodied reality, expressed in the way our buildings are structured in relation to wider public space, shows a shift from the traditional place at the heart of the public realm, in constant conversation with government and community, to a position at the margins, more closely identified with the private, a part of the commuter life that allows faith to be compartmentalised as one isolated element among many. The symbolic reality has two dimensions: formal and informal. The formal reality, the relationship between church and state, reflects the complexity of Australian history. While there seems to have been a *de facto* establishment in operation in the early days of the colonies in New South Wales and Tasmania, the pluralism of Australian society, even in the early days, led to a swift move away from any privileging of the Church of England over other denominations and to the eventual loss of all state funding of religious groups. What resulted was a clearer distinction between church and state, albeit one that is more flexible than its American counterpart, allowing for funding of church-sponsored schools (as long as all religions are treated equally) but no basis for state interference in church affairs. The informal symbolic reality is more complex: Anglicans have continued to exercise power and influence on a personal level in the public sphere, and civil religion has maintained a carefully guarded place for the church. It is, however, in the area of ethics that the church has faced the greatest challenges, enduring pressure to retreat to a circumscribed realm of morality on the one hand, while being condemned as wowsers and hypocrites on the other. Here the church needs to claim its distinctive identity as both part of and other than the public realm, clearly articulating its mission as a critical and independent voice.

The theological reality consists in the themes that underpin the church's self-understanding in relation to public space. The church is incarnational, redemptive and communal: these characteristics underpin its claim to be actively involved in the public realm. Finally, two practical realties, where the church is in relationship with public space, concern church in cyberspace and prophetic speech. While cyberspace spirituality can act as a support for church, it is in itself inadequate to be church, lacking the embodied and communal dimensions as fundamental parts of its constitution. Prophetic speech, on the other hand, is an expression of the church's incarnational, redemptive, and communal character, and as such is valuable vehicle for its interaction with public space.

The church remains a central contributor to public life in twenty-first century Australia, albeit one that owes more to its informal than its formal influences. What has emerged in recent years is the need for it to be more confident in articulating this place, grounded in its fundamental identity and mission, offering a renewed vision grounded firmly in the identity of the triune God.

Contributors

Peter Adam is currently the Principal of Ridley College, Melbourne, where he teaches theology and preaching. He has studied and lectured at St John's College, Durham and was minister of St Jude's, Carlton in Melbourne for twenty years. He is a Canon of St Paul's Cathedral, Melbourne. He holds a PhD from Durham University and has published books on theology and preaching and a commentary on Hebrews.

Email: principal@ridley.unimelb.edu.au

Peter G Bolt is Head of New Testament at Moore College, Sydney. He holds a PhD from London University and has published several books on the gospel of Mark and on mission. He has also contributed to and co-edited numerous other publications on the New Testament and the contemporary church. He is a member of General Synod and the executive editor of *The Australian Church Record*.

Email: peter.bolt@moore.edu.au

Alan Cadwallader, formerly in parish ministry in Melbourne and teaching at Ridley College and Trinity Theological School, has taught New Testament at St Barnabas Theological College since 1993. He gained his doctorate in Biblical and historical studies from Flinders University. His over-arching passion is in the exchange between culture and gospel in both early and modern times, yet he remains an interested observer of the synodal organism.

Email: alan.cadwallader@flinders.edu.au

Ray Cleary is Chief Executive Officer of Anglicare Victoria. The agency provides a range of services to children, young people and families. He has a Doctor of Ministry Degree from the Melbourne College of Divinity on the subject of welfare and justice as integral to the Church's mission. He recently chaired the Victorian Government's Homelessness Strategy. He is a Canon of St Paul's Anglican Cathedral,

Melbourne, Chairman of Anglicare Australia and the General Synod's Public Affairs Commission.

Email: ray.cleary@anglicarevic.org.au

David Cole is Chaplain and Head of Divinity at Overnewton Anglican Community College, Keilor, Victoria. Holding both a PhD and DMin, he is Chair of Examiners (Ministry Studies) for the Melbourne College of Divinity and an associated teacher of the United Faculty of Theology. Prior to his current appointment, David was Senior Chaplain of Trinity College (University of Melbourne) and Frank Woods Lecturer and Director of the Theological School. He was President of the United Faculty of Theology and a member of the Melbourne College of Divinity. He chairs the Australian Hymn Book Editorial Committee.

Email: david.cole@overnewton.vic.edu.au

Scott Cowdell is Rector of St Paul's, Manuka, in Canberra. He teaches part-time at Charles Sturt University (St Mark's National Theological Centre), edits *St Mark's Review* and serves on the Doctrine Commission of General Synod. He is the author of four books, most recently *God's Next Big Thing: Discovering the Future Church*. He holds a PhD from the University of Queensland. He has worked in parishes in Brisbane and has been Director of Trinity Theological School, Melbourne and Principal of St Barnabas College, Adelaide.

Email: scowdell@csu.edu.au

Jane Foulcher is currently Senior Priest at St John's, Canberra. She spent the previous seven years in Coffs Harbour, first as Chaplain of Bishop Druitt College, then as Rector of Coffs Harbour. Her most recent passion is for Orthodox icons.

Email: jane@stjohnscanberra.org

Bruce Kaye was General Secretary of the Anglican Church of Australia, General Synod (1994–2004), prior to which he was Master of New College at the University of New South Wales, founder of the New College Institute for Values Research and the New College Lectures, and Fellow in the Science and Technology School. Before returning to Australia in 1983 he was Vice Principal of St John's College and University Lecturer in the University of Durham. A graduate of the universities of Sydney, London and Basel, he has held

Fellowships at Freiburg in Germany, Cambridge England and Seattle in the USA. He is the Editor of the *Journal of Anglican Studies*.

Email: bnkaye@optusnet.com.au

Sarah Macneil is an Anglican priest and is currently Rector of All Saints, Ainslie, and Diocesan Archdeacon of the Diocese of Canberra and Goulburn. Before training for ordination she spent over a decade as a public servant, first as a diplomat in the Department of Foreign Affairs and then as a policy officer in the Department of Trade. She is fascinated by the way we humans organise ourselves and wrote her PhD thesis on the nexus between governance and identity in the Anglican Church in Australia.

Email: rector@allsaintsainslie.org.au

Stephen Pickard is currently Director, St. Mark's National Theological Centre and Associate Professor and Head of the School of Theology, Charles Sturt University. He holds a PhD from the University of Durham. He began working life with BHP in Industrial Relations before ordination and parish work in Newcastle and England. He was Resident Chaplain, Trevelyan and Van Mildert Colleges, University of Durham, UK and in Australia, Lecturer in Theology, United Theological College, Sydney and Vice-Principal. He was a member of the National Anglican/Uniting Church Dialogue, 1995–2001 and the Inter Anglican Theological and Doctrinal Commission. He has written extensively on episcopacy and mission. He is currently a member of the Charles Sturt University Public and Contextual Theology (PACT) community of scholars.

Email: spickard@csu.edu.au

Keith Rayner was formerly the Archbishop of Melbourne and Primate of the Anglican Church of Australia, before which he was the Archbishop of Adelaide. He has been the Chair of the Inter Anglican Theological and Doctrinal Commission and of the Design Group for the Lambeth Conference 1998. He has a PhD from the University of Queensland, and has lectured at St Francis College Brisbane and was Rotary Foundation Fellow at Harvard University.

Email: krayner@senet.com.au

Duncan Reid has worked as a secondary school teacher, a parish priest, and a lecturer in systematic theology both in Adelaide and Melbourne. He received his doctorate in theology from the University of Tübingen, in Germany, and most recently he has been Dean of the United Faculty of Theology, Melbourne.

Email: duncan.reid@optusnet.com.au

Geoff Smith is currently Rector of the parish of Surfers Paradise and Archdeacon of the Gold Coast in the Diocese of Brisbane. He worked as a parish priest in the Grafton diocese and spent three years in the Anglican Church of Papua New Guinea before becoming National Director of the Anglican Board of Mission-Australia in 2000–05. He has an MPhil in Practical Theology from the Australian Catholic University and is now a part time PhD student examining the impact that the rise of the single-person household will have on the Anglican Church in Australia.

Email: sprector@bigpond.net.au

Mark D Thompson is Academic Dean and Senior Lecturer in Theology at Moore College in Sydney, where he has taught since 1991. He studied at Macquarie University, Moore College and the University of Oxford. He has published numerous articles and books, his latest being *A Clear and Present Word: The Clarity of Scripture* (IVP, 2006).

Email: mark.thompson@moore.edu.au

Heather Thomson is Lecturer in Theology and Academic Dean at St Mark's National Theological Centre, School of Theology, Charles Sturt University. She received her doctorate from Charles Sturt University and her publications show a range of theological interests. In 2004 she spent six weeks as scholar-in-residence at St Paul's, Limuru in Kenya. She is currently on the Editorial Board of *St Mark's Review*, and of the *Journal of Anglican Studies*, and is a member of AUSTARC, the Australian Anglican and Roman Catholic dialogue group. She is also a member of the Charles Sturt University Public and Contextual Theology (PACT) community of scholars.

Email: hthomson@csu.edu.au

Richard Treloar studied Medicine at the University of NSW, before testing a vocation to ordained ministry at Trinity College, the University of Melbourne, where he currently serves as Chaplain and

Stewart Lecturer in Theology. A graduate of the Melbourne College of Divinity and Monash University, he has worked in rural and urban parishes, is a regular columnist for *Eureka Street*, and has published in the areas of Hebrew biblical narrative and hermeneutics. His PhD thesis on theodicy, literary theory, and the book of Esther has been accepted for publication in ATF's dissertation series. Richard is a member of the World Council of Churches Faith and Order Standing Commission, and of the Carlton Football Club.

Email: rtreloar@trinity.unimelb.edu.au

Raewynne J Whiteley trained in the Diocese of Melbourne and has served in Hunters Hill in Sydney and Charlestown in Newcastle. After completing a PhD in Practical Theology focussing on Homiletics at Princeton Theological Seminary in the United States, she became Vicar of Trinity Episcopal 'Old Swedes' Church in Swedesboro, New Jersey. She was co-editor of *Get Up Off Your Knees: Preaching the U2 Catalog* (Cowley Publications, 2003) and is currently working on a book on preaching as a spiritual practice. She continues to be involved with the Australian Anglican Church through her online teaching for Trinity College Theological School, as well as preaching and teaching when she visits home.

Email: office@trinityswedesboro.org

Author Index

CPSIA information can be obtained
at www.ICGtesting.com
Printed in the USA
BVHW072036301219
568171BV00005B/53/P

9 781925 612301